# Communications
# in Computer and Information Science 2330

## Series Editors

Gang Li⬤, *School of Information Technology, Deakin University, Burwood, VIC, Australia*

Joaquim Filipe⬤, *Polytechnic Institute of Setúbal, Setúbal, Portugal*

Ashish Ghosh⬤, *Indian Statistical Institute, Kolkata, West Bengal, India*

Zhiwei Xu, *Chinese Academy of Sciences, Beijing, China*

**Rationale**
The CCIS series is devoted to the publication of proceedings of computer science conferences. Its aim is to efficiently disseminate original research results in informatics in printed and electronic form. While the focus is on publication of peer-reviewed full papers presenting mature work, inclusion of reviewed short papers reporting on work in progress is welcome, too. Besides globally relevant meetings with internationally representative program committees guaranteeing a strict peer-reviewing and paper selection process, conferences run by societies or of high regional or national relevance are also considered for publication.

**Topics**
The topical scope of CCIS spans the entire spectrum of informatics ranging from foundational topics in the theory of computing to information and communications science and technology and a broad variety of interdisciplinary application fields.

**Information for Volume Editors and Authors**
Publication in CCIS is free of charge. No royalties are paid, however, we offer registered conference participants temporary free access to the online version of the conference proceedings on SpringerLink (http://link.springer.com) by means of an http referrer from the conference website and/or a number of complimentary printed copies, as specified in the official acceptance email of the event.

CCIS proceedings can be published in time for distribution at conferences or as post-proceedings, and delivered in the form of printed books and/or electronically as USBs and/or e-content licenses for accessing proceedings at SpringerLink. Furthermore, CCIS proceedings are included in the CCIS electronic book series hosted in the SpringerLink digital library at http://link.springer.com/bookseries/7899. Conferences publishing in CCIS are allowed to use Online Conference Service (OCS) for managing the whole proceedings lifecycle (from submission and reviewing to preparing for publication) free of charge.

**Publication process**
The language of publication is exclusively English. Authors publishing in CCIS have to sign the Springer CCIS copyright transfer form, however, they are free to use their material published in CCIS for substantially changed, more elaborate subsequent publications elsewhere. For the preparation of the camera-ready papers/files, authors have to strictly adhere to the Springer CCIS Authors' Instructions and are strongly encouraged to use the CCIS LaTeX style files or templates.

**Abstracting/Indexing**
CCIS is abstracted/indexed in DBLP, Google Scholar, EI-Compendex, Mathematical Reviews, SCImago, Scopus. CCIS volumes are also submitted for the inclusion in ISI Proceedings.

**How to start**
To start the evaluation of your proposal for inclusion in the CCIS series, please send an e-mail to ccis@springer.com.

Lap-Kei Lee · Petra Poulova · Kwok Tai Chui ·
Miloslava Černá · Fu Lee Wang ·
Simon K. S. Cheung
Editors

# Technology in Education

## Digital and Intelligent Education

7th International Conference
on Technology in Education, ICTE 2024
Hradec Kralove, Czech Republic, December 2–5, 2024
Proceedings

*Editors*
Lap-Kei Lee
Hong Kong Metropolitan University
Hong Kong SAR, China

Kwok Tai Chui
Hong Kong Metropolitan University
Hong Kong SAR, China

Fu Lee Wang
Hong Kong Metropolitan University
Hong Kong SAR, China

Petra Poulova
University of Hradec Králové
Hradec Kralove, Czech Republic

Miloslava Černá
University of Hradec Králové
Hradec Kralove, Czech Republic

Simon K. S. Cheung
Hong Kong Metropolitan University
Hong Kong SAR, China

ISSN 1865-0929  ISSN 1865-0937 (electronic)
Communications in Computer and Information Science
ISBN 978-981-96-0204-9  ISBN 978-981-96-0205-6 (eBook)
https://doi.org/10.1007/978-981-96-0205-6

© The Editor(s) (if applicable) and The Author(s), under exclusive license
to Springer Nature Singapore Pte Ltd. 2024

This work is subject to copyright. All rights are solely and exclusively licensed by the Publisher, whether the whole or part of the material is concerned, specifically the rights of translation, reprinting, reuse of illustrations, recitation, broadcasting, reproduction on microfilms or in any other physical way, and transmission or information storage and retrieval, electronic adaptation, computer software, or by similar or dissimilar methodology now known or hereafter developed.
The use of general descriptive names, registered names, trademarks, service marks, etc. in this publication does not imply, even in the absence of a specific statement, that such names are exempt from the relevant protective laws and regulations and therefore free for general use.
The publisher, the authors and the editors are safe to assume that the advice and information in this book are believed to be true and accurate at the date of publication. Neither the publisher nor the authors or the editors give a warranty, expressed or implied, with respect to the material contained herein or for any errors or omissions that may have been made. The publisher remains neutral with regard to jurisdictional claims in published maps and institutional affiliations.

This Springer imprint is published by the registered company Springer Nature Singapore Pte Ltd.
The registered company address is: 152 Beach Road, #21-01/04 Gateway East, Singapore 189721, Singapore

If disposing of this product, please recycle the paper.

# Preface

This edited volume consists of the extended papers selected from the 7th International Conference on Technology in Education (ICTE 2024), held on 2–5 December 2024.

Technology has become an integral part of virtually all aspects of education, broadly covering curriculum planning, content development and delivery, communication among learners, instructors and institutions, assessment and programme evaluation. Under the theme of *Digital and Intelligent Education,* the 7th International Conference on Technology in Education (ICTE 2024) aimed to serve as a platform for relevant academic exchanges across higher education institutions, focusing especially on the sharing of good practices and results from studies.

ICTE 2024 attracted a total of 65 submissions. After a careful paper review process, 21 papers were selected for inclusion in this volume. These papers are organized into 5 groups: (1) online learning, innovation learning, and digital learning, (2) artificial intelligence in education, (3) institutional strategies and practices, (4) personalized and individual learning, and (5) smart learning environment.

Our sincere thanks go to the conference's organizing committee for their effective administration and unfailing support. Our thanks also go to the international programme committee. The high quality of the papers could not have been maintained without their professional comments and advice in the paper review process.

December 2024

Lap-Kei Lee
Petra Poulova
Kwok Tai Chui
Miloslava Černá
Fu Lee Wang
Simon K. S. Cheung

# Organizing Committee

## Conference Chairs

Jan Kriz — University of Hradec Králové, Czech Republic
Reggie Kwan — Hong Kong Metropolitan University, Hong Kong SAR, China

## Programme Chairs

Petra Poulova — University of Hradec Králové, Czech Republic
Miloslava Černá — University of Hradec Králové, Czech Republic
Kwok Tai Chui — Hong Kong Metropolitan University, Hong Kong SAR, China
Lap-Kei Lee — Hong Kong Metropolitan University, Hong Kong SAR, China

## Organizing Chairs

Blanka Klimova — University of Hradec Králové, Czech Republic
Stepan Hubalovsky — University of Hradec Králové, Czech Republic
Leung-Pun Wong — Tung Wah College, Hong Kong SAR, China

## Financial Chairs

Petra Poulova — University of Hradec Králové, Czech Republic
Steven Ng — Ming-Ai (London) Institute, UK

## Registration Chairs

Marie Hubalovska — University of Hradec Králové, Czech Republic
Edmond King Sing Fong — Hong Kong Metropolitan University, Hong Kong SAR, China

## Publication Chairs

Petra Poulova University of Hradec Králové, Czech Republic
Miloslava Černá University of Hradec Králové, Czech Republic
Louise Luk Hong Kong Metropolitan University, Hong Kong SAR, China

## Webmaster

Yin-Chun Fung Hong Kong Metropolitan University, Hong Kong SAR, China

# International Programme Committee Chairs

## Programme Chairs

| | |
|---|---|
| Petra Poulova | University of Hradec Králové, Czech Republic |
| Miloslava Černá | University of Hradec Králové, Czech Republic |
| Kwok Tai Chui | Hong Kong Metropolitan University, Hong Kong SAR, China |
| Lap-Kei Lee | Hong Kong Metropolitan University, Hong Kong SAR, China |

## Members

| | |
|---|---|
| Jan Kriz | University of Hradec Králové, Czech Republic |
| Reggie Kwan | Hong Kong Metropolitan University, Hong Kong SAR, China |
| Blanka Klimova | University of Hradec Králové, Czech Republic |
| Stepan Hubalovsky | University of Hradec Králové, Czech Republic |
| Leung-Pun Wong | Tung Wah College, Hong Kong SAR, China |
| Steven Ng | Ming-Ai (London) Institute, UK |
| Marie Hubalovska | University of Hradec Králové, Czech Republic |
| Lam For Kwok | HKCT Institute of Higher Education, Hong Kong SAR, China |
| Louise Luk | Hong Kong Metropolitan University, Hong Kong SAR, China |
| John Hui | Vocational Training Council, Hong Kong SAR, China |
| Kam Cheong Li | Hong Kong Metropolitan University, Hong Kong SAR, China |
| Lucie Rohlíková | University of West Bohemia, Czech Republic |
| Zehui Zhan | South China Normal University, China |
| Jianli Jiao | South China Normal University, China |
| Billy T. M. Wong | Hong Kong Metropolitan University, Hong Kong SAR, China |
| Kongkiti Phusavat | Kasetsart University, Thailand |
| Naraphorn Paoprasert | Kasetsart University, Thailand |
| Haoran Xie | Lingnan University, Hong Kong SAR, China |
| Xiaojun Liu | Shenzhen Institute of Technology, Shenzhen, China |

x  International Programme Committee Chairs

| | |
|---|---|
| Ramidayu Yousuk | Kasetsart University, Thailand |
| Praewpran Payadsab | Kasetsart University, Thailand |
| Will W. K. Ma | Tung Wah College, Hong Kong SAR, China |
| Chen Li | Hong Kong Polytechnic University, Hong Kong SAR, China |
| Edmond King Sing Fong | Hong Kong Metropolitan University, Hong Kong SAR, China |
| Yin-Chun Fung | Hong Kong Metropolitan University, Hong Kong SAR, China |

## Organizer

International Hybrid Learning Society

## Co-organizers

University of Hradec Králové

Hong Kong Metropolitan University

Tung Wah College

# Contents

**Keynote Papers**

Flexible Learning: From Theory to Practical Implications .................. 3
   *Lucie Rohlíková*

Human-AI Co-Innovation: Navigating the Innovative Problem-Solving
Landscape with the Process Model and Technology Empowerment ........... 15
   *Zehui Zhan, Chaocheng Zhong, Jiayi Zheng, and Weisen Zhong*

**Online Learning, Innovation Learning, and Digital Learning**

Does More Frequently Mean Better? The Current Teacher View of the Use
of Digital Technologies in Higher Education ............................. 41
   *Katerina Kostolanyova, Tomas Javorcik, Tomas Barot,*
   *and Ivana Simonova*

Empowering Open Educational Practices Through Open-Source Software:
A Grounded Theory Approach in the Context of a University in Hong Kong ... 55
   *Chenggui Duan*

The Practice of Digital Education: Findings and Lessons Based on Urgent
Outreach Activities .................................................... 71
   *Shao-Fu Li, Shun-Neng Yang, Jzung-Lu Lin, Kwan-Keung Ng,*
   *Lap-Kei Lee, and Louise Luk*

A Study of Improvements in Educational Accessibility and Adaptability
Using Digital and Intelligent Education ................................. 85
   *Jiaqi Liu, Kwok Tai Chui, Lap-Kei Lee, Naraphorn Paoprasert,*
   *Leung Pun Wong, and Kwan-Keung Ng*

**Artificial Intelligence in Education**

Mapping the Landscape of AI Implementation in STEM and STEAM
Education: A Bibliometric Analysis ...................................... 99
   *Ningwei Sun and Salmiza Saleh*

Can Generative AI Really Empower Teachers' Professional Practices? Comparative Study on Human-Tailored and GenAI-Designed Reading Comprehension Learning Materials .................................... 112
*Fen-Lan Jen, Xingyun Huang, Xiaoting Liu, and Jianli Jiao*

Can Generative AI Really Empower Teachers' Professional Practices? A Quasi-Experiment on Human-GenAI Collaborative Rubric Design .......... 124
*Xingyun Huang, Fen-Lan Jen, Yuting Lian, and Jianli Jiao*

Empowering Assessors in Providing Quality Feedback with GenAI Assistance: A Preliminary Exploration .................................. 134
*Zexuan Chen, Simon Cross, and Bart Rienties*

**Institutional Strategies and Practices**

Assessing College Students' Peer Feedback Literacy ...................... 151
*Wenyi Chen and Linlin Jia*

The Relationship Between Mentor Role and Teachers' Practical Knowledge in the Process of Mentor-Apprentice Dialogue – Based on Epistemic Network Analysis ........................................ 164
*Yating Jin, Yaxuan Wang, and Ling Chen*

Graduate Study Program Improvement: A Case Study of Industrial Engineering Programs .................................................. 173
*Pongthorn Ruksorn, Naraphorn Paoprasert, Kongkiti Phusavat, and Pornthep Anussornnitisarn*

Specific Aspects of MOOC's Use in Czech Universities .................... 185
*Miloslava Cerna and Petra Poulova*

**Learning Analytics in Education**

Identification of Potential At-Risk Students Through an Intelligent Multi-model Academic Analytics Platform ............................... 199
*Kam Cheong Li, Billy T. M. Wong, and Mengjin Liu*

An Investigation into the Application of Learning Analytics in Collaborative Learning .............................................. 210
*Billy T. M. Wong, Kam Cheong Li, and Mengjin Liu*

Enhancing a Probabilistic Auto-regressive Model with Gaussian Noise
and Savitzky–Golay Filter for the Data Generation of Small-Scale
Education Datasets .................................................... 222
   *Kwok Tai Chui, Jackson Tsz Wah Chan, Ramidayu Yousuk,
   Lap-Kei Lee, and Fu Lee Wang*

**Smart Learning Environments**

Review Study "Virtual Reality in Biology Education" ...................... 235
   *Michaela Toman and Marie Hubálovská*

Use of Virtual Reality for Improving Students' Learning Attention
in Higher Vocational Education .......................................... 246
   *Xiaojun Liu, Liang Liu, Yong Cai, and Simon K. S. Cheung*

A Study on the Effectiveness of a VR Training Programme in the Property
Management Industry .................................................... 257
   *Yan-Wai Chan, Simon K. S. Cheung, Kwan-Keung Ng,
   Aaron S. Y. Chiang, Pius Lam, and Kwok Tai Chui*

A Virtual Reality Serious Game for Improving Pet Dog Care Skills .......... 269
   *Lap-Kei Lee, Yukai Cai, Ho-Yin Chui, Chun-Hei Lam,
   Edmond King Sing Fong, Praewpran Prayadsab, and Nga-In Wu*

**Author Index** ......................................................... 283

# Keynote Papers

# Flexible Learning: From Theory to Practical Implications

Lucie Rohlíková(✉)

Faculty of Education, University of West Bohemia, Plzeň, Czech Republic
lrohik@kvd.zcu.cz

**Abstract.** This theoretical study pays special attention to flexible learning, the development of which is closely related to societal changes in the 21st century. Flexible forms of education are specific in terms of study organization (unusual time, space, schedule, combination of forms), non-traditional target groups (open access to education, second chance studies, mastery-oriented learning, teaching in a foreign language), and the use of technology (multimedia, digital technology, electronic communication, information systems). This paper discusses theories that support the idea of flexibility in education and their practical implications. Attention is paid to philosophical starting points (empiricism, rationalism, pragmatism and humanism), related psychological theories of learning (behaviourism, cognitivism, constructivism) and other specific theories that are important in the field of open, online, flexible, and distance education (connectivism, systems theory, communication theory, media theory, independence and autonomy theory, interaction and communication theory, equivalence theory, industrialized learning theory, learning community theory, teaching-learning congruence theory, transactional distance theory, self-regulated learning theory, situated learning theory, collaborative learning theory, and cognitive flexibility).

**Keywords:** flexible learning · flexible forms of teaching and learning · higher education · theory

## 1 Introduction

The digital revolution has permeated many areas of society and the economy, and has profoundly changed our lives. Learning is ubiquitous; blurring the boundaries of time and place even between traditionally compartmentalized tools, such as audio, video, textbooks, games, and more (Livingstone, Haddon, Görzig, Ólafsson, 2011). In order to achieve better learning experiences and learning outcomes, the system must adapt to the needs of the students, and not the other way around (Green, Pearson, Stockton, 2006).

In recent years, universities have therefore faced the following questions:

- Which forms, methods, and strategies of teaching and learning can be used to develop key skills for the 21st century?
- How can we adapt teaching and learning to the needs of individual students?

- How can we provide education to clients who can't go to an educational institution, and need to be educated at the workplace or at home?
- How can we use the potential of digital technologies in education?

Practical answers to the above questions are hidden in the idea of flexible forms of education.

The importance of flexible learning increased even more during the 2020–2022 period, when the world faced a specific situation due to the epidemic of COVID-19 (European University Association, 2024). COVID-19 has led to the lockdown of cities and the closing of university buildings around the world, bringing the necessity to find alternatives to work, teach, and study (Quacquarelli, 2020). Universities were looking for ways to adjust the teaching of students who were temporarily unable to attend classrooms, and flexible forms of education were a tool that could be used more or less successfully at this time (Anderton, Vitali, Blackmore, Bakeberg, 2021, Lo, Han, Wong, Tang, 2021, Dayagbil, Palompon, Garcia, Olvido, 2021, Tarrayo, Anudin, 2021). Most teaching during the epidemic relied on digital technologies, but sometimes it was necessary to find other ways of distance learning for students with poor Internet connections or insufficient technical equipment (Essel, Vlachopoulos, Adom, Tachie-Menson, 2020). Universities were not prepared for a similar situation, with the exception of open universities, which normally offer flexible forms of education as standard, and therefore had previous experience not only in the field of distance learning and its technical provision, but also in the field of the solving social problems of students, as well as in the field of verification of learning outcomes (Shishakly, 2021). It has been shown that resilient higher education systems can only be created if traditional institutional boundaries of learning are broken down, and students are offered the opportunity to acquire knowledge and skills in flexible ways.

Today, students and lifelong learners expect to find a rich learning environment, supported by well-designed resources, and with quality support services at universities. Increasingly, they are looking to choose a combination of traditional and new learning approaches and technologies, and want to study at their own time and place, and at their own pace. There are a huge number of possibilities for designing and implementing flexible forms of education. A flexible form of education acquires specific value only in relation to a specific student, his or her needs, personal goals, previous knowledge and skills, his or her learning styles, possibilities, and limits.

This study is based on literature review, and aims to map the theoretical frameworks of flexible learning. Due to the diversity that is characteristic of flexible forms of education, we can't talk about just one theory, but we encounter a whole range of diverse approaches.

## 2 Philosophical Foundations of Flexible Learning

Pedagogical approaches applied within flexible forms of education are built on the foundations of general philosophical and psychological theories, as well as learning theories. The theoretical frameworks presented in this paper are based on the theoretical foundations of distance education, which is a significant stream of flexible forms of education, and whose theory has been developed over a long period of time, precisely with an emphasis on flexible approaches to learning.

Table 1 shows the relationship between selected philosophical approaches and basic psychological theories of learning, which influence flexible learning and flexible forms of education, and are reflected in diverse approaches in this area.

**Table 1.** The relationship between the philosophical and psychological foundations of flexible forms of education

| Philosophical foundations | Psychological foundations |
| --- | --- |
| empiricism | behaviourism, cognitivism |
| rationalism | cognitivism, cognitive constructivism |
| pragmatism | behaviourism, cognitivism |
| humanism | constructivism |

Source: Cheng, Rushing, Xu, Dogan, 2017

Empiricism is based on the Persian philosopher Avicenna's idea that man is a "tabula rasa" (Rizvi, 2006), and knowledge can only be gained through the use of the five senses (sight, hearing, taste, smell and touch), while evidence is obtained through observation. The theories of behaviourism and cognitivism, created on the basis of empirical research, have similar starting points. It is typical to carry out a whole host of experiments for them, that try to demonstrate the effectiveness of various learning strategies.

Rationalism, like empiricism, sees knowledge outside of the individual, and truth as universal and verifiable (Reigeluth, 2012), but rationalists are convinced that not everything can be known through experiment and sensory perception. A part of knowledge may be derived by deduction. Cognitivism and cognitive constructivism reject the concept of man as an unwritten sheet of paper, and reflect the approach of rationalism. An example of the application of rationalism in flexible forms of education could be a teacher who chooses an appropriate learning strategy according to the needs of the student. The teacher cannot experimentally verify the choice of the best strategy, but he/she can use observation and deduction in order to choose an appropriate strategy, based on his/her experience and logical reasoning (Cheng, Rushing, Xu, Dogan, 2017).

Pragmatism focuses on action, practicality, and practical problem solving. The usefulness of knowledge and things is in their practical application. James (1907) described pragmatism as a hotel corridor that leads to many different rooms. Flexible forms of education can be seen as a pragmatic paradigm, as they allow studying from different places, at different times, in different ways, as it is most practical for students.

Humanism reflects a person's individual needs, desires, and experiences, as does constructivism, which emphasizes the learner's motivation to learn, and the context itself. According to Lamont (1984), humanists use the methods of reason, science, and democracy to solve human problems. Unlike behaviourism and cognitivism, constructivism does not view the learner as a passive receiver of knowledge, but rather as an active creator of it. Learning is contextual – it takes place in a certain context, and information needs to be related to that context (Anderson, 2008).

## 3 Psychological Foundations of Flexible Learning

Behaviourism sees learning as an observable change in the learner's behaviour that has been caused by a stimulus from the external environment (Skinner, 1974). Behaviourists examine learning and students in order to determine when is the best time to begin learning, and what support is most effective for a particular student (Ertmer, Newby, 2013). The focus is on ongoing practice and feedback on learning outcomes, where decisions are made on this basis about further learning progress (Schunk, 1991). Behaviourism theory brings a number of inspiring implications for flexible forms of education (to paraphrase Cheng et al., 2017):

- Teachers should explicitly explain expected learning outcomes to students so that the students can focus on the teacher's expectations and assess their learning progress.
- Learning should include ongoing assessment of student learning outcomes. Assessment feedback can direct teachers and students to further interventions.
- Learning can be positively influenced by modular learning materials that can be arranged in different ways – simple–difficult, familiar–new, theoretical–practical (Anderson, 2008).
- A student needs analysis must be designed to show the gap between current skills and expected learning outcomes. In addition, it is appropriate to include an analysis of the student's learning styles.
- It is important to include practical activities.

Cognitivists emphasize the importance of cognition, thinking, mental abilities and skills, and intellect. According to them, humans are naturally inquisitive. Memory, which has a limited capacity, plays an important role in learning, so teachers must dose the learning content in an appropriate way. When a student watches a video in an online course, he/she receives visual and auditory information that he/she stores in his/her sensory memory. It then transfers it to short-term working memory, where it combines with previous information that was previously stored in long-term memory. In this way, the student remembers the key parts of the video. These conclusions of cognitivism are inspiring for the practice of flexible forms of education (to paraphrase Cheng et al., 2017):

- It is appropriate to use strategies and techniques such as highlighting, justifying, commenting, and selecting materials appropriate to the student's reasoning and knowledge level, because these strategies help the student transfer information to his/her working memory.
- Strategies that use the learner's prior knowledge and experience allow the learner to use information from long-term memory to understand new information.
- Breaking down information into smaller chunks can prevent working memory from being overloaded.
- It is appropriate to use different strategies to adapt learning to different students.
- Teachers can design different forms of study materials for different sensory channels (visual and auditory) in order to facilitate the students' processing of information in working memory.
- Teachers should strive to gain students' attention, and support their self-confidence and motivation to learn.

- In the study materials, it is advisable to connect knowledge with the possibilities of its application in real life, and to support the application of knowledge.

Rohlíková, Vejvodová (2012) state that constructivism considers learning to be a deeply individual process, and emphasizes that knowledge and reality do not have an objective or absolute value (or that we do not know the way of knowing this reality). Man constructs and interprets reality based on his own individual experience. When applying constructivism in practice, the student, based on familiarization with several different theories (at the level of scientific and sensitive approach), in an active discussion with the teacher, classmates, and in a critical re-evaluation of his/her original opinions, comes to build his/her own and unique structure of knowledge and attitudes. The basic methodological starting points are the active concept of teaching, experiential learning in a real context and self-reflection. Emphasis is placed on the social dimension of education (forming one's own opinions in confrontation with the opinions of others). A student needs to actively do something, discuss, and confront his opinions with the opinions of others, create, and gain real experience.

Cognitive constructivism is based on the European genetic epistemology of Jean Piaget and the American cognitive psychology (J.S. Brunner and others). He bases his didactic procedures on the assumption that cognition occurs through construction in such a way that the cognizant subject (student) connects fragments of information from the external environment into meaningful structures, and performs mental operations, with them conditioned to the corresponding level of his cognitive development. Social constructivism is based on works on the social dimension of learning (L.S. Vygotsky and others), and emphasizes the irreplaceable role of social interaction and culture in the process of knowledge construction. In didactics, his principles are implemented primarily in co-operative learning. In practice, there is a synthesis of both mentioned concepts in the pedagogical movement, which promotes solving problems from life, creative thinking, working in groups, and less theory and drill in teaching.

The constructivist concept is referred to as an ideal pedagogical starting point for flexible forms of education based on e-learning (Rohlíková, Vejvodová, 2012). Information and communication technologies are a tool capable of creating very good conditions for a constructivist educational programme. Constructivist pedagogy places the student at the centre of the educational process. In the same way, e-learning assumes an independent student who manages and organizes his/her learning in an online system. The traditional role of the teacher naturally changes in e-learning, and the teacher becomes a constructivist tutor, facilitator, and guide. E-learning, by its nature of guided self-study, forces the learner to take responsibility for their learning, control their results, and evaluate their progress. At the same time, online technology allows students to record and monitor their own learning and reflect on their style and methodology. Synchronous or asynchronous interactions between online education participants are possible in e-learning without the barriers of place and time. However, communication needs to be encouraged, both by creating a pleasant atmosphere of an open space for sharing opinions, and by an appropriate concept of group work (Rohlíková, Vejvodová, 2012). Working together with other students gives students a real experience of working in a team, and forces them to utilise their metacognitive skills (Anderson, 2008).

Implications of constructivism inspiring flexible forms of education (to paraphrase Cheng et al., 2017):

- Learning is an active process, so students should be at the centre, and teachers should facilitate learning, rather than acting as an authority for imparting knowledge.
- Students construct their own knowledge based on prior knowledge, experience, and interaction with peers and teachers, rather than receiving information from teachers.
- Education should offer students opportunities to individualize, personalize, and contextualize knowledge to adapt to the needs of different learners.
- Teachers should use collaborative student activities to facilitate learning.
- Knowledge should come from related real-life problems and phenomena to make learning meaningful to students.

Behaviourism, cognitivism, and constructivism are theories that were developed before technology entered our lives. These theories have general validity, and as theoretical frameworks, we can also apply them to forms of learning in which technology plays a very significant role. However, with the advent of technology and its significant influence on our daily lives, the way we communicate and learn, questions have arisen whether existing learning theories meet the needs of students, or whether we need to work on a new theory. Siemens (2005) integrated the principles of chaos theory, network theory, complexity theory, and self-organization theory, and brought a new concept and term – connectivism. Behaviourism, cognitivism, and constructivism all describe learning as occurring within the learner, but connectivists believe that learning does not occur under the control of the individual.

## 4 Flexible Learning and Connectivism

According to Brdička (2008), the basic idea of connectivism is that the increasing amount of existing information and its easy availability leads to the need to understand understanding as a property of a network in which each member manages only a certain part of knowledge. The need to solve a given problem then leads to the temporary creation of dynamically changing connections for the specific task that network users need to solve, including available information sources.

The main principles of connectivism (Siemens, 2005, Anderson, 2008, Brdička, 2008):

- Learning is a process during which specialized nodes of a general complex network are connected (sharing access to information resources, knowledge).
- Cognition is based on a number of diverse experiences (combination of different cultures, use of different technologies).

Siemens' ideas (2005) have been elaborated by Anderson (2008), and have important implications for flexible forms of education (to paraphrase Cheng et al., 2017):

- The teacher should encourage students to research current information from a variety of sources.
- The teacher should provide guidance on how to recognize the reliability and importance of information from different sources.

- Students should be able to share knowledge with other students and teachers, using different kinds of communication technologies.
- Students should be able to choose appropriate learning technology for different learning objectives.
- Students should be able to adapt to the constant changes in technology that are used in flexible forms of education.

## 5 Other Theories Relevant to Flexible Learning

Flexible forms of education are based on systems theory, communication theory, and media theory (Cheng et al., 2017). Systems theory describes flexible forms of education as systems composed of interconnected parts. These systems can take different forms, from the robust organizational structure of a global company, to small local and independent learning communities, and are influenced by many factors in the creation, adoption, and application of flexible forms of learning. Communication theory helps to describe how communication works, which is a very important part of flexible forms of education. Media theory helps explain how to use different media effectively in different forms of communication. Richey, Tracey, Klein (2011) emphasize that visual elements facilitate the learning process by motivating (attracting students' attention, being realistic), facilitating the understanding of content (explaining, illustrating, analogizing), or helping to recall content.

According to the independence and autonomy theory, the concept of autonomous learning includes the student's ability to make independent decisions regarding his/her own learning (Moore, Kearsley, 2012).

Interaction and communication theory emphasizes the importance of students' interaction with other people and the environment. Interaction occurs when students transform inert information into knowledge, with personal application and value (Dewey, 1916, 1938).

Equivalency theory strives for flexible forms of education (here, specifically distance courses) to provide equivalent educational experiences and learning outcomes as traditional forms. However, it is very problematic to ensure identical educational experiences while not taking into account when and where students of flexible forms of education learn. Therefore, Simonson, Smaldino, Albright, Zvacek (2008) suggest that instead of providing equivalent learning experiences and expecting equivalent learning outcomes from students of both traditional and flexible forms, it is better to focus on equitable outcomes and equitable educational experiences for all students.

The theory of industrialized learning is based on the fact that, just as the industrial revolution made it possible to produce a huge number of products (serial production), distance education makes it possible to educate a large number of people (Peters, 2007). It can be said that distance education is based on economies of scale. If a centrally developed course is easily accessible to dozens, hundreds, or even thousands of students, for example as a MOOC course, the number of students is no longer decisive – with a larger number of students, the costs increase only minimally. Another important idea of the theory of industrialized learning is the division of labour between specialists in the conception, creation, and implementation of courses. In face-to-face education, a large part of the agenda is usually handled by the teacher, while in distance education the roles are divided among a larger number of people.

Holmberg (2007) works with a theory based on teaching-learning conversations, and focuses on feelings, empathy, and the relationship between the student and the educational institution. His theory is based on the following hypotheses:

- the greater the harmony between teaching and learning, the stronger the students' relationship with the educational institution,
- the stronger the students' relationship with the educational institution, the greater their personal involvement,
- the stronger the students' relationship with the educational institution, and the greater their personal involvement, the stronger the motivation, and therefore the more effective the learning.

Garrison and Arbaugh (2007) develop the concept of learning communities (community of inquiry) within flexible forms of education. This approach is based on the close co-operation of students, with an emphasis on personal communication (through synchronous and asynchronous forms).

Moore's transactional distance theory draws attention to the relationship between dialogue (communication in the course), course structure, and student autonomy (Moore, 2007).

In flexible forms of education, and especially in distance education, it is important to take into account the principles of self-regulatory learning, because the active role of the teacher is missing, and there are significant demands on student autonomy (Hsu, Ching, Mathews, Carr-Chellman, 2009).

The theory of situated learning emphasizes the close connection between learning and the real context. Brown, Collins, and Duguid (1989) state that learning is meaningful when there is an opportunity to apply the knowledge we have acquired in a social and real context. One learns best through concrete real-life activities and social interaction.

A very important component of flexible forms of education is collaborative learning, in which two or more students work together to solve a certain problem (Swan, Shen, Hiltz, 2006).

The development of flexible forms of education is also supported by the theory of cognitive flexibility (Spiro, Coulson, Feltovich, Anderson, 1988). This theory focuses on the nature of learning in complex systems. It emphasizes advanced knowledge acquisition that allows flexible re-arrangement of pre-existing knowledge to adapt to the needs of a new situation (Spiro, Feltovich, Jacobson, Coulson, 1991).

The means to achieve the cognitive flexibility of the student is to modify the way in which knowledge is represented, and to influence the process of processing these mental representations. The main principles of how to do this are to (Spiro et al., 1991):

- Reflect the complexity of knowledge – The system should provide students with opportunities to create interconnections between concepts and principles. Teaching should avoid presenting problems as simple linear sequences of a decision-making process.
- Offer multiple representations of content – Learners should be able to access content at different times, in different contexts, for different purposes, and from different

perspectives. Multiple thematic organization of content and multiple views of content can help students create multiple representations of content. Different examples can be used to illustrate different topics and perspectives, as well as to support different contexts for knowledge applications.
- Support context-dependent knowledge – Knowledge cannot be oversimplified. Oversimplification isolates knowledge from its context of use, and segments knowledge into separate components. It is essential to provide contextual variability for different representations, and multiple interconnectedness of knowledge components.

The implementation of flexible forms of education must be seen in the context of basic philosophical and psychological theories, and theories of learning at the university. There are definitely a number of possible ways to build specific educational programmes, and what impact the selected theoretical framework will have on the study activities and relationships of individual actors. Nowadays, flexible learning can rely on the results and findings of a whole range of research projects that describe the advantages, disadvantages, possibilities, and also the limits of individual forms. When searching in this area, it is necessary to work with many keywords, because only a fraction of relevant resources can be found under the term "flexible learning". It is then necessary to search for further professional literature using sub-terms and the names of individual types of flexible forms of education.

## 6 Conclusion

Flexible forms of education are based on the ideas of empiricism, rationalism, pragmatism, and humanism, and are based on basic psychological theories of learning (behaviourism, cognitivism, constructivism). Technology and the demand for flexibility then lead to the development of other specific theories that are an inspiration for the conception and implementation of flexible forms of education (e.g. connectivism, communication theory, independence and autonomy theory, transactional distance theory, cognitive flexibility theory, and others).

We often find that authors of flexible educational programmes are looking for simple templates and clear methodological guidelines on how to design programmes. However, it is clear from the previous text that the theoretical framework in which the authors will operate must be the guide for the author's creation and implementation of flexible forms of education. It is necessary to think about this framework thoroughly, and then derive from it the specific parameters of the conceptual and author's work (e.g. educational programmes based on the ideas of social constructivism will differ significantly from forms based on behaviourism in the type, form, and organization of individual learning activities, in the way of communication within the programme etc.).

Higher education institutions will increasingly open educational opportunities to other groups of adult students who place a high priority on study flexibility, and who want educational programmes to fit their life and work schedules and opportunities. The university of the future will be more practical and experiential, with more social interaction between students. It will offer a new range of services, such as micro-certificates, electronic assessment of learning outcomes, including learning monitoring and data collection for continuous assessment of activities (not just assessment in exams), and lifelong learning (personalised, discontinuous, and implemented at different paces). It will offer personalized learning to immediately address specific needs. Such a change in approach will require flexibility and agility. Educational programmes will be more open, modular, recognizable, and supplemented by a specific offer of services according to needs (modules, content, tutoring, evaluation, certification, personalization).

The issue of flexible learning and flexible forms of education is extremely broad, and deserves due attention. It is important to look at this whole area much less from a technological point of view, and much more from the point of view of pedagogy and related social science fields (psychology, philosophy, ethics, etc.). Enabling each student to find the right individual educational path, and gradually harmonize it in accordance with their personal, family, and work needs, while developing an in-depth approach to learning, is a major challenge for universities.

## References

Anderson, T. (ed.): The Theory and Practice of Online Learning. Athabasca University Press (2008). https://doi.org/10.15215/aupress/9781897425084.01

Anderton, R.S., Vitali, J., Blackmore, C., Bakeberg, M.C.: Flexible teaching and learning modalities in undergraduate science amid the COVID-19 pandemic. Fron. Educ. (2021). https://doi.org/10.3389/feduc.2020.609703

Brdička, B.: Konektivismus–teorie vzdělávání v prostředí sociálních sítí. (Connectivism – the theory of education in the environment of social networks) Metodický portál: inspirace a zkušenosti učitelů (2008)

Brown, J.S., Collins, A., Duguid, P.: Situated cognition and the culture of learning. Educ. Res. **18**(1), 32–42 (1989)

Cheng, L., Rushing, R., Xu, Z., Dogan, N.: Theoretical Foundations of Distance Education. In: Distance Education: A Guide for Theory and Practice. Open Educational Resource (2017). https://www.aritzhaupt.com/distance_education/theoretical-frameworks/

Dewey, J.: Democracy and Education. Macmillan (1916)

Dewey, J.: Experience and Education. Collier Macmillan (1938)

Ertmer, P.A., Newby, T.J.: Behaviorism, cognitivism, constructivism – Comparing critical features from an instructional design perspective. Perform. Improv. Q. **26**(2), 43–71 (2013)

Essel, H.B., Vlachopoulos, D., Adom, D., Tachie-Menson, A.: Transforming higher education in Ghana in times of disruption: flexible learning in rural communities with high latency internet connectivity. J. Enterprising Commun.: People Places Glob. Econ. **15**(2), 296–312 (2021). https://doi.org/10.1108/JEC-08-2020-0151

European University Association: Flexible learning and teaching. Thematic Peer Group Report (2024). https://www.eua.eu/publications/reports/flexible-learning-and-teaching.html

Randy Garrison, D., Arbaugh, J.B.: Researching the community of inquiry framework: review, issues, and future directions. Internet High. Educ. **10**(3), 157–172 (2007). https://doi.org/10.1016/j.iheduc.2007.04.001

Green, S., Pearson, E., Stockton, C.: Personal learning environments: accessibility and adaptability in the design of an inclusive learning management system. In: Pearson, E., Bohman, P. (eds.) Proceedings of ED-MEDIA 2006 – World Conference on Educational Multimedia, Hypermedia and Telecommunications, pp. 2934–2941. Association for the Advancement of Computing in Education (AACE), Orlando, FL USA (2006). https://www.learntechlib.org/p/23425/

Holmberg, B.: A theory of teaching-learning conversations. In: Moore, M.G. (ed.) Handbook of Distance Education, pp. 69–75. Lawrence Erlbaum Associates (2007)

Hsu, Y.C., Ching, Y.H., Mathews, J.P., Carr-Chellman, A.: Undergraduate students' self-regulated learning experience in web-based learning environments. Quart. Rev. Distance Educ. **10**(2), 109–121 (2009)

James, W.: Pragmatism. Prometheus (1907)

Lamont, C.: Humanism. In: Runes, D.D. (ed.) Dictionary of philosophy. Rowman & Allanheld, Totowas, NJ (1984)

Livingstone, S., Haddon, L., Görzig, A., Ólafsson, K.: Risks and safety on the internet: The perspective of European children. Full Findings. LSE, EU Kids Online (2011)

Lo, C.-M., Han, J., Wong, E.S.W., Tang, C.-C.: Flexible learning with multicomponent blended learning mode for undergraduate chemistry courses in the pandemic of COVID-19. Interact. Technol. Smart Educ. **18**(2), 175–188 (2021). https://doi.org/10.1108/ITSE-05-2020-0061

Moore, M.G.: The theory of transactional distance. In: Moore, M.G. (ed.) Handbook of Distance Education, pp. 89–105. Lawrence Erlbaum Associates, Mahwah, NJ (2007)

Moore, M.G., Kearsley, G.: Distance education – a systems view of online learning. Wadsworth Cengage Learning (2012)

Peters, O.: The most industrialized form of education. In: Moore, M.G. (ed.) Handbook of Distance Education, pp. 57–68. Lawrence Erlbaum Associates (2007)

Quacquarelli, N.: Introduction. The Impact of the Coronavirus on Global Higher Education (2020). https://www.qs.com

Reigeluth, C.: Instructional Theory and Technology for the New Paradigm of Education (160). Revista de Educación a Distancia (RED) (2012). https://doi.org/10.6018/red/50/1b

Richey, R., Tracey, M.W., Klein, J.D.: The Instructional Design Knowledge Base – Theory, Research, and Practice. Routledge (2011)

Rizvi, S.H.: Avicenna/Ibn Sina (c. 980–1037), Internet Encyclopedia of Philosophy (2006). https://iep.utm.edu/avicenna-ibn-sina/

Rohlíková, L., Vejvodová, J.: Vyučovací metody. (Teaching methods) GRADA Publishing (2012)

Schunk, D.H.: Learning Theories – An Educational Perspective. Macmillan (1991)

Shishakly, R.: Challenges of online learning systems during COVID-19 in the UAE universities and its Effect on Business Students' Academic Performance. Am. J. Online Distance Learn. **3**(1), 1–24 (2021)

Siemens, G.: Connectivism: a Learning Theory for the Digital Age, Elearnspace (2005). http://www.elearnspace.org/Articles/connectivism.htm

Simonson, M., Smaldino, S., Albright, M., Zvacek, S.: Teaching and Learning at a Distance. Pearson Education Inc. (2008)

Skinner, B.F.: About Behaviorism. Knopf (1974)

Spiro, R.J., Coulson, R.L., Feltovich, P.J., Anderson, D.: Cognitive flexibility theory: Advanced knowledge acquisition in ill-structured domains. In: Tenth Annual Conference of the Cognitive Science Society, pp. 375–383. Lawrence Erlbaum Associates (1988)

Spiro, R.J., Feltovich, P.J., Jacobson, M.J., Coulson, R.L.: Cognitive flexibility, constructivism and hypertext: Random access instruction for advanced knowledge acquisition in ill-structured domains. Educational Technology, May, pp. 24–33 (1991)

Swan, K., Shen, J., Hiltz, S.R.: Assessment and collaboration in online learning. J. Asynchronous Learn. Netw. **10**(1), 45–62 (2006)

Tarrayo, V.N., Anudin, A.G.: Materials development in flexible learning amid the pandemic: perspectives from English language teachers in a Philippine state university. Innov. Lang. Learn. Teach. **17**(1), 102–113 (2023). https://doi.org/10.1080/17501229.2021.1939703

Shaheen, M., Pradhan, S., Ranajee: Sampling in qualitative research. In: Qualitative Techniques for Workplace Data Analysis, pp. 25–51 (2019). https://doi.org/10.4018/978-1-5225-5366-3.ch002

Rudolph, J., Tan, Sh., Tan. S.: War of the chatbots: Bard, Bing Chat, ChatGPT, Ernie and beyond. The new AI gold rush and its impact on higher education. J. Appl. Learn. Teach. **6**(1), 364–389 (2023). https://doi.org/10.37074/jalt.2023.6.1.23

Kim, J., Cho, Y.H.: My teammate is AI: understanding students' perceptions of student-AI collaboration in drawing tasks. Asia Pac. J. Edu. (2023). https://doi.org/10.1080/02188791.2023.2286206

Pesovski, I., Santos, R., Henriques, R., Trajkovik, R.: Generative AI for customizable learning experiences. Sustainability (2024). https://doi.org/10.3390/su16073034

Hosseini, M., Resnik, D.B., Holmes, K.: The ethics of disclosing the use of artificial intelligence tools in writing scholarly manuscripts. Res. Ethics **19**(4), 449–465 (2023). https://doi.org/10.1177/17470161231180449

# Human-AI Co-Innovation: Navigating the Innovative Problem-Solving Landscape with the Process Model and Technology Empowerment

Zehui Zhan[✉], Chaocheng Zhong, Jiayi Zheng, and Weisen Zhong

School of Information Technology in Education, South China Normal University, Tianhe District, No. 55 West Zhongshan Avanue, Guangzhou, China
zhanzehui@m.scnu.edu.cn

**Abstract.** This paper introduces a 5P model for guiding innovative problem-solving process and explores the role of artificial intelligence (AI) in facilitating the teaching and learning process. The complexity of innovative problem-solving necessitates the alternating application of divergent and convergent thinking along with phenomenon analysis, problem exploration, Plan design, prototype iteration, and value promotion. Considering the double helix development path of knowledge and thinking in this process, AI could deepen the leverage of innovative thinking by cognitive acceleration, social construction and Dual-Instructor Collaboration. Accordingly, a Human-AI Co-Innovation Framework is set up to further elaborate the AI empowerment mechanism. Looking forward, research should focus on refining human-computer collaboration and igniting students' passion for exploration. The AI-driven augmented intelligence paradigm opens new avenues for cultivating innovative talents with interdisciplinary perspectives and skills in human-computer collaboration.

**Keywords:** innovative problem-solving · Human-AI Co-Innovation · 5P model · artificial intelligence · innovation and entrepreneurship education

## 1 Introduction

Under the new round of technological revolution and industrial transformation, innovation has emerged as a crucial factor in the competition among major powers. Leading economies worldwide have positioned innovation at the heart of national development strategies, such as the United States' "Innovation and Competition Act," Japan's "Sixth Basic Plan for Science and Technology Innovation," and China's emphasis on "accelerating the implementation of the innovation-driven development strategy" in the report from its 20th National Congress, all striving to gain an edge in innovation-driven growth. Innovation and entrepreneurship education, serving as a pivotal platform for higher education to nurture innovative talents, is not only a significant strategic initiative for building innovative nations but also a crucial means to cultivate students' innovative spirit and practical skills.

However, innovation and entrepreneurship education at universities has encountered challenges such as outdated educational philosophies in nurturing innovative talents (Qiu et al., 2023), students' innovative thinking being constrained by prolonged indoctrination and restrictions (He, 2017), and the inability to resonate with the spirit of innovation in the curriculum, which hampers the effectiveness of overall teaching. Unlike disciplinary education, the essence of innovation and entrepreneurship education lies in fostering the entrepreneurial spirits, emphasizing enhancing students' overall qualities through problem-solving, and nurturing their entrepreneurial spirit, awareness, and capabilities (Mei et al., 2022). Students are often faced not with rigid knowledge questions but with how to apply interdisciplinary knowledge and skills to tackle complex problems in real-world situations.

Generally, problems are defined as unconventional situations lacking clear solutions. In another word, problems emerge when there is a definite goal, but without specific methods or actions to achieve the goal (Carlson & Bloom, 2005). Facing situations with ambiguous definitions, complex resolution paths, and uncertain outcomes, it becomes particularly crucial to address problems in a flexible and original way. In this context, the alternating use of divergent and convergent thinking is crucial: divergent thinking aids in exploring a broader range of innovative ideas, while convergent thinking assists in filtering, integrating, and making decisions among numerous perspectives and proposals, to get the most practical, reasonable, and viable solution. The core value of innovation not only lies in its novelty, practicality, and feasibility but also in its capacity to generate economic value, referred to as the "outcome effect" (Zhan et al., 2022). As a distinct type of task, innovative problem-solving emphasizes the full utilization of an individual's creativity in real-world scenarios to develop more pragmatic and efficient solutions as the problem transitions from its initial to its goal state. In essence, innovative problem-solving is the process of addressing uncertainties in real-world scenarios through innovative methods.

With the dawn of the cognitive intelligence era, artificial intelligence (AI) has become a pivotal support for solving innovative problems. An increasing array of AI tools are showcasing their significant advantages in identifying problems and generating solutions. According to their objectives and operational principles, AI can be categorized into two main types: discriminative AI and generative AI (Banh & Strobel, 2023). Discriminative AI (DAI) focuses on decision-making based on existing data, such as classification, regression, or clustering, aiming to identify decision boundaries through data analysis. Common models of DAI include support vector machines, decision trees, and K-nearest neighbors, among others. During the innovative problem-solving process, DAI can extract structured creative pathways from unstructured data, thereby accelerating the decision-making process (Jebara, 2004). For instance, discriminative models based on deep learning can analyze vast amounts of historical innovation cases to identify key features and patterns, thus providing fresh insights for new problems (Balcan & Blum, 2010).

Conversely, generative AI (GAI) is dedicated to creatively generating new contents, such as texts, images, and audio. It generates new samples that are similar yet not identical to the training data by learning the intrinsic distribution and structure of the data. Prominent models of GAI include Generative Adversarial Networks (GAN) and

Variational Autoencoders (VAE) (Gui et al., 2023; Wei & Mahmood, 2021). In innovative problem-solving, GAI has demonstrated remarkable advantages (Atchley et al., 2024). For example, large language models based on the Transformer architecture, such as GPT-3, can generate coherent and creative long texts from a small input of text (Ray, 2023). Image generation models based on GAN can transform text descriptions into high-quality images, providing intuitive visual feedback for creative design. By learning abstract concepts and patterns from vast data, GAI can explore multiple possibilities for problem-solving and inspire innovation (Li et al., 2024). Together, DAI and GAI complement each other and are expected to maximize the potential of AI in innovative problem-solving to the fullest extent.

In the evolution from perceptual to cognitive intelligence among humans, understanding the essence of things is largely based on problem-solving. Integrating the problem-solving pedagogy into innovation and entrepreneurship education has become a key task for cultivating innovative talents. However, there is not sufficient theoretical support from an epistemological perspective, and the mechanism by which AI facilitates the innovative problem-solving process remains unclear. In light of this, this study aims to explore the mechanism of AI-enhanced innovative problem-solving in entrepreneurship education. Specifically, this study seeks to address the following questions:

(1) How to guide the process of innovative problem-solving in innovation and entrepreneurship education?
(2) What's the hierarchical epistemological mechanism during the innovative problem-solving process and how to effectively deepen the leverage with AI?
(3) How could AI empower the innovative problem-solving process, and what are its specific mechanisms of action?

## 2 Navigating the Innovative Problem-Solving Landscape: The 5P Process Model of Innovative Problem-Solving

In the concrete operational aspect of problem-solving, contemporary research has delineated various stage-based methodologies from the initial to the target state of problem resolution, including the six-stage model (Dewey, 1910), the seven-stage model (Bransford et al., 1993), the eight-stage model (Bardach & Patashnik, 2019), and the five-stage model (Aarikka-Stenroos et al., 2012). These seminal problem-solving frameworks lay the groundwork for the development of innovative problem-solving models. Unlike traditional problem-solving, innovative problem-solving underscores the complexity and uncertainty of real-world problems within practical contexts, the diversity of solutions and strategies, the human-centric nature, and the value and scalability of the outcomes (Zhan et al., 2024). Serving as a conduit between creativity and innovation, design thinking is deemed an apt foundational model for this study and has been restructured within the entrepreneurship courses (Li & Zhan, 2022), which bifurcated the design process into problem definition and resolution phases. The problem definition phase encompasses divergent problem identification and convergent problem framing, whereas the problem resolution phase involves divergent solution development and convergent solution implementation.

Leveraging this divergent and convergent framework, in the entrepreneurship course, the "business plan" is utilized as a generative product that traverses the entire course, also acting as the linchpin of problem definition and resolution. Specifically, on one hand, "problem definition" is segmented into a problem discovery process based on "phenomenon analysis" and a pain point determination process based on "problem exploration," enabling students to undergo observation, analysis, contemplation, and decision-making within the innovation process, thereby facilitating "solution design" upon thoroughly understanding the problem; on the other hand, "problem resolution" is segmented into a testing and evaluation process for the Minimum Viable Product (MVP) based on "prototype iteration" and a solution demonstration and promotion process based on "value propagation." Accordingly, we interpret the innovative problem-solving process as comprising five phases: Phenomenon Analysis, Problem Exploration, Plan Design, Prototype Iteration, and Value Promotion, as depicted in Fig. 1. Due to the contextual complexity inherent in the innovative problem-solving process, it necessitates deconstructing each phase into a series of specific segments through tiered thinking. Each segment must rigorously adhere to the dual standards of creativity and value, progressing under the alternating influence of divergent and convergent thinking.

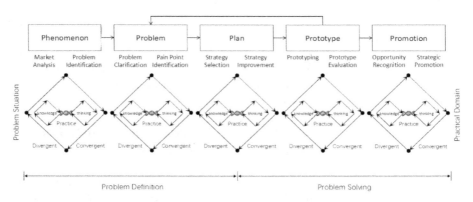

**Fig. 1.** The 5P Bead String Model of Creative Problem-Solving

Each node in this model starts with the letter P and is connected by multiple diamonds, forming a sequence that resembles a string of diamonds. That's why it is also named as "5P Bead Chain Model." The model aims to depict the abstract process of thinking development as a series of logical and interconnected steps, offering a vivid guide for solving innovative problems.

Within this framework, the problem situation is depicted as a "continuum," linking performance tasks in practical contexts. Each phase of the 5P Model encompasses three pivotal points: the first is the "starting point," which represents the demand point of the task to be accomplished and serves as the goal and starting point for divergent thinking. The second is the "divergence endpoint," achieved after extensive exploration, where the culmination of all perspectives and wisdom represents the peak of divergent thinking. The more creative ideas and new perspectives generated at the "divergence endpoint," the more innovative the problem-solving at this stage. The third is the "convergence endpoint," which begins with the divergence endpoint and involves convergent thinking to examine, integrate, optimize, and decide among the numerous perspectives and plans developed. The more effective the solutions generated at the "convergence endpoint," the greater the value of the problem-solving. The final solution obtained after the processes of divergence and convergence in each stage of solving innovative problems becomes the initial basis for the next stage, thereby gradually advancing the resolution of innovative problems.

## 3 How AI Help to Deepen the Leverage of Innovative Thinking

### 3.1 The "Knowledge-Thinking" Spiral

Innovative problem-solving is grounded in the problem representation, which encompasses the problem situation and problem space. The problem situation is situated within a practical context, highlighting the individual's organization and cognition of the facts, concepts, and their interrelationships that constitute the problem, through "transformation" and "correspondence" in a real, challenging, and complex environment, ensuring the embodied participation of multiple senses. The problem space refers to the individual's process of encoding the components of the problem (such as specified conditions, goals, rules, and other relevant contexts) into interpretable internal mental representations, visualizing the transition of the problem from an initial state through an intermediate state to a goal state in a spatial form. The essence of problem-solving is a series of purposeful, goal-directed cognitive activities aimed at achieving a goal state (Simon & Newell, 1971). When contradictions are reflected in consciousness, the individual focuses on the problem goal to gather and process information, employing various cognitive activities and skills in an attempt to solve the problem. Thus, the problem situation and problem space are not only central elements of innovative problem-solving but also the mediums through which knowledge and thinking exert their effects, determining the rational representation of the problem and its solution.

Learning is a social and practical process mediated by differential resources, entailing participation. The internal and external, virtual and real places and environments where humans conduct practical activities form the practice field (Bourdieu, 1980). Human rationality and sensibility are always embedded within specific practice fields, with an individual's desire for problem-solving serving as the foundation for inducing, guiding, and supporting learning behaviors. Differences in individuals' understanding and cognition of behavioral norms within the practice field lead to various innovative motivations and behavioral outcomes. Since human cognition is not a static representation of a fixed mind towards a fixed world but a dynamic, embodied engagement (Vallet et al., 2016), the "visibility" of the practice field is determined by the state of individual embodied involvement. Therefore, based on the level of human embodied participation, the practice field can be segmented into five sub-fields: initial field, marginal field, progressive field, central field, and comprehensive field, as shown in Fig. 2.

## 3.2 The Five-Tier Hierarchy of Innovative Problem-Solving

During innovative problem-solving, the cognitive structure is modified through "adaptation" and "restructuring"; fragmented knowledge within the brain also becomes hierarchical and systematized as the cognitive structure is refined during the innovation process. The linkage between thinking and knowledge is depicted as a double helix structure, embedding and supporting each other. Considering the intrinsic unity of knowledge and thinking, innovative problem-solving can be categorized into five progressive levels: pre-scattered structure, single-point horizontal structure, multi-point cross structure, associative multidirectional structure, and abstract expansion-synthetic structure, which are elaborated as follow:

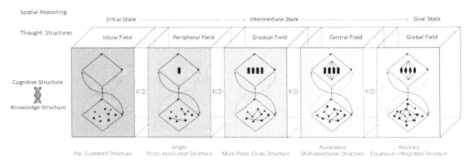

**Fig. 2.** Five-Tier Hierarchical Structure for Innovative Problem-Solving

### 3.2.1 Initial Field: Pre-scattered Structure

In the initial field, the practical field is separate from cognition. It gains value only through subjective mental actions (Chambon et al., 2014). Facing complex problems, individuals perceive phenomena open-mindedly, aiming for insights. Their judgments, based on past experiences, are influenced by prior knowledge, focusing on details and leaving the thought structure blank. Their fragmented knowledge is weakly related to the problem, insufficient for filtering irrelevant info (Stamovlasis et al., 2013). Thus, they rely on incidental info, causing logical disarray and redundancy in understanding. In the pre-scattered structure, learners have not yet probed into the clues of the problem, but the fragmented knowledge still enables learners to establish an intuitive understanding of the problem clues.

### 3.2.2 Peripheral Field: Single Point—Horizontal Structure

In the peripheral field, individuals gradually shift their practice from phenomenological cognition to exploring the essence of the problems. Within the single point—horizontal structure, the discrimination and filtration of information are fundamental to the formation of problem clues, constituting a generalization of a single event under the influence of thinking and knowledge. However, this generalization lacks precision and comprehensiveness, as the learners' thinking is characterized by a bundle-like single-point structure formed by the lateral transfer of similar types of knowledge. The insufficient expansiveness and transferability of thought make it easy for learners to overlook potential contradictions within responses, resulting in solutions that focus on horizontal connections but lack vertical depth.

### 3.2.3 Progressive Field: Multi-point – Cross-Structure

In the progressive field, as individuals deepen their state of embodied engagement, they move from peripheral participation to progressive participation. At this point, a bilateral or multilateral network formed by structural relationships has not yet emerged, necessitating individuals to undertake more practical activities to strengthen their subjective position (Eberle et al., 2014). In the multi-point—cross-structure, learners perceive an increasing number of correct features related to the problem within the problem context, uncover limited problem clues around several problem features, and use these clues as anchors to inductively summarize and generalize surrounding isolated events. However, learners at this stage are unable to perceive the connection between problem clues and information, often providing "possible solutions" that are fragmented.

### 3.2.4 Central Field: Associative-Multidirectional Structure

In the central field, individuals are less affected by external events and information, and under the influence of subjective spirit, they gradually build a network that reflects the essential connections among concepts, facts, and problem-solving situations (Cattaneo, 2023). This construction is often specific and multidirectional, characterized by its rich extensiveness and associativity. In the associative-multidirectional structure, due to the high transferability between knowledge nodes, the alternation frequency between knowledge and thinking is increased, enabling learners to link multiple events and achieve high-throughput transfer in problem-solving through reverse operations and feedback mechanisms. Consequently, the strategies generated for problem-solving are more diverse and appropriate.

### 3.2.5 Holistic Field: Abstract Expansion—Integrated Structure

Within the holistic field, individuals are fully immersed in the practice field, with the external world seamlessly integrated into their cognition. This integration facilitates the emergence of knowledge and thinking at a higher level of abstraction through the dynamic relationship of the "brain-body-field" (Madsen & Aggerholm, 2020). In the holistic field, learners transcend existing information and data, venturing into a new mode of reasoning that expands the intrinsic meaning of the problem, making solutions or conclusions more open-ended and abstract. These "classes" or "domains" represent a unique expression of knowledge, characterized by their distinct interdisciplinary attributes and structured features, with the relationships between nodes being deep, intrinsic, and transcending superficial appearances. In this stage, learners are able to distill the essential characteristics of problems and apply what they have learned to seemingly highly dissimilar situations on the surface, thus achieving solutions to innovative problems.

## 3.3 The Mechanism of AI in Enhancing Innovative Thinking

Artificial intelligence, by integrating into the entire chain of innovators' cognitive processes, practical scenarios, and the transformation of creativity, has redefined the intrinsic mechanisms of innovative problem-solving across three dimensions: cognitive processing, social structuring, and collaborative mentorship. This integration has led to the establishment of a practice paradigm characterized by a synergistic augmentation of human-computer interaction.

### 3.3.1 Cognitive Acceleration: Reshaping the Individual Cognitive Processing Flow

AI's intervention in the individual's process of solving innovative problems fosters a profound integration between human intelligence and machine intelligence, breaking through the constraints of human cognition. On one side, intelligent algorithms powered by machine learning can swiftly search, compare, filter, and link massive volumes of heterogeneous data, uncovering hidden complex patterns and laws. This aids individuals in breaking away from conventional thought patterns, creating multidimensional and interdisciplinary information landscapes, and providing a rich source of nourishment for divergent thinking. On the other side, artificial intelligence can monitor the data of the innovation process in real-time, uncover patterns of innovative behaviors, and establish an interpretable and transferable strategic knowledge base. It offers heuristic cues that go beyond previous experiences when innovators face deadlocks, guiding the continuous deepening of thought and preventing aimless divergence. Thus, artificial intelligence merges the advantages of human cognitive and computational thinking, propelling the reconstruction of the "information processing-knowledge extraction-strategy optimization" process. This promotes a beneficial interaction between "knowledge and thinking," accelerating the spiral iteration of innovative thought.

### 3.3.2 Social Construction: Catalyzing Collaborative Innovation in Teams

Innovative problem-solving cannot be separated from social interaction and collaboration. AI has created an intelligent social construct for innovation practices, serving as a "catalyst" for the collaborative emergence of innovation within groups. AI is capable of precisely connecting innovators from different fields, intelligently matching them based on their knowledge backgrounds, research interests, and complementary skills to form highly creative heterogeneous teams. Additionally, AI provides a variety of intelligent tools for collaborative innovation, such as online brainstorming platforms, virtual collaboration spaces, and intelligent project management systems, breaking the barriers of time and space to enhance the efficiency of collaboration. Throughout this process, AI also continuously records and analyzes data from the collaboration process, identifying patterns of collective intelligence emergence and optimizing the routes for collaborative innovation. For instance, it identifies and reinforces the conditions for generating key creative ideas, adjusts the modes of interaction among team members, and guides the convergence and clash of different perspectives. Consequently, AI acts as the "social adhesive" for collaborative innovation, fostering the emergence and leap of group intelligence.

### 3.3.3 Dual-Instructor Collaboration: Fostering a New Model of Student-Centered Education

AI and teachers collaborate as a "dual-instructor" team to foster an intelligent, interactive, and tailored educational ecosystem. In this human-computer collaborative teaching paradigm, AI and teachers leverage their respective strengths to complement each other and collectively enhance students' innovative abilities. AI excels at processing vast amounts of information quickly, establishing knowledge connections, and creating accurate student profiles. It provides personalized learning resources, real-time feedback, and adaptive learning pathways to achieve precise instruction. Teachers, on the other hand, draw on their extensive teaching experience and deep understanding of students to design innovative teaching activities. They create a classroom atmosphere conducive to innovation, guide students in inquiry-based and project-based learning, and subtly influence students' innovation consciousness and beliefs through demonstrating innovative thinking methods and sharing innovative cases.

## 4 Human-AI Co-Innovation Framework: The AI Empowerment

The need for technology acts as the direct driving force behind an individual's technological behavior. The logic of technology serving education is the alignment between the needs of teachers and students and the tools available. The distinguished German sociologist Weber, M. (1978) divided technological rationality into two types: instrumental rationality and value rationality. From the standpoint of instrumental rationality, the application of AI in the problem-solving process must adhere to the norms of normalization, convenience, efficiency, and practicality. On the other hand, from the perspective of value rationality, the application of AI should integrate human emotional preferences and value pursuits, highlighting the rationality of AI applications and their congruence with human essence and genuine needs. Only AI that is practical and targeted can be normalized in educational applications.

In entrepreneurship education, given the intricate nature of innovative issues, it is imperative to leverage AI for its capabilities in acquiring and organizing information, presenting and evaluating knowledge, facilitating divergent and convergent thinking, and managing planning and project execution. The "solution assistance" and "creation assistance" role of AI supports enhances the uniqueness, practicality, and viability of solutions throughout the practical process. Therefore, this study developed a Human-AI Co-Innovation Framework (see Fig. 3), representing the function of AI grounded in the 5P Model. On one hand, it can offer personalized support to students based on data on their learning behaviors; on the other hand, it can also reduce the cost of solving problems by optimizing resource allocation.

### 4.1 AI Empowerment in the Construction of Practical Fields

Practical fields are spaces designated for the identification, resolution, iterative development, and validation of solutions to problems. In the educational process, the creation of problem scenarios, personalized teaching, and real-time feedback are all indispensable elements supported by intelligent learning environments. AI can empower the construction of practical fields with two types of intelligent learning environments: The first is by creating adaptive learning environments through technologies such as machine learning and knowledge graphs. These environments can accurately capture data on students' learning behaviors, analyze their grasp of knowledge and learning preferences, and thus recommend personalized learning resources and paths. This approach meets the individualized learning needs of students during the process of solving innovative problems, thereby enhancing their learning outcomes. The second is by establishing intelligent interactive environments through natural language processing and intelligent dialogue systems. These environments can provide students with intelligent learning assistant services, facilitating automatic answers to questions, real-time instructional guidance, and guidance throughout the problem-solving process via human-computer dialogue. Furthermore, they can encourage interactive exploration between students and intelligent assistants, thereby stimulating students' creativity and imagination.

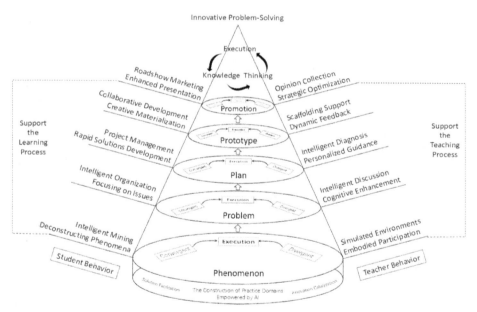

**Fig. 3.** Mechanism Diagram of Innovation Problem-Solving Empowered by Technology

## 4.2 AI Empowers the Learning Process

From the perspective of students, the empowerment of innovative learning by AI manifests in two aspects: (1) accelerate the divergence and convergence of thought; (2) assist students in transforming ideas into schemes or products with certain economic value. Specifically, the support of AI in learning process is reflected in the following five aspects:

First, intelligent exploration and deconstruction of phenomena. Faced with uncertain events, students will develop an intuitive understanding, which can only be transformed into various problem clues by collecting a large amount of information and meticulously analyzing it. The application of AI can aid students in gathering extensive information and materials, as well as acquiring multi-sensory experiences. For instance, intelligent information collectors like WiseFlow and MindSearch are specifically designed for collecting and organizing online information. By employing specific AI algorithms, they enable learners to capture data from multiple websites and resources in real time, compiling it into a comprehensive report. This allows students to delve into issues from multiple perspectives and dimensions, enhancing research efficiency. Moreover, integrating the ChatGPT API into WeChat groups, group members can engage in multiple rounds of dialogue with Chat GPT on a particular phenomenon or topic, obtaining multifaceted answers and comprehensive informational materials. By embracing the advantageous aspects of intelligent solutions, a unique insight is ultimately formed through human-computer collaboration.

Secondly, intelligent organization and focus on the problem. After a deep analysis of the phenomena, the focus and characterization of the problem determine the direction of its resolution. The application of AI can help students efficiently organize and process information, quickly converge their thoughts, eliminate irrelevant information, reason through problem clues, and form logical and innovative conclusions for solving problems. For example, when students are confronted with messy information and multiple complex clues, AI tutors and learning assistants, such as Tutor.ai and Syntea, can provide personalized guidance to help students solve problems, making the learning process more focused and engaging. Furthermore, ChatGPT can start from a first-person perspective, assisting individuals in selecting information through Socratic dialogue, gradually focusing on the issue, and helping students distinguish between pain points and difficulties until identifying the "real problem" to be solved. This achieves a comprehensive organization of textual information based on the learner's thought framework.

Third, project management, expedited solutions. Once the problem is clearly defined, students are tasked with creating targeted solutions, a process complicated by the constraints of time and space. Thus, the judicious use of AI and tools can significantly enhance the flow of information and knowledge among team members, facilitate a multidimensional approach to problem-solving strategies, and streamline project management. Team members can employ smart meeting note-taking tools such as Feishu Miaoji, Tongyi Tingwu, and Tencent Meeting AI Assistant to simplify the documentation process, improve information management and task execution, and further the development and organization of strategies. Additionally, leveraging ChatGPT, which possesses a level of expert thinking, to identify issues in the preliminary design solutions and offer suggestions for adjustments can aid students in refining their problem-solving approaches in a timely manner, thereby reducing time costs.

Fourth, collaborative development and the materialization of creativity. The specific presentation of design schemes depends on the materialized products that match them. Developing the simplest viable product through team collaboration forms the foundation of advancing projects. AI can facilitate efficient collaborative development among team members, enhancing the transformation of creative ideas into tangible products.

For instance, AI-assisted design software like Uizard can automatically analyze user inputs and generate optimal layout plans, thereby streamlining the application design process for teams. Moreover, through collaborative features, such software can ignite the exceptional skills, knowledge, and ideas of each team member, bridging the gaps between inspiration, thought, creation, management, presentation, and collaboration, thus achieving efficient team management and comprehensive task collaboration. In the aspect of rapid prototyping, AI technologies like Codedesign.ai can quickly generate UI elements and design interfaces based on text inputs, facilitating the swift creation of product prototypes. Additionally, by employing AI methods such as machine learning to analyze user behavior data, these technologies can further the verification of a product's effectiveness, credibility, and security, thereby enabling iterative optimization of the product.

Fifth, roadshow promotion to enhance display. The final stage of innovative problem-solving is to have students undergo entrepreneurial simulation training or incubation. By building scenario-based business logic, identifying the most advantageous scenes and opportunities for product promotion, students can clarify the forms, plans, and presentation tools of product promotion through both divergent and convergent thinking. The application of AI can aid in precisely targeting the intended audience, effectively conducting market research, creating product demonstrations, and collecting consumer feedback, thereby enhancing their business acumen. For example, students can leverage Baidu's ERNIE-ViLG 2.0 and other large language models such as DALL-E 2 and Midjourney to generate cross-modal product posters or virtual spokespersons for promotion, displaying results, and sharing creativity. In terms of collecting feedback, a variety of AI technologies, such as Natural Language Processing (NLP), can be utilized. For instance, the Sauce platform employs NLP technology to automatically collect and analyze customer feedback from multiple channels, assisting product teams in understanding customer needs and providing data-driven decision support, effectively evaluating the impact and effectiveness of the innovative outcomes.

## 4.3 AI Empowers the Teaching Process

The complexity of innovative teaching stems from the inherent dynamic generation, uniqueness, and uncertainty of teaching activities. From the perspective of teacher behavior, the essence of leveraging AI for innovative problem-solving lies in the simplification of "complexity". Teachers should enhance their educational and instructional capabilities through the use of various AI technologies, grounded in their own subjectivity and creativity. This approach enables them to comprehensively understand the process of students' problem-solving and guide them towards achieving their goals.

First, Simulation Situations, Embodied Participation. The entire process of innovative problem-solving is transitioning from physical to digital spaces, underscoring the importance of creating a practice field for innovation and entrepreneurship that blends the virtual with the real. It is essential for teachers to establish learning environments that are relaxed, open for discussion, conducive to collaboration, and supportive of autonomous exploration and intellectual engagement. This approach facilitates a deeper understanding of problems among students through embodied participation. For example, AI-supported virtual laboratory, such as Labster and PhET Interactive Simulations, offer students a highly interactive and immersive learning experience. These platforms enable students to engage in the innovative problem-solving process in various roles, thereby enhancing their initiative and sense of involvement, and promoting sensory perception, behavioral control, and the construction of meaning. From the perspective of problem-solving, virtual platforms driven by AI not only make the presentation of problem situations more vivid but also ensure the dissemination of knowledge within these problems is more efficient.

Secondly, intellectual seminars and stimulation of thought. In the face of complex and fragmented information, students are required to judge, filter, and construct their own conceptual networks. Teachers can utilize AI to establish virtual learning communities, such as through intelligent educational platforms like Zhihai-Sanle (sanle.hep.com.cn), offering opportunities for discussion and conceptualization. This enables the continuous feedback of information and knowledge within the group into the knowledge system, fostering a positive cycle between individual and organizational knowledge (Zamiri & Esmaeili, 2024). Furthermore, AI-powered knowledge graphs can be employed to assist students in organizing the connections between different subject areas, creating a meaningful mechanism for knowledge transformation, and accelerating the evolution and optimization of knowledge and thinking. At this stage, teachers should also leverage AI tools to gather students' ideas, comprehend the origins of innovative problems, and provide their insights. They can even inspire students through ChatGPT to generate meaningful viewpoints, facilitating the aggregation of wisdom in the problem-solving process and achieving the regenerative accumulation of collective knowledge.

Third, intelligent diagnostics and personalized guidance. Problem diagnostics involve utilizing various AI technologies to unearth issues within design schemes, promptly detecting imbalances in learning progress. This allows for the control of the teaching pace and the flexible adjustment of teaching plans and strategies to achieve educational goals. For example, adaptive learning systems like the "Smart AI Assistant System for University Physics Courses" at Southeast University in China, by constructing knowledge graphs and student profiles, can timely understand students' learning statuses and needs. These systems are capable of diagnosing the progress of resolving issues in design schemes, pushing personalized reference materials to students, guiding them to maximize their individual potential, assisting in "failure management," and precisely providing the necessary support and guidance.

Fourth, Scaffolding Support and Dynamic Feedback. During the process of constructing prototypes based on design schemes, students are required to integrate interdisciplinary knowledge and various AI tools. Therefore, it is imperative for teachers to provide timely scaffolding to assist students in overcoming challenges. On one hand, teachers utilize AI-driven intelligent tutoring systems, such as the GLM4 model developed by Tsinghua University, which boasts hundreds of billions of parameters. This system acquaints students with the usage and operation of AI tools, thereby aiding them in verifying user segmentation, product or service modality, application effects, and market responses. This continuous support facilitates the refinement of product prototype development and application. On the other hand, teachers must constantly monitor the issues students face during prototype construction. With the aid of AI tools for intelligent monitoring and data analysis, teachers can obtain real-time insights into students' subtle behavioral changes during problem-solving. These insights, marked by time, create a behavioral footprint (Ouyang et al., 2023), allowing for the provision of timely feedback on issues. This, in turn, supports students in the iterative optimization of the prototype product.

Fifth, gathering opinions and optimizing strategies. During the value promotion phase, teachers can utilize AI to construct scenario-based business logics. For instance, by employing AI-driven virtual characters to create simulated business scenarios, students can be engaged in playing various roles within a virtual environment, such as investors or customers, to interact and make decisions, culminating in the publication of outcomes. In the aspect of roadshow promotion, teachers can take advantage of AI to establish intelligent roadshow platforms, like the "National Science and Technology Plan Achievement Roadshow Promotion Platform," which centrally publishes and showcases roadshow activities and results, providing a linkage channel for both supply and demand sides. Throughout this process, teachers should fully leverage AI to empower the evaluation of teaching, accurately assess the creativity generated by students, and make strategic adjustments and optimizations to teaching strategies based on these creative outcomes, thereby enhancing the decision-making's effectiveness and adaptability. For example, by using AI systems to simulate the thought processes of expert reviews and employing AI feedback generators, such as integrating ChatGPT to automatically generate detailed and constructive feedback, teachers can offer professional guidance for students' projects.

## 4.4 Typical Cases

### 4.4.1 Phenomenon Analysis

Innovative problem-solving begins with a thorough analysis of phenomena related to the issue at hand. This process necessitates that learners extensively gather data and information, through which they can identify key features and patterns. Traditional methods of data collection and analysis are often time-consuming and labor-intensive. However, the advent of large language models and intelligent data analysis tools has provided significant intelligent support for this phase. Learners can utilize large language models with internet search capabilities, such as KimiChat, to efficiently acquire background information pertinent to the problem. By simply using natural language to describe the issue of concern, KimiChat can swiftly return highly relevant background information, research reports, news events, and more, based on vast web data, encompassing texts, data, charts, among other formats. Leveraging the model's robust capabilities for semantic understanding and information integration, learners can quickly access multidimensional information about the problem, thereby constructing a comprehensive picture of the phenomenon.

Based on the collection of information, learners can further utilize intelligent data analysis tools such as TableFinder to automate the organization and exploration of the gathered structured data. By uploading the data to TableFinder and posing questions in natural language, learners are able to swiftly compute various statistical metrics, create charts depicting data distribution, and intuitively understand the characteristics of the data (Figs. 4 and 5). For unstructured text data, learners can employ advanced language

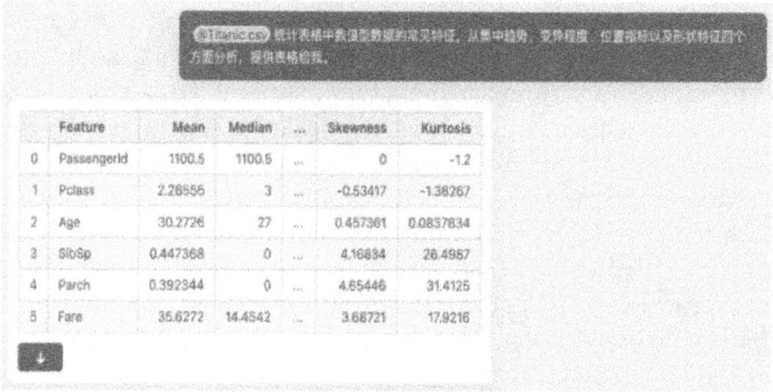

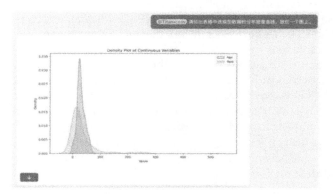

**Fig. 4.** Return a table based on structured data

models like Claude, using prompts to guide the model in automatically extracting key informational elements, summarizing the essence of the text, and deeply mining the valuable insights concealed within the text.

**Fig. 5.** Return a chart based on structured data

### 4.4.2 Problem Exploration

The Zoddy platform, built on the cutting-edge Large Language Model algorithms, is endowed with formidable capabilities in semantic understanding and information processing. It is capable of interfacing with multi-source heterogeneous data, swiftly accessing a vast array of information, and utilizing technologies such as natural language processing and knowledge graphs for intelligent parsing, extraction, association, and integration, thereby eliminating redundancies to create a structured knowledge base. Building on this foundation, Zoddy guides users to systematically identify the causes of issues using tools like the Ishikawa fishbone diagram. Through the use of visualization technology, the platform vividly displays the analysis process and leverages its accumulated interdisciplinary knowledge to intelligently recommend and supplement potential causes, assisting users in a comprehensive examination of the issues at hand.

Through human-machine collaboration, the Zoddy platform reduces the users' burden of manually sorting information and accelerates the accurate understanding of problem contexts. More importantly, with deep learning models trained on vast amounts of data, the platform can acutely capture the semantic implications of user inputs, proactively connect with enlightening new perspectives, break through traditional thought patterns, and uncover truly significant issues. For example, when an innovative team used the Zoddy platform to explore ways to enhance meeting efficiency, the platform quickly identified key influencing factors and guided the team to focus on deep-rooted causes such as "insufficient preparation before meetings" and "large differences in participants' backgrounds," thereby broadening the team members' perspectives.

### 4.4.3 Plan Design

The AI tutor and teaching assistant, Khanmigo, co-developed by Khan Academy and OpenAI, plays a crucial role in assisting students with identifying solutions to problems. After learners draft an initial solution for a specific issue on the platform, they have the opportunity to engage in deep dialogue with Khanmigo, who is equipped with expert-level thinking. Through Socratic questioning, Khanmigo encourages learners to scrutinize their solutions from various angles, pinpointing potential flaws and areas for improvement. For instance, Khanmigo might pose thought-provoking questions like, "What challenges could arise during the implementation of this solution?" or "Are there alternative solutions that could be considered?" Such questions prompt learners to reflect and self-question, leading to the continuous refinement of their solutions.

Khanmigo, drawing from an extensive knowledge base and cutting-edge algorithms, is adept at holistically considering the myriad factors affecting a plan, simulating the scenario of its implementation, forecasting potential risks, and offering viable optimization recommendations. This intelligence-led guidance, rooted in expert experience, aids learners in thoroughly evaluating the viability of a plan, refining its details, and substantially reducing the time and cost associated with repeated trials and errors. Engaging with Khanmigo, learners receive tailored professional advice, and through proactive thinking and iterative refinement, they gradually develop solutions that are not only more comprehensive but also more innovative.

### 4.4.4 Prototype Iteration

Galileo AI, powered by the cutting-edge Large Language Model algorithms and embracing the "Text to UI" philosophy, not only can generate high-fidelity user interface designs from textual descriptions but also supports importing these design outcomes into Figma for detailed refinement and iteration. Its core driving force stems from its deep learning model, which can precisely interpret users' textual inputs and swiftly produce design prototypes. This procedure significantly reduces the transition time from abstract concepts to concrete visual prototypes, enabling both professional designers and novices to quickly explore and iterate over diverse design ideas. With just a concise text description from the user, Galileo AI can unveil a multitude of visual design options, encompassing layout, user interface elements, imagery, and text, thereby aiding users in accurately capturing the essence of the design and making rapid adjustments.

In the domain of AI co-creation, Galileo AI not only boosts the efficiency of design but also unleashes boundless potential for innovation. It sharply captures the semantic implications embedded in user inputs through advanced deep learning models, actively connects with insightful new perspectives, breaks free from traditional cognitive molds, and uncovers the truly vital elements of design. For instance, when users upload an initial interface sketch, Galileo AI is capable of analyzing and suggesting a variety of optimization strategies, directing users to concentrate on the crucial interactive and visual components within the design, thus fostering innovation and refinement. This form of intelligent design support streamlines and enhances the prototype iteration process.

### 4.4.5 Promotion and Value Distribution

In the final stage of solving innovative problems, teams are required to demonstrate the value of their innovative outcomes to potential users or investors, to carry out effective promotion. The Yidong AI Platform, through the customization of digital human avatars, enables teams to interact with investors in a more vivid and personalized way during product presentations. These digital humans can simulate realistic appearances and voices, providing a targeted interactive experience, thereby enhancing investors' sense of engagement and their recognition of the company's value. Moreover, Yidong AI also offers intelligent analysis report services, which analyze the participation data and behavioral patterns of investors, aiding entrepreneurial teams in better understanding the needs and feedback of investors. This service leverages AI to conduct in-depth analysis of vast amounts of data, providing the company with profound insights and recommendations, thereby optimizing future investor relations strategies.

## 5 Research Evidence on Effectiveness of AI in Innovative Problem-Solving

Extensive research has provided robust evidence demonstrating the efficacy of AI in problem-solving. For example, Gizzi et al. (2022) introduced a framework that encompasses problem formalization, knowledge representation, knowledge manipulation, and evaluation as core components, offering a theoretical basis for AI-driven problem-solving. They found AI has exceptional capability in processing and manipulating a variety of abstract concepts related to problems, particularly in the areas of problem representation, knowledge reasoning, and solution generation. These findings are consistent with Garbuio and Lin (2021)'s, who argue that AI fundamentally transforms the innovation process by augmenting human causal reasoning abilities. AI can swiftly process a vast array of structured and unstructured data, extracting valuable insights and significantly broadening the cognitive horizons of innovators. Further experimental studies have corroborated the positive contribution of AI to creative problem-solving. For instance, AI-powered assistants, by providing timely feedback and posing challenging questions, along with immersive learning experiences, effectively stimulate students' thinking and creativity (Winkler et al., 2019). Students assisted by ChatGPT notably surpassed the control group in terms of solution quality, detail, and originality (Urban et al., 2024).

However, the full potential of AI in solving innovative problems can only be unleashed through effective human-computer collaboration and meticulously designed educational applications. Boussioux et al. (2024) conducted an empirical study to compare the effectiveness of human crowdsourcing (HC) versus human-AI collaboration (HAI) in generating innovative solutions. The findings revealed that solutions developed through human-AI collaboration (HAI) were significantly superior to those from human crowdsourcing (HC) in strategic feasibility, environmental value, financial value, and overall quality. More importantly, HAI solutions generated under human-guided differentiated search outperformed those from AI-alone search configurations in terms of novelty and overall quality, underscoring the crucial role of human guidance in optimizing AI outputs. Despite AI's substantial enhancement of the process for solving innovative problems, human creativity and insight remain indispensable. Future research should focus on optimizing human-computer collaboration to maintain unique human creative thinking while leveraging AI capabilities (Garbuio & Lin, 2021).

Integrating AI into practical problem-solving not only promotes the innovative problem-solving process but also enhances students' creativity. AI teaching platforms are capable of collecting vast amounts of multimodal data generated by students throughout their learning journey and perform in-depth analyses using machine learning algorithms to precisely diagnose students' learning difficulties, offering personalized interventions and support (Zhong & Zhan, 2024). For instance, AI can analyze the learning data of students or groups with weaker entrepreneurial skills, pinpoint their difficulties, and provide targeted assistance for accurate problem resolution. AI-driven adaptive learning platforms, virtual labs, and collaborative platforms offer students personalized learning pathways, secure experimental settings, and opportunities for interdisciplinary collaboration, thereby sparking their enthusiasm for exploration and innovative thinking (Pane et al., 2015; Johnson et al., 2016). The integration of AI tools into problem-oriented project-based learning significantly boosts students' capabilities in tackling complex real-world problems (Shneiderman, 2020).

## 6 Challenges and Opportunities

### 6.1 Challenges

In the integration of AI into the practice of solving innovative problems, we encounter several key challenges. The complexity of integrating technology cannot be ignored. To seamlessly integrate AI with current educational and innovative practices, it is necessary to address issues such as data compatibility and system interoperability to ensure the effective application of the technology. Different learning management systems and AI platforms might use varying data formats and interface standards, making it difficult for data to flow between systems and thus affecting the efficacy of AI. Furthermore, issues of data privacy and security are of utmost importance. Strict measures must be taken to protect privacy and ensure the confidentiality and integrity of students' learning data and personal information, which is crucial for building user trust and meeting regulatory requirements. However, finding a balance between effective data protection and full utilization is not an easy task (Friedrich et al., 2024).

The application of AI presents new challenges for the roles and capabilities of teachers. Not only must teachers understand the fundamental principles and methods of AI, but they must also be able to apply it creatively in their teaching practices. This requires a shift in teaching philosophies and a proactive exploration of new models for human-computer collaboration. However, many teachers are still relatively unfamiliar with AI and lack the necessary training and support. Addressing how to assist teachers in quickly mastering AI and seamlessly integrating it with teaching content and strategies is an urgent issue (Zawacki-Richter et al., 2019). Additionally, teachers must be wary of over-relying on technology to the detriment of interpersonal interaction and emotional communication.

The swift advancement of AI brings forth new challenges to the education of ethics and values. During the process of solving problems innovatively, students might become overly dependent on the solutions and suggestions provided by AI, thus neglecting the development of independent and critical thinking (Zhong et al., 2024). Concurrently, AI could exacerbate the inherent biases within data, adversely influencing students' value systems. For instance, should the data used for training AI models exhibit gender bias, the output generated by these models could reinforce such biases, potentially eluding the students' awareness of these underlying prejudices (O'Connor & Liu, 2023). Hence, it is imperative to bolster ethical education while employing AI, guiding students towards a proper understanding and utilization of technology, and fostering the establishment of sound values.

## 6.2 Opportunities

Despite facing numerous challenges in applying AI to the resolution of innovative problems, it has also ushered in tremendous opportunities for educational reform. AI provides a robust tool for facilitating personalized and adaptive learning. Traditional teaching models often employ a "one-size-fits-all" approach, which struggles to address the individual differences among students. AI, however, can analyze students' learning behavior data to accurately identify their levels of knowledge, learning styles, and interests, thereby offering learning content and strategies tailored to their unique characteristics. For instance, the Cognitive Tutor intelligent tutoring system developed by Carnegie Mellon University is capable of adjusting the difficulty level of learning content and hinting strategies in real-time based on students' performance, achieving personalized instruction (Koedinger et al., 2013). This form of personalized learning support can significantly enhance students' learning efficiency and motivation.

AI can also offer students immersive and interactive learning experiences, kindling their passion for exploration and creativity. Unlike traditional classroom instruction, which primarily revolves around teacher lectures and passive knowledge absorption by students, AI enables the creation of lifelike virtual environments. Within these environments, students are encouraged to actively explore, manipulate, and create. For instance, virtual reality drawing tools such as Google's Tilt Brush and Oculus's Medium permit students to craft freely in three-dimensional spaces, thus sparking their artistic imagination. Moreover, intelligent conversational systems and virtual assistants facilitate natural interactions with students, offering immediate feedback and guidance to foster a learning atmosphere that feels real and engaging.

Ultimately, AI opens up new avenues for fostering interdisciplinary integration and collaborative innovation. Innovation often arises from the intersection and collision of knowledge across different disciplines, yet traditional disciplinary barriers and knowledge silos have impeded such integration. AI, however, can act as a robust platform for integrating knowledge, linking and reasoning across diverse fields to ignite the spark of cross-disciplinary thinking. For instance, IBM's Watson system is capable of conducting associative analyses across extensive medical, pharmaceutical, and chemical literature, offering clues for the development of new drugs (Pfizer, 2016). Similarly, in the context of teaching innovative problem-solving, AI can assist students in connecting knowledge from various disciplines, uncovering hidden associations, and providing a range of solution approaches. This significantly broadens students' horizons of knowledge and cultivates their capacity for cross-disciplinary innovation.

## 7 Vision and Future Directions

The swift advancement of AI is revolutionizing the patterns and pathways of innovative activities, carving out new realms of possibility for research into creative problem-solving. Looking ahead, it is imperative to deeply investigate the mechanisms by which AI can be applied in crucial stages such as problem representation, strategy optimization, and knowledge accumulation, to enhance the paradigm of human-computer collaboration, and to transcend the inherent cognitive limitations of humanity (Partarakis & Zabulis, 2024). On the theoretical front, there is a pressing need to further refine the process models and knowledge structure theories related to creative problem-solving, and to elucidate the operating principles of innovative thinking across various contexts (Qiu et al., 2022); on the empirical side, it is essential to conduct extensive cross-disciplinary and multi-contextual empirical studies, leveraging big data and learning analytics to uncover the patterns underlying innovative behavior trajectories (Lee et al., 2020), thereby ensuring a precise integration of theoretical models with practical applications. Furthermore, the prospective application of cutting-edge technologies such as the metaverse and brain-computer interfaces in innovative practices warrants sustained attention, as environments that blend virtual and real elements with high immersion and strong interaction are expected to foster entirely new paradigms of innovation.

In the context of higher education, it is crucial to actively adapt to the demands of the intelligent era by deeply integrating cutting-edge technology with teaching methodologies. Constructing an intelligent innovation practice environment and developing personalized learning systems and creative support tools based on AI to provide students with precise guidance and services is of immediate importance (Chen et al, 2024). The teaching models should highlight openness, interactivity, and collaboration, fostering communication and idea exchange among teachers and students, integrating multidisciplinary approaches, and stimulating collective intelligence. The mechanisms for integrating industry with education and partnerships between schools and enterprises need to be further deepened to establish a collaborative platform for innovation that spans industry, education, research, and application, immersing students in real-world scenarios and honing their innovative abilities through human-machine collaboration. Moreover, the curriculum system must be further refined to include systematic training in innovative methodologies, guiding students to grasp a comprehensive innovation paradigm that seamlessly integrates "knowledge, strategy, and practice." Most importantly, cultivating students' literacy in human-machine collaboration, shaping a vision of innovation characterized by human-machine complementarity and mutual prosperity, and developing habits of human-machine interactive thinking are essential.

**Funding.** This research was financially supported by the National Natural Science Foundation in China (62277018; 62237001), the Ministry of Education in China Project of Humanities and Social Sciences (22YJC880106), the Special Funds for the Cultivation of Guangdong College Students' Scientific and Technological Innovation (pdjh2023b0154), the University Student Innovation and Entrepreneurship Training Program (202410574002X).

# References

Aarikka-Stenroos, L., Jaakkola, E.: Value co-creation in knowledge intensive business services: a dyadic perspective on the joint problem solving process. Ind. Mark. Manage. **41**(1), 15–26 (2012). https://doi.org/10.1016/j.indmarman.2011.11.008

Atchley, P., Pannell, H., Wofford, K., Hopkins, M., Atchley, R.A.: Human and AI collaboration in the higher education environment: opportunities and concerns. Cogn. Res. Principles Implications (2024). https://doi.org/10.1186/s41235-024-00547-9

Balcan, M., Blum, A.: A discriminative model for semi-supervised learning. J. ACM **57**(3), 1–46 (2010). https://doi.org/10.1145/1706591.1706599

Banh, L., Strobel, G.: Generative artificial intelligence. Electron. Markets (2023). https://doi.org/10.1007/s12525-023-00680-1

Bardach, E., Patashnik, E. M.: A Practical Guide for Policy Analysis: The Eightfold Path to More Effective Problem Solving (2019). http://www.gbv.de/dms/sub-hamburg/30636509X.pdf

Bourdieu, P.: The logic of practice (1980). https://ci.nii.ac.jp/ncid/BA1050996X

Boussioux, L., Lane, J.N., Zhang, M., Jacimovic, V., Lakhani, K.R.: The crowdless future? Generative AI and creative Problem-Solving. Organ. Sci. (2024). https://doi.org/10.1287/orsc.2023.18430

Bransford, J.D., Stein, B.S.: The ideal problem solver. Georgia Southern Commons (1993). https://digitalcommons.georgiasouthern.edu/ct2-library/46/

Carlson, M.P., Bloom, I.: The cyclic nature of problem solving: an emergent multidimensional problem-solving framework. Educ. Stud. Math. **58**(1), 45–75 (2005). https://doi.org/10.1007/s10649-005-0808-x

Cattaneo, C.: Community of Practices. In: Idowu, S.O., Schmidpeter, R., Capaldi, N., Liangrong, Z., Del Baldo, M., Abreu, R. (eds.) Encyclopedia of Sustainable Management, pp. 652–662. Springer International Publishing, Cham (2023). https://doi.org/10.1007/978-3-031-25984-5_921

Chambon, V., Sidarus, N., Haggard, P.: From action intentions to action effects: how does the sense of agency come about? Front. Hum. Neurosci. (2014). https://doi.org/10.3389/fnhum.2014.00320

Chen, L., Ifenthaler, D., Yau, J.Y., Sun, W.: Artificial intelligence in entrepreneurship education: a scoping review. Education + Training (2024). https://doi.org/10.1108/et-05-2023-0169

Dewey, J.: The Influence of Darwin on Philosophy, and Other Essays in Contemporary Thought. H. Holt, New York (1910). https://doi.org/10.5962/bhl.title.17966

Eberle, J., Stegmann, K., Fischer, F.: Legitimate peripheral participation in communities of practice: participation support structures for newcomers in faculty student councils. J. Learn. Sci. **23**(2), 216–244 (2014). https://doi.org/10.1080/10508406.2014.883978

Friedrich, J., Brückner, A., Mayan, J., Schumann, S., Kirschenbaum, A., Zinke-Wehlmann, C.: Human-centered AI development in practice—Insights from a multidisciplinary approach. Zeitschrift Für Arbeitswissenschaft (2024). https://doi.org/10.1007/s41449-024-00434-5

Garbuio, M., Lin, N.: Innovative idea generation in problem finding: abductive reasoning, cognitive impediments, and the promise of artificial intelligence. J. Prod. Innov. Manag. **38**(6), 701–725 (2021). https://doi.org/10.1111/jpim.12602

Gizzi, E., Nair, L., Chernova, S., Sinapov, J.: Creative problem solving in artificially intelligent agents: a survey and framework. J. Artif. Intell. Res. (2022). https://doi.org/10.1613/jair.1.13864

Gui, J., Sun, Z., Wen, Y., Tao, D., Ye, J.: A review on generative adversarial networks: algorithms, theory, and applications. IEEE Trans. Knowl. Data Eng. **35**(4), 3313–3332 (2023). https://doi.org/10.1109/tkde.2021.3130191

He, L.-l: Reflections on the dilemma and solutions of college students' innovation and entrepreneurship education under the background of "Internet Plus." DEStech Trans. Soc. Sci. Educ. Hum. Sci. (2017). https://doi.org/10.12783/dtssehs/icsste2017/9379

Jebara, T.: Generative versus discriminative learning. In: Jebara, T. (ed.) Machine Learning, pp. 17–60. Springer US, Boston, MA (2004). https://doi.org/10.1007/978-1-4419-9011-2_2

Johnson, B.C.E.H.F.: The NMC Horizon Report: 2016 Higher Education Edition. Zenodo (CERN European Organization for Nuclear Research) (2016). https://doi.org/10.5281/zenodo.5825548

Koedinger, K.R., Brunskill, E., Baker, R.S.J.D., McLaughlin, E.A., Stamper, J.: New potentials for data-driven intelligent tutoring system development and optimization. AI Mag. **34**(3), 27–41 (2013). https://doi.org/10.1609/aimag.v34i3.2484

Lee, L., Cheung, S.K.S., Kwok, L.: Learning analytics: current trends and innovative practices. J. Comput. Educ. **7**(1), 1–6 (2020). https://doi.org/10.1007/s40692-020-00155-8

Li, T., Zhan, Z.: A systematic review on design thinking integrated learning in K-12 education. Appl. Sci. **12**(16), 8077 (2022). https://doi.org/10.3390/app12168077

Li, T., Ji, Y., Zhan, Z.: Expert or machine? Comparing the effect of pairing student teacher with in-service teacher and ChatGPT on their critical thinking, learning performance, and cognitive load in an integrated-STEM course. Asia Pac. J. Educ. **44**(1), 45–60 (2024). https://doi.org/10.1080/02188791.2024.2305163

Madsen, K.L., Aggerholm, K.: Embodying education – a bildung theoretical approach to movement integration. Nordic J. Stud. Educ. Policy **6**(2), 157–164 (2020). https://doi.org/10.1080/20020317.2019.1710949

Mei, H., et al.: University students' successive development from entrepreneurial intention to behavior: the mediating role of commitment and moderating role of family support. Front. Psychol. (2022). https://doi.org/10.3389/fpsyg.2022.859210

O'Connor, S., Liu, H.: Gender bias perpetuation and mitigation in AI technologies: challenges and opportunities. AI Soc. (2023). https://doi.org/10.1007/s00146-023-01675-4

Ouyang, F., Xu, W., Cukurova, M.: An artificial intelligence-driven learning analytics method to examine the collaborative problem-solving process from the complex adaptive systems perspective. Int. J. Comput.-Support. Collab. Learn. **18**(1), 39–66 (2023). https://doi.org/10.1007/s11412-023-09387-z

Pane, J., Steiner, E., Baird, M., Hamilton, L.: Continued progress: promising evidence on personalized learning. In RAND Corporation eBooks (2015). https://doi.org/10.7249/rr1365

Partarakis, N., Zabulis, X.: A review of immersive Technologies, knowledge representation, and AI for Human-Centered Digital Experiences. Electronics **13**(2), 269 (2024). https://doi.org/10.3390/electronics13020269

Pfizer: IBM and Pfizer to accelerate immuno-oncology research with Watson for Drug Discovery. Pfizer (2016). https://www.pfizer.com/news/press-release/press-release-detail/ibm_and_pfizer_to_accelerate_immuno_oncology_research_with_watson_for_drug_discovery

Qiu, C., Tan, J., Liu, Z., Mao, H., Hu, W.: Design theory and method of complex products: a review. Chin. J. Mech. Eng. (2022). https://doi.org/10.1186/s10033-022-00779-0

Qiu, Y., García-Aracil, A., Isusi-Fagoaga, R.: Critical issues and trends in innovation and entrepreneurship education in higher education in the post-COVID-19 era in China and Spain. Educ. Sci. **13**(4), 407 (2023). https://doi.org/10.3390/educsci13040407

Ray, P.P.: ChatGPT: a comprehensive review on background, applications, key challenges, bias, ethics, limitations and future scope. Internet of Things and Cyber-Phys. Syst. **3**, 121–154 (2023). https://doi.org/10.1016/j.iotcps.2023.04.003

Shneiderman, B.: Human-Centered AI. In Oxford University Press eBooks (2022). https://doi.org/10.1093/oso/9780192845290.001.0001

Simon, H.A., Newell, A.: Human problem solving: the state of the theory in 1970. Am. Psychol. **26**(2), 145–159 (1971). https://doi.org/10.1037/h0030806

Stamovlasis, D., Papageorgiou, G., Tsitsipis, G.: The coherent versus fragmented knowledge hypotheses for the structure of matter: an investigation with a robust statistical methodology. Chem. Educ. Res. Pract. **14**(4), 485–495 (2013). https://doi.org/10.1039/c3rp00042g

Urban, M., et al.: ChatGPT improves creative problem-solving performance in university students: an experimental study. Comput. Educ. **215**, 105031 (2024). https://doi.org/10.1016/j.compedu.2024.105031

Vallet, G., Brunel, L., Riou, B., Vermeulen, N.: Editorial: dynamics of sensorimotor interactions in embodied cognition. Front. Psychol. (2016). https://doi.org/10.3389/fpsyg.2015.01929

Weber, M.: Economy and Society: An Outline of Interpretive Sociology, vol. 1. University of California press (1978)

Wei, R., Mahmood, A.: Recent advances in variational autoencoders with representation learning for biomedical informatics: a survey. IEEE Access **9**, 4939–4956 (2021). https://doi.org/10.1109/access.2020.3048309

Winkler, R., Büchi, C., Söllner, M.: Improving problem-solving skills with smart personal assistants: insights from a quasi field experiment. In: International Conference on Information Systems (2019). https://aisel.aisnet.org/cgi/viewcontent.cgi?article=1434&context=icis2019

Zamiri, M., Esmaeili, A.: Methods and technologies for supporting knowledge sharing within learning communities: a systematic literature review. Adm. Sci. **14**(1), 17 (2024). https://doi.org/10.3390/admsci14010017

Zawacki-Richter, O., Marín, V.I., Bond, M., Gouverneur, F.: Systematic review of research on artificial intelligence applications in higher education – where are the educators? Int. J. Educ. Technol. High. Educ. (2019). https://doi.org/10.1186/s41239-019-0171-0

Zhan, Z., Fong, P.S.W., Lin, K., Zhong, B., Yang, H.H.: Editorial: creativity, innovation, and entrepreneurship: the learning science toward higher order abilities. Front. Psychol. (2022). https://doi.org/10.3389/fpsyg.2022.1063370

Zhan, Z., He, L., Zhong, X.: How does problem-solving pedagogy affect creativity? A meta-analysis of empirical studies. Front. Psychol. (2024). https://doi.org/10.3389/fpsyg.2024.1287082

Zhong, X., Zhan, Z.: An intelligent tutoring system for programming education based on informative tutoring feedback: system development, algorithm design, and empirical study. Interact. Technol. Smart Educ. (2024). https://doi.org/10.1108/itse-09-2023-0182

Zhong, X., Xin, H., Li, W., Zhan, Z., Cheng, M.: The Design and application of RAG-based conversational agents for collaborative problem solving. In: ICDEL. Association for Computing Machinery, pp. 62–68 (2024). https://doi.org/10.1145/3675812.3675871

# Online Learning, Innovation Learning, and Digital Learning

# Does More Frequently Mean Better? The Current Teacher View of the Use of Digital Technologies in Higher Education

Katerina Kostolanyova, Tomas Javorcik, Tomas Barot, and Ivana Simonova(✉)

Faculty of Education, University of Ostrava, F. Sramka 3, Ostrava, Czech Republic
{katerina.kostolanyova,tomas.javorcik,tomas.barot,
ivana.simonova}@osu.cz

**Abstract.** The paper deals with the research that focuses on three areas within the higher education: (1) the frequency of the use of digital technology, in particular, types of digital devices, resources, tools for collecting feedback on student learning, and preferences for classroom management systems; (2) what digital devices teachers expect that students have available for learning; (3) whether teachers think that a more frequent use of digital technologies can improve the quality of the process of instruction in the future. Applying the IMRaD structure, six hypotheses were set. Data were collected using the online questionnaire from 176 respondents working for four faculties of one Czech university. Findings reveal that a computer/notebook and presentation are the leaders in the field of digital technology area. However, more than half of respondents do not think that a more frequent use of technology can improve teaching in the higher education environment in the future.

**Keywords:** digital technologies · higher education · teacher view · frequency

## 1 Introduction

Currently, after almost three decades of using information and communication or digital (IC/D) technologies, they have penetrated all spheres of human activities, including education. They have primarily appeared and stayed in higher education making use of the autonomy in learning of adult university and college students. Bringing new elements into education, the process of instruction enhanced by IC/D technologies has been continuously under research. However, the field is wide, and wide areas have not been examined.

As summarized by and Leyer (2023), numerous extensive studies were carried out that examined problems related to the use of the IC/D technologies in higher education. Attention was paid to various fields, for example, what the process of instruction looks like in different geographical parts of the world, e.g., in Northern Europe (Lindfors et al., 2021; Elm et al., 2023), Eastern Europe (Grosseck et al., 2024), Asia (Yu & Lin, 2023); Kaushik & Kaushik, 2024), Southern America (Luna & Breternitz, 2021), Africa

(Lumadi, 2024), how teacher digital competency was developed (Peters et al., 2022; Rêgo et al., 2024; Santoveña-Casal & López, 2024), what teacher opinions and experience in the development were (Lindfors et al., 2021; Ferreira, 2022; Sundgren et al., 2023), what their opinions might be in the future (Tondeur et al., 2023; Lang & Šorgo, 2024), in what rather non-traditional courses the technologies were applied, e.g., in physiotherapy, academic writing, arts (Ødegaard et al., 2022; Ducasse et al., 2023; Cisneros-Alvarez & de las Heras-Fernández, 2023), and what the efficiency of teaching and learning was, if any (Vale & Martins, 2023). Furthermore, teaching methodologies were analyzed (Santoveña-Casal & López, 2024), as well as barriers to the technology-enhanced process of instruction (Gkrimpizi et al., 2023; Svetsky & Moravcik, 2018). Researchers also monitor what form of instruction is preferred by teachers and students (Bitakou et al., 2023), what students recommend reflecting their opinions (Damsa, 2019), whether the student gender plays a role in the process of instruction (Mercader & Duran-Bellonch, 2021), and many other criteria are being investigated. The equipment of schools with digital technologies is one of them. Usually, it is not considered separately but together with the learner satisfaction with the process of learning and teaching, the efficiency and learner progress, and other criteria.

One of the current problems that has not been sufficiently examined is the frequency of digital technologies implementation in higher education. Therefore, we asked the question how frequently teachers use the technologies in their lessons and preparation for them. And if they do so, that is, if they claim the use, do they also think that a more frequent implementation of digital technologies results in better teaching?

Within the research, following questions were examined:

1) How frequently do teachers use digital technologies? *Types of devices* are considered within this research question.
2) How frequently do teachers use digital technologies? Types of *digital resources for student learning* are considered within this research question.
3) How frequently do teachers use digital technologies? Digital technologies the teachers use to *collect student feedback on the process of instruction* are considered within this research question, mainly, what digital technologies enable them to see how students *acquire* a new learning content and what technologies are exploited for *testing* their newly gained knowledge.
4) How frequently do teachers use digital technologies? Types of *systems for classroom management* are considered within this research question.
5) What digital devices do teachers expect *students will have available* for the process of instruction enhanced by digital technologies?
6) Do teachers working for different faculties think that *a more frequent use of digital technologies* in the process of instruction can improve it in the future?

Based on these research questions, the **main objective** of the research is to discover how frequently the respondents use digital technologies in their courses and during the preparation for them, and consider whether a more frequent use of digital technologies can improve the quality of the process of instruction.

## 2 Method

### 2.1 Methods, Hypotheses, and Statistic Tests

The research description follows the IMRaD structure. The data were collected using the ex post facto method. Six null hypotheses were tested to answer the research questions.

H01: There is no significant difference in the frequency the teachers use the monitored digital devices.
H02: There is no significant difference in the frequency the teachers use the monitored digital resources.
H03: There is no significant difference in the frequency the teachers use digital technologies to collect feedback on student learning.
H04: There is no significant difference in the frequency the teachers use the monitored classroom management systems.
H05: There is no significant difference in the frequency of teacher expectations regarding digital technologies students have available for the process of instruction enhanced by digital technologies.
H06: There is no significant difference in the number of teachers working for different faculties who think that a more frequent use of digital technologies in the process of instruction can improve it in the future.

The hypotheses were tested using following statistic tests.

Chi-square test checks whether two categorical variables are related or independent so that we could understand if the observed datasets differ significantly from the expected data and draw conclusions about whether the variables have a meaningful association.

Monte Carlo p simulation is used to predict the probability of a variety of outcomes, when the potential for random variables is present. It shows the expected results if the null hypothesis is accepted and thus helps explain the impact of risk and uncertainty in prediction.

Cramer´s V shows an effect size measurement for the chi-square test of independence. Using values from 0 to 1 it measures how strongly two categorical fields are associated.

Contingency C is a coefficient of association stating whether two variables or data sets are independent or dependent of each other. It is a chi-square-based measure of association for categorical data that relies on the chi-square test for independence. If C is close or equal to zero, the variables are independent of each other and there is no association between them. If C is away from zero, there is a relationship; C can only reach positive values.

### 2.2 Research Tool and Sample

Data were collected using an online questionnaire. The questionnaire was devoted to new approaches to teaching and learning and consisted of 50 items. Below, we analyzed one part of the questionnaire (six items) that focused on the use of digital technologies. The items were formulated as statements. Respondents expressed themselves using two Likert scales: never (hardly ever) – sometimes – often – (almost) always; Yes, in all courses – Yes, in some courses – No, current state suits my courses – I do not know;

and the Yes/No choice. The questionnaire was available for three weeks online. All academics of the university were addressed to express their opinions.

Respondents were from four faculties of the University of Ostrava: Faculty of Medicine (FM, 76 respondents), Faculty of Social Faculty of Science (FS, 53), Faculty of Education (FE, 41), Faculty of Social Studies (FSS, six respondents). In total, 176 respondents participated in the research. Data were also collected from the respondents of other faculties of the university (Faculty of Fine Arts &Music, Faculty of Arts, Institute of Fuzzy Modeling); however, due to the narrow specialization of these institutions they were not considered within this research. The respondents´ age was not considered in this research; however, we monitored their academic degree. In total, nine professors, 43 associate professors, 93 PhDs, and 31 academics still not reaching the PhD degree participated in the research.

## 3 Results

The results are presented in six subchapters; each of them is devoted to one hypothesis. First, statistic data are presented in Table 1. Then, the results are displayed in six figures (Figs. 1, 2, 3, 4, 5 and 6).

The hypotheses were tested at the significance level alpha 0.05 using the above described tools. In Table 1, the results are structured in separate columns, one for each hypothesis, showing (1) a number of rows and columns in the table, (2) degrees of freedom, (3) chi-square value, (4) p-value, (5) Monte Carlo p, (6) Cramer´s V test, and (7) contingency C value. The final result is displayed on line 8 stating whether the hypothesis was accepted or rejected. A figure is added to each hypothesis (Figs. 1, 2, 3, 4, 5 and 6) that displays the absolute occurrence of frequencies (N).

**Table 1.** Testing hypotheses.

|   |   | H01 | H02 | H03 | H04 | H05 | H06 |
|---|---|---|---|---|---|---|---|
| 1 | Rows, columns | 4; 4 | 5; 4 | 6; 4 | 3; 4 | 6; 2 | 4; 4 |
| 2 | Degrees of freedom | 9 | 12 | 15 | 6 | 5 | 9 |
| 3 | Chi2 | 403.08 | 193.59 | 214.22 | 199.49 | 464.2 | 12.404 |
| 4 | p (no assoc.) | 3.0173E-81 | 6.8605E-35 | 2.698E-37 | 2.4415E-40 | 4.2495E-98 | **0.19149** |
| 5 | Monte Carlo p | 0.0001 | 0.0001 | 0.0001 | 0.0001 | 0.0001 | 0.192 |
| 6 | Cramer's V | 0.42872 | 0.27079 | 0.26004 | 0.43463 | 0.66301 | 0.15371 |
| 7 | Contingency C | 0.59617 | 0.42464 | 0.41067 | 0.52365 | 0.55259 | 0.25727 |
| 8 | Null hypothesis H0 | Rejected | Rejected | Rejected | Rejected | Rejected | **Accepted** |

### 3.1 Hypothesis H01: Results

In hypothesis H01, research question 1 is answered that focuses on how frequently the teachers use digital technologies, in particular, what types of digital devices they preferably implement in the preparation and teaching their courses. Results are displayed in Fig. 1. Respondents gave their opinion to the digital device(s) that are available to them in each classroom: personal computer (PC) with a data-projector (DP), interactive board (IB), visualizer, and mobile devices, which in this case include a smartphone, or tablet. They expressed their opinion using the four-level Likert scale *never (hardly ever) – sometimes – often – (almost) always*.

Figure 1 shows that PC with a data projector is the most frequently used device; it is *(almost) always* exploited by 122 respondents (out of 176, i.e., 69%); 34 respondents (19%) *often* use the device. Contrary to this, other three devices are *never (hardly ever)* exploited for teaching: a visualizer is the least frequently used, when marked by 130 respondents (74%), followed by mobile devices selected by 99 respondents (56%), and an interactive board ticked by 81 respondents (46%). However, for example, mobile devices are *often* used by 47 respondents (27%), an interactive board by 31 respondents (18%) and *sometimes* by 48 respondents (27%).

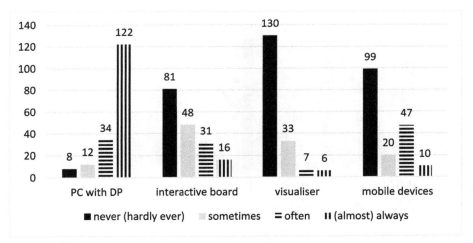

**Fig. 1.** Frequency of DT use: types of digital devices (Source: own) (DT: digital technologies; PC: personal computer; DP: data-projector)

Based on the statistics we can conclude that hypothesis H01 stating that *there is no significant difference in the frequency the teachers use the monitored digital devices* was rejected.

### 3.2 Hypothesis H02: Results

In hypothesis H02, research question 2 is answered that focuses on how frequently the teachers use digital technologies, in particular, what types of digital resources for student learning they preferably implement in the preparation and teaching their courses. Results are displayed in Fig. 2. Respondents gave their opinion to the digital resource(s) that are commonly available to them. Some time ago, LMS Moodle was agreed as a unified tool to be used at all universities. It is available to all teachers and students free of charge at the monitored faculties.

Figure 2 shows that in spite of the wide availability of the LMS Moodle, 72 respondents (41%) expressed they *never (hardly ever)* used this tool and 50 respondents (28%) selected the choice *sometimes*. In total, this result shows is not exploited too much extent in practice, i.e. by 69% within this sample. Similar results were received in applications and shared materials, where highest frequencies are in *never (hardly ever)* used: 70 respondents (40%) in applications; 66 (82%) in shared materials; *sometimes* was selected by 66 respondents (38%) in applications; 50 (28%) in shared materials. Video-lectures were *never (hardly ever)* used by 53 respondents (30%), 77 respondents (44%) marked the choice *sometimes*. Contrary to these data, presentations were the most frequently exploited type of digital resource that was *(almost) always* used by 89 respondents (51%), and 38 respondents (22%) *often* implement them in courses.

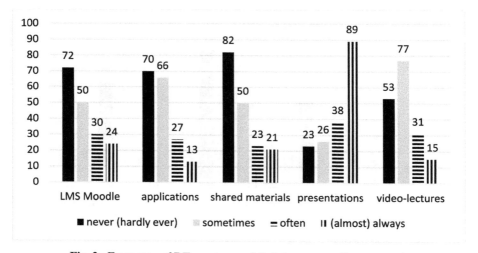

**Fig. 2.** Frequency of DT use: types of digital resources (Source: own).

Based on the statistics we can conclude that hypothesis H02 stating that *there is no significant difference in the frequency the teachers use the monitored digital resources* was rejected.

### 3.3 Hypothesis H03: Results

In hypothesis H03, research question 3 is answered that focuses on how frequently the teachers use digital technologies when collecting student feedback on the process of instruction, mainly, what digital technologies they explore to see how students acquire a new learning content and what technologies they use for testing student newly gained knowledge. Results are displayed in Fig. 3. Respondents gave their opinion to the digital tools that are commonly available to them.

Figure 3 shows that never (hardly ever) is the most frequently marked choice from all. The not-use is the lowest in MS Forms: 64 respondents (36%) expressed that they never (hardly ever) use this tool and 53 respondents (30%) sometimes use it. When comparing data of other digital tools, the not-use is the highest in applications (135 respondents, 77% for never (hardly ever); 34 respondents, 19% for sometimes), followed by shared materials (129, 73%; 31, 18%). Presentations and LMS Moodle have similar frequencies; a reason could be that another tool to collect feedback must be added to them, neither presentation nor LMS itself can serve to monitor student learning. Another choice Others was also added to the questionnaire; however, only three respondents selected this choice and proposed to use the tool Socrative.com. This is a tool that effortlessly assesses and engages learners while visualizing learning progress in real-time with instant results. It enables them to choose an activity type, which provides an efficient way to monitor and evaluate learning and saves time for educators while delivering fun and engaging interactions for learners. Thus, this tool can be considered useful for collecting feedback; however, only a few respondents use it.

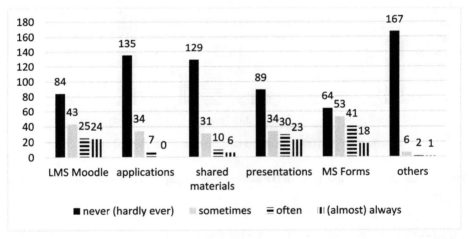

**Fig. 3.** Frequency of DT use: types of DT to collect feedback (Source: own) (DT: digital technologies).

Based on the statistics we can conclude that hypothesis H03 stating that *there is no significant difference in the frequency the teachers use digital technologies to collect feedback on student learning* was rejected.

### 3.4 Hypothesis H04: Results

In hypothesis H04, research question 4 is answered that focuses on how frequently the teachers use digital technologies, in particular, what types of systems for classroom management they use. Results are displayed in Fig. 4. Respondents gave their opinion on three classroom management systems that are commonly available to them: LMS Moodle, MS Teams, and Google Classroom.

At first sight, it is clearly visible from Fig. 4 that Google Classroom does not belong to the widely used tools because 161 respondents (91%) *never (hardly ever)* exploited this tool for classroom management, and so do 83 respondents (47%) in LMS Moodle. Contrary to these, MS Teams is *(almost) always* used by 38 respondents (22%); 53 respondents (30%) *often* exploit the tool, and another group of 53 respondents (30%) *sometimes* work with MS Teams. MS Teams has similar number of complete supporters *(almost) always)* and complete rejectors *(never (hardly ever)* (38 versus 32 respondents; 22% versus 18%) while in LMS Moodle the amount of supporters and rejectors differs (17 versus 83 respondents; 10% versus 47%).

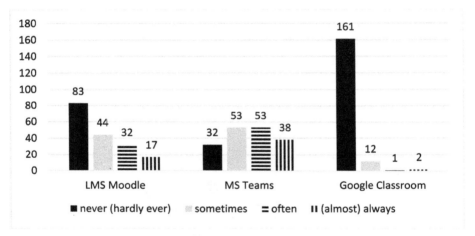

**Fig. 4.** Frequency of DT use: types of DT for classroom management (Source: own) (DT: digital technologies).

Based on the statistics we can conclude that hypothesis H04 stating that *there is no significant difference in the frequency the teachers use the monitored classroom management systems* was rejected.

### 3.5 Hypothesis H05: Results

In hypothesis H05, research question 5 is answered that focuses on what digital devices the teachers expect that *students have available* for process of instruction enhanced by digital technologies. Results are displayed in Fig. 5. Respondents gave their opinion on the use of each of the listed digital devices.

Figure 5 shows that a personal computer or notebook are the most frequently exploited devices; 156 respondents (89%) expect that one or both are available to students for the current process of instruction. Furthermore, 42 teachers (24%) expect that students can use mobile devices, that is, smartphones and/or tablets, 29 respondents (16%) count on students having a web camera, 24 respondents (14%) suppose students have a printer available, 10 respondents (6%) expect a copier, and 9 respondents (5%) a scanner.

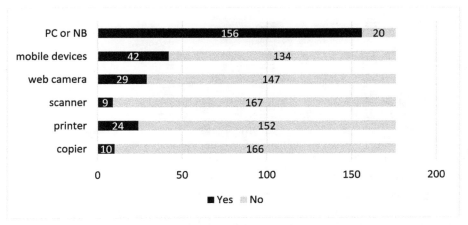

**Fig. 5.** Frequency of DT use: teacher expectations regarding DT students have available for the current process of instruction (Source: own) (DT: digital technologies; PC: personal computer; NB: notebook).

Based on the statistics we can conclude that hypothesis H05 stating that *there is no significant difference in the frequency of teacher expectations regarding digital technologies students have available for the current process of instruction* was rejected.

### 3.6 Hypothesis H06: Results

In hypothesis H06, research question 6 is answered that focuses on the problem whether the teachers working for different faculties think that *a more frequent use of digital technologies* in the process of instruction can improve it in the future. Results are displayed in Fig. 6. Respondents opinions are structured according to the faculty they work for.

Figure 6 clearly shows that most teachers regardless of the faculty they work for do not think that *a more frequent use of digital technologies in the process of instruction can improve it in the future.* In three faculties, the choice *No, current state suits my courses* was the most frequent. In particular, they were 35 respondents (46%) working for the Faculty of Medicine (FM), 33 respondents (62%) for the Faculty of Science (FS), 19 respondents (46%) for the Faculty of Education (FE), and two for the Faculty of Social Studies (FSS). However, almost the same number of respondents selected the *Yes* answer, either in *all courses* or in *some courses* (FM: 14%, 29%; FS: 11%, 21%; FE: 22%, 32%).

Moreover, in our previous research we discovered that digital technologies had been implemented in a half and more courses by 80% of teachers at FM, 92% at FS, and 85% at FE (Kostolanyova et al., in print).

Based on the statistics we can conclude that hypothesis H06 stating that *there is no significant difference in teachers regarding the faculties who think that a more frequent*

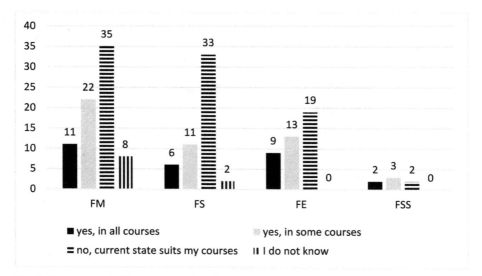

**Fig. 6.** Frequency of DT use: more DT can improve the process of instruction in the future (Source: own) (DT: digital technologies; FM: Faculty of Medicine; FS: Faculty of Science; FE: Faculty of Education; FSS: Faculty of Social Studies).

*use of digital technologies in the process of instruction can improve it in the future* was accepted.

## 4 Discussion and Conclusion

The purpose of this research was to discover how frequently the university teachers implement digital technologies in their lessons, including the preparation for them. Special attention was mainly paid to the types of devices the teachers use, digital resources they offer for student learning, digital technologies for feedback collection that show how students acquire a new learning content and enable teachers to test the newly gained knowledge. Types of preferred classroom management systems were monitored, too. Logically, it was also detected what digital devices teachers expect that students will have available for the process of instruction and whether they think that a more frequent use of digital technologies can improve the quality of teaching.

Findings reveal that computer/notebook with data-projector are the most frequently used devices and presentations are the most frequently used digital resources, LMS Moodle and presentations are the most frequently applied ways to collect feedback on student learning, MS Teams is the most frequently used classroom management system, students are expected to have available or own a computer/notebook and/or smartphone/tablet, web camera, printer. Despite all these, most teachers do not think that a more frequent use of digital technologies can improve the process of instruction in the future.

In the context of the Czech education system, the above presented findings were collected regardless of the course the teacher designed and taught. However, depending on the learning content, specific digital tools are selected and implemented. For example, when teaching the course of English for Specific Purposes, Duolingo and Google Translate are frequently used in lessons by both teachers and students; ChatGPT can be helpful throughout all courses (Pikhart et al., 2024). Pikhart et al. (2024) also discovered a wide variety in the frequency the students use these tools, from regular everyday 30-min usage to a rare random logging in less than 30 min per month. When considering this finding and our results, it can be also stated that there is a wide difference in the frequency of use of digital technologies. In another study, the implementation of digital technologies in Mathematics and Arts is under focus. For example, Abar et al. (2024) examined the use of classroom management system MS Teams; this system was also preferred in our study. Their study (Abar et al., 2024) aimed at developing mathematical skills through artistic techniques and reflections on products and actions through Geogebra commands. The approach they applied was positively accepted, although there were two participants in the study only. In addition, as mentioned by Abar et al. (2024), the classroom management system MS Teams portrays as a helpful digital technology.

Koutska (2023) conducted a study in the Czech higher education environment. The study quantitatively analyzed the frequency of the use of digital technology during and after the covid-19 pandemic period. She collected 2.674 respondents´ answers; the respondents came from 128 countries. The findings discovered that pandemic conditions increased the usage of collaborative, communicative, and interactive synchronous tools and portable devices, and the variety of educational software solutions. This factor was not mention by the respondents in our study. Furthermore, Koutska (2023) proves that currently, i.e., in the post-pandemic period, more tools are available to the users, and they are more competent to work with them. Her study does not focus on one course, which aligns the findings with our results.

The implementation of latest digital technology in education is one of the ways how to support education, innovate the instruction, and keep it sustainable and competitive. Information and communication, digital or other type of technologies can enhance this process. How frequent this support should be is a question. As defined by Comenius (1948) in the $17^{th}$ century in his didactic principles, various factors play a role in this process; however, the main criterion is to use digital technologies *appropriately*, that is, when designing university courses, teachers as designers should consider the level of learner knowledge, learning content, and form of study as minimum. The application of this principle can be found in the answers of teachers who do not think that a more frequent use of digital technologies in the process of instruction can improve it in the future. In practical implications, we are sure that new types of technologies will appear, and teachers will consider whether they are appropriate to mediate or not the learning content they are going to teach, regardless of the fact how attractive they are for them and might be for the students.

To conclude, the main didactic recommendation, both for teachers and learners, is to consider whether the use of digital technologies for teaching/learning is appropriate, helpful for the process. If so, then, to collect the one/s that will work most productively for you and the course, that is, that will suit your teaching/learning style, learning content you are going to teach/acquire, level of student knowledge, and other criteria. The SAMR model by Puentedura (Nearpodteam, 2024) can serve for practical implications.

## 4.1 Limitations, Added Value, Future Research

The study has some limitations.

Firstly, it is a quantitative study, which means that it does not include any qualitative data to provide a more objective insight. The reason is that the analyzed items were part of a large questionnaire that collected quantitative data only.

Secondly, more items could be included in the questionnaire so that to receive a deeper insight in the problem; however, it was not the purpose of this study.

Thirdly, the research sample was rather homogenous – it included students from one university (from three faculties in our research) but more respondents would improve the quality of results. On the contrary, the fact that in total respondents from seven faculties of the university filled in the whole questionnaire prepared a basis for didactic interventions within various areas of higher education in the future. This feature can be considered the added value of the study. Consequently, it can be expanded to other Czech higher education institutions so that to collect adequate data there.

On the other hand, hardly any studies have been available that deal with all three criteria: frequency, digital technologies, and the Czech higher education environment. So, it is not possible to consider the results in a detailed context. Current findings could work as a foundation for further studies examining the use of latest technologies by teachers at particular faculties, monitoring and assessing the appropriateness to learning content, and formulating didactic recommendations for courses in which digital technologies have not been settled. Permanent attention should be also paid to the role of teacher. It has been under development as well as the digital technologies are.

## References

Abar, C.A.P., de Almeida, M.V., Lavicza, Z.: Arts and mathematics: geogebra focused on isometric transformations. J. Math. Arts. (2024). https://doi.org/10.1080/17513472.2024.2365361

Bitakou, E., Ntaliani, M., Demestichas, K., Costopoulou, C.: Assessing massive open online courses for developing digital competences among higher education teachers. Educ. Sci. **13**(9), 900 (2023). https://doi.org/10.3390/educsci13090900

Cisneros-Alvarez, P., de las Heras-Fernández, R.: The implementation of digital technology in arts education: a review of the scientific literature. Artseduca **35**, 53–65 (2023). https://doi.org/10.6035/artseduca.6929

Comenius, J.A.: Velka didaktika [Great didactics]. Komenium, Brno (1948)

Damsa, C.: Learning with digital technologies in higher education. J. Educ. Sci. Psychol. **9**(1), 5–9 (2019)

Ducasse, A.M., Ferrero, C.L., Mateo-Girona, M.T.: Technology-enabled higher education academic writing feedback: Practices, needs and preferences. Australasian J. Educ. Technol. **39**(4), 48–73 (2023). https://doi.org/10.14742/ajet.8557

Elm, A., Nilsson, K.S., Björkman, A., Sjöberg, J.: Academic teachers' experiences of technology enhanced learning (TEL) in higher education – A Swedish case. Cogent Educ. (2023). https://doi.org/10.1080/2331186X.2023.2237329

Ferreira, J.G.B.: The higher education teacher and the new challenges of teaching in the context of digital technologies: a socio-cognitive approach. Revista Crítica de Ciências Sociais **129**, 177–202 (2022). https://doi.org/10.4000/rccs.14048

Gkrimpizi, T., Peristeras, V., Magnisalis, I.: Classification of barriers to digital transformation in higher education institutions: systematic literature review. Educ. Sci. **13**(7), 746 (2023). https://doi.org/10.3390/educsci13070746

Grosseck, G., Bran, R.A., Tîru, L.G.: Digital assessment: a survey of Romanian higher education teachers´ practices and needs. Educ. Sci. **14**(1), 32 (2024). https://doi.org/10.3390/educsci14010032

Kabakus, A.K., Bahcekapili, E., Ayaz, A.: The effect of digital literacy on technology acceptance: an evaluation on administrative staff in higher education. J. Inform. Sci. (2023). https://doi.org/10.1177/01655515231160028

Kaushik, H., Kaushik, S.: A study on the associations among the factors influencing digital education with reference to Indian higher education. Educ. Inf. Technol. (2024). https://doi.org/10.1007/s10639-023-12410-3

Kostolanyova, K., Barot, T., Javorcik, T., Simonova. I.: The implementation of field-oriented digital technologies by university teachers (2024)

Koutska, I.: Tecnología educativa 'introducida' por la pandemia COVID-19. Innoeduca. Int. J. Technol. Educ. Innov. **9**(2), 115–133 (2023). https://doi.org/10.24310/innoeduca.2023.v9i2.15481

Lang, V., Šorgo, A.: Views of students, parents, and teachers on smartphones and tablets in the development of 21st-century skills as a prerequisite for a sustainable future. Sustainability **16**(7), 3004 (2024). https://doi.org/10.3390/su16073004

Lindfors, M., Pettersson, F., Olofsson, A.D.: Conditions for professional digital competence: the teacher educators' view. Educ. Inquiry **12**(4), 390–409 (2021). https://doi.org/10.1080/20004508.2021.1890936

Lumadi, M.W.: Exploring the use of digital technologies to tackle inequities in assessment at higher education institutions. S. Afr. J. Higher Educ. **38**(3), 77–96 (2024). https://doi.org/10.20853/38-3-6368

Luna, F.D.S., Breternitz, V.J.: Digital transformation in private Brazilian higher education institutions: pre-coronavirus baseline. Revista de Administração Mackenzie. **22**(6), 1–31 (2021). https://doi.org/10.1590/1678-6971/eRAMD210127

Peters, M., Ejjaberi, A.E., Martínez, M.J., Fabregues, S.: Teacher digital competence development in higher education: Overview of systematic reviews. Australasian J. Educ. Technol. **38**(3), 122–139 (2022). https://doi.org/10.14742/ajet.7543

Mercader, C., Duran-Bellonch, M.: Female higher education teachers use digital technologies more and better than they think. Digit. Educ. Review. **40**, 172–184 (2021). https://doi.org/10.1344/der.2021.40.172-184

Müller, W., Leyer, M.: Understanding intention and use of digital elements in higher education teaching. Educ. Inf. Technol. **28**(1), 15571–15597 (2023). https://doi.org/10.1007/s10639-023-11798-2

Nearpodteam: Practical SAMR model examples to integrate educational technology. Practical SAMR model examples to integrate education technology (nearpod.com) (2024)

Often vs. frequently. grammarhow.com/often-vs-frequently/ (n.d.)

Ødegaard, N.B., Røe, Y., Dahl-Michelsen, T.: Learning is about being active, but the digital is not really active: physiotherapy teachers´ attitudes toward and experiences with digital education. Physiother. Theory Pract. **40**(3), 494–504 (2022). https://doi.org/10.1080/09593985.2022.2119907

Pikhart, M., Klimova, B., Al-Obaydi, L.H.: Exploring university students' preferences and satisfaction in utilizing digital tools for foreign language learning. Front. Educ. (2024). https://doi.org/10.3389/feduc.2024.1412377

Rêgo, B.S., Lourenço, D., Moreira, F., Pereira, C.S.: Digital transformation, skills and education: a systematic literature review. Ind. High. Educ. **38**(4), 336–349 (2024). https://doi.org/10.1177/09504222231208969

Sundgren, M., Jaldemark, J., Cleveland-Innes, M.: Disciplinary differences and emotional presence in communities of inquiry: Teachers' expressions of digital technology-enabled teaching. Comput. Educ. Open **4**, 100134 (2023). https://doi.org/10.1016/j.caeo.2023.100134

Svetsky, S., Moravcik, O.: Some barriers regarding the sustainability of digital technology for long-term teaching. In K. Arai, R. Bhatia, S. Kapoor, (Eds.). Advances in Intelligent Systems and Computing. Future Technologies Conference (FTC), pp. 950–961. Vancouver, Canada, 13–14 Nov 2018. 880 (2018). https://doi.org/10.1007/978-3-030-02686-8-71

Vale, A., Martins, A.:. The experience of remote teaching in higher education: a scenario of challenges and opportunities. J. Higher Educ. Theory Pract. 23(2), 8–17 (2023). https://doi.org/10.33423/jhetp.v23i2.5805

Yu, Y., Lin, G.R.: Why and how digital technology empowers the high-quality development of postgraduate education. Front. Educ. China **18**(1), 83–101 (2023). https://doi.org/10.3868/s110-008-023-0006-9

Sánchez-Caballé, A., Esteve-Mon, F.M.: Analysis of teaching methodologies using digital technologies in higher education: a systematic review. Ried-Revista Iberoamericana De Educacion A Distancia. **26**(1), 181–199 (2023). https://doi.org/10.5944/ried.26.1.33964

Santoveña-Casal, S., López, S.R.: Mapping of digital pedagogies in higher education. Educ. Inf. Technol. **29**(2), 2437–2458 (2024). https://doi.org/10.1007/s10639-023-11888-1

Tondeur, J., et al.: The HeDiCom framework: Higher Education teachers' digital competencies for the future. Educ. Technol. Res. Dev. **71**(1), 33–53 (2023). https://doi.org/10.1007/s11423-023-10193-5

# Empowering Open Educational Practices Through Open-Source Software: A Grounded Theory Approach in the Context of a University in Hong Kong

Chenggui Duan[1,2]

[1] School of Information Technology in Education, South China Normal University, Guangzhou, China
dduan@hkmu.edu.hk
[2] School of Open Learning, Hong Kong Metropolitan University, Hong Kong, China

**Abstract. Purpose** – The study aims to understand university teachers' perceptions and experiences of adopting open educational resources and open-source software (OSS) in their teaching practices at a University in Hong Kong. The research seeks to develop a theoretical framework explaining the motivation and challenges of OSS adoption in higher education.

**Design/methodology/approach** – The research employs a qualitative approach using grounded theory methodology. Semi-structured interviews were conducted with eight academic staff from various schools at Hong Kong Metropolitan University (HKMU). Data analysis followed the three-stage coding process of grounded theory: open coding, axial coding, and selective coding.

**Findings** – The study identified three core categories emerging from the data: Open Educational Technology, Open Educational Resources, and Open Pedagogy. These categories interact to shape the adoption and implementation of OSS-empowered open educational practices at HKMU. The research resulted in the development of an Open TPACK (Technological Pedagogical Content Knowledge) model, which extends the traditional TPACK framework to encompass open educational practices. This model illustrates how open technology, open resources, and open pedagogy intersect and influence each other in the context of higher education.

**Originality/value/implications** – This research provides novel insights into the motivations, challenges, and support needed for OSS adoption in higher education. The Open TPACK model offers a theoretical framework for understanding the complex interplay between technology, resources, and pedagogy in open educational practices. It highlights the importance of considering openness as a key dimension in educational technology integration. The findings can inform policy development to support university teachers in fully utilizing the potential of OSS in education. Moreover, the study contributes to the growing body of literature on open education by providing a contextualized understanding of OSS adoption in a Hong Kong higher education institution.

**Keywords:** Open educational practices · Open-source software · Grounded theory · Higher education · Hong Kong

## 1 Introduction

The emergence of innovative education technology has transformed the landscape of higher education. With the integration of digital educational tools, such as visual aids, multi-media and artificial-intelligent (AI) agents, teaching and learning at university facilitated a dynamic mode of interaction between teachers and students which differs from the established traditional practice of classroom tutorials (Chen et al., 2020). Meanwhile, online Open Education Resources (OERs), such as Massive Open Online Courses (MOOCs), MIT open courseware, and open textbooks, have become prevalent. OERs has changed the traditional teacher-focused pedagogy to a student-centred approach, through which students are centre of the teaching and are allowed the flexibility to learn at their own pace (Li & Wong, 2021). Besides digitalized educational tools and online OERs, open-source software (OSS) also provides teachers with a wide range of useful and assessable educational tools and resources which can be utilized in their educational practices. OSS refers to software whose source code is open and free to access, use (O'Neil et al., 2021), re-distribute (Sharp & Huett, 2006) and developed in a collaborative manner (Alrawashdeh et al., 2020). The wide use of Moodle and MySQL, two open-source learning management systems, in tertiary institutions shows how OSS can be integrated into the educational practice in higher education to facilitate teaching and academic administrations (Luk et al., 2018). In addition to learning management systems, there exists a variety of OSS which serves different academic purposes. Zotero, an open-source reference management software, is adopted by university teachers with the aim to enhance their students' proficiency with literature (Kim, 2011). Alnassar (2023) shows an example of adopting OSS in undergraduate-level Physics classes.

However, there is still a stereotype amongst many educators that OSS requires users' specialized knowledge in computer science which is difficult to be picked up by educators without experience in programming. Implementation of OSS in teaching also faces challenges such as the lack of infrastructure and budget and lack of manpower in supporting software developments (Thankachan & Moore, 2017). Currently many discussions of OSS-empowered educational practices at university only focus on STEM subjects, e.g., Computer Science, Mathematics, Chemistry, Engineering. In this way, the potential of empowering open-educational practice with open-source software (OSS) has not been fully utilized. This paper presents a qualitative study through grounded-theory analysis which aim at understanding university teachers' perceptions and experience of adopting open education resource and OSS in their teaching, curriculum developments and open education practices. The scope of our research is restricted to teachers at the Hong Kong Metropolitan University (HKMU). A theory explaining the motivation and challenges of OSS adoption is developed and extracted from the data using the grounded theory approach. It provides a casual explanation for teachers' OSS adoption and explores the challenges faced and support needed by teachers in developing OSS-empowered open educational practice. Our research findings show how future policy should be structured to support university teachers at HKMU to fully utilize the potential of OSS in education.

## 2 Research Context

In Hong Kong, there have been many successful examples of empowering university's educational practice by OSS. Moodle, a free and open-source teaching and learning management system, is adopted by the University of Hong Kong, the Education University of Hong Kong (EdUHK) and Hong Kong Baptist University. Apart from Moodle, there exists a wide variety of open-source software, e.g., Zotero, Firefox, Linux, Open Office. OSS offers a comprehensive package for academic, teaching, and research that have been adopted by university teachers and students from diverse backgrounds. Hong Kong Metropolitan University (HKMU), formerly The Open University of Hong Kong, was established in 1989 offering distance-learning educations to mature students. Over time, the university has expanded and added full-time degree programs at undergraduate, master and doctoral level. As such, HKMU has been playing a major role in carrying forward the research and development of open-educational resources (OERs) and open pedagogy, including publishing Open Textbooks for Hong Kong, the establishment of the Institute for Research in Open and Innovative Education (IROPINE), and organizing annually the International Conference on Open and Innovative Education (ICOIE) (Li et al., 2014).

In this study, 8 semi-structured interviews were carried out with academic staff at Hong Kong Metropolitan University who had experience in both teaching face-to-face and distance learning classes. The interview questions were structured around six key areas related to teachers' perception of and experience with the use of open educational resources, open pedagogy, and adoption of OSS open-source software.

## 3 Methods

*Data Collection and Analysis Procedures*
In total 11 teachers were shortlisted for interviews. As the first stage of open coding went in parallel with the interview, we stopped conducting more interviews after no new emerging code which indicated that our themes were "saturated". As a result, 8 face-to-face semi-structured interviews were conducted in total, of which the respondents are teachers from School of Nursing and Health Studies (N&HS) School of Education and Languages, School of Arts and Social Sciences, Lee Shau Kee School of Business and Administration, School of Nursing and Health Studies (N&HS), School of Science and Technology (S&T) of HKMU. The list of teachers interviewed is detailed in the following Table 1.

**Table 1.** Participants list

|   | Gender | School | Date |
|---|---|---|---|
| A | Female | School of Nursing and Health Studies (N&HS) | 10/April/2024 |
| B | Female | School of Education and Languages | 12/ April /2024 |
| C | Male | School of Education and Languages | 19/ April /2024 |

(*continued*)

## Table 1. (*continued*)

|   | Gender | School | Date |
|---|---|---|---|
| D | Male | School of Arts and Social Sciences | 23/ April /2024 |
| E | Male | School of Science and Technology (S&T) | 6/May/2024 |
| F | Male | Lee Shau Kee School of Business and Administration | 7/ May /2024 |
| G | Female | School of Science and Technology (S&T) | 10/ May /2024 |
| H | Male | School of Nursing and Health Studies (N&HS) | 3/June/2024 |

All interviews were conducted between April and June 2024. Each interview lasted from 30 to 60 min, depending on the length of the participants' sharing. The conversation between the researchers and the interviewee was audio-recorded and written notes for follow-up analysis. The audio-recordings were then transcribed into text format by an AI-empowered tool, Memo, followed with refinements and vetting by researching through comparing the AI-generated texts with the audio content of the recordings. Subsequent coding was conducted by two researchers with the aid of Nvivo12, a qualitative data analysis software.

The grounded theory method (GTM), developed by Strauss and Glaser in The Discovery of Grounded Theory in 1967, is adopted as the data analysis paradigm of this study. Grounded theory aims at extracting and conceptualizing theoretical themes and core categories emerging from the data to construct a theory. It is characterized as a qualitative research method to construct, or as Corbin and Strauss put it, to "mine" theories from data through researchers' interactions with it.

According to Corbin and Strauss (2012), the coding process in GTM consists of three stages: Open Coding, Axial Coding and Selective Coding. In open coding, initial labels were attached to data by the method of constant comparison. The stage of open coding ends when no more new concepts emerge from the data. Next, axial coding was

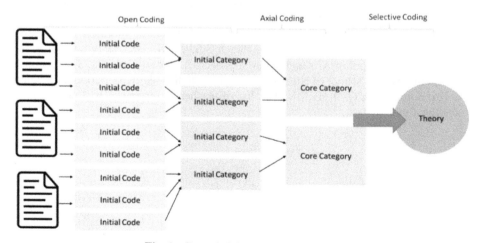

**Fig. 1.** Grounded theory coding process

used to identify relationships between categories that emerged during open coding. This involved reassembling the fractured data and exploring connections between categories and subcategories. Finally, selective coding was performed to identify the core category and systematically relate all other categories to it, refining the theory and filling in any gaps. Throughout this process, the constant comparative method was used to ensure the emerging theory was grounded in the data. The coding process is shown in the following Fig. 1.

*Interview Guide and Research Questions*

The questions in the interview guide were structured around four key areas: 1) respondents' experiences with Open Educational Practices (OEP) and OSS, 2) their attitudes towards and perspectives on OEP and OSS, 3) the role and impacts of educators in OEP and OSS, 4) educators' needs and expectations for OSS-empowered OEP. The specific research areas and questions are detailed in Table 2.

**Table 2.** Research areas and questions

|   | Areas | Interview Questions |
|---|---|---|
| 1 | Experiences with OEP and OSS | What classes have you taught? |
|   |   | Have you ever adopted OEP or OSS in your teaching? |
|   |   | What are the impacts of OEP and OSS? |
|   |   | Have you ever faced any difficulties or challenges when implementing OEPs and OSS? What are they? |
| 2 | Attitudes towards and perspectives on OEP and OSS | What are your views upon OEP? |
|   |   | How do you anticipate the development of OEP in the future? |
|   |   | What do you think maybe the impacts of OEP on teachers? |
|   |   | Compared with proprietary software, how do you find your user experience with OSS? |
| 3 | The role and impacts of educators in OEP and OSS | What is your role in OEP? |
|   |   | What are the roles played by teachers in OEP? |
|   |   | How do you evaluate your job in carrying forward the development of OEP? |
| 4 | Educators' needs and expectations for OSS-empowered OEP | What do you think are the supports needed for the future development of OSS-empowered OEP? |
|   |   | What are your expectations on the development of OEP? |
|   |   | What are the resources or institutional supports you hope to receive in your teaching? |
|   |   | Have you ever received any training from a third-party on the use of OSS? |

## 4 Data Analysis

**Open Coding**

In the first stage of data analysis, open coding was conducted in which a line-by-line analysis was carried out. At this stage, lines of data recorded in the interview transcripts were constantly compared with each other and with the notes in the memo. The similarity and difference were then encoded by attaching initial labels to concepts which emerge from the data (Urquhart, 2017). The conceptualizations are conducted in a bottom-up in-vivo approach, meaning that the data label is suggested by the data and is put in terms of the interviewee's own wordings. In this way, the initial labels are free of the theoretical preconception of the researchers and adequately reflect and communicate the participants' view (Bose, 2021; Urquhart, 2017).

In this study, the open coding process was conducted rigorously to analyze the collected data. Initially, this process yielded 301 coding units. Following this, two researchers engaged in an iterative process of reading, coding, refining, and comparing these units.

Through this collaborative and meticulous approach, the researchers were able to distill the initial 301 coding units down to a more focused set of 285 coding units. This refinement process involved careful consideration of each unit, ensuring that the codes accurately reflected the data while eliminating redundancies and clarifying ambiguities. The codes were further organized into categories by the method of constant comparative analysis (Glaser & Strauss, 1967).

From these 285 coding units, the researchers then proceeded to group and categorize the data, resulting in the preliminary identification of 49 initial categories. These categories represent the first level of abstraction from the raw data, capturing key concepts and themes that emerged from the coding process (Table 3).

**Table 3.** Open coding (example)

| Initial Categories | Coding Units | Original Interview Sentences |
| --- | --- | --- |
| a1: Benefits and Challenges of Open Education | A1: Open education reduces educational inequality | When I was a student, I used Coursera, including some open courses, and the related resources were indeed very abundant. I think one benefit of this kind of open education is that it can help reduce educational inequality |
| | F7: The accessibility /popularity of open educational resources | In the past, when there were no open resources, children had less exposure to these things. Now, it is easier to access these resources, and more students can benefit from them |
| c2: The Use of Technology in Teaching and Its Challenges | C36: The technical barriers/thresholds to using plugins | We don't have much because once plugins are involved, it becomes somewhat challenging and requires an IT background |
| | D27: The resistance teachers face in using open-source software | With so many tools available, I need to understand this technology myself, and the teacher has to spend time preparing. The teacher may already be teaching a lot of things and might not be willing to spend additional time learning about an open-source software |

## Axial Coding

In the axial coding phase, we aimed to uncover potential logical relationships between the initial categories identified during open coding. Through progressive categorization and refinement, we organically integrated and connected the categories that emerged from the open coding process.

Two researchers collaboratively classified, compared, and clustered the initial categories. This process resulted in the consolidation of the original 48 initial concepts into 21 more refined concepts. This consolidation allowed for the preliminary emergence of a second-level framework for the Open Educational Practices model.

Building upon the initial hypotheses about Open Educational Practices mentioned in the literature review, we conducted further comparison, association, and refinement of these 21 concepts. This process led to the distillation of six categories:

1) Open Educational Resources
2) Policy and Institutional Support
3) Technological Infrastructure and Development
4) Educational Software and Tools
5) Teacher and Student Support
6) Pedagogical Development

## Selective Coding

In the selective coding phase, the core category should be a central concept that can explain and integrate other categories. Based on the continued analysis of the original materials, the following three categories could serve as core categories:

1) Open Educational Technology

This is a key category as it directly involves the application and enabling role of technology in open education. It includes aspects such as the development of technological infrastructure, the use of software tools, and technological support in teaching.

2) Open Educational Resources

This category is critical because open educational resources are foundational to open educational practices. It covers multiple aspects, including the access, use, and diversification of resources.

3) Open Pedagogy

This category emphasizes the instructional methods and practices within open education, focusing on student engagement, teacher roles, and the integration of open resources and technology into teaching practices.

The relationships among the concepts, categories, and core categories are as shown in Table 4.

## Relationship Between Core Categories and Other Categories

Open Educational Technology is a crucial enabling factor that interacts with all other

**Table 4.** Axial and selective coding

|    | Concept | Category | Core Category |
|----|---------|----------|---------------|
| 1  | Initial Understanding of Open Educational Resources and Practices | Open Educational Resources | Open Educational Resources |
| 2  | Utilization and Diversification of Teaching Resources | | |
| 3  | Use of Teaching Resources and Tools | | |
| 4  | Standardization and Recommendations for School Resources | | |
| 5  | Perspectives on Open Education and Future Development | Policy and Institutional Support | |
| 6  | Benefits and Challenges of Open Education | | |
| 7  | Need for Policies and Support | | |
| 8  | Need for Support for Schools and Teachers | | |
| 9  | Impact and Challenges of Technological Development | Technological Infrastructure and Development | Open Educational Technology |
| 10 | Technological Challenges and Support in Teaching | | |
| 11 | Technological Support and Resource Needs | | |
| 12 | Importance of Information Literacy | | |
| 13 | Use and Evaluation of Software and Tools | Educational Software and Tools | |
| 14 | Views and Experiences with Open-Source Software | | |
| 15 | Perspectives on Open Education and Artificial Intelligence | | |
| 16 | Guidance and Support for Students | Teacher and Student Support | Open Pedagogy |
| 17 | Impact of Open Education on Teachers | | |

(*continued*)

**Table 4.** (*continued*)

|    | Concept | Category | Core Category |
|----|---------|----------|---------------|
| 18 | Teacher Professional Development Needs | | |
| 19 | Need for Teacher Training | | |
| 20 | Teaching Practices and Student Engagement | Pedagogical Development | |
| 21 | Importance of the Teacher's Role | | |

categories, particularly with Open Educational Resources and Open Pedagogy. Technology not only supports teaching but also significantly determines the possibilities and effectiveness of open educational practices.

Open Educational Resources forms the foundation of open educational practices; the accessibility and diversity of resources directly influence the quality of teaching content and the choice of pedagogy.

Open Pedagogy emphasizes the instructional strategies and methods that integrate open educational resources and technology. It highlights the importance of student engagement, teacher roles, and the overall impact of open education on teaching practices.

Teacher and Student Support and Policy and Institutional Support are critical conditions for ensuring that technology, resources, and pedagogy are effectively integrated into teaching practices.

**Suggestions for Further Development of the Theory**

The theory of open education empowerment through technology can be further developed by examining several key aspects. Causal relationships play a crucial role in this framework. The development and support of technology serve as prerequisites for the effective utilization of open educational resources, which in turn impacts teaching effectiveness and student engagement. Additionally, Open Pedagogy is shaped by the availability of resources and the technological tools used to deliver and manage educational content.

Certain conditions are necessary for the successful integration of technology, resources, and pedagogy. Effective policy support and teacher training are essential to ensure this integration. Moreover, the emphasis on teacher roles and professional development within Open Pedagogy is crucial for the effective implementation of open educational practices.

The theory also recognizes significant interactions between its components. There is a high degree of interplay between technology, resources, and pedagogy. Technological advancements not only change how resources are accessed but also how pedagogy is implemented. Open Pedagogy relies on this interplay to create engaging, inclusive, and effective learning experiences.

Contextual factors also play a vital role in the theory. Socioeconomic background, educational policy environment, and the level of technological development are key factors influencing the empowerment of open education through technology. Additionally, institutional support and cultural factors significantly shape the adoption and effectiveness of open pedagogy.

**Theoretical Propositions or Hypotheses**
Building on these aspects, several theoretical propositions can be formulated. Firstly, the level of technological infrastructure directly determines the accessibility and effectiveness of open educational resources, which in turn influences the success of open pedagogy. Secondly, effective policy support can significantly enhance the impact of technology in empowering open educational practices, particularly in the standardization and diversification of educational resources and the implementation of innovative pedagogical approaches.

The third proposition suggests that the integration of open educational resources and technology within open pedagogy leads to improved student engagement, teacher effectiveness, and overall educational outcomes. Lastly, teachers' technological proficiency and students' digital literacy play significant mediating roles in the effectiveness of open educational technology and resources in enhancing open pedagogy.

These propositions provide a framework for future research and can guide the further development and refinement of the theory of open education empowerment through technology.

## 5 Discussion

**The Evolution of Open Education**
Open education has emerged as one of the most significant themes in contemporary education, evolving far beyond its initial focus on open educational resources (OER). Knox (2013) highlights that the open education movement actively positions digital technologies as central means of engagement and inclusion, with Open Educational Resources (OERs) and Massive Open Online Courses (MOOCs) at the forefront of this development.

The Cape Town Open Education Declaration (2007) emphasizes that open education encompasses not only OER but also open technologies that facilitate collaborative learning and the sharing of teaching practices. This broader conception of open education includes new approaches to assessment, accreditation, and collaborative learning, underscoring the importance of embracing these innovations for the long-term vision of the movement.

**The Role of Technology in Open Education**
The role of technology in open education is multifaceted and central to its philosophy. Weller (2018) identifies three core premises of the current open education movement: open universities, open-source software, and Web 2.0 culture, highlighting the technological underpinnings of open education. Cronin (2017) goes further, prioritizing open technologies over the use and reuse of OER in open educational practices.

However, Knox (2013) points out a paradox: despite the centrality of networks, systems, and software in open education, there is a lack of in-depth consideration of these technologies beyond user interpretation analyses. This observation suggests a need for more critical examination of the technological aspects of open education.

The OpenEdu framework, as described by Inamorato dos Santos et al. (2016), views open education as a tool for modernizing education through technology and new teaching practices. This framework aims to reduce educational barriers at various levels, including opportunity, cost, technology, and pedagogy. Importantly, the authors assert that the degree of openness in an institution's technology reflects its culture of openness, emphasizing the symbiotic relationship between technological and cultural aspects of openness in education.

Hegarty (2015) argues that OER alone cannot guarantee the development of a participatory culture where people connect through social media to share ideas, knowledge, and resources. Instead, Hegarty proposes eight attributes of open pedagogy, with participatory technologies being the foremost, highlighting the crucial role of technology in open teaching practices.

Expanding on this idea, Fahrer et al. (2022) define participatory pedagogy as an approach aimed at fully involving students as co-creators in the learning process. They emphasize that participatory technologies, in particular, facilitate this by providing digital tools for interaction among all participants. This perspective reinforces the idea that technology is not merely a tool in open education but an integral component that shapes the nature of educational interactions and experiences.

In conclusion, the literature consistently emphasizes the critical role of technology in open education. From facilitating collaborative learning to reflecting institutional culture, technology is portrayed as a fundamental element that enables and shapes open educational practices. As the field continues to evolve, it is clear that a deep understanding and strategic implementation of educational technologies will be crucial for the advancement and success of open education initiatives.

**Open TPACK Framework**

In 2006, Punya Mishra and Matthew J. Koehler introduced a groundbreaking framework for incorporating educational technology: the Technology Pedagogical Content Knowledge (TPACK) model. This framework, illustrated in Fig. 2, has since become one of the most significant and widely-recognized approaches in the field of instructional technology integration (Mishra & Koehler, 2006).

The TPACK framework categorizes educator knowledge into three primary domains: Technological Knowledge (TK), Pedagogical Knowledge (PK), and Content Knowledge (CK). This model has become a cornerstone in understanding the complex interplay between these knowledge areas in modern education.

- Technological Knowledge (TK): This encompasses an educator's understanding of various technologies, from basic classroom tools to advanced digital platforms.
- Pedagogical Knowledge (PK): This refers to the methods and practices of teaching and learning, including classroom management, assessment strategies, and student engagement techniques.
- Content Knowledge (CK): This represents the subject matter expertise that educators possess in their specific fields.

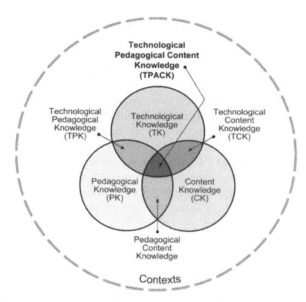

**Fig. 2.** Technological, Pedagogical, and Content Knowledge (TPACK) Framework

The TPACK framework goes beyond these individual components to explore their intersections:

- Pedagogical Content Knowledge (PCK): The ability to teach specific content effectively.
- Technological Content Knowledge (TCK): Understanding how technology and content influence each other.
- Technological Pedagogical Knowledge (TPK): Knowing how to use technology to support various teaching methods.

At the center of these intersections lies Technological Pedagogical Content Knowledge (TPACK), representing the ideal integration of all three knowledge domains.

This model helps address challenges in implementing classroom technology by emphasizing that effective technology integration must support both content delivery and pedagogical methods to enhance learning. It encourages educators to consider not just what technology to use, but how and why to use it in the context of their subject matter and teaching approaches.

Open educational practices mirror these TPACK elements, focusing on open technology, pedagogy, and content. This similarity leads to the proposal of an Open TPACK framework (Fig. 3), adapting TPACK principles to open education contexts. The Open TPACK framework considers:

- Open Technological Knowledge: Understanding and utilizing open-source technologies and platforms.
- Open Pedagogical Knowledge: Embracing teaching methods that promote openness, collaboration, and sharing.

- Open Content Knowledge: Leveraging and creating openly licensed educational resources.

The intersections in the Open TPACK framework are particularly interesting:

- Open Pedagogical Content Knowledge: How to teach specific subjects using open educational resources and methodologies.
- Open Technological Content Knowledge: Understanding how open technologies can be used to represent and manipulate subject matter.
- Open Technological Pedagogical Knowledge: Knowing how open technologies can support and enhance open teaching practices.

At the core of Open TPACK is the synergy of all these elements, representing a comprehensive approach to open education that integrates open technologies, open content, and open pedagogies.

This adaptation of TPACK to open educational contexts provides a valuable framework for educators and institutions looking to implement open education practices effectively. It encourages a holistic view of open education, where technology, pedagogy, and content are not considered in isolation but as interconnected elements that, when properly integrated, can significantly enhance the educational experience.

**Future Research Directions**
Future research could explore the integration of technology, resources, and pedagogy, examining how different tools can be effectively combined with educational resources and teaching practices to improve outcomes. Additionally, studies could investigate the interaction between policy, technology, and pedagogy, focusing on how policy-making

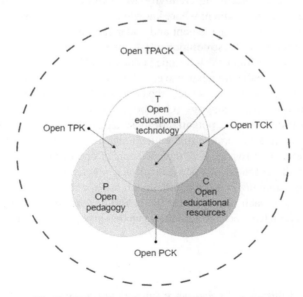

**Fig. 3.** Open Education Practice Framework Map

influences the application of technology and resources in open education, and how this impact translates to pedagogical practices. Lastly, research could examine the role of teacher training in empowering open education, particularly how it can enhance educators' ability to apply open pedagogy effectively using technology and resources. These research directions aim to provide insights for creating more effective open educational environments, inform policy-making, and improve teacher preparation programmes.

## 6 Conclusion

This study has explored the adoption of open educational resources (OER) and open-source software (OSS) within the context of Hong Kong Metropolitan University (HKMU) through a grounded theory approach. By examining the perceptions and experiences of university teachers, we have developed a comprehensive understanding of the motivations, challenges, and support needed for the effective integration of these open educational practices.

Our findings reveal that the true potential of open educational practices (OEP) lies not just in the use of open content, but in the synergistic interaction between open content, open tools, and open pedagogy. The development of the Open TPACK framework in this study underscores this holistic approach, illustrating how these three elements—technology, resources, and pedagogy—interconnect to create a comprehensive and transformative educational experience.

Open content provides the essential foundation for equitable access to knowledge, addressing issues of educational inequality. However, equity alone is insufficient to foster the creative and collaborative skills necessary for modern education. Open tools empower educators and learners to not only consume but also create, modify, and share educational resources, thereby nurturing creativity. Meanwhile, open pedagogy promotes a collaborative learning environment where knowledge is co-created by both teachers and students, fostering a deeper engagement and understanding.

The interdependence of these components—open content, open tools, and open pedagogy—creates a robust framework for open educational practices. This framework not only enhances access to education but also enriches the learning experience by encouraging creativity and collaboration. As such, the equation "Open Content (Equity) + Open Tools (Creativity) + Open Pedagogy (Collaboration) = Open Educational Practices" encapsulates the transformative potential of these elements when integrated effectively.

Looking ahead, it is imperative that educational institutions and policymakers recognize the importance of fostering all three aspects of open education. By doing so, we can fully realize the potential of open educational practices to revolutionize the educational landscape, making it more equitable, creative, and collaborative for all learners. This holistic approach is crucial for the future development of education and the empowerment of both teachers and students in an increasingly digital and interconnected world.

## References

Alnassar, M.S.N.: Utilization of open-source software in teaching the physics of P-N diodes. Comput. Appl. Eng. Educ. **31**(4), 867–883 (2023). https://doi.org/10.1002/cae.22611

Bose, S.: Using grounded theory approach for examining the problems faced by teachers enrolled in a distance education programme. Open Praxis **13**(2), 160 (2021). https://doi.org/10.5944/openpraxis.13.2.128

Cape Town Open Education Declaration: Cape Town Open Education Declaration: Unlocking the promise of open educational resources (2007). http://www.capetowndeclaration.org/read-the-declaration

Chen, L., Chen, P., Lin, Z.: Artificial intelligence in education: a review. IEEE Access **8**, 75264–75278 (2020). https://doi.org/10.1109/ACCESS.2020.2988510

Corbin, J., Strauss, A.: Basics of Qualitative Research (3rd ed.): Techniques and Procedures for Developing Grounded Theory. SAGE Publications, Inc., 2455 Teller Road, Thousand Oaks California 91320 United States (2008). https://doi.org/10.4135/9781452230153

Cronin, C.: Openness and praxis: Exploring the use of open educational practices in higher education. Int. Rev. Res. Open Distrib. Learn. **18**(5), 15–34 (2017)

Fahrer, R.R., Ellegaard, M., Nørgård, R.T.: Participatory pedagogy and participatory technologies: a critical perspective on digital teaching and learning in higher education. Teach. Higher Educ. 1–16 (2022)

Glaser, B. G., Strauss, A.L.: The Discovery of Grounded Theory: Strategies for Qualitative Research. Routledge (1967)

Hegarty, B.: Attributes of open pedagogy: a model for using open educational resources. Educ. Technol. **55**(4), 3–13 (2015)

Hepburn, G.: Open source software and schools: new opportunities and directions. Canadian J. Learn. Technol./La revue canadienne de l'apprentissage et de la technologie (2005). https://doi.org/10.21432/T25P5B

Inamorato dos Santos, A., Punie, Y., Castaño-Muñoz, J. : Opening up education: A support framework for higher education institutions. JRC Science for Policy Report, EUR 27938 EN (2016)

Knox, J.: Five critiques of the open educational resources movement. Teach. High. Educ. **18**(8), 821–832 (2013)

Kim, T.: Building student proficiency with scientific literature using the Zotero reference manager platform. Biochem. Mol. Biol. Educ. **39**(6), 412–415 (2011). https://doi.org/10.1002/bmb.20551

Li, K., Wong, B.: A review of the use of open educational resources: the benefits, challenges and good practices in higher education. Int. J. Innov. Learn. **30**(3), 279–298 (2021)

Li, K. C., Yuen, K. S., Wong, B. T.-M.: Readiness for open educational resources: a study of Hong Kong. In: Proceedings of the 2nd Regional Symposium on Open Educational Resources: Beyond Advocacy, Research and Policy, pp. 35–41 (2014)

Luk, C.-H., Ng, K.-K., Lam, W.-M.: The acceptance of using open-source learning platform (moodle) for learning in hong kong's higher education. In: Cheung, S.K.S., Lam, J., Li, K.C., Au, O., Ma, W.W.K., Ho, W.S. (eds.) Technology in Education. Innovative Solutions and Practices, pp. 249–257. Springer Singapore, Singapore (2018). https://doi.org/10.1007/978-981-13-0008-0_23

Mishra, P., Koehler, M.J.: Technological pedagogical content knowledge: a framework for teacher knowledge. Teachers College Record: The Voice Scholarsh. Educ. **108**(6), 1017–1054 (2006). https://doi.org/10.1111/j.1467-9620.2006.00684.x

Sharp, J.H., Huett, J.B.: The use of open-source software in education. Inform. Syst. Educ. J. **4**(45) (2006). http://isedj.org/4/45/. ISSN: 1545-679X

Somaraj, S.: Unveiling the potential of open-source software integration in education: advantages, challenges, and effective strategies. Int. Res. J. Adv. Engg. Mgt. **2**(05), 1309–1314 (2024). https://doi.org/10.47392/IRJAEM.2024.0178

Thankachan, B., Moore, D.R.: Challenges of implementing free and open source software (FOSS): evidence from the Indian educational setting. Int. Rev. Res. Open Distrib. Learn. (2017). https://doi.org/10.19173/irrodl.v18i6.2781

Urquhart, C.: Grounded theory for qualitative research: a practical guide. SAGE Publications, Ltd. (2017). https://doi.org/10.4135/9781526402196

Weller, M.: Twenty years of EdTech. Educause Rev. Online **53**(4), 34–48 (2018)

# The Practice of Digital Education: Findings and Lessons Based on Urgent Outreach Activities

Shao-Fu Li[1], Shun-Neng Yang[1], Jzung-Lu Lin[2], Kwan-Keung Ng[3](✉), Lap-Kei Lee[4], and Louise Luk[4]

[1] Chung Hua University, Taiwan, China
{shaofu,simonyang}@g.chu.edu.tw
[2] Hsinchu Community University, Taiwan, China
[3] Shenzhen City Polytechnic, Shenzhen, China
ngkwankeung@outlook.com
[4] Hong Kong Metropolitan University, Hong Kong, China
{lklee,lluk}@hkmu.edu.hk

**Abstract.** By a stroke of luck, a boring digital technology course was transformed into a university social responsibility programme that serves the community. As a result of the time limit, the programme requirements were completed in a joint effort between the school and the community university. This paper uses the assistance of the Faculty of Architecture as an example of how a department can quickly adapt its curriculum to maintain student satisfaction. Teachers and authors are involved in observing all activities and conducting semi-structured student interviews. Although there were many setbacks in the process, the stakeholders of the project were satisfied and even considered it a rare experience. This paper aims to compile the student part of the process, making it a reference point for future curriculum design.

**Keywords:** digital education · reality games · outreach activity · social innovation (SI) · university social responsibility (USR)

## 1 Introduction

The demand for computer-related positions will continue to grow for the foreseeable future. This presents a great opportunity to address employment issues but is also a challenge as it requires addressing diversity issues (Mano et al., 2010). This phenomenon of need or pursuit is seen in most higher education in Taiwan. Schools at all levels are developing new digital learning programmes, which are often targeted at professional disciplines with non-IT backgrounds. This paper uses the example of architecture students to illustrate how to teach digital technology. On the other hand, the authorities in charge of higher education are also constantly asking schools to enhance students' social participation skills. This is now commonly known as a university social responsibility (USR) programme or service-learning project.

By chance, a local community university requested assistance from the Department of Architecture and Urban Planning (DAUP) to support their ongoing project. The school's USR office found this to be a unique opportunity (Nuncio et al., 2020) to experiment with the social design of the digital curriculum. Mano (2010) also found that students could learn about various computer science topics through regular classroom activities. These activities can be used to create an effective curriculum for other outreach programmes (Harris et al., 2018). After a quick internal discussion, the College's mandatory APP Design and Application (APP Course) was selected as a counterpart to respond to an urgent request from the community university.

The paper underscores the critical intersection of digital education and community engagement, highlighting the necessity of adaptive curriculum design in response to employment demands and diversity challenges in the tech sector. It illustrates how higher education can enhance student skills while fostering social responsibility and cultural preservation by transforming a digital technology course into a university social responsibility program. The collaboration between architecture students and local elders in developing an outdoor reality game is presented as a model for integrating experiential learning with community needs, promoting intergenerational dialogue and cultural memory. This research emphasizes the importance of innovative, inclusive educational practices that equip students to meet the challenges of a rapidly evolving world, while positively impacting their communities.

## 2 Research Approach and Methodology

Universities are increasingly endeavouring to strengthen their public commitment to their city, local economy and wider society through research and higher education activities to impact the local community and increase the relevance of higher education (McCann et al., 2015; Resch et al., 2016). This paper believes universities are drivers and responsible agents of societal well-being, growth and innovation – through their excellence in research and teaching. USR requires engagement and commitment from within the University and an understanding of external stakeholders (business partners, regional non-profit organisations, associations, local politics, etc.). Coe et al. (2006) also believe that exchanging experiences, innovations and good practices among universities will contribute to a better understanding of the importance of social responsibility in public higher education institutions. It also provides relevant insights for action planning of social responsibility activities. In discussions with the community university team, the DAUP hopes to take this opportunity to create new course offerings. In this social practice, "new" represents innovation, while social ends and social means indicate that society is the goal and means of SI (Effendi, 2023). The social sciences' main goal is to meet society's needs through social action (Mulgan, 2006). This article provides and analyses qualitative information from a sample of course students and their community partners to address three questions of core interest in collaboration:

- Does community participation in college-led external programs (outdoor reality games) help universities expand community outreach?
- What types of partnerships do academic institutions have with various organisations in the community?

- How and to what extent have universities institutionalised community outreach and cooperation activities?
- Evaluate the programme and specify lessons learned that can guide similar projects, researchers, policymakers and other stakeholders in the school's IT department.

This study adopts a case study methodology, drawing on a similar approach to news interviews to explore student outreach day activities as part of a recording and memory community. Journalism is a method and practice, an evolving system of collecting, organising and communicating information. Its goals include accuracy and truthfulness, as well as creating space for criticism and compromise, as in the activities of outreach day (Lindgren & Phillips, 2011; Carroll, 2019). Parks (2021) explained that the interview allowed for an in-depth exploration of the community of practice as it was centred on context, environment, organisational culture and participant frames of reference. In addition, because field notes are rooted in a "commitment to accurately reflecting the perspectives and feelings of participants," they allow researchers to investigate the informational behaviours of the communities targeted by the outreach efforts (Roeschley, 2023). These activities were created through the active participation of two stakeholder groups, community elders and students who contributed records to the real-life game. Two collection methods were used to gain a thorough understanding of these two groups and the outreach activities themselves: direct observation and semi-structured interviews.

## 2.1 Outdoor Reality Game Project for Senior Citizens

The Community University plans to take the ancient city of Hsinchu as the core and take the elders and the public on a journey through time and space that spans a hundred years through an enlarged version of the city's "Outdoor Reality Game" model. According to the findings of the planning team, living and ageing in place is what the elders expect for the rest of their lives. The collective memory of time and space of the elders is full of emotions of local culture, local knowledge and local stories, which need to be preserved and promoted. Therefore, this project is to link up with local elders over 65 years old in Hsinchu City to jointly develop a reality game. The basic order of the plan is as follows:

(1) Interviews and recordings of elders' collective memories of temporality.
(2) Taking stock of spatial cultural resources with elders.
(3) Convene a workshop with elders to confirm the characteristics of local symbols for reality games.
(4) Invite elders to discuss the process and methods of reality games with manufacturers
(5) After the reality game is developed, the elders will experience and verify the game.
(6) The programme is corrected and post-produced to promote it to seniors and residents across the city.

From the above process arrangement, we can see that the space of the elders is part of daily life, and the time is part of childhood memories. The gaze is the discursive text between the two, representing urban memory. The project's vision is based on the fact that the entire old city is the playground of the elders so that the elders' memories of the city can be preserved, promoted, passed on, and have educational significance. These include 'the moat, market, city gate, parks, temples, museums, and the city hall,' all familiar to the elders of Hsinchu City. This project is based on the old city walking map (Fig. 1) defined by the local government as the spatial scope of the reality game. The Qing Dynasty City Gate on the moat on the east side of the picture is the only remaining city tower. In contrast, the city towers in the other three directions were destroyed during the Japanese occupation. This picture shows the corresponding locations of historical attractions with the East Gate Tower as the core, and is the main scene range of this reality game.

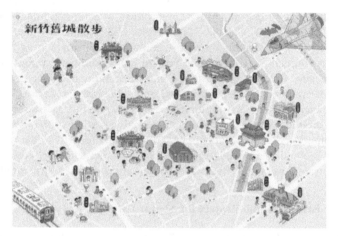

**Fig. 1.** Walking map of Old Town Hsinchu. (Source: Hsinchu City Government, 2020)

## 2.2 Data Collection: Direct Observation of Outreach Activities

Direct observations of outreach activities involve the study of group and individual behaviour in the natural environment. The observer records in real time the behaviour of individuals in the environment as they interact with each other and the environment. The observer then encodes the observed phenomena and creates a data-driven narrative of the observation, providing insights into the observed event and the subjects involved in the event. This approach can be beneficial to researchers and others seeking to understand specific outreach activities. In this study, a total of five events arranged by the community university from 25 April to 28 May 2023 were observed. However, this was not an entirely unobtrusive observation, as both study subjects and participants were verbally informed of this observation. Coding was used to categorise the data and identify common topics or themes regarding subject demographics, subject behaviours, and interactions with each other and the physical space.

## 2.3 Data Collection: Semi-structured Interviews with Student Participants

Semi-structured interviews are a method between structured and unstructured interviews, containing both preset questions and allowing the interviewer to ask free-form questions based on the students' responses. This is particularly suitable for exploratory research and contexts that require a deeper understanding of respondents' perspectives, allowing for more flexible information while ensuring the research objectives are met (Georgakopoulou, 2015). Compared with fully structured interviews, semi-structured interviews are more likely to establish an informal atmosphere of dialogue and help build trust between the interviewer and the respondent. During the interviews, when the interviewees revealed new insights, new follow-up questions were asked to further understand their experiences in outreach activities. A purposive sampling of students was conducted with a sample size of 7 subjects, as these were the only students who participated in the entire session.

## 2.4 Method of Analysis: Qualitative Content Analysis

In response to this request for activities, in addition to meeting the needs of the community university to create reality games, we also need to take care of the experience and feelings of students. The research must aim to identify patterns, themes, concepts or other meaningful elements of such activities to gain a deeper understanding of the object of study. The main step in qualitative content analysis, apart from identifying the research question or objective and the data to be analysed, is to code the data and break it down into small, meaningful units (Elo et al., 2014). Based on the coding, similar content is grouped, and recurring themes or patterns are identified. Analyse the generalised themes, explain their meaning and relate them to the research question. This process may involve several reviews and adjustments to ensure an accurate and in-depth understanding of the data.

# 3 Findings and Analysis of the Study

The department's decision to participate in the Hsinchu Community University's reality game programme was urgent but time-consuming to plan, and it was indeed a long and complex process. Inspired by the participatory action research process in the context of multi-stakeholder partnerships, each project stage's process and key activities are listed below.

Phase A: The prologue discussion helps students communicate with elders by sharing childhood memories and discussing meaningful experiences. Students express past experiences through pictures and receive praise for their ability and attitude. The group discussion in Fig. 2 is conducted in two groups, with two elderly participants.

Phase B: Five students participated during the first discussion session, and the implementation was considered satisfactory. A field trip to the Old City was successful, with 16 students attending. The author, also the president of the community university, led a walking tour for students and seniors, collecting visual symbols and exploring buildings of historical significance. The old city centre of Hsinchu was the focal point, and the field investigation took place in the afternoon. The photo gallery in Fig. 3 depicts the current condition of the old town business district.

Phase C: Urbanism and architecture students deeply understand the built environment. The principal discussed defining geographic elements for a realistic game plan in Fig. 4. Scenic spots in old towns play a strategic role in tourism promotion. Graphics from selected photos were processed to create recognisable symbols for mobile game interfaces. Figure 5 shows a city landscape and a student's hand-drawn tonal work.

**Fig. 2.** Phase A. Learning how to work with the Elders. (Source: Hsinchu Community University, 2020)

**Fig. 3.** Phase B. Collection of symbolic characteristics of Old Town Areas. (Source: Hsinchu Community University, 2020)

Phase D: The student outreach program consists of three phases, technical learning and application, and guidance from game developers. The university arranged two full days for study groups (CHU, 2024). On the first day, students study on campus, and the next day, they visit the old city to test their learning results. During the visit, the game developer introduced real-life game engines for the students to practice with, including Playreal (Playreal Co., 2022), which involves using mobile phones and props to solve puzzles in real environments. The game designer (Clubon Co., 2023) led the

**Fig. 4.** Phase C. Filtering of symbolic characteristics (Seminar Format). (Source: Hsinchu Community University, 2020)

students through physical games and the Playreal amusement program. Figure 6 shows an example of Playreal's mobile phone interface.

Phase E: After practising on campus the day before, the students quickly settled into the rhythm of things at the old town site. About seven students arrived early at the market office to work in groups. Figure 7 showcases their work. Other students who arrived late were assigned to different groups. These students generally had higher expectations for themselves in class and put in extra effort to ensure quality work.

**Fig. 5.** Examples of visual works created by students. (Source: Hsinchu Community University, 2022)

**Fig. 6.** Phase D. Treasure Hunt Game for Beginners (On Campus). (Source: Hsinchu Community University, 2022)

**Fig. 7.** Phase E. Realistic Treasure Hunt Game (Hsinchu Old City). (Source: Hsinchu Community University, 2022)

### 3.1 Direct Observation of Various Off-Campus Activities

As mentioned before, APP Courses have no prior subsidy to participate in this game development program. Students are only required to participate in at least one of the scheduled activities, so this is a voluntary outreach programme. However, the department will provide hourly credits equivalent to participation in required on-campus activities (Turner et al., 2011). The number of students taking the course this semester reached 63, among which 22 had not participated in the course once, with a participation rate of about 65.1%. Of these 41 students, 2 participated the whole time and another 5 from the 2nd to the last. Table 1 Statistics on the basic information of each activity. The above five stages of student participation resulted from multiple discussions and designs. The main thing is to plan a gradual investment so that students can have a good impression of the activity.

The observation started with a discussion session and continued with five activities on and off campus, totalling about 23 h. According to the aforementioned cases of Phases A to E, whether the students are proactive or not can be seen. In particular, seven of these students performed the best overall:

**Table 1.** Table of time spent and number of participants in each activity.

|  | Date/Time | Place | Number of students who volunteer | Number of elderly participants |
|---|---|---|---|---|
| Phase A | Tuesday 25 April 2023<br>14:00 – 17:00 (3 h) | Community Activity Centre, Hsinchu | 5 | 2 |
| Phase B | Monday 8 May 2023<br>13:00 – 17:00 (4 h) | Old Town District, Hsinchu City | 16 | 2 |
| Phase C | Monday 15 May 2023<br>13:00 – 17:00 (4 h) | Community Activity Centre, Hsinchu | 11 | 2 |
| Phase D | Saturday 27 May 2023<br>09:00 – 16:00 (6 h) | CHU Campus | 29 | 2 |
| Phase E | Sunday 28 May 2023<br>09:00 – 16:00 (6 h) | Old Town District, Hsinchu City | 28 | 2 |

- *Actively Seek Resources and Help:* Proactive students actively seek solutions when faced with a problem. They may use online resources, and ask teachers or classmates to help them understand the problem.
- *Questioning and Critical Thinking:* These students not only accept the requirements of the assignment but also ask questions to further explore the topic of the assignment. They may challenge assumptions made in the assignment or look for more in-depth answers.
- *Self-checks and Corrections:* After completing their assignments, proactive students check their answers and take the initiative to correct errors as they are found.
- *Attitude of Continuous Learning:* They don't just study to complete their homework, but see it as part of learning. They take the initiative to look for more learning materials to expand their knowledge.

## 3.2 Themes Present in Direct Observation

The direct observations mentioned above were made at outreach events and in the classroom during the programme. In coding and recoding the observation notes, clear themes emerge in treasure hunting, such as physical environment and space, moments of purpose and spontaneity, and human connection. The physical and spatial presence of the old city is very evident. The layout of the old town business district ensures that the space itself is conducive to pedestrian movement, allowing participants to move smoothly through the various streets and alleys while engaging in a dialogue about the character of the city. When a participant finds a feature, it is photographed to stimulate dialogue and interest in the features that are being actively created in the city.

What is being wrestled with in these moments is the question of whether or not the subject of human connection is a recognised so-called characteristic or symbol. This was evident in the presentation of relevant photographs by the participants and in the way the elders listened to each other as they told the stories behind a particular photograph (place). The serendipitous interactions among participating elders illustrate the possibilities for community building and human connection during outreach. Recurring themes in the observation data illustrate the role of on-site outreach days in event-based participatory and memory community building. This well-designed programme by the community university allows for successful outreach activities and enables participants to build a unique mechanism of mutual trust with each other.

## 3.3 Semi-Structured Interviews with Participants

The project was repeatedly described as being full of heightened emotion, with the final two days relying on a face-to-face atmosphere centred on sharing historical stories and spatial relationships. According to the Community University Principal and staff, the Reality Treasure Hunt event was a purposeful effort to bring community participants together. While these efforts were purposeful for the programme implementers, participants saw them as unexpected moments of connection. For example, Student Participant #07 described such a moment:

> *During the process, it was found that the elderly people who were willing to participate in the programme were all very lively and lovely. They also liked to*

make friends. Apart from being willing to interact with us, they were also willing to keep up with the times and learn more about electronic products.

As these activities were designed to be a part of the community's history and the participants' family memories, it is not surprising that strong emotions were present in the interview data. Student Participant #06 describes how the experience of interacting with elders motivated her to participate in the collection activities:

*Although it is said that the general public does not know much about reality games, or understand that they are a product of the young people. However, this is not true; nowadays, the world has evolved into a social pattern of living and learning until old age, and the silver-haired people also have the right to participate in the activities of young people. It's a great experience to see yourself in miniature during the event! ... ...Memories come flooding back! We hope that they will be able to rekindle their passion for life and desire for freshness in the rest of their lives, and regain the craziness of their youth!*

Although Participant #05 is an architecture student, she has never entered a religious building. In the interview, she talked about how her family rarely took her to certain places:

*What impressed me most about this location was that the front half belonged to a traditional Chinese medicine store, but when I walked to the back, I found that it still had historic buildings that had been completed....... For me, the chance of entering a church was zero, so that was my first time stepping into a church. Its interior space is particularly high, giving people a sacred feeling when they walk in.*

Student Participant #04 expressed that one of the benefits of participating in off-campus activities is the expansion of one's capabilities:

*About this app development out-of-school activity, I think it was a lot more absorbing than just attending classes at school. Not only did it allow us to get in touch with the history of the Hsinchu City God Temple neighbourhood, but it also allowed us to interact with the elders and promote conversation and bonding between the young and the old. I was impressed by the fact that at the beginning we collected historical information about each site, and in the process, we tried to understand what this 50 to 60-year-old building has gone through by asking for their biographies and even communicating with them directly. We were also able to be more outgoing and brave in our ability to try more things.*

Whilst the vast majority of participants positively described their engagement with the immersive play, some students also described hesitations about the activity, such as 'expressing reluctance to participate'. Student Participant 3 explained his situation:

*After cooperating with the community college for about two months, it can be seen that both parties attach great importance to the activities. As members of the Architecture Department, we are more than happy to participate in this kind of* service, but the time arrangement is the problem we need to overcome. Our own time may conflict with the event, but we try to cooperate as much as possible.

The interactive nature of outreach services was noted in each interview. Immersion in the programme and face-to-face interactions were the focus of several interviews. Student Participant #02 stated that the atmosphere of the programme itself was crucial to the success of the programme:

*At first, I didn't quite understand what the APP Course meant to the architecture department. It wasn't until the teacher arranged for us to work with a community college that I learnt from the four events that there is a very different kind of fieldwork experience than sitting in a classroom all day. The Rector of the Community University explained to us that these experiences would be used in our research for our future Master's degree. ... ...I am very fortunate to have this opportunity to work with the Community University, and I have enjoyed myself at every event. Whether it is listening to the elders of the Community University share their stories or exploring the world on your own two feet, there are so many details that need to be experienced to be savoured.*

As he explains, the outreach programme is an immersive experience, dependent on the interaction between participants at a particular time and place. Student Participant #01 found it very meaningful, combining the memories of elders and modern game technology. The student portion of the work is now over, and it is hoped that the programming portion of the work is going well too:

*This day was the most tiring but fun of the past few days. Not only did we design puzzles to solve, but we also travelled all over the place. After the experience, I think it was worth all the hard work.*

The above seven students can be considered the most serious participants in the class, and the model of independent learning can be seen in them. Apart from these seven who were the focus of the interviews, a dozen or so others were interviewed in the form of casual conversations. There was a common feeling among them, and that was about the designer of the game developer:

*At the beginning of the course, the teacher led us to play games in a relaxed and fun way. Later, we also had group competitions and group recreation games to unite the group's centripetal force. We will become more enthusiastic when we all work towards a common goal. In our free time, we can extend our communication from discussion activities to daily life, so we don't have to be afraid of drying out throughout the whole process.*

*But honestly, I think that teaching by example is more important than exciting and fun games. The teacher has a smile on his face even when he is physically challenged, and he is passionate about life, his future, and what they are doing.*

## 4 Discussion and Conclusion

The main focus of the Senior Outdoor Reality Game Project is to promote the co-creation of real-life puzzles between young and old people. Through the interaction between elders and university students, the project will cover the basic operation of computer and mobile phone apps for real-life games, outdoor symbols and memory collection, as well as the development and testing of game-specific workshops and in-situ levels. Students discuss with elders the collective memory of childhood and the operation mode of the APP human factors interface and then follow the conclusions and survey items to further process the APP requirement writing and game box project construction. System development will begin after the APP requirement writing and game box project construction are completed. After the system is developed, it will accept the APP requirement writing and game box project construction, and invite the co-development students and elders to participate in the system acceptance, including functionality, interface, reliability, ease of use, performance, compatibility, security, etc. to conduct the acceptance and testing operations.

During the activities, the elders fully express their stories of childhood memories and symbols. At the same time, the students gain the experience of space and time, which fully demonstrates 'Learning with the Elderly and the Young, Learning with the Generation' (Hamner, 2007). The students will be able to communicate, interact and share their experiences, and change their perceptions and attitudes through the learning of each other's skills (German & LeMire, 2018; Gall et al., 2020). The programme emphasises the importance of intergenerational assistance to complete the learning tasks and enable all participants, young and old, to gain and grow.

The transition of the digital technology course into a university social responsibility program proved to be highly effective. It significantly heightened student engagement by linking academic learning with real-world applications. Students acquired crucial digital skills through the design and execution of an outdoor reality game targeted at local senior citizens, fostering a sense of purpose and community involvement. This integration safeguarded local cultural heritage and encouraged intergenerational dialogue, highlighting the value of experiential learning. Furthermore, the adaptability of the curriculum sets a precedent for future collaborations between educational institutions and communities, showcasing the potential for social engagement in higher education.

The transformation process encountered several key challenges, including time constraints due to the urgent nature of the community request, which restricted comprehensive planning and execution. Balancing educational objectives with the community's needs required careful negotiation to meet learning outcomes and community expectations. Resource limitations, such as funding and personnel, further complicated the project, necessitating effective coordination with external partners. Additionally, involving local elders in the development process posed challenges in accurately capturing their input and memories. At the same time, the need for ongoing feedback and iterations added complexity to project timelines and outcomes.

The research findings from observations and semi-structured interviews conducted with students and stakeholders in the program have revealed several significant insights. Students reported an enriched learning experience through hands-on engagement with real-world applications of digital technology, which enhanced their motivation and sense of purpose. Collaboration among students, educators, and community stakeholders was vital, fostering teamwork and interpersonal skills while emphasising the importance of feedback loops for iterative improvements. Challenges in engaging local elders necessitated adaptability and sensitivity. However, students and community members expressed high satisfaction with the project, appreciating its role in preserving local culture. These findings underscore the potential for integrating community engagement into higher education curricula, reinforcing the value of experiential learning and social responsibility in academic programmes.

The programme significantly enhanced students' social participation skills and understanding of digital education, reality games, outreach activities, social innovation, and university social responsibility. By collaborating with local elders to develop an outdoor reality game, students engaged directly with the community, improving their communication, teamwork, and adaptability skills. They applied their digital knowledge practically, fostering innovative problem-solving and understanding of how digital education can address real-world challenges. The project provided firsthand experience in planning and executing outreach activities while cultivating a mindset oriented toward social innovation. Ultimately, students developed a commitment to university social responsibility, recognising the role of educational institutions in contributing to societal well-being and enhancing their capacity to create positive social change.

The development of real-life games provides a sense of excitement and achievement that cannot be found outside of school. In addition, the elders have rich social experience, and with the accumulation of age, they have many life experiences, which are valuable life wisdom. All of these are valuable life wisdom that can be passed on to young individuals and groups, and the process of admiration for the elders' life history and recognition of their hometowns, as well as the value of the local culture of Hsinchu, is also seen.

The project follows the principles of feasibility, creativity, and impact, and identifies the expectations of the public, elders, or elders' family members in the process of participating in the launch of the system, as well as the process of experiencing and learning about elders' life stories. In addition, the game process of experiencing and understanding the life stories of elders and grandmothers resolves the intergenerational gap (understanding the life stories of grandparents) and promotes the interaction between families. To deepen the intergenerational integration, it is suggested that the content of the development of the real-life puzzle game should be in addition to the memories of the elders in their childhood. It can add topics that young people are interested in the living space, popular culture and social facts so that the content is not only one-way, but also two-way to achieve communication and integration.

## References

Carroll, E.C.: Promoting Journalism as Method. Drexel L. Rev. **12**, 691 (2019)

Chung Hua University (CHU): 提升資訊力:運算思維與程式設計 [Enhancing Information Competence: Computational Thinking and Programming] (2024), https://coding.chu.edu.tw/. Retrieved 28 July 2024

Clubon Creativity Corporation: Clubon Space (2023), https://clubon.medium.com/. Retrieved 28 July 2024

Coe, K., Wilson, C., Eisenberg, M., Attakai, A., Lobell, M.: Creating the environment for a successful community partnership. Cancer **107**(S8), 1980–1986 (2006). https://doi.org/10.1002/cncr.22156

Effendi, T.D.: Student-centered innovation project as university social responsibility (usr). Innov. Soc. Sci. **1**(1), 150–174 (2023). https://doi.org/10.1163/27730611-bja10002

Elo, S., Kääriäinen, M., Kanste, O., Pölkki, T., Utriainen, K., Kyngäs, H.: Qualitative content analysis: a focus on trustworthiness. SAGE Open **4**(1), 2158244014522633 (2014). https://doi.org/10.1177/2158244014522633

Gall, A.J., Vollbrecht, P.J., Tobias, T.: Developing outreach events that impact underrepresented students: are we doing it right? Eur. J. Neurosci. **52**(6), 3499–3506 (2020). https://doi.org/10.1111/ejn.14719

Georgakopoulou, A.: Small stories research: methods–analysis–outreach. Handbook Narrative Anal. (2015). https://doi.org/10.1002/9781118458204.ch13

German, E., LeMire, S.: Sharing the value and impact of outreach: taking a multifaceted approach to outreach assessment. J. Acad. Librariansh. **44**(1), 66–74 (2018). https://doi.org/10.1016/j.acalib.2017.11.001

Hamner, J.B., Wilder, B., Byrd, L.: Lessons learned: Integrating a service learning community-based partnership into the curriculum. Nurs. Outlook **55**(2), 106–110 (2007). https://doi.org/10.1016/j.outlook.2007.01.008

Harris, M.A., Grange, S., Feeney, A., Odorico, S.K.: Undergraduate students are the key to community science outreach partnerships. Proc. Assoc. Biol. Lab. Educ. **39**, 30 (2018)

Lindgren, M., Phillips, G.: Conceptualising journalism as research: two paradigms. Australian J. Rev. **33**(2), 73–83 (2011). https://doi.org/10.3316/ielapa.047652749712227

Mano, C., Allan, V., Cooley, D.: Effective in-class activities for middle school outreach programs. In: 2010 IEEE Frontiers in Education Conference (FIE), pp. F2E-1 (2010). IEEE. https://doi.org/10.1109/FIE.2010.5673587

McCann, B.M., Cramer, C.B., Taylor, L.G.: Assessing the impact of education and outreach activities on research scientists. J. High. Educ. Outreach Engagem. **19**(1), 65–78 (2015)

Mulgan, G.: The process of social innovation (2006). https://doi.org/10.1162/itgg.2006.1.2.145

Nuncio, R.V., Arcinas, M.M., Lucas, R.I.G., Alontaga, J.V.Q., Neri, S.G.T., Carpena, J.M.: An E-learning outreach program for public schools: Findings and lessons learned based on a pilot program in Makati City and Cabuyao City, Laguna, Philippines. Eval. Program Plann. **82**, 101846 (2020). https://doi.org/10.1016/j.evalprogplan.2020.101846

Parks, P.: Choosing joy as methodology in journalism research. J. Commun. Inq. **45**(2), 119–137 (2021). https://doi.org/10.1177/019685992092439

Playreal Corporation (2022). Create an exciting gaming experience at your fingertips. Retrieved 28 July 2024. https://playreal.com.tw/

Resch, K., et al.: Unibility: USR-Toolkit of practices (2016)

Roeschley, A.: "They care enough to document people's stories": using ethnographic methods to understand collection day outreach events in participatory archives. Libr. Inf. Sci. Res. **45**(2), 101234 (2023). https://doi.org/10.1016/j.lisr.2023.101234

Turner, A.W., Mulholland, W., Taylor, H.R.: Funding models for outreach ophthalmology services. Clin. Exp. Ophthalmol. **39**(4), 350–357 (2011). https://doi.org/10.1111/j.1442-9071.2010.02475.x

# A Study of Improvements in Educational Accessibility and Adaptability Using Digital and Intelligent Education

Jiaqi Liu[1], Kwok Tai Chui[1(✉)], Lap-Kei Lee[1], Naraphorn Paoprasert[2], Leung Pun Wong[3], and Kwan-Keung Ng[4]

[1] School of Science and Technology, Hong Kong Metropolitan University Ho Man Tin, Kowloon, Hong Kong SAR, China
s1304012@live.hkmu.edu.hk, {jktchui,lklee}@hkmu.edu.hk

[2] Department of Industrial Engineering, Faculty of Engineering, Kasetsart University, 50 Ngamwongwan Road, Lat Yao, Chatuchak, Bangkok 10900, Thailand
naraphorn.p@ku.th

[3] Tung Wah College, Hong Kong SAR, China
lpwong@twc.edu.hk

[4] Shenzhen City Polytechnic, Shenzhen, China
ngkwankeung@outlook.com

**Abstract.** This study examines recent advancements in digital and intelligent education, focusing on their impact on learning outcomes and student engagement. By analyzing studies from 2022 to 2024, we identify key trends such as the integration of AI-driven personalized learning and immersive virtual environments. The findings suggest significant improvements in accessibility and adaptability, though challenges remain in ensuring equitable access. Future research should address these disparities and explore the long-term effects of digital tools on educational achievement.

**Keywords:** artificial intelligence · educational accessibility · educational adaptability · digital education · intelligent education

## 1 Introduction

Technology, productivity, and social patterns all have an impact on educational development. With the rapid advancement of science and technology in today's world, the field of education has undergone enormous changes, highlighting the critical role of digital and intelligent education in transforming the traditional learning environment (Ali et al., 2024). As more educational institutions and educators incorporate new technologies, such as artificial intelligence and digital tools, into their classrooms, it is critical to understand and assess their impact.

This study aims to examine the most recent developments in digital education, focusing on the benefits and challenges of implementing smart education systems. By analyzing current studies, we assess the impact of smart educational technologies and propose future research directions. We conducted a comprehensive search on the Web of Science Database using the keywords "digital and intelligent education," initially retrieving 659 results. Our search was refined by applying several filters (as exclusion criteria): we included only English peer-reviewed journal articles published between 2022 and 2024. We further excluded conference proceedings, retracted articles, and other non-peer-reviewed documents, resulting in 208 articles. Finally, we filtered for titles including "education," narrowing it down to a final selection of 65 articles as shown in Fig. 1.

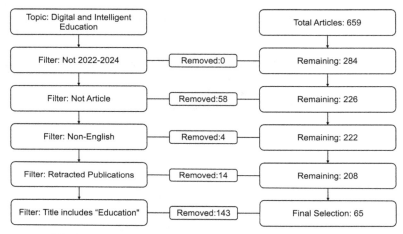

**Fig. 1.** The article search process, including exclusion criteria.

To emphasize influential studies, we prioritized articles with high citation counts or significant impact. This approach helps highlight key contributions and trends within the digital and intelligent education domain, providing a robust foundation for further analysis.

In our investigation of digital and intelligent education, we draw on and contrast our methods with existing works. Notably, the works of Pinto and Leite (2020), Huang et al. (2021) and Munir et al. (2022) provided significant insights into the application of AI and ML in educational contexts, though from slightly different perspectives.

Pinto and Leite (2020) investigated how digital technologies support student learning in higher education. Their research systematically examined the use of various digital technologies, such as learning management systems and artificial intelligence (AI)-powered tools, to improve educational experiences in higher education institutions. Their emphasis on integrating technology into teaching processes and categorizing educational technologies provided a structured view of how digital tools facilitate learning. Meanwhile, Munir et al. (2022) presented a more focused examination of AI algorithms (including machine learning (ML) algorithms) in the context of digital education through a systematic revision. Their study thoroughly examined how various machine learning algorithms, such as neural networks and support vector machines, were used to predict educational outcomes such as student dropouts or performance improvements. This granular focus on algorithmic application provided an in-depth look at the operational aspects of AI in education, as opposed to broader thematic discussions. Huang et al. (2021) contributed to this discussion by investigating specific applications of AI in education, such as adaptive learning, teaching evaluation, and the development of smart campuses, and discussing how technologies such as face recognition and virtual classrooms improve the educational experience. Their analysis thoroughly integrated AI's role in optimizing learning and administrative processes, emphasizing AI's ability to transform educational practices.

Our study aims to comprehensively understand digital and intelligent education by integrating these three dimensions: technological, societal, and policy-focused. This approach allows us to identify gaps in the current literature, such as digital equity considerations and ethical technology use in education. These are critical for developing comprehensive strategies to effectively leverage technology across diverse educational settings.

In essence, while Pinto and Leite (2020), Huang et al. (2021) and Munir et al. (2022) suggested insights into the integration and application of specific technologies within education, our study expands the scope to include a more comprehensive array of technologies and their implications, advocating for a multifaceted approach to understanding and advancing digital and intelligent education.

## 2 Related Works

In this section, we provide a comprehensive overview of key points and emerging trends in the literature. We also summarize and analyze the data types and smart tools used in education, as illustrated in Fig. 2.

| Data Types | Intelligent Tools |
|---|---|
| Learner Data | Intelligent Tutoring Systems |
| Performance and Assessment Data | Chatbots |
| Ethical and Privacy Data | Digital Teaching Resources |
| Audio Data | Automated Grading Systems |
| Environment-aware Data | Data Analytics Tools |
| Knowledge Mapping Data | Interactive Audio Analysing Systems |
| Educational Accessibility Data | Internet of Things |
| Educator Insights Data | Blockchain Technology |
|  | Virtual Reality and Augmented Reality |
|  | Digital Twins |

**Fig. 2.** Summary of data types and intelligent tools used in digital and intelligent education.

## 2.1 Key Insights

The use of technologies such as 5G, artificial intelligence, the Internet of Things (IoT) and digital audio technology is reshaping the educational environment, making it more interactive, personalized and efficient. These technologies facilitate innovative teaching methods, improve access to educational resources, enhance communication and support personalized learning paths.

**Integration of Digital Technologies in Education.** Kalaman et al. (2023) examined the integration of digital and intellectual tools in education, outlining three potential integration scenarios—inertial, transformational, and divergent. Each scenario offered different impacts on educational culture, operations, and management. The study also emphasized the need for substantial shifts to effectively utilize digital innovations, helping to guide strategic decisions in educational technology.

**Smart Education in the 5G Era.** Yang et al. (2022) and Al-Malah et al. (2023) both emphasized the crucial role of 5G technology in transforming education systems. The key advancements include faster speeds, lower latency, and enhanced connectivity. 5G supports immersive learning through IoT, augmented reality (AR) and virtual reality (VR), facilitating large online classrooms and improving the integration of educational resources. In addition, it enables interactive learning environments, smart classrooms, and better data management, ultimately correlating with improved educational outcomes and innovation.

**Technology-Driven Innovations in Education.** Xu (2024) discussed how digital audio technologies, such as voice-activated robots, were innovating preschool music education by customizing content to enhance young learners' engagement and skills. Similarly, Feng et al. (2023) highlighted the rise of smart textbooks and adaptive learning systems that used AI to tailor content and assessments, supporting and transforming traditional learning methods. In engineering education, Shi et al. (2023) presented an intelligent English teaching system that employs advanced algorithms to improve interactions and outcomes, underscoring the role of technology in enhancing student engagement across disciplines.

**AI's Transformative Role in Education.** Sappaile et al. (2024) delved into the profound influence of artificial intelligence (AI) on educational progress within the digital era, highlighting its pivotal role in fostering personalized learning, enhancing accessibility, and empowering educators. The study employed a qualitative, multifaceted approach, incorporating theoretical analysis and empirical evidence to elucidate the transformative potential of AI. It underscored the need to carefully consider ethical issues like data privacy and algorithmic bias. Harry and Sayudin (2023) explored the integration of artificial intelligence (AI) in education, highlighting its potential to personalize and enhance learning processes. This work identified key applications of AI, such as intelligent tutoring systems, chatbots, and automated grading, which contributed to more efficient and engaging educational experiences. Kamalov, Santandreu, and Gurrib (2023) discussed the burgeoning influence of artificial intelligence (AI) within the educational sector, underscoring its potential to fundamentally alter teaching, learning, and administrative processes. The study systematically reviewed the current literature to unpack AI's applications, benefits, and challenges, suggesting a sustainable, multifaceted approach to integrating AI technologies. Key areas such as personalized learning, intelligent tutoring systems, automated assessments, and enhanced teacher-student collaboration are explored.

While these studies have made promising advances, they also highlighted significant challenges, such as concerns about data privacy, algorithmic bias, and the possibility of academic fraud. In response, researchers advocated for more interdisciplinary research to improve AI's application in education and create a more equitable and innovative learning environment. They suggested a balanced approach to maximizing AI's benefits while minimizing risks.

Furthermore, researchers emphasized the importance of ethical considerations, particularly in ensuring fairness, accessibility, and transparency, all required for AI's responsible integration into educational settings. They advocated strategically using AI technologies to foster a more inclusive and effective educational environment.

## 2.2 Data Types in Digital and Intelligent Education

In the integration of AI within educational systems, several specific data types are utilized to enhance the effectiveness of learning environments and administrative operations:

**Learner Data.** Learner Data includes behavioural data, grades, and interaction records in digital profiles (Feng et al., 2023). Learner behaviour data encapsulates how students interact with digital learning platforms, tracking metrics such as click rates, time spent on tasks, and navigation paths through course materials. These insights allow educators to understand student engagement levels and learning habits, crucial for customizing the learning experience to better suit individual needs. For example, student access and usage data reflect the frequency and manner in which students access various learning resources. It is used to analyze resource utilization patterns, helping educational institutions optimize digital content availability and delivery across different learner demographics and ensuring equitable access to educational tools.

Interaction records were generated using 5G-enabled multimedia and interactive teaching and learning tools (like chatbots or adaptive learning systems) to improve teaching and learning methods (Al-Malah et al., 2023). Captured during interactions between students and AI tools, this data includes student queries, the responses generated by AI, and the effectiveness of those interactions in resolving student issues. This data helps refine AI algorithms to improve their accuracy and responsiveness, which was pointed out in various research studies by Okunlaya et al. (2022) and Yang et al. (2022). Al-Malah et al. (2023), Kamalov et al. (2023) and Hu et al. (2023) utilized learner data to adapt educational content dynamically, ensuring it aligns with the student's learning progress and preferences. Grades and interaction recorded data collected through intelligent assessment systems to adjust and optimize personalized learning paths.

**Performance and Assessment Data.** Performance data was collected along with the assessment function for real-time feedback and adjustment of teaching strategies (Feng et al., 2023). It included scores from assessments, rate of assignment completion, and qualitative feedback from educators. The analysis of performance data helped identify learning gaps and strengths, enabling targeted interventions. As Yang et al. (2022) and

Kamalov et al. (2023) discussed, AI systems use performance data to adjust the learning pathway for each student, ensuring that instructional content is neither too challenging nor too simplistic.

**Ethical and Privacy Data.** It considers the information related to compliance with educational standards and regulations concerning data privacy and ethical AI usage. This includes data on user consent, data anonymization practices, and the fairness of AI algorithms. As noted by Abdurahman et al. (2023) and Alneyadi et al. (2023), addressing these concerns is critical to maintaining the integrity and trustworthiness of AI applications in education.

**Audio Data.** This data type is crucial in applications where sound plays a fundamental role, such as music education. Xu (2024) emphasized the context of preschool music education, audio data includes recordings of musical pieces, student vocalizations and instrument sounds, and interactive audio feedback. This data was used to analyze students' music engagement, performance, and progression. It allowed for detailed assessments of a student's rhythm, pitch accuracy, and overall musicality, essential for personalized music education.

**Environment-Aware Data.** Al-Malah et al. (2023) and Yang et al. (2022) used IoT technologies to collect environment-aware data, such as the usage of learning spaces and the status of devices and 5G networks, to optimize the teaching and learning experience and environment.

**Knowledge Mapping Data.** Feng et al. (2023) highlighted that knowledge mapping in intelligent textbooks facilitates the dynamic organization of content and personalized learning paths, enhancing functions like intelligent adaptation and guidance. Hou et al. (2023) supplemented that knowledge graphs define relationships among knowledge points, integrating resources effectively and optimizing educational decision-making through personalized teaching.

**Educational Accessibility Data.** Sappaile et al. (2024) discussed data, including language translation, text transcription, and accessibility features to enhance educational content accessibility for learners with disabilities or from marginalized communities. Zhang et al. (2020) emphasized the accessibility of educational resources by designing open educational resources (OER) and open educational practices (OEP) to meet the needs of disabled learners, adhering to principles of perceivability, operability, understandability, and robustness, thus improving e-inclusion in educational settings.

### 2.3 Intelligent Tools in Digital and Intelligent Education

Several AI-driven tools have been employed to address various educational needs, enhancing learning experiences and operational efficiency:

**Intelligent Tutoring System (ITS).** ITS provides customized tutoring services by analyzing individual learning patterns and adapting the instructional content accordingly. Intelligent algorithms were used to analyze student data and adapt teaching content or methods based on the results in an important and useful way (Shi and Shi, 2022). Complex algorithms were also used in ITS to offer real-time feedback, personalized assessments, and adaptive learning paths, which are crucial for meeting diverse educational needs efficiently. Yang et al. (2022) and Kamalov et al. (2023) highlighted that it is pivotal in offering personalized education that adjusts to the learner's pace and understanding.

**AI-Powered Educational Tools.** AI-powered chatbots interact with students via text or voice, providing instant responses to inquiries, tutoring assistance, and administrative support. These tools are instrumental in reducing response times and increasing student engagement through interactive and responsive communication. Interactive learning platforms could support real-time teacher-student interaction, including virtual classrooms, instant feedback systems, etc. (Shi and Shi, 2022). Yang et al. (2022) and Okunlaya et al. (2022) discussed the implementation of chatbots in libraries to enhance user interaction and information retrieval. Sappaile et al. (2024) analyzed AI-powered tools to help educators understand student learning patterns and progress.

**Digital Teaching Resources.** Digital teaching resources encompass online teaching materials, interactive videos, dynamic mathematical technologies, and online platforms. Recall the works (Clark-Wilson et al., 2020; Shi and Shi, 2022), intelligent systems used algorithms to personalize learning experiences and process interactive data, enhancing the quality of English teaching in engineering education and supporting mathematics instruction at the secondary school level. These technologies facilitated active engagement, promoted teacher collaboration, and enabled multimedia content presentation for improved teaching and learning outcomes.

**Automated Grading Systems.** Chen and Ward (2022) proposed automated grading systems that leveraged data from student submissions to provide immediate feedback, assessed code correctness and monitored engagement and performance. These systems facilitated rapid grading of multiple attempts and code-based assignments, allowing educators to focus on pedagogical strategies rather than manual grading tasks. Utilizing natural language processing and machine learning, they evaluate various responses, from multiple-choice questions to essays, ensuring quick and unbiased grading. It was noted that these tools streamline the feedback process and offer predictive insights into student performance, effectively guiding instructional resource allocation and reducing the administrative burden on educators, enabling them to dedicate more time to instructional duties (Kamalov et al., 2023).

**Data Analytics Tools.** Data analytics tools are instrumental in transforming educational methodologies by leveraging sophisticated technologies such as machine learning and natural language processing. These tools meticulously analyze educational data to identify trends, forecast student performance, and offer actionable insights that facilitate curriculum enhancements. Kamalov et al. (2023) emphasized that these analytics systems not only streamlined the grading process by efficiently evaluating a range of student submissions—from multiple-choice questions to comprehensive essays—but also ensured quick, consistent, and unbiased results. By significantly alleviating the administrative workload, these tools enabled educators to focus more on teaching and less on logistical tasks.

**Interactive Audio Analysing Systems.** This system processes audio recordings to evaluate pitch, tempo, and rhythm elements. It provides educators and learners with feedback to improve students' musical skills. For example, AI algorithms interacted with students in real-time, providing auditory instructions, feedback, and encouragement (Xu, 2024). They are designed to be engaging for young learners, making music education both effective and enjoyable.

**Internet of Things (IoT).** IoT technology integrates sensors, RFID, and wide connectivity to enhance educational environments (Yang et al., 2022). These technologies enable real-time data capture and environment sensing, improving interaction between educational content delivery and learner engagement through personalized learning experiences. Recent research investigated how IoT applications leverage connectivity and smart devices to improve communication between students and educational systems (Al-Taai et al., 2023). By integrating these technologies, they supported real-time data capture and personalized learning scenarios, enhancing the educational experience and facilitating remote and flexible learning environments.

**Blockchain Technology.** Yang et al. (2022) explored how blockchain technology integrates with 5G and other smart technologies to enhance data security and intellectual property rights management. This integration supported a secure educational system through decentralized, transparent, immutable record-keeping. Blockchain was confirmed as a transformative tool for ensuring data security, privacy protection, and copyright management. By facilitating secure storage of educational records and credentials, blockchain enables global sharing and verification without risk of tampering, enhancing transparency and efficiency in educational processes (Bhaskar et al., 2021).

**Virtual Reality (VR) and Augmented Reality (AR).** VR and AR technologies, when integrated with 5G, enhanced the educational sector by providing immersive, interactive learning environments (Yang et al., 2022). These technologies facilitated deeper engagement and understanding through simulations and virtual field trips, making learning more accessible and effective. The integration with 5G technology ensured high-speed, low-latency experiences, creating seamless and responsive educational interactions. As Al-Ansi et al. (2023) highlighted, the rapid advancement of AR and VR offers transformative potentials in education, enabling immersive digital experiences that enhance student engagement and understanding of complex concepts. Their applications have grown rapidly, significantly benefiting educational outcomes by providing platforms for simulation-based learning and interactive environments.

**Digital Twins.** The role of digital twins in education was highlighted, and they used real-time data to create virtual replicas of learners to enhance personalized learning (Akhmedov, 2023). By applying the Internet of Things, chronobiology and bioinformatics, digital twins could monitor and tailor educational content to the individual, improving engagement and learning outcomes. This coincided with modern education reforms aimed at providing high-quality, personalized education. Another research work suggested that digital twins could be used to create visual and interactive learning and teaching environments that enhanced the understanding of complex concepts and experimental simulations (Yang et al., 2022).

## 2.4 Emerging Trends

The deployment of 5G technology provides ultra-fast internet speeds, lower latency, and more connectivity options and is completely transforming the educational sector. In conjunction with the IoT, this technology is being used to develop connected learning environments. This allows for more complex use of AR/VR and digital textbooks in classrooms and enables more immersive and responsive virtual learning environments using smart boards, IoT-enabled lab equipment, and other smart devices, promoting interactive and engaging learning.

Using robots and automated systems as teaching tools and assistants is a growing trend in AI-powered learning systems. These systems use student data to personalize learning paths and content, offering tailored support and assessment to improve learning outcomes. Personalized learning abilities and collaborative group learning environments are becoming more important. Digital and intelligent technologies enable a more personalized learning experience while facilitating collaborative projects and student interactions, critical for developing key skills such as problem-solving and communication.

The further application of AI, such as ITS and AI-powered chatbots, is demonstrating their impact on personalized learning paths and content within the educational field. These technologies use student performance and assessment data to improve the learning experience through real-time feedback and the adjustment of teaching strategies.

The introduction of blockchain technology, especially in ensuring data security and maintaining intellectual property rights, is beginning to show its potential in educational management. Its decentralized, transparent, and immutable record-keeping features provide a secure support framework for the educational system.

Digital twin technology enables educators to create virtual replicas of learners from real-time data, thereby improving personalized learning. This technology, which combines IoT, bioinformatics, and other features, enhances learning outcomes by monitoring and adjusting educational content.

In the future, the rapid advancement of educational technology will continue to drive trends toward personalization and automation in the education sector. As more emerging technologies, such as big data and cloud computing, are introduced into the educational field, the system emphasizes flexibility and student-led learning methods. Educators and policymakers must continue to adapt to technological changes to use these advanced tools to optimize learning outcomes and improve students' overall educational experience.

## 3 Conclusion and Discussion

Digital and intelligent education has emerged as a transformative force in the educational sector, propelled by rapid technological advancements such as AI, 5G, and various smart tools. These technologies have not only transformed traditional learning environments, but they have also ushered in new paradigms in educational accessibility, teaching methodologies, and student engagement.

Throughout this paper, we explored integrating and applying digital tools and AI in education, emphasizing their significant contributions to personalized learning experiences and better educational outcomes. AI-powered tutoring systems, interactive audio analysis systems, and virtual reality all help to create dynamic, responsive, and engaging learning environments that meet students' diverse needs. Furthermore, advancements in 5G and IoT technologies enable seamless and immersive educational experiences that are more accessible and efficient.

However, the digital divide remains a major issue. As technology advances, there is a growing disparity in access between wealthy and underprivileged communities. This divide limits the availability of digital tools and impacts how these technologies are integrated into educational systems across regions. To address this, comprehensive policy interventions are urgently required to ensure equitable access to technology for all students. Such policies should prioritize the development of infrastructure for reliable internet connectivity, particularly in rural and underserved areas, and provide necessary devices and technological support to all educational institutions.

Furthermore, the role of educators is evolving. There is an urgent need for professional development programs that provide teachers with the necessary skills to effectively incorporate and leverage new technologies into their teaching practices. Emphasizing collaborative, interactive, and problem-based learning approaches can help maximize the benefits of educational technology, resulting in a more inclusive and effective learning environment.

Additionally, as more educational institutions use data analytics and AI, the importance of protecting data privacy and security cannot be overstated. Ethical issues surrounding AI and automation in education are becoming more prominent. It is critical to address concerns about bias, equity, and the overall impact of technology on learning. Ensuring that these technologies are used responsibly and that all students have equal access to their benefits is critical.

Looking ahead, the rapid advancement of educational technology indicates that personalization and automation will play even more important roles in education. Emerging technologies like big data and cloud computing will improve learning flexibility and student-centred educational methods. Educators and policymakers must stay ahead of these trends, adapting to technological changes to improve learning outcomes and prepare students for a technologically driven world.

In conclusion, while digital and intelligent education can potentially transform the educational landscape, they also necessitate a balanced approach to fully realize their benefits. This entails incorporating emerging technologies and a strong emphasis on ethical standards, equitable access, and ongoing professional development for educators. As we progress, we must continue researching innovative educational technologies while addressing the challenges and disparities that arise, ensuring a more equitable and advanced educational system for future generations.

## References

Akhmedov, B.: Prospects and trends of digital twins in education. Uzbek Scholar J. **23**, 6–15 (2023)

Al-Ansi, A.M., Jaboob, M., Garad, A., Al-Ansi, A.: Analyzing augmented reality (AR) and virtual reality (VR) recent development in education. Soc. Sci. Humanit. Open. **8**(1), 100532 (2023)

Al-Malah, D.K.A.-R., Majeed, B.H., ALRikabi, H. T. S.: Enhancement the educational technology by using 5G networks. Int. J. Emerg. Technol. Learn. **18**(1), 137 (2023)

Al-Taai, S.H.H., Kanber, H.A., Al-Dulaimi, W.A.M.: The importance of using the internet of things in education. Int. J. Emerg. Technol. Learn. **18**(1), 19–39 (2023)

Ali, O., Murray, P.A., Momin, M., Dwivedi, Y.K., Malik, T.: The effects of artificial intelligence applications in educational settings: challenges and strategies. Technol. Forecast. Soc. Chang. **199**, 123076 (2024)

Bhaskar, P., Tiwari, C.K., Joshi, A.: Blockchain in education management: Present and future applications. Interact. Technol. Smart Educ. **18**(1), 1–17 (2021)

Chen, H., Ward, P.A.: Predicting student performance using data from an auto-grading system. arXiv Preprint arXiv:2102.01270 (2021)

Clark-Wilson, A., Robutti, O., Thomas, M.: Teaching with digital technology. Zdm. **52**(2020–7), 1–20 (2020)

Feng, L., Jie, S., Wei, H.: Design and implementation of intelligent textbooks: from a perspective of digital transformation in education. Front. Educ. China **18**(4), 460–478 (2023)

Harry, A., Sayudin, S.: Role of AI in education. Interdiciplinary J. Hummanity **2**(3), 260–268 (2023)

Hou, Y., Liu, B., Fan, Q., Zhou, J.: Research on the application mode of knowledge graph in education. In: Proceedings of the 2023 6th International Conference on Educational Technology Management, pp. 215–220 (2023)

Hu, K.H.: An exploration of the key determinants for the application of AI-enabled higher education based on a hybrid Soft-computing technique and a DEMATEL approach. Expert Syst. Appl. **212**, 118762 (2023)

Huang, J., Saleh, S., Liu, Y.: A review on artificial intelligence in education. Acad. J. Interdisciplinary Stud. **10**(3), 206–217 (2021)

Kalaman, O., Bondarenko, S., Telovata, M., Petrenko, N., Yershova, O., Sagan, O.: Management of digital and intellectual technologies integration in education informatization. TEM J. **12**(3), 1645 (2023)

Kamalov, F., Santandreu Calonge, D., Gurrib, I.: New era of artificial intelligence in education: towards a sustainable multifaceted revolution. Sustainability **15**(16), 12451 (2023)

Munir, H., Vogel, B., Jacobsson, A.: Artificial intelligence and machine learning approaches in digital education: a systematic revision. Information **13**(4), 203 (2022)

Okunlaya, R.O., Syed Abdullah, N., Alias, R.A.: Artificial intelligence (AI) library services innovative conceptual framework for the digital transformation of university education. Library Hi Tech. **40**(6), 1869–1892 (2022)

Pinto, M., Leite, C.: Digital technologies in support of students learning in Higher Education: Literature review. Digit. Educ. Rev. **37**, 343–360 (2020)

Sappaile, B.I., Vandika, A.Y., Deiniatur, M., Nuridayanti, N., Arifudin, O.: The role of artificial intelligence in the development of digital era educational progress. J. Artif. Intell. Dev. **3**(1), 1–8 (2024)

Shi, H., Shi, C.: Intelligent interactive English teaching system for engineering education. Adv. Multimed. **2022**(1), 4676776 (2022)

Xu, Y.: Intelligent e-learning system in the development of preschool music education based on digital audio technology. Entertainment Comput. **50**, 100682 (2024)

Yang, J., Shi, G., Zhuang, R., Wang, Y., Huang, R.: 5G and smart education: educational reform based on intelligent technology. Front. Educ. China **17**(4), 490–509 (2022)

Zhang, X., et al.: Accessibility within open educational resources and practices for disabled learners: a systematic literature review. Smart Learn. Environ. **7**, 1–19 (2020)

# Artificial Intelligence in Education

# Mapping the Landscape of AI Implementation in STEM and STEAM Education: A Bibliometric Analysis

Ningwei Sun[1,2] and Salmiza Saleh[1(✉)]

[1] School of Educational Studies, Jalan Sungai Dua, Georgetown Pulau Penang, University Science Malaysia, Penang, Malaysia
salmiza@usm.my
[2] Department of Research and Development, Guangdong Women's Polytechnic College, No. 2, Nanpu Village Section, Shilian Road, Panyu District, Guangzhou, China

**Abstract.** The purpose of this paper is to explore the applications, research trends and research gaps of AI in STEM and STEAM education through bibliometric analysis. Despite the increasing application of AI technology in education, systematic research on its specific role and developmental trends in STEM and STEAM education is still relatively lacking. In this paper, literature data on the application of AI in STEM/STEAM education between 2014 and 2024 were collected using the Web of Science database, and analyzed using the Bibliometrix R package and VOSviewer to identify the research hotspots, development **trends**, and future research gaps in the field. The results of the study show that the research on the application of AI in STEM/STEAM education has shown a significant growth trend since 2019, especially in China and the United States. Keyword analysis shows that emerging topics such as generative AI, personalized learning and AI literacy have gradually become the focus of research in recent years. At the same time, the study also reveals that the existing literature has paid less attention to AI in the field of arts education, and that the long-term impact and cross-disciplinary integration of AI technologies in STEM and STEAM education still need to be further explored. The research in this paper provides new perspectives for a deeper understanding of the potentials and challenges of AI in STEM and STEAM education and suggests directions for future research.

**Keywords:** STEAM education · STEM education · bibliometric analysis · artificial intelligence

## 1 Introduction

Artificial Intelligence (AI) is rapidly converging with science, technology, engineering, and mathematics (STEM) and science, technology, engineering, arts, and mathematics (STEAM) education, revolutionizing the educational landscape. This study employs bibliometric analysis to map the development of AI in these domains from 2014 to 2024, revealing intricate trends and unexpected research gaps.

© The Author(s), under exclusive license to Springer Nature Singapore Pte Ltd. 2024
L.-K. Lee et al. (Eds.): ICTE 2024, CCIS 2330, pp. 99–111, 2024.
https://doi.org/10.1007/978-981-96-0205-6_7

## 1.1 Background

The utilization of artificial intelligence in education has demonstrated significant promise in revolutionizing the field of education in recent years. Specific instances of these applications encompass tutoring-exclusive systems, adaptive learning platforms, and AI-supported evaluation tools (Zawacki-Richter et al., 2019). The use of AI in education can enhance student learning by providing personalized learning paths that cater to individual student requirements (Qingsong et al., 2024). This, in addition, improves student engagement and comprehension, contributing to enhanced learning outcomes.

## 1.2 Importance of AI in STEM and STEAM Education

The integration of AI in STEM and STEAM education is pivotal for enhancing learning experiences, personalizing education, and preparing students for future challenges. Applications of AI, such as intelligent tutoring systems, help reduce teachers' workloads and provide contextualized learning opportunities for students (Chaudhry & Kazim, 2021). AI's role in STEAM education emphasizes the importance of a multidisciplinary approach, integrating technical training with social sciences, arts, ethics, and business. This holistic education model prepares students to creatively address complex global challenges, such as climate change and social inequalities (Skowronek et al., 2022). While AI offers numerous benefits, its success in education still faces challenges such as ethical considerations and teacher confidence in the use of AI in STEAM education (Sun et al., 2024).

## 1.3 Research Questions

Previous research has provided insights into the various functions of AI in current educational settings and research trends. However, comprehensive analyses specifically examining research related to AI in STEM and STEAM education are lacking. Hence, the objective of this study is to address this gap, and the initial inquiries that will be addressed are as follows:

RQ1: What is the productivity distribution of the field of AI implementation in STEM and STEAM education research in terms of authorship, country/region, institution and journal?
RQ2: What is the development trend of research on AI implementation in STEM and STEAM education?
RQ3: What are the current frontiers and potential research gaps in AI applications for STEM and STEAM education?

# 2 Literature Review

## 2.1 Implementation of Artificial Intelligence in STEM and STEAM Education

At present, the implementation of AI in STEM and STEAM education is transforming traditional educational paradigms by enhancing learning experiences, personalizing education, and equipping students with essential skills for the future. The use of AI tools like the MIT App Inventor platform and its Personal Image Classifier (PIC) tool has been shown to significantly improve learning outcomes in STEAM education. These tools help students grasp complex concepts such as programming logic and image recognition through experiential learning, making the learning process more engaging and effective for young students (Hsu et al., 2021). The development of AI-aided computational thinking models in STEM education has shown promising results in enhancing students' understanding and competence in STEM education (Wu et al., 2021). Despite the benefits, the implementation of AI in education comes with challenges such as the need for adequate teacher training and the development of appropriate curricula. Strategies for successful implementation include developing comprehensive models and guides to help educational institutions integrate AI technologies effectively (Owoc et al., 2021).

## 2.2 Bibliometric Analysis in STEM and STEAM Education

Li et al. (2020) conducted a bibliometric analysis of STEM education research between 2000 and 2018. Their study pointed out not only the most productive countries, institutions, and authors in the field but also the dynamics of the research topics and the relationships among coauthors. This work demonstrated that bibliometric analysis could provide an exhaustive picture of a fast-emerging area of education.

More focused on the application of AI in education, Xie et al. (2023) conducted a bibliometric analysis of ITS research conducted between 2012 and 2021. In their study, they depicted an intellectual map of ITS research, defined research areas, and predicted future trends in ITS research. This work exemplifies the application of bibliometrics to analyze trends in the development of AI technologies in education and forecasts future directions of their evolution.

These studies also show that through bibliometric analysis, it is possible to identify aspects such as the nature, evolution, and mapping of a research domain. As a result, this study seeks to fill this gap by providing a detailed bibliometric analysis, with a particular focus on the implementation of AI in STEM and STEAM education.

## 3 Methodology and Data Collection

### 3.1 Method

Bibliometrics is a quantitative analysis method that employs mathematical and statistical tools to measure the interrelationships and influence of publications within a specific field of study (Öztürk, 2024). Academic and professional communities express that bibliometric analysis is an effective instrument for reducing human error (Ellegaard & Wallin, 2015) and subjective bias (Zupic & Čater, 2015). Therefore, this study uses a comprehensive bibliometric analysis to map the landscape of AI implementation in STEM and STEAM education.

In this study, we selected the Bibliometrix package of R, which includes the graphical interface Biblioshiny (Aria & Cuccurullo, 2017), and the VOSviewer to create and visualize bibliometric networks (Van Eck & Waltman, 2010). The Biblioshiny analysis function generates an annual analysis of the scientific output of the study, the most productive authors, the most frequently used terms, the most popular journals, national collaborations, and more. The advantages of using the R package for data analysis are simplicity and speed, clearer visualization of data, greater functionality, and the fact that the Biblioshiny interface is constantly maintained and updated (Rashid, 2023).

## 3.2 Data Retrieval

The research is based on data retrieved from the Web of Science (WoS) database, which was chosen for its broad representation of high-quality, peer-reviewed publications in a variety of fields (Gaviria-Marin et al., 2019; Merigó, 2017). Moreover, WoS is considered one of the most suitable databases for bibliometric analysis (Ding & Yang, 2020). After identifying the data sources, it is necessary to determine the retrieval strategy (Jing et al., 2023). We used the topic search (TS) function in the Web of Science for specific screening. The specific criteria used to screen the literature for this study are shown in Table 1.

**Table 1.** Summary of the data sources and selection.

| Category | Specific standard requirements |
|---|---|
| Research database | Web of Science Core Collection |
| Citation indexes | SSCI,SCIE |
| Searching period | 2014 to July 2024 |
| Searching keywords | TS = ("STEM" OR "STEAM" OR "science" OR "technology" OR "engineering" OR "art" OR "math")AND ("instruct*" OR "teach*" OR "education")AND("artificial intelligence" or "AI") |
| Document types | Articles |
| Data extraction | Export with full records and cited references in plain text format |
| Sample size | *553(before manual screening)* |

## 3.3 Literature Screening

To ensure that the literature included in the analysis was closely related to the research topic, this study conducted a two-step manual screening process after the initial literature retrieval was completed. First, two members of the research team eliminated irrelevant literature on the basis of titles and abstracts, removing 316 articles and retaining 237 articles. A comprehensive review of the full texts was subsequently conducted to identify the literature required for the study accurately. To conduct the second stage of screening effectively and scientifically and to minimize researcher bias, the research team established inclusion criteria, as shown in Table 2. After careful screening at this stage, 123 articles were retained. The entire selection process, as shown in Fig. 1, followed the PRISMA guidelines (Page et al., 2021).

**Table 2.** Inclusion and exclusion criteria.

| Inclusion Criteria | Exclusion Criteria |
| --- | --- |
| • The research topics included in the literature should focus on AI technology in education within the STEM or STEAM fields, and the included literature should thoroughly investigate and evaluate the impact and value of AI in all aspects of education, not limited to the STEM or STEAM teaching and learning process but also covering educational assessment, curriculum design, professional development of STEAM educators within the field, increasing student engagement, and learning outcomes monitoring and feedback | • Review articles, editorials, or opinion pieces without original research content |
| • Consideration should also be given to incorporating the potential contribution of AI in enhancing the learning experience, optimizing the allocation of educational resources and educational equity in STEM or STEAM education | • Conference abstracts or proceedings without full-text availability |

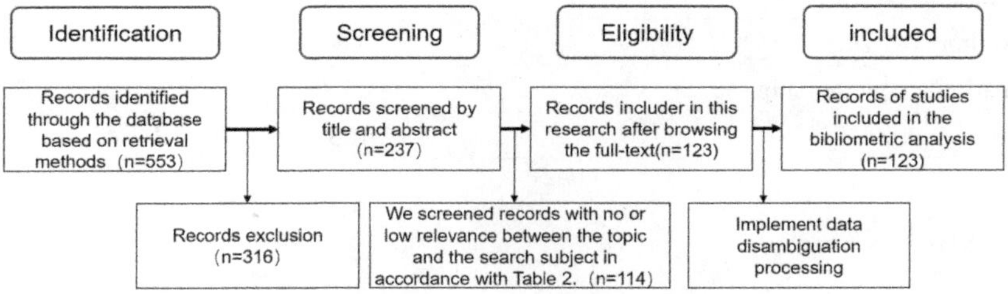

**Fig. 1.** Process flowchart for obtaining and filtering the necessary literature data for research

## 4 Results of Analysis

### 4.1 Performance Analysis (RQ1)

The performance analysis of AI implementation in STEM and STEAM education from 2014–2024 revealed a marked increase in research output, as evidenced by the 123 publications distributed across 89 distinct sources (Table 3). The annual growth rate of 38.25% indicates a burgeoning academic interest in this field, while the average document age of 1.42 years underscores the relatively recent emergence of this research area. Zawacki-Richter et al. (2019) reported a similar pattern of growth in their systematic review of AI implementation in higher education. Notably, the analysis of author productivity reveals that no individual author has contributed more than two publications, suggesting that the field of AI implementation in STEM and STEAM education is still in its nascent stages and has yet to establish a cohort of highly prolific researchers. As shown in Fig. 2, the number of articles and citations has risen sharply since 2019. This trend suggests that increasing research is beginning to focus on the transformative potential of AI technologies in STEM and STEAM education.

**Table 3.** Main information on the publications (Source: Biblioshiny R package).

| Description | Results |
|---|---|
| Timespan | 2014:2024 |
| Sources (Journals, Books, etc.) | 89 |
| Documents | 123 |
| Annual Growth Rate % | 38.25 |
| Document Average Age | 1.42 |
| Average citations per doc | 8.073 |
| References | 5987 |
| Keywords Plus (ID) | 196 |
| Author's Keywords (DE) | 413 |
| Authors | 414 |
| Authors of single-authored docs | 19 |
| Single-authored docs | 20 |
| Co-Authors per Doc | 3.54 |
| International coauthorships % | 25.2 |
| article | 123 |

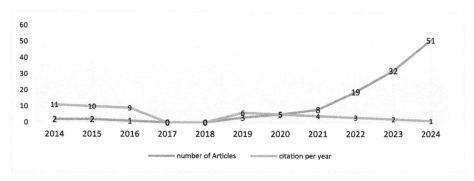

**Fig. 2.** Process article production and citation (Source: Biblioshiny R package)

The details of the productivity distribution of journals in this field are shown in Table 4. The journal "Computer Applications in Engineering Education" has the highest number of published articles, with a total of 6. The "International Journal of Artificial

Intelligence in Education" has fewer articles (5); however, its H-index of 3 and total number of citations of 55 indicate its significant influence. Additional notable journals include "Science & Education" with 5 articles, "Frontiers in Education" with 4 articles and an H-index of 3, and "Sustainability" with 4 articles.

Table 4. Top 5 journals (Source: Biblioshiny R package).

| Sources | Articles | H-index | TC |
| --- | --- | --- | --- |
| Computer Applications in Engineering Education | 6 | 2 | 15 |
| International Journal of Artificial Intelligence in Education | 5 | 3 | 55 |
| Science & Education | 5 | 1 | 2 |
| Frontiers in Education | 4 | 3 | 28 |
| Sustainability | 4 | 2 | 12 |

Through the analysis of highly cited articles, Table 5 lists the most cited papers in the field, with Cooper G.'s (2023) paper about Science Education in ChatGPT topping the list with 174 citations. This reflects the popularity of AI-driven tool applications such as ChatGPT. Other high-impact articles discussed mixed-reality AI systems, the use of AI in engineering education assessment, and the role of AI in STEAM education.

Table 5. Top 6 cited papers (Source: Biblioshiny R package).

| Article | Main theme | Source title | TC | Citations per years |
| --- | --- | --- | --- | --- |
| Cooper, G. (2023) | Science Education in ChatGPT | Journal of Science Education and Technology | 174 | 87.00 |
| Yannier, N. (2020) | A Mixed-Reality AI System to Support STEM Education | International Journal of Artificial Intelligence in Education | 35 | 7.00 |
| Nikolic, S. (2023) | ChatGPT versus engineering education assessment | European Journal of Engineering Education | 34 | 17.00 |
| Sánchez-Ruiz, L. M., et al. (2023) | ChatGPT Challenges Blended Learning Methodologies in Engineering Education | Applied Sciences | 29 | 14.5 |
| How, M., et al. (2019) | Educing AI-Thinking STEAM Education | Education Sciences | 29 | 4.83 |
| Wu, C. H., et al. (2022) | exploration of continuous learning intention in STEAM use teaching material design based on artificial intelligence-based concepts | International Journal of STEM Education | 28 | 9.33 |

By analyzing the 10 countries with the most publications and author affiliations, the results in Fig. 3 show the global situation of AI research in STEM and STEAM education. In terms of the number of papers published by each country, China tops the list with 78 papers, followed by the United States with 76 papers. South Korea ranked third with 19 publications, Australia with 15 publications and the UK with 13 publications. The top ten countries span Asia, North America, Europe, South America and the Middle East, indicating that this field is attracting increasing attention from an increasing number of regions and countries, but there is still relatively little research in this field except for China and the United States.

From the perspective of author affiliation (shown in Fig. 3), Hong Kong University of Education leads the list with 9 articles, followed by National Cheng Kung University with 8 articles. Several institutions, including North Carolina State University, Seoul National University and Virginia Tech, published five articles each. Clemson University and South China Normal University were among the top ten with four articles each. The Asian and U.S. institutions had the most articles. The papers from these top institutions are relatively evenly distributed, with several professional organizations contributing to the advancement of AI in STEM and STEAM education.

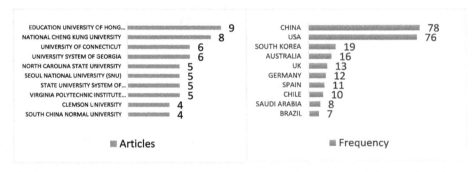

**Fig. 3.** Top 10 countries of publication and authors' affiliation (Source: Biblioshiny R package)

### 4.2 Keyword Analysis and Catographic Analysis (RQ2 &RQ3)

The keyword trends in Fig. 4 indicate a shift from general discussions of AI in STEM and STEAM education to more specific and application-oriented terms. In addition to the initial search terms, emerging keywords such as "personalized learning", "machine learning", "data analytics" and "intelligent tutoring systems" provide insight into how AI is implied in STEM and STEAM education.

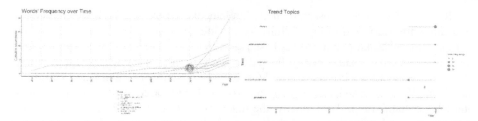

**Fig. 4.** Words frequency over time and topic trends (Source: Biblioshiny R package)

Based on the analysis of word frequency over time and topic trends, Fig. 4 clearly illustrates the dynamic evolution of the research theme. The continued growth of "engineering education", the earliest keyword, reflects the long-term importance of AI in engineering education. From the early years of 2014–2018, the keywords "engineering education" and "STEAM education" dominated, reflecting the focus of early research on integrating AI into traditional STEM disciplines, and engineering education remained a key focus for AI technology integration. From 2019–2021, the keywords "science education" and "STEAM education" dominated, reflecting the focus of early research on integrating AI into traditional STEM disciplines. From 2019–2021, the keywords "engineering education" and "STEAM education" dominated. From 2019–2021, "science education" and "technology" grew rapidly, indicating that the scope of research is expanding to a wider range of scientific fields. Emerging themes such as "ChatGPT", "generative AI" and "large language models" have emerged in the past three years, reflecting the explosive growth of emerging AI technologies in STEM and STEAM education and the high level of attention given to generative AI application research. Notably, the emergence and rapid growth of "AI literacy" indicate that research in this field not only focuses on the application of AI technology but also begins to emphasize the cultivation of students' AI competence. This indicates that research on AI in the context of STEAM education is gradually developing to a deeper level.

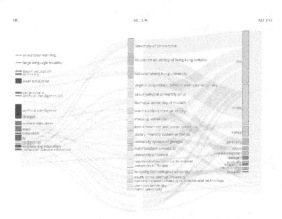

**Fig. 5.** Three-field plot (or Sankey diagram) associated with keywords, authors, and countries (Source: Biblioshiny R package)

Some of the trends in research on the implementation of AI in STEM and STEAM education are illustrated in Fig. 5. Initially, a wide range of research topics, including computational thinking and project-based learning, as well as emerging technologies such as augmented reality, was reflected in the diversity of keywords. Furthermore, the close connections between institutions, including National Cheng Kung University and Hong Kong University of Education, indicate that research institutions are increasing their collaboration. Additionally, the integration of AI with advanced educational technologies and methods is currently being actively investigated in STEM and STEAM education research, as evidenced by the integration of innovative pedagogical approaches (e.g., gamified learning) and emerging technologies (e.g., virtual reality). In general, the field of AI in STEM and STEAM education research is advancing in a more innovative, collaborative, and diverse way.

Figure 6 illustrates the co-occurrence network of keywords pertaining to AI in the context of STEM and STEAM education research. The VOSviewer Cartography illustrates that the research field comprises five main color-coded clusters. The green cluster, at the heart of the network, closely links "artificial intelligence" to emerging concepts such as "ChatGPT," "large language models," and "generative artificial intelligence." This highlights the latest trends in the application of AI technologies in STEM education. The topics of "ChatGPT," "large language models," and "generative artificial intelligence" center the red cluster. The red cluster is centered on the themes of "engineering education" and "students," encompassing keywords such as "assessment," "AI literacy," and "computer science education." This cluster underscores the importance of AI in engineering and computer science education, as well as the emphasis on evaluating students' AI capabilities. The emphasis on AI literacy and computer science education underscores the importance of AI in engineering and computer science education, as well as the importance of assessing students' AI literacy. The blue cluster centers around "computational thinking" and "science education," highlighting the crucial role of computational thinking in science education. "Technology" and "augmented reality" dominate the purple cluster, demonstrating the integration of emerging technologies in STEM education. The yellow cluster contains the keywords "higher education," "motivation," and "deep learning," indicating the field's focus on the application of AI technologies at the higher education level and their impact on the motivation to learn.

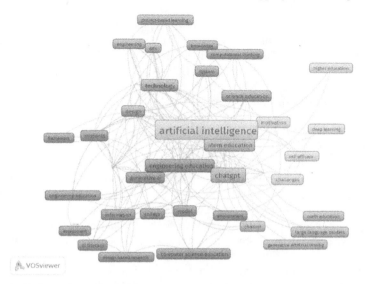

**Fig. 6.** Cartography with 3 minimum cooccurring keywords (Source: VOSviewer)

## 5 Discussion and Conclusion

The analysis of research growth and distribution revealed that since 2019, research results have shown a significant upward trend, which is consistent with the research of Zawacki-Richter et al. (2019). However, in terms of geographical distribution, the papers are concentrated mainly in China and the United States. Despite the growing interest in artificial intelligence in STEM/STEAM education, research in other regions, especially developing countries, is still lacking. The analysis identifies several research gaps in the application of AI in STEM and STEAM education. Research on pedagogical approaches to developing AI literacy in STEM and STEAM subjects is insufficient despite its growing importance. Furthermore, not much study has been conducted on the integration of AI technologies for the humanities and arts with STEM. Finally, there is a lack of research on effective models for preparing and supporting teachers as they integrate AI into their STEM and STEAM teaching practices.

With respect to emerging technologies and application trends, interest in emerging AI technologies has increased in recent years, such as large language models and generative AI, especially the application of the Chat GPT in STEM and STEAM education, which is also consistent with Cooper (2023). Although emerging technologies are quickly being applied to STEM/STEAM fields, there is little research on the long-term impact of technology applications on student learning outcomes and skill development. Luan et al. (2022) also noted this gap when discussing the challenges of AI in education. In particular, there is a lack of empirical research on the integration of these AI tools into existing STEM/STEAM curricula and pedagogies, as noted by Hwang et al. (2020). There is also limited research on the effectiveness and comparison of the many AI applications currently in use (e.g., intelligent tutoring systems and virtual reality).

The keywords "AI literacy" and "interdisciplinary integration" show that there is an increasing focus on AI literacy, which is also mentioned in the study by How et al. (2019) on AI thinking in STEAM education. However, there is limited research on how to effectively integrate AI literacy into all STEM and STEAM fields. As Perignat & Katz-Buonincontro (2019) noted, research on the integration of STEAM education needs to be extended to the specific context of AI literacy. In addition, although the data show the connection between AI and various STEM fields, they also reflect the lack of attention given to the Art field and the lack of research on how to play a role in STEAM interdisciplinary learning.

Ethical considerations and challenges. It is clear from the research data that limited attention has been given to the ethical implications of artificial intelligence in STEM/STEAM education. Holmes et al. (2022) also raised the ethical issues of artificial intelligence in education. In the future, it is necessary to conduct relevant research to develop and evaluate an ethical framework for the use of artificial intelligence in STEM/STEAM education, addressing issues such as data privacy, algorithmic bias, and equitable access.

Nevertheless, this study possesses limitations. It depends on only one data source and bibliometric analysis, which are mainly based on citation data. This methodology may not reliably reflect actual study impacts, and publication bias may influence the outcomes. Future research ought to broaden the database sources, considering both extensively cited and minimally cited literature, to furnish a more comprehensive overview of the field.

## References

Aria, M., Cuccurullo, C.: Bibliometrix: an R-tool for comprehensive science mapping analysis. J. Informet. **11**(4), 959–975 (2017)

Chaudhry, M., Kazim, E.: Artificial Intelligence in Education (AIEd) a High-Level Academic and Industry Note 2021. SSRN Electron. J. 1–14 (2021)

Cooper, G.: Examining science education in ChatGPT: an exploratory study of generative artificial intelligence. J. Sci. Educ. Technol. **32**(3), 444–452 (2023)

Ding, X., Yang, Z.: Knowledge mapping of platform research: a visual analysis using VOSviewer and CiteSpace. Electron. Commer. Res. **20**(3), 593–612 (2020)

Ellegaard, O., Wallin, J.A.: The bibliometric analysis of scholarly production: How great is the impact? Scientometrics **105**(3), 1809–1831 (2015)

Gaviria-Marin, M., Merigó, J.M., Baier-Fuentes, H.: Knowledge management: a global examination based on bibliometric analysis. Technol. Forecast. Soc. Chang. **140**, 194–220 (2019)

Holmes, W., et al.: Ethics of AI in education: toward a community-wide framework. Int. J. Artif. Intell. Educ. **32**(1), 61–94 (2022)

How, M.L., Hung, W.L.D.: Educing ai-thinking in science, technology, engineering, arts, and mathematics (STEAM) education. Education Sciences **9**(3), 184 (2019)

Hsu, T.C., Abelson, H., Lao, N., Chen, S.C.: Is It Possible for young students to learn the AI-STEAM application with experiential learning? Sustainability **13**(19), 11114 (2021)

Hwang, G.J., Xie, H., Wah, B.W., Gašević, D.: Vision, challenges, roles and research issues of Artificial Intelligence in Education. Comput. Educ: Artif. Intell. **1**, 100001 (2020)

Jing, Y., Wang, C.L., Chen, Y., Wang, H., Yu, T., Shadiev, R.: Bibliometric mapping techniques in educational technology research: a systematic literature review. Educ. Inf. Technol. **28**(5), 5873–5901 (2023)

Li, Y., Wang, K., Xiao, Y., Froyd, J.E.: Research and trends in STEM education: a systematic review of journal publications. Int. J. STEM Educ. **7**(1), 1–16 (2020)

Luan, H., et al.: Challenges and future directions of big data and artificial intelligence in education. Front. Psychol. **13**, 871065 (2022)

Owoc, M. L., Sawicka, A., Weichbroth, P.: Artificial Intelligence Technologies in Education: Benefits, Challenges and Strategies of Implementation. arXiv preprint arXiv:2106.15033 (2021)

Page, M.J., et al.: The PRISMA 2020 statement: an updated guideline for reporting systematic reviews. Int. J. Surg. **88**, 105906 (2021)

Perignat, E., Katz-Buonincontro, J.: STEAM in practice and research: an integrative literature review. Thinking Skills Creativity **31**, 31–43 (2019)

Rashid, M.F.A.: How to conduct a bibliometric analysis using r packages: a comprehensive guidelines. J. Tourism, Hospitality Culinary Arts **15**(1), 24–39 (2023)

Skowronek, M., Gilberti, R.M., Petro, M., Sancomb, C., Maddern, S.W., Jankovic, J.: Inclusive STEAM education in diverse disciplines of sustainable energy and AI. Energy and AI **7**, 100124 (2022)

Sun, F., Tian, P., Sun, D., Fan, Y., Yang, Y.: Preservice teachers' inclination to integrate AI into STEM education: analysis of influencing factors. Br. J. Edu. Technol. **55**(2), 489–511 (2024)

Van Eck, N.J., Waltman, L.: Software survey: VOSviewer, a computer program for bibliometric mapping. Scientometrics **84**(2), 523–538 (2010)

Wen, Q., et al.: AI for education (AI4EDU): advancing personalized education with LLM and adaptive learning. ACM Trans. Comput. Educ. **1**(1), 6743–6744 (2024)

Wu, L., et al.: Advancing AI-aided Computational Thinking in STEM Education. In: Computational Science – ICCS 2021, pp. 684–697. Springer, Cham (2021)

Xie, H., Chu, H.C., Hwang, G.J., Wang, C.C.: Trends and research issues of intelligent tutoring systems: a bibliometric analysis of publications from 2012 to 2021. Interact. Learn. Environ. **31**(3), 1435–1458 (2023)

Zawacki-Richter, O., Marín, V.I., Bond, M., Gouverneur, F.: Systematic review of research on artificial intelligence applications in higher education - Where are the educators? Int. J. Educ. Technol. High. Educ. **16**(1), 39 (2019)

Zupic, I., Čater, T.: Bibliometric methods in management and organization. Organ. Res. Methods **18**(3), 429–472 (2015)

# Can Generative AI Really Empower Teachers' Professional Practices? Comparative Study on Human-Tailored and GenAI-Designed Reading Comprehension Learning Materials

Fen-Lan Jen[✉], Xingyun Huang, Xiaoting Liu, and Jianli Jiao

School of Information Technology in Education, South China Normal University, No.55, West of Zhongshan Avenue, Tianhe District, Guangzhou City, Guangdong Province, China
cassiejen@qq.com

**Abstract.** This study compares the efficiency and quality of reading comprehension materials designed by human teachers and Generative Artificial Intelligence (GenAI) for middle school English classes. Six K-12 English teachers in China and two GenAI tools, Twee and Kimi, each created five multiple-choice reading comprehension questions based on the exact text. The time taken to design the materials and their quality were evaluated by experts and participating teachers using a specifically designed rubric. Additionally, open-ended questionnaires were used to explore the teachers' logic and principles in material design and to analyze the strengths, weaknesses, and complementarities of human versus GenAI-assisted creation. This research aims to identify collaborative pathways and methods for human-GenAI co-design in educational tasks to enhance effectiveness. By examining how GenAI can support and augment teachers' work, the study seeks to discover innovative strategies for improving educational outcomes through human-AI collaboration.

**Keywords:** Generative Artificial Intelligence · comparative study · learning material design · human-AI collaboration

## 1 Research Background

The rapid integration of Generative Artificial Intelligence (GenAI) into education reshapes how teaching materials are created and delivered. However, a gap remains in evaluating how GenAI-generated materials compare with those created by human educators, particularly in middle school English reading comprehension in China. This study addresses the critical gap by exploring the effectiveness, quality, and potential for collaboration between GenAI and human educators.

### 1.1 Uniqueness of Human-Tailored Materials

Human teachers, particularly in China's rigorously structured educational system, design reading materials based on their deep pedagogical knowledge and an understanding of student needs. These human-crafted materials are tailored to the specific learning objectives and classroom dynamics, ensuring they are contextually and culturally relevant (Farrelly & Baker, 2023). Studies have shown that human-designed content adapts more flexibly to diverse learning environments as teachers continuously adjust materials based on real-time student feedback and classroom challenges (Kadaruddin, 2023). In Chinese K-12 education, the emphasis on aligning materials with national standards while addressing students' diverse learning needs makes human-created content highly effective.

## 1.2 The Role of GenAI in Educational Material Design

The emergence of GenAI tools such as Twee and Kimi entirely revolutionizes educational content creation for its speed and scalability, mostly in high quality. Both GenAI-powered tools were selected because Twee focused on English language modules and Kimi focused on content summarization and multilingual tasks, automating content creation for practical use. These GenAI tools can produce educational materials that are aligned with curriculum standards rather well, lowering the workload for educators. According to Nguyen et al. (2024), GenAI tools are very good at automating tasks efficiently but might fail to replicate adaptive and culturally nuanced properties designed by humans. While GenAI is indeed efficient, human educators may need more contextual understanding and sensitivity to design the materials, leading to less engaging and effective educational experiences. As Johri et al. (2023) posit, despite these issues, the potential to support teachers through automating routine tasks and providing a range of content options makes GenAI an attractive tool in contemporary educational settings.

## 1.3 Impact on Teachers' Professional Practices

GenAI tools can enhance teaching efficiency by freeing up time for teachers to focus on student engagement. However, they also challenge traditional views of teacher autonomy and creativity. In China, where the educational system is both centralized and highly competitive, Dron (2023) points out that using GenAI could either support or undermine the teacher's role, depending on how these technologies are integrated into the classroom.

## 1.4 Research Contributions

This study makes several key contributions as following: (1) Fills a Research Gap: Provides empirical data on the comparative effectiveness of human-tailored versus GenAI-generated reading comprehension materials. (2) Enhances Understanding of Human-AI Collaboration: Explores human and AI-assisted material creation's strengths, weaknesses, and complementarities. (3) Informs Educational Practices and Policies: Offers insights that can guide educators, policymakers, and developers in integrating GenAI tools to support teaching and learning.

## 1.5 Alignment with Policy and Educational Goals

China's national policies, including the Development Plan of the New Generation of Artificial Intelligence issued by the State Council (2017) and the Ministry of Education's 2024 "Four Action Push Intelligent Technology Power Education," highlight the growing emphasis on AI's role in education. In addition, on a global scale, UNESCO has been a prominent advocate for the ethical use of AI in education. Their 2021 "Recommendation on the Ethics of Artificial Intelligence" stresses the importance of inclusivity, transparency, and human-centered values in AI deployment within educational contexts (Silva & Janes, 2023). This research aligns with these goals by critically evaluating how AI can be integrated into the educational process without undermining the critical human elements essential for effective teaching and learning.

## 1.6 Research Questions

Given the increasing integration of GenAI into educational practices and the significant role of human teachers in creating pedagogically sound learning materials, this study seeks to explore two key research questions: (1) How do GenAI tools compare to human teachers in terms of efficiency and quality when designing middle school English reading comprehension materials? (2) What are the strengths and weaknesses of Generative AI and human teachers in co-designing educational tasks, and what are the potential collaborative pathways?

# 2 Literature Review

The integration of Generative AI (GenAI) in education is set to transform educators' professional practices, particularly in designing middle school English reading comprehension materials. This literature review explores how GenAI affects teaching practices, comparing the efficiency and quality of AI-generated versus human-created materials and examines collaborative opportunities between GenAI and educators. It highlights the opportunities and challenges of AI integration in education by Drawing on technological determinism, sociocultural theory, affordance theory, distributed cognition, and transformative learning.

## 2.1 Technological Determinism and GenAI Efficiency

Technological determinism posits that technology drives societal change, including in education. GenAI, a disruptive innovation, offers scalable, customizable, and efficient alternatives to traditional content creation methods (Creely & Blannin, 2023). This transformation aligns with digital pedagogy frameworks, which emphasize the integration of digital tools to enhance learning outcomes and streamline routine teaching tasks (Farrelly & Baker, 2023). In terms of efficiency, AI-powered platforms reduce the time teachers spend on routine tasks, enabling them to focus on critical thinking and student engagement (Nguyen, 2024; Kim, 2024a, Kim, 2024b). However, while AI excels in efficiency, its quality can vary. Studies show that human teachers are better at tailoring materials to meet individual student needs, particularly in fostering deep comprehension and adapting lessons in real-time (Alwaqdani, 2024).

## 2.2 Sociocultural and Affordance Theories in GenAI-Enhanced Interaction

Sociocultural theory, especially Vygotsky's concept of the Zone of Proximal Development (ZPD), explains how GenAI enhances teachers' capabilities by enabling them to create more personalized learning materials. This shift allows educators to focus on higher-order tasks like critical thinking and student engagement (van den Berg & du Plessis, 2023). Hence, the affordance theory further supports this by examining how GenAI offers new possibilities for generating diverse content and adapting materials to specific learning needs (Jauhiainen & Guerra, 2023). Tools such as Twee provide customizable lesson templates and multimedia integration options, while Kimi, as a large language model, allows for interactive dialogue and content generation through prompts. However, AI's limitations include its inability to fully grasp classroom dynamics and student emotions and the risk of over-reliance on technology, which may diminish educators' creativity and pedagogical judgment. Professional development is essential to balance using GenAI while maintaining teacher autonomy (Alwaqdani, 2024).

## 2.3 Distributed Cognition and Teacher-GenAI Collaboration

Distributed cognition posits that knowledge is shared across individuals, tools, and environments. In this framework, GenAI is a cognitive tool that supports teachers by automating mundane tasks and providing real-time data, allowing for more informed instructional decisions (Kim, 2024a, Kim, 2024b). This collaboration between GenAI and human educators improves teaching efficiency and learning outcomes (Vallis et al., 2023). Transformative learning theory highlights how GenAI enables more interactive and personalized instructional strategies, meeting the needs of 21st-century learners (Nguyen, 2024; Kadaruddin, 2023). For instance, AI can generate a basic lesson structure, which teachers can refine based on classroom dynamics and student feedback. This collaboration maximizes AI's and educators' strengths, ensuring that AI enhances rather than diminishes teacher autonomy.

# 3 Method

This study employs a mixed-methods research design, integrating both quantitative and qualitative approaches to comprehensively analyze the comparative effectiveness of human-designed and AI-generated reading comprehension materials. The mixed-methods design is particularly suited for this research as it allows for an in-depth examination of the measurable outcomes (efficiency and quality of content) and participants' subjective experiences (teacher perceptions and willingness for collaboration). By combining quantitative data (time measurement, quality assessment scores) and qualitative data (open-ended questionnaire responses), the study ensures a robust exploration of human-AI collaboration in educational content creation.

## 3.1 Sample Selection and Justification

This study's sample includes six English language teachers from Shenzhen, China, and two GenAI tools, Twee and Kimi. The teachers selected for their expertise in AI-empowered education represent different educational levels, from elementary to senior high school, providing a diverse perspective on the educational process. While the sample size is small, it is strategically chosen to yield meaningful insights, though its limitations in generalizability are acknowledged.

Given the teachers' diverse backgrounds, the study set content difficulty at the "middle school" level. This level ensures compatibility with both basic and advanced content, challenging teachers. The English reading passage was from the 2023 Henan Province High School Entrance Examination (Zhongkao) English test. It was chosen for its scientific rigor and appropriate challenge, avoiding bias or obscure content.

The inclusion of GenAI tools, Twee and Kimi, was based on their ability to generate educational content and relevance in contemporary AI-empowered teaching environments. The sample size of six teachers and two GenAI tools was determined to provide sufficient data for a meaningful comparison while allowing for detailed qualitative insights.

### 3.2 Data Collection Procedures

The data collection process was divided into two primary phases: content design and qualitative feedback collection.

**Phase 1: Content Design and Evaluation**
*Task Description.* The six teachers and the two GenAI tools (Twee and Kimi) designed five multiple-choice questions based on the selected English reading passage from the 2023 Henan Province Middle School Entrance Examination. The teachers were instructed to complete the task without AI assistance, ensuring the materials were purely human-generated.*Time Measurement.* The time taken by each participant to complete the task was recorded, capturing both the start and end times. This data allowed for the efficient comparison between human and AI-generated content.

*Quality Evaluation.* A panel of nine expert raters evaluated the questions generated by teachers and the GenAI tools using a standardized rubric. The rubric assessed relevance, clarity, difficulty balance, logical consistency, and alignment with teaching objectives. The evaluation scores were averaged to provide a comparative content quality analysis.

**Phase 2: Feedback Collection and Thematic Analysis**
*Evaluator Feedback.* This data set consists of evaluations provided by nine evaluators, including six human teachers and three GenAI tools, including GPTs-Assessment Generator and Evaluator, iFLYTEK Spark, and ChatGLM, and assessing five multiple-choice reading comprehension questions generated by different teachers (T1-T8). These evaluations were based on nine criteria categorized into three main dimensions: Question Design, Alignment with Teaching Objectives, and Feedback and Evaluation. The evaluators provided both quantitative scores and qualitative feedback for each question set.

*Open-Ended Questionnaires.* This data set comprises reflective feedback from teachers who participated in the design of the multiple-choice questions. This questionnaire was designed to capture their reflections on the design process, challenges, strategies for overcoming these challenges, and perceptions of human-AI collaboration.

*Questionnaire Content.* Specific questions included design and generation logic, challenges faced during the process, comparisons between AI and human-generated content, and willingness to engage in future human-AI collaborations.

*Data Analysis.* The responses were analyzed using thematic analysis, which helped identify key themes and insights related to the strengths, weaknesses, and potential pathways for human-AI collaboration in educational content design.

### 3.3 Data Analysis

**Quantitative Analysis.** A multivariate analysis of variance (MANOVA) was conducted using SPSS 26 to compare the efficiency (time spent) and effectiveness (quality scores) between GenAI tools (Twee and Kimi) and human teachers in designing middle school English reading comprehension materials. The goal was to determine whether the two groups had significant differences in efficiency and quality, with Time_Spent_Minutes and Average_Score as the dependent variables.

The results indicated a significant difference in time spent: GenAI tools completed the tasks in an average of 1 min, much faster than human teachers, who took 61.33 min on average ($F = 62.362$, $p = 0.000$). However, no significant difference was observed in the Average_Score between the two groups ($F = 1.779$, $p = 0.231$), suggesting that GenAI tools and human teachers produced materials of comparable quality.

**Table 1.** The detailed results of the Multivariate Analysis of Variance (MANOVA).

| Source | Dependent Variable | Sum of Squares | df | MS | F | p |
|---|---|---|---|---|---|---|
| Group | Time_Spent_Minutes | 5460.167 | 1 | 5460.167 | 62.362 | 0.000 |
|  | Average_Score | 0.034 | 1 | 0.034 | 1.779 | 0.231 |
| Error | Time_Spent_Minutes | 525.333 | 6 | 87.556 |  |  |
|  | Average_Score | 0.114 | 6 | 0.019 |  |  |
| Total | Time_Spent_Minutes | 23098.000 | 8 |  |  |  |
|  | Average_Score | 127.988 | 8 |  |  |  |

Table 1 provides detailed results from the MANOVA, highlighting the significant differences in time spent while showing no statistical differences in content quality. The overall MANOVA result supports these findings with a Wilks' Lambda of 0.912 and $F = 25.998$ ($p = 0.002$).

Figure 1 visually illustrates the comparison of time spent and average scores between GenAI tools and human teachers, emphasizing the significant time-saving advantage of GenAI tools without compromising the quality of the generated content. These results suggest that GenAI tools can significantly enhance efficiency while maintaining quality standards like human teachers.

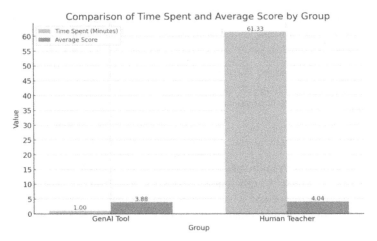

**Fig. 1.** Comparison of Time Spent and Average Score by Group.

**Qualitative Analysis.** Thematic analysis conducted two data sets: evaluator feedback on reading comprehension questions and teacher reflections on the question design process. This analysis identified key themes related to the challenges and benefits of human-AI collaboration and insights into future collaboration potential.

Firstly, the feedback emphasized that most questions were relevant to the material, but some misalignments were noted. Clarity was mostly praised, but wording needed improvement for some questions to prevent confusion. The difficulty level was suitable for junior high students, though some questions were too easy or difficult. Answer choices were logically consistent, but some options could be misleading. Language usage was accurate, but suggestions were made for more concise wording to improve readability.

The questions aligned with teaching goals but often needed more emphasis on critical thinking. They provided insights into students' abilities but could offer more specific guidance for improvement. Teachers used a systematic approach to question design, facing challenges with distractors, difficulty balancing, and wording clarity. GenAI tools aided in creating drafts and maintaining consistency, but significant revisions were needed. Teachers are open to collaborating with GenAI, recognizing its potential to improve efficiency and creativity while stressing the importance of human oversight. Improvements suggested include more advanced GenAI tools and precise guidelines for integrating AI with human expertise.

## 4 Results

The study compared the quality and efficiency of reading comprehension materials generated by human teachers and GenAI tools, specifically Twee and Kimi. The results demonstrate that GenAI tools significantly outperformed human teachers in terms of time efficiency, completing tasks much faster. However, human-generated materials were superior in key areas such as relevance to the reading material, clarity of questions, and alignment with educational objectives. These findings highlight the strengths and limitations of both AI-generated and human-generated content, suggesting the need for human oversight in the creation of educational materials involving GenAI tools.

### 4.1 Time Efficiency

Results showed that the Twee and Kimi GenAI tools outperformed the human teachers regarding task completion time. Specifically, from the MANOVA, the average time spent by GenAI tools was 1 min per set of questions, compared to the human teachers' average time of 61.33 min, with $F = 62.362$ and $p = 0.000$. This result signifies that GenAI tools are more efficient when generating reading comprehension materials. However, there was no significant difference in the quality of the questions, as represented by the Average_Score, between the two groups, $F = 1.779, p = 0.231$. This information supports that even though the GenAI tools were highly efficient, their speed did not compromise the quality of the content. Efficiency gains from GenAI tools do not necessarily result in reduced material quality. This statement supports the position that human teachers and GenAI tools can produce content of comparable quality, with GenAI being more time-efficient.

### 4.2 Content Quality

The quality of human-designed questions was rated higher in several key dimensions:
  **Relevance.** Human-created questions were more closely aligned with the reading material, effectively covering the text's themes and details. **Clarity.** Human questions were more precise, with fewer ambiguities compared to GenAI-generated ones. **Logical Consistency.** The options provided by human teachers were logically sound and free from errors, while GenAI-generated options sometimes contained logical inconsistencies. **Alignment with Educational Objectives.** Human-designed questions were better aligned with teaching goals, particularly in covering a broader range of reading comprehension skills, including higher-order thinking. For example, Participant T4 highlighted that *"GenAI-generated content often required substantial simplification to ensure clarity and appropriateness."* At the same time, Participant T6 pointed out that *"GenAI-generated questions frequently lacked logical coherence, necessitating human refinement to meet pedagogical standards."*

### 4.3 Feedback and Evaluation

Evaluators found that human-tailored questions provided more actionable feedback to students, helping to identify strengths and weaknesses in reading comprehension. GenAI-generated feedback could have been more specific, limiting its usefulness in guiding students toward improvement. For instance, Participant T5 noted that *"GenAI-generated questions often lacked the depth required for engaging middle school students,"* indicating that GenAI tools alone cannot fully address the complexity of educational content creation.

## 5 Discussion

This study evaluated the effectiveness of GenAI tools like Twee and Kimi compared to human teachers in creating reading comprehension materials for middle school English. While previous research has touched on various aspects of AI in education, our study uniquely contributes by directly comparing AI-generated content with that produced by educators and introducing a novel framework for AI integration in teaching.

### 5.1 Key Findings and Implications

The quantitative analysis revealed a moderate, though not statistically significant, positive correlation between the time spent on content creation and the quality of the materials produced. This suggests that while time is a factor, other elements—such as teacher expertise and alignment with curricular goals—play a more substantial role in determining content quality.

Additionally, our study contributes to filling this gap by examining the practical application of GenAI tools in educational content creation. This topic has yet to receive much attention in the existing literature. GenAI tools like ChatGPT and Kimi consistently produced content with strong logical structures and precise language use. However, the performance of human teachers varied significantly, with top performers like Participant T5 excelling and others like Participant T7 exhibiting deficiencies. This variability underscores the diverse design styles and strategies that human teachers bring to content creation. While GenAI offers efficiency and consistency, the human element introduces depth, adaptability, and the potential for more nuanced and compelling educational materials.

### 5.2 Introducing a Novel Model for AI Integration

Building on the findings of this study and the original framework proposed by Professor Jianli Jiao, we present a refined five-tier model for integrating Generative AI (GenAI) into education (Fig. 2). This model incorporates recent research insights, including Kim's (2024) Teacher-AI Collaboration (TAC) stages, which highlight the evolving roles of teachers—from passive users to active collaborators and, ultimately, co-creators in partnership with AI. This refined model provides a structured pathway for educators, guiding them from initial AI awareness (Level 1) to full mastery and integration (Level 5), where teachers and AI collaborate in co-designing learning experiences.

The five-tier pyramid model shows the gradual integration of GenAI in education, where each level reflects increasing task complexity and teacher proficiency. The left side highlights teachers' growth from Level 1 (Awareness without Application) to Level 5 (Integration / Mastery) in using GenAI for advanced educational tasks. On the right, the model illustrates the evolving relationship: At Levels 1 and 2, teachers passively use GenAI for basic tasks like content automation. As they reach Levels 3 and 4, they customize GenAI outputs for personalized teaching. By Level 5, teachers collaborate with GenAI to co-design teaching strategies, marking a shift from user to partner. This model guides educators from passive AI usage to active collaboration, improving teaching and student outcomes.

This model aligns with the observations of Xia et al. (2023), who noted that while tools like ChatGPT are effective for collective teaching tasks—such as designing syllabi, generating lecture notes, and creating teaching strategies—they require expert input for precise instructional dialogues. As GenAI capabilities evolve, our model suggests that educators should progress toward higher levels of integration, where GenAI complements human expertise to enhance learning outcomes.

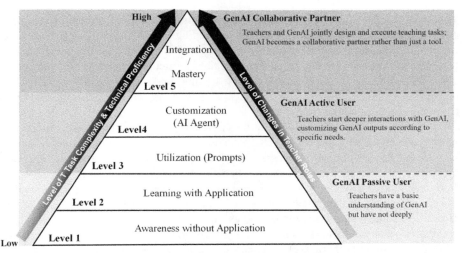

**Fig. 2.** A Five-tiered model for Teacher-Generative AI collaboration in education that was originally proposed by Prof. Jianli Jiao (Jen et al., 2024)

## 5.3 Limitations

While the study provides significant insights, it is important to acknowledge its limitations, particularly the small sample size, which may affect the generalizability of the findings. Additionally, the study's focus on middle school English education limits the applicability of the findings to other subjects or educational levels.

## 5.4 Future Research Directions

Further studies that build on these findings seek to enlarge the sample size in a way that tests the effectiveness of the five-tiered GenAI integration model at different educational levels and settings. Future research should be conducted to delve more deeply into various ways in which each level of this model has different layers of AI-human collaboration affecting the efficiency of teachers in improving student outcomes. Preliminary data from our present study on teacher feedback, gains in efficiency, and quality of content show promising opportunities for further improvement in AI-human collaboration, especially in balancing automation tasks with creative and critical thinking tasks. Further research is needed to study how the levels—especially Levels 4 and 5, where teachers are advanced active users and collaborators—can be honed to align even more strongly with Bloom's Taxonomy. In other words, instructors can do more high-order cognitive tasks of analyzing, evaluating, and creating, while the GenAI tools help with remembering and understanding lower-level tasks.

## 6 Conclusion

This study assessed the effectiveness of GenAI tools, specifically Twee and Kimi, compared to human teachers in creating middle school English reading comprehension materials. While GenAI tools demonstrated efficiency and consistency in content generation, human teachers produced higher-quality materials, particularly in relevance, clarity, and alignment with educational objectives. These findings underscore the indispensable role of human expertise in ensuring pedagogical soundness despite the potential of GenAI to streamline certain educational tasks.

Our proposed five-tiered model for teacher-GenAI collaboration in education highlights the need for educators to move beyond primary GenAI usage toward more sophisticated, integrated applications where GenAI complements human expertise. This progression is essential for maximizing the benefits of GenAI in education. However, the study's limitations, including a small sample size and potential bias in qualitative evaluations, suggest that further research is needed. Future studies should focus on developing GenAI tools that support this model and exploring the impacts of advanced AI-human collaboration on educational outcomes. In conclusion, while AI has a valuable role in education, it must be harnessed to enhance, not replace, the critical contributions of educators.

**Acknowledgment.** We sincerely appreciate all the teachers who completed the materials designed and the survey. Their valuable response made this work possible.

## References

Alwaqdani, M.: Investigating teachers' perceptions of artificial intelligence tools in education: potential and difficulties. Educ. Inf. Technol. (2024). https://doi.org/10.1007/s10639-024-12903-9

Creely, E., Blannin, J.: The implications of generative AI for creative composition in higher education and initial teacher education. ASCILITE Publ. (2023). https://doi.org/10.14742/apubs.2023.618

Dron, J.: The human nature of generative AIs and the technological nature of humanity: Implications for education. Digital **3**(4), 319–335 (2023). https://doi.org/10.3390/digital3040020

Farrelly, T., Baker, N.: Generative artificial intelligence: implications and considerations for higher education practice. Educ. Sci. **13**(11), 1109 (2023). https://doi.org/10.3390/educsci13111109

Jauhiainen, J.S., Guerra, A.G.: Generative AI and ChatGPT in school children's education: evidence from a school lesson. Sustainability (2023). https://doi.org/10.3390/su151814025

Johri, A., Katz, A., Qadir, J., Hingle, A.: Generative artificial intelligence and engineering education. J. Eng. Educ. (2023). https://doi.org/10.1002/jee.20537

Kadaruddin, K.: Empowering education through generative AI: innovative instructional strategies for tomorrow's learners. Int. J. Bus., Law, Educ. **4**(2), 618–625 (2023). https://doi.org/10.56442/ijble.v4i2.215

Kim, J.: Leading teachers' perspective on teacher-AI collaboration in education. Educ. Inf. Technol. **29**(7), 8693–8724 (2024). https://doi.org/10.1007/s10639-023-12109-5

Kim, J.: Types of teacher-AI collaboration in K-12 classroom instruction: Chinese teachers' perspective. Educ. Inf. Technol. (2024). https://doi.org/10.1007/s10639-024-12523-3

Ministry of Education of the People's Republic of China: The Ministry of Education releases four actions to promote AI empowerment in education. Ministry of Education of the People's Republic of China (2024). http://www.moe.gov.cn/jyb_xwfb/xw_zt/moe_357/2024/2024_zt05/mtbd/202403/t20240329_1123025.html

Nguyen, A., Hong, Y., Dang, B., Huang, X.: Human-AI collaboration patterns in AI-assisted academic writing. Stud. High. Educ. (2024). https://doi.org/10.1080/03075079.2024.2323593

Nguyen, T.H.C.: Exploring the role of artificial intelligence-powered facilitator in enhancing digital competencies of primary school teachers. Eur. J. Educ. Res. **13**(1), 219–231 (2024). https://doi.org/10.12973/eu-jer.13.1.219

de Oliveira Silva, A., dos Santos Janes, D.: Artificial intelligence in education: What are the opportunities and challenges? Rev. Artif. Intell. Educ. **5**(00), e018 (2023). https://doi.org/10.37497/rev.artif.intell.educ.v5i00.18

The State Council: Notice on issuing the development plan of the new generation of artificial intelligence. The State Council of the People's Republic of China (2017). https://www.gov.cn/zhengce/content/2017-07/20/content_5211996.htm

Vallis, C., et al.: Collaborative sensemaking with generative AI: a muse, amuse, muse. ASCILITE Publ. (2023). https://doi.org/10.14742/apubs.2023.514

van den Berg, G., du Plessis, E.: ChatGPT and generative AI: Possibilities for its contribution to lesson planning, critical thinking and openness in teacher education. Educ. Sci. (2023). https://doi.org/10.3390/educsci13100998

Xia, Q., Cheng, M., Zhao, J., Lai, J.: How to effectively integrate ChatGPT into education from an international perspective——Based on a systematic review on 72 literature. Mod. Educ. Technol. **33**(6), 26–33 (2023)

# Can Generative AI Really Empower Teachers' Professional Practices? A Quasi-Experiment on Human-GenAI Collaborative Rubric Design

Xingyun Huang[✉], Fen-Lan Jen, Yuting Lian, and Jianli Jiao

School of Information Technology in Education, South China Normal University, No.55, West of Zhongshan Avenue, Tianhe District, Guangzhou City, Guangdong Province, China
10826762@qq.com

**Abstract.** Rubric design traditionally relies heavily on the personal experience and professional understanding of teachers, which, to a certain extent, limits the effectiveness and scope of rubrics and renders the task of designing and assessing particularly burdensome for frontline teachers. Emerging as a technological tool, generative AI enables the generation of text and diagrams by mimicking human thought and creativity. Therefore, this study examines the potential of integrating generative AI into rubric design. In study, teachers collaborated with GenAI to craft rubrics assessing students' competencies and skills. The findings reveal that GenAI significantly enhances design efficiency and expands the evaluative dimensions of rubrics. By analyzing 38 experimental data sets, the study recommends that teachers collaborate with GenAI in rubric design to harness the full benefits of AI and human expertise. The study offers insights and guidance for achieving a more scientific, precise, and efficient instructional design through human-computer synergy.

**Keywords:** generative AI · rubric design · human-AI collaboration

## 1 Introduction

As a set of criteria for evaluating students' academic performance, including behaviors, cognitive attitudes, and various learning outcomes (e.g., artwork, oral presentations, research reports, essays, etc.) during the learning process (Zhong et al., 2007), rubrics have become a common tool in all levels of educational settings around the world. Educators and policy makers trust rubrics because they are effective in judging the quality of students' performance against predetermined criteria and increase the reliability of ratings (Jönsson & Svingby, 2007).

However, teachers are faced with the dilemma of designing and applying rubrics, which takes a lot of time and effort. Artificial Intelligence technology, as a key driver of ecological change in education, has received a lot of attention in terms of how it can empower teaching and learning to improve quality and efficiency.

Since 2022, applications of generative AI in the direction of text generation (e.g., GPT model) have emerged, triggering changes in the way of educational content production (Zhao et al., 2023). Generative AI adopts the Pre-train-Prompt learning model, and combines user-input text with feedback and reinforcement learning to provide multiple rounds of smooth and natural content generation (Liu et al., 2024), becoming an important tool for teachers to develop instructional materials. So, this study seeks to explore the key research questions: *Can this type of generative AI help teachers improve the efficiency and quality of rubric design?*

To answer this question, this study will conduct a quasi-experiment in terms of both efficiency and quality of rubric design to explore how effective this type of generative AI is in assisting teachers in rubric design.

## 2 Literature Review

### 2.1 Generative AI-Empowered Educational Practices

The rise of generative AI is gradually penetrating and reshaping multiple dimensions of the education industry by virtue of its excellence in text generation, comprehension, and interaction.

Scholars Dai Ling et al. (2023) proposed four dimensions of applying generative AI to education and teaching, namely student learning, teacher teaching, education management and learning evaluation, pointing out that GenAI will empower the transformation of students' knowledge assessment and competence evaluation to process, dynamic, higher-order, and comprehensive, and promote the exploration of the practice of process, value-added, and comprehensive evaluation. Lee(2023) showed that ChatGPT significantly reduced teachers' workload in automating the generation of teaching resources and the creation of assessment questions, allowing teachers to devote more energy to other parts of the curriculum as well as their own professional development practices.

Meanwhile, Wang and Chen (2023) found that ChatGPT enhanced student-teacher interactions in distance and online education environments by providing personalized scheduling, timely feedback, and flexible pedagogical adjustments. Verma (2023) regards ChatGPT as a powerful tool in the teaching and assessment process, believing that teachers can actively apply ChatGPT in curriculum planning, resource development, and assessment activities to gain teaching support.

In addition, ChatGPT can be used to develop grading criteria, provide detailed feedback on student work, and even act as an automated assessment system (Kasneci et al., 2023). In conclusion, generative AI such as ChatGPT shows great potential to transform teaching practice and empower teachers to develop their professional practice.

### 2.2 Teaching Rubrics

In the 20th century, rubrics were devised as a tool to improve the reliability and validity of grading student performance. Over time, the use of rubrics has gradually increased, especially at the beginning of the 21st century, with an exponential growth in their use in education (Jönsson & Svingby, 2007). Currently, rubrics are widely used as an educational assessment tool at all levels of education worldwide (Panadero et al., 2023).

Rubrics can increase the transparency of marking by clearly demonstrating the assessment criteria and the level of expectation for a task. Students can better understand task requirements, clarify learning goals, and self-regulate their learning accordingly by using scales (Brookhart, 2013). Andrade etal.'s (2009) study found that the long-term use of scales increasedstudents' self-efficacy, especially in writing tasks. Panadero etal.'s meta-analytic study (2023) found that the use of rubrics had a moderate positive effect onstudents' academic performance, and a standardized mean difference analysis showed that rubrics significantly improvedstudents' performance on the task.

As the design of rubrics requires teachers to have the expertise and skills to ensure that the criteria for rubrics are both clear and actionable (Brookhart, 2013). Poorly designed scales may lead to inconsistent understanding between students and teachers, affecting the fairness and validity of the assessment. At the same time, teachers need to use scales continuously for assessment and feedback during the teaching and learning process, which will take a lot of time and effort. Inefficiency and difficulty in maintaining quality have become the main difficulties faced by teachers in designing rubrics.

## 3 Method

### 3.1 Participants

In digital instruction capabilities enhanced workshops, 38 K-12 teachers were recruited to participate in this study, who all had more than two years of teaching experience and had learnt about teaching rubrics. The participants contained 18 males (47.37%) and 20 females (52.63%), with an age range of 28–47 years old. Table 1 details the participants' background variables.

**Table 1.** Distribution of participants' background variables

| Variables | Variable description | No. Participant | Participant (%) |
|---|---|---|---|
| Gender | Male | 18 | 47% |
|  | Female | 20 | 53% |
| School | Primary | 17 | 45% |
|  | Middle | 12 | 31% |
|  | High | 9 | 24% |

### 3.2 Procedures

A quasi-experimental study design was employed to answer the proposed research question. Each teacher was required to select a rubric topic relevant to their teaching practice and complete the design of two rubrics around the same topic.

*Human-designed Rubric (Group 1).* The research participants completed the design of the rubrics independently, without the use of generative AI.

*GenAI-designed Rubric (Group 2).* Based on the prompt framework provided by the researcher, the teacher collaborated with GenAI to complete the second set of rubrics under the theme. To avoid language barriers, this study used the SparkDesk Model 3.5, which is based on Chinese. The design process is shown in Fig. 1.

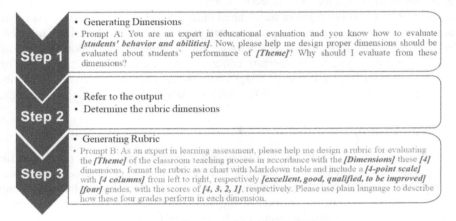

**Fig. 1.** The process of rubric designed with GenAI.

## 3.3 Instrument

### 3.3.1 Efficiency Assessment

This study controlled for participant design time, with each rubric taking 20 min to complete. To compare the efficiency of Group 1 and Group 2, the completeness and number of dimensions of the rubrics will be analyzed.

### 3.3.2 Quality Assessment

The present study focuses on the elements of rubric design (Phillip Dawson, 2015), and principles of rubric design (Li & Lu, 2018) to assess the quality of teaching rubrics. This instrument assessed four dimensions of rubric quality: rationality, readability, measurability and equidistance.

Rationality means that the rubrics are set up in a scientific and rational manner with reference to the teaching objectives, content and level of the students, and contain all the key elements affecting the evaluation results. Readability pertains to ascertaining the text easy to read and understand. Measurability refers to the use of concrete and operational descriptive language, avoiding the use of abstract and conceptual language. For example, when assessing a student's information-gathering skills, if the indicator is described as 'the student has good information-gathering skills', then the indicator is very vague and unworkable. A much clearer and more specific description would be 'able to collect information from multiple electronic and non-electronic sources, with proper attribution'. Equidistance indicates that the indicator levels are clearly distinguishable from each other and are evenly spaced and largely equidistant.

### 3.4 Training of Raters and Interrater Reliability

Two graduate students received a 60-min training session and completely participated in the entire process of designing rubrics by participants. During the training, the researcher provided instructions on how to rate each rubric dimension with examples. After the training, the raters were required to achieve a minimum of 80% agreement with the researcher across three sets of rubrics before they started rating the rubrics for the study. After the completion of the training, the raters, who were blind to the study conditions, independently coded each rubric. Interrater reliability was established by randomly selecting 20% of the rubrics and having both raters code them. Any discrepancies in coding were resolved through consensus meetings between the raters. The interrater reliability percentage score was 95% (range = 90%–100%), while the Kappa coefficient was 0.87.

### 3.5 Data Analysis

To answer the research question, the mean scores on the rubrics were calculated for each group, and the Independent-samples T Test was used to determine if there was a statistically significant difference in mean scores between the Group 1 (control) and Group 2 (GenAI). Meanwhile, the percentage of completion of the rubrics and the mean value of the number of rubric dimensions were calculated for the assessment of efficiency.

## 4 Results

### 4.1 Efficiency

*Percentage of Completion.* In the same time frame, GenAI co-design had a completion rate of 100 percent (Group 2), compared to 81.6 percent for independent manual design by teachers (Group 1).

*Number of Dimensions.* The control group had a mean score of 3.16 (SD = 1.31), while the GenAI group had a mean score of 4.16 (SD = 0.89). Results showed a statistically significant difference between the two groups ($t = -3.907, p < 0.01$), indicating that the efficiency of rubrics designed by teachers with GenAI group was significantly higher than that of the control group (see Table 2).

**Table 2.** The Independent-samples T test of the experimental group and the control group on the Number of Dimensions

| Name | Group | Averages | SD | t | p |
|---|---|---|---|---|---|
| Number of Dimensions | 1(control) | 3.16 | 1.31 | −3.907 | .00 |
| | 2(GenAI) | 4.16 | 0.89 | | |

As far as efficiency is concerned, GenAI has a clear advantage in designing rubrics. With the support of massive data, generative AI can generate text content quickly, while teachers can only rely on personal experience. Therefore, through the collaboration of GenAI, teachers will design rubrics more efficiently and make up for the lack of experience in instructional evaluation.

### 4.2 Quality

The Independent-samples T Test was employed to examine the differences between the experimental and control groups. The analysis considered the scores obtained for four dimensions, as detailed in Table 3.

**Table 3.** The Independent-samples T test of the experimental group and the control group on the content quality

| Name | Group | Averages | SD | t | p |
|---|---|---|---|---|---|
| Rationality | 1 (control) | 3.63 | 1.28 | −2.423 | .018 |
| | 2 (GenAI) | 4.24 | 0.85 | | |
| Readability | 1 (control) | 4.11 | 1.27 | −3.612 | .001 |
| | 2 (GenAI) | 4.89 | 0.45 | | |
| Measurability | 1 (control) | 3.53 | 1.33 | −4.168 | .000 |
| | 2 (GenAI) | 4.53 | 0.65 | | |
| Equidistance | 1 (control) | 4.05 | 1.31 | −3.930 | .000 |
| | 2 (GenAI) | 4.92 | 0.36 | | |

For the dimension of rationality, the mean scores for the experimental and control groups were 4.24 and 3.93. The difference was statistically significant ($t = -2.423$, $p < 0.05$), indicating a notable difference in the rationality dimension.

In the dimension of readability, the experimental group scored a mean of 4.89, while the control group scored 4.50. The difference was also statistically significant ($t = -3.612$, $p < 0.01$), suggesting a discernible difference between the two types of rubrics.

For the dimension of measurability, the experimental group scored a mean of 4.53, and the control group scored 4.03. The difference was statistically significant ($t = -4.168$, $p < 0.01$), indicating a significant advantage of the experimental group.

In the dimension of equidistance, the experimental group scored a mean of 4.92, while the control group scored 4.49. The difference was statistically significant ($t = -3.930$, $p < 0.01$), leading to the conclusion that GenAI did better in equidistance.

Overall, the GenAI co-designed rubrics showed significant advantages in terms of rationality, readability, measurability, and equidistance compared to those done independently by teachers. These findings shed light on the usability of generative AI in the design of rubrics, suggesting that the novel use of generative AI can help teachers optimise the quality of their rubrics to some extent in these dimensions.

## 5 Discussions

### 5.1 Key Findings

#### 5.1.1 Work Efficiency is Enhanced with the GenAI

One of the most striking findings of this study is the significant enhancement in work efficiency experienced by educators when incorporating generative AI into their professional practices. Traditionally, the creation of teaching materials and resources has been a time-consuming and labor-intensive process. However, the integration of GenAI tools into this workflow has shown remarkable results in streamlining the preparation of teaching resources. By automating the generation of lesson plans, quizzes and rubrics, generative AI has alleviated the workload on teachers, thereby freeing up valuable time that can be redirected towards more pressing aspects of instruction and professional development. This finding aligns with previous research suggesting that generative AI can serve as a powerful ally in reducing the administrative burden on educators.

#### 5.1.2 The Quality of Rubric Design is Elevated

Another key finding of our study highlights the substantial improvement in the quality of rubrics designed with the assistance of generative AI. Specifically, the rubrics produced through human-GenAI collaboration exhibited a higher degree of measurability and equidistance, crucial qualities that ensure the rubric's effectiveness in fair and accurate assessment. The rubrics generated by AI were notably consistent in their structure and language, making them easier to interpret and apply consistently across different student assessments. While the text generated by AI was found to be well-formulated, it tended to follow a more templated approach, potentially lacking the nuanced personal touch that human educators bring to the table. Therefore, teachers are encouraged to collaborate with GenAI to maintain the standardisation of the rubrics while reflecting individual teaching experience.

#### 5.1.3 Challenges of Discipline-Specific

Despite the numerous advantages offered by generative AI in rubric design, the study uncovered limitations in scenarios where the evaluation pertained to specific disciplines or detailed curricular contexts. When dealing with subject-specific assessments, the AI's performance was less impressive, often falling short in capturing the intricacies and nuances of the course material. This suggests that generative AI, while adept at generating generalized content, may struggle with specialized educational domains that require deep domain knowledge. To mitigate this issue, we recommend that teachers provide the AI with contextual information and specific subject-matter content. This collaborative approach leverages the strengths of both parties: the AI's ability to generate structured and consistent rubrics, and the teacher's expertise in subject matter, thus creating a more robust and tailored evaluation tool.

## 5.2 P-P-P Framework

To better enhance the collaboration between teachers and GenAI in the creation of educational resources, the Provision-Prompt-Polish framework is proposed (Fig. 2). The P-P-P framework emphasizes human-GenAI collaboration based on the teacher's understanding of educational teaching and learning, taking full advantage of both human and GenAI capabilities so that it can improve the quality and efficiency of instructional materials.

Provision: The first step in the P-P-P Framework involves providing GenAI with the necessary background materials and context. This includes relevant pedagogical knowledge, teaching objectives, and textbook content. By supplying GenAI with comprehensive and detailed information, educators ensure that the AI has a solid foundation to build upon. This step is crucial as it sets the stage for the AI to generate content that aligns with the educational goals and standards.

Prompt: The second step is to prompt it to generate the corresponding teaching resources. This is done using the Role-Purpose-Requirements (RPR) framework, which guides the AI in understanding the specific roles it needs to fulfill, the purpose of the generated content, and the requirements that must be met.

Polish: The final step involves polishing and revising the GenAI-generated resources according to the needs of specific teaching practices. While the AI-generated content may be well-structured and consistent, it may lack the nuanced personal touch that human educators bring to the table. Therefore, it is essential for educators to review and refine the AI-generated materials, ensuring that they are aligned with the specific learning objectives and the unique characteristics of their students. This step also allows educators to incorporate their own pedagogical expertise and creativity, making the final product more engaging and effective.

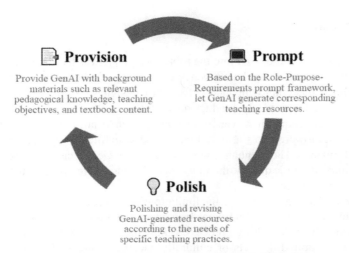

**Fig. 2.** P-P-P Framework of Human-GenAI Collaboration.

By following the P-P-P Framework, educators can harness the power of generative AI to enhance their professional practices, while still maintaining control over the educational content and ensuring that it meets the specific needs of their students. This collaborative approach not only improves the efficiency of resource creation but also elevates the quality of educational materials, ultimately leading to a more effective and engaging learning experience for students.

### 5.3 Limitations

While this paper provides valuable insights into the potential of GenAI in enhancing teachers' professional practices, particularly in the collaborative design of rubrics, we acknowledge several limitations inherent in our research approach.

Firstly, the present study was conducted with a limited sample size, comprising 38 experimental datasets. Although these samples offer preliminary evidence supporting the efficacy of integrating GenAI into rubric design, they may not fully represent the broader landscape of educational settings where such tools could be applied. Future investigations should aim to include a larger and more diverse dataset to ensure the generalizability of the findings across different contexts and demographics.

Secondly, this study utilized only one type of GenAI tool for the experiment, which might introduce tool-specific biases. Given the rapid evolution of AI technologies and the emergence of various GenAI models, each with unique functionalities and performance metrics, relying on a single tool limits our understanding of the differential impacts that distinct AI systems might have on the rubric design process. It would be beneficial for future research to explore the effects of multiple AI platforms, thereby providing a comparative analysis that can inform educators about the most suitable AI tools for their specific needs.

## 6 Conclusion

The integration of generative AI into the rubric design process has demonstrated significant potential for enhancing the efficiency and quality of educational assessment. The findings indicate that employing GenAI for rubric design shows marked improvements over traditional methods solely conducted by educators. By shortening the design time and increasing the comprehensiveness of rubrics, GenAI not only eases the workload on teachers but also promotes a more precise and scientifically rigorous evaluation of student performance. These enhancements suggest that GenAI can serve as an effective tool for optimizing rubric quality, thereby supporting more effective instructional design and assessment practices.

However, we also acknowledge the limitations and ethical considerations associated with the integration of AI technologies into educational practices. For instance, while AI can expedite the rubric design process, it may introduce biases or errors, especially when based on limited datasets or culturally specific contexts. Therefore, educators should remain vigilant and perform necessary validations to ensure the accuracy and fairness of rubrics created with AI assistance.

Moreover, the practical implications of integrating generative AI into rubric design include providing teachers with more time for professional development, allowing them to focus on pedagogical innovations and the development of personalized learning pathways for students. For example, teachers can utilize the saved time to develop richer instructional resources or offer more personalized feedback, which in turn could enhance students' academic performance. Specifically, rubrics co-designed with AI assistance can aid students in better understanding assignment requirements, clarifying learning goals, and regulating their learning behavior accordingly, thus enhancing their sense of self-efficacy, particularly in tasks such as writing. Such an approach ultimately contributes to improved student learning outcomes while supporting teachers' professional practices.

**Acknowledgment.** We sincerely appreciate all the teachers who completed the materials designed. Their valuable response made this work possible.

# References

Andrade, H.L., Wang, X., Du, Y., Akawi, R.L.: Rubric-referenced self-assessment and self-efficacy for writing. J. Educ. Res. **102**(4), 287–302 (2009)

Brookhart, S.M.: How to create and use rubrics for formative assessment and grading. ASCD (2013)

Dai, L., Hu, J., Zhu, Z.: New strategies for digital transformation of education under the empowerment of ChatGPT. Open Educ. Res. **29**(4), 41–48 (2023)

Jönsson, A., Svingby, G.: The use of scoring rubrics: reliability, validity and educational consequences. Educ. Res. Rev. **2**(2), 130–144 (2007)

Kasneci, E., Sessler, K., Küchemann, S., et al.: ChatGPT for good? On opportunities and challenges of large language models for education. Learn. Individ. Differ. **103**, 1–13 (2023)

Lee, H.: The rise of ChatGPT: Exploring its potential in medical education. Anat. Sci. Educ. (2023)

Liu, B.Q., Nie, X.L., Wang, S.J., et al.: Generative artificial intelligence and the reshaping of future education: technical framework, capability Characteristics, and application trends. Educ. Res. **45**(1), 13–20 (2024)

Panadero, E., Jonsson, A., Pinedo, L., Fernández-Castilla, B.: Effects of rubrics on academic performance, self-regulated learning, and self-efficacy: a meta-analytic review. Educ. Psychol. Rev. **35**(4), 113 (2023). https://doi.org/10.1007/s10648-023-09823-4

Verma, M.: The digital circular economy: ChatGPT and the future of STEM education and research. In. J. Trend Sci. Res. Dev. **7**(3), 178–182 (2023)

Wang, M., Chen, Y.: Research on the future vision of the Intelligent Integration of ChatGPT and Online Education. Adv. Educ. Technol. Psychol. **7**(2), 128–134 (2023)

Zhao, W.X., Zhou, K., Li, J., et al.: A survey of large language models [EB/OL]. arXiv preprint. https://doi.org/10.48550/arXiv.2303.18223. Retrieved 3 Aug 2024

Zhong, Z.X., Wang, M., Lin, A.Q.: Rubrics: a modern method of teaching evaluation. Chin. J. Distance Educ. **10**, 43–46 (2007)

Dawson, P.: Assessment rubrics: towards clearer and more replicable design, research and practice. Assess. Eval. High. Educ. **42**(3), 347–360 (2015)

Li, G., Lu, L.J.: Visible assessment: development and application of rubric-based core literacy assessment sheets. Educ. Theory Pract. **29**, 12–15 (2018)

# Empowering Assessors in Providing Quality Feedback with GenAI Assistance: A Preliminary Exploration

Zexuan Chen[1,2(✉)], Simon Cross[2], and Bart Rienties[2]

[1] School of Foreign Studies, Southern Medical University, No. 1023-1063, Sha Tai Nan Road, Baiyun District, Guangzhou 510515, Guangdong Province, China
SerlinaChen@163.com
[2] Institute of Educational Technology, The Open University, Walton Hall, Milton Keynes, Buckinghamshire MK7 6AA, UK
{simon.j.cross,bart.rienties}@open.ac.uk

**Abstract.** This study examines the impact of GenAI on assessors' ability to provide feedback during peer assessment. Utilizing a customized peer assessment system, PeerGrader, six undergraduate participants used either a GenAI-facilitated or non-GenAI-facilitated condition to provide feedback on their peers' English as a Foreign Language (EFL) writings. The assessors were categorized as three types based on their utilization of GenAI tools for feedback refinement: Self-sufficient Masters, Cautious Adopters, and Sustained Users. An analysis of the feedback provided by the six assessors in the three peer assessments revealed a positive influence of GenAI, as it helped assessors focus more on discourse-level aspects, apply more helpful feedback as indicated in more specific praise and criticism, more reasoning and exemplification. Post-course interviews indicated that participants strategically employed GenAI due to language challenges but also highlighted its benefits in assisting with feedback delivery. These findings tentatively suggest that integrating GenAI into peer assessment can positively impact the feedback quality.

**Keywords:** peer assessment · assessor · GenAI-facilitated feedback · quality feedback

## 1 Introduction

Peer assessment is a learning activity where learners act as assessors, providing feedback and suggestions for each others' learning processes and outputs (Topping & Ehly, 1998; Yu & Lee, 2016; van den Bos & Tan, 2019) grounded in a common set of rubrics or criteria (Adachi et al., 2018). As a cornerstone of educational practices, peer assessment has long been recognized for its potential to foster critical thinking (Strijbos & Sluijsmans, 2010), self-regulated learning (Topping, 2018; 2021; Alemdag & Yildirim, 2022), and co-regulated learning (Alemdag & Yildirim, 2022) among learners.

However, "traditional" peer assessment practices frequently encounter challenges, including the provision of relatively low-quality feedback from assessors (Darvishi et al., 2022a; Darvishi et al., 2022b; Gielen & De Wever; 2015a; Gielen & De Wever; 2015b; Nelson & Carson, 1998), which can stem from inadequate feedback skills (Adachi et al., 2018; Planas Lladó et al., 2014; etc.) and/or a lack of experience in conducting peer assessments by assessors (Adachi et al., 2018; Planas Lladó et al., 2014; Weaver and Cotrell, 1986; etc.).

The emergence of Generative Artificial Intelligence (GenAI) as a potential tool for educational enhancement (Giannakos et al., 2024; Owoc et al., 2019; Rienties et al., 2024; etc.) may present new opportunities to address some of the limitations of "traditional" peer assessment (Limna et al., 2022). This is because GenAI, by leveraging vast amounts of data and advanced algorithms (Alier et al., 2024), can offer personalized and augmented insights and feedback that may not be readily accessible among student peers. Despite the promising aspects of GenAI-facilitated peer assessment, there is still a notable research gap in exploring its potential effects in enhancing feedback quality and understanding participants' experiences and perceptions with this innovative method.

Therefore, this study aims to tentatively bridge this gap by investigating the effects of enhancing assessors' feedback using GenAI in peer assessment contexts. Guided by the above research purpose, the following research question was formulated: To what extent can the use of GenAI by undergraduate peer assessors augment and improve the quality of feedback they give?

## 2 Literature Review

### 2.1 Improving the Quality of Assessors' Feedback

The quality of feedback provided by assessors plays a crucial role in enhancing student learning in peer assessment (Hattie & Timperley, 2007). Assessors in peer assessment need to be able to recognize and apply particular criteria to judge the learning process and outputs of their peers, and eventually provide peer feedback (Gielen & De Wever; 2015a; Gielen & De Wever; 2015b). Giving feedback demands higher-order thinking skills (Coleman et al., 2001, Kollar & Fischer, 2010), hence one of the key challenges in peer assessment is how to ensure the student assessors provide constructive, informative and actionable feedback that is both accurate and relevant to the assessed work.

In order to address this challenge, some researchers have examined the factors that influence feedback quality, including assessor expertise (Govaerts et al., 2013; Hovardas et al., 2014, etc.). Another group of researchers have investigated intervention strategies to support peer feedback, such as providing assessors with comprehensive guidelines, checklists (Baker, 2006; Topping, 2009; Ware & O'Dowd, 2008), and structured peer feedback templates (Gielen & De Wever, 2015) as a means to facilitate the process of giving high-quality feedback. Furthermore, Suzuki's (2008) coding scheme of text revision following peer assessment has provided valuable insights into feedback focus in peer assessment. While these interventions have indeed contributed to assisting students in providing feedback, there is still room for improvement in terms of their overall effectiveness.

## 2.2 Empowering Assessors with GenAI Assistance

More recently, researchers have turned their attention to the potential of intelligent assistance in enhancing the quality of assessors' feedback. For example, many studies have investigated the effect of utilizing GenAI techniques to select and design rubrics for educational assessment, including peer assessment, as reviewed by Mendoza et al. (2020).

Other studies tend to use GenAI as quality-control assistance to help assessors improve peer feedback quality (Darvishi et al., 2022a; 2022b; Ou et al., 2024). For example, Darvishi et al. (2022a; 2022b) have developed a set of GenAI facilitated quality control functions in their self-developed system, RiPPLE, that automatically assess the quality of the submitted feedback and prompt the participants to improve the feedback. Meanwhile, recent studies have started to explore the possibility of empowering assessors with GenAI assistance in peer assessment. For example, Oliveira et al. (2023) have developed a GenAI-facilitated review process to substitute the students in conducting peer assessment in traditional Computer Science education for reducing software errors and enhancing the overall quality of software projects.

However, there is a lack of research exploring how GenAI can be leveraged to facilitate assessors in formulating and delivering high-quality feedback. Consequently, the primary objective of the current study is to delve into the effects of assessors utilizing GenAI as an assistive technology for providing feedback.

Based on the major research question of "To what extent can the use of GenAI by undergraduate peer assessors augment and improve the quality of feedback they give?", three sub-research questions are put forward:

(1) To what extent is the quality of feedback by assessors improved with GenAI assistance?
(2) How did the student assessors make use of GenAI to support their peer feedback writing?
(3) What are the challenges and opportunities assessors encountered while using GenAI assistance?

## 3 Methodology

This study adopted a mixed method approach to gain insights into the assessors' feedback quality, their experiences and perceptions of GenAI-assisted peer assessment.

### 3.1 Participants

The study was carried out in a natural classroom environment, encompassing three classes (N = 179) within a blended learning course called College English II at a major university in southern China. Students were encouraged to bring and use their personal devices during class.

Six students, aged 18–19, voluntarily participated in the study after an open invitation was extended to all students enrolled in the course. To ensure anonymity they have been coded S1–S6.

## 3.2 The Peer Assessment Procedure

The course included standard in-person teaching sessions and featured three peer assessment tasks carried out during the Spring semester of 2024, with each task scheduled at monthly intervals (April 9th, May 7th, and June 11th).

The three peer assessment tasks followed the same learning design using a flipped classroom approach to ensure time in class was used to maximum advantage (Divjak et al., 2022): Prior to the peer assessment session, students completed their writing out of class and submitted it to the peer assessment system; during the face-to-face peer assessment session, the assessors then accessed their own computing device to give feedback in class with/without GenAI-assistance (assessors could choose to provide feedback to more than one other fellow student).

## 3.3 The Feedback Training

Feedback training consists of four essential components: feedback focus, feedback strategies, GenAI-assisted feedback tools, and a peer assessment system.

Firstly, the assessors were instructed with a "Feedback Focus Checklist" adapted from Suzuki's (2008) "Coding Scheme of Text Changes" in students' revision of writings. This categorization divided the assessors' focus on their peers' writings into three distinct levels: discourse-level, sentence-level, and lexical-level (see Appendix I).

Secondly, an "Assessors' Feedback and Feedforward Strategies Checklist" was developed and implemented during the feedback training session (see Appendix II). This study categorized feedback strategies into four main types: general praise, specific praise, general criticism, and specific criticism, drawing inspiration from Baker's (2006) taxonomy of "helpful and unhelpful comments" and Ware & O'Dowd's (2008) emphasis on "specific feedback." Additionally, this study introduces three feedforward strategies—reasoning, exampling, and direct editing—which are based on the feedforward template proposed by Gielen & De Wever (2015).

Thirdly, during the feedback sessions, participants were presented with the option to utilize external GenAI tools, such as Xinghuo and Yiyan (analogous to ChatGPT), to provide prompt suggestions and guidance throughout the feedback process. It was suggested to them that this could be useful in facilitating and improving the development and refinement of their feedback comments but use of GenAI across all three tasks was not mandatory.

Last but not least, a specifically designed peer assessment system called PeerGrader (http://peergrader.cn/) was used to facilitate the learning activities and research data collection. This system allowed participants to submit their work, give and receive feedback from their peers anonymously.

## 3.4 Data Collection and Analysis

**Feedback Given by Assessors.** The feedback provided by each participant was downloaded from PeerGrader and then sorted and coded by author one and a second locally-based researcher, delving into the feedback focus of the assessors and the corresponding feedback and feedforward strategies employed by them. Note that the "Feedback Focus

Checklist" (see Appendix I) and the "Assessors' Feedback and Feedforward Strategies Checklist" (see Appendix II) were employed as the coding scheme for feedback focus and feedback strategies, respectively.

After the coding was completed, this study used the line chart function of Excel to visually present the use of GenAI by the six assessors in the three peer assessment tasks and their performance in feedback giving.

**Experience and Perceptions in Giving GenAI-Facilitated Peer Feedback.** Post-course interviews were conducted utilizing a tailored interview outline, which was adapted and refined from Kim et al.'s (2024) guiding questions, specifically focusing on the participants' experiences and perceptions of GenAI-assisted writing, given that providing written feedback constitutes a form of writing itself. The interview outline comprised three main sections: Experience of GenAI-assisted feedback giving, limitations and advantages of GenAI-assisted feedback giving.

The interviews were recorded with the consent of the participants and were transcribed afterwards. Thematic analysis was performed to explore the experiences, challenges, and opportunities faced by the six assessors in adopting GenAI assistance.

## 4 Results

### 4.1 Quality of Feedback by Assessors with GenAI Assistance

This section delves into comparing and contrasting the focal points and strategies employed in feedbacks that are facilitated by GenAI and those that are not, with the aim of exploring the impact of GenAI assistance on the quality of feedback provided by assessors.

As participants were free to choose whether (or not) to incorporate GenAI in any of the three peer assessment tasks, three types of assessors were identified amongst the six participants (Table 1), and every type was then assigned a provisional descriptor: Type 1 (S1, S2), labelled "Self-sufficient Master", initially chose to utilize GenAI-assisted feedback for the first and second tasks but subsequently decided to deliver feedback without AI intervention for the remaining tasks. Type 2 (S3, S4), termed "Cautious Adopter", ventured into GenAI-facilitated feedback generation exclusively during the third task. Finally, Type 3 (S5, S6), the "Sustained User", consistently used GenAI-facilitated feedback throughout the entire semester (see Table 1).

As indicated in Table 1, the independent decision to incorporate GenAI into any of the three peer assessment tasks resulted in not only three distinct types of assessors based on the extent of GenAI usage, but also the emergence of two types of feedback giving: GenAI-facilitated and non-GenAI-facilitated.

**Assessors' Feedback Focus.** As depicted in Table 1, the Self-sufficient Masters collectively provided 24 feedbacks, with 18 (75%) of them facilitated by GenAI in Peer Assessments 1 and 2. In contrast, the Cautious Adopters generated a total of 14 feedbacks, of which only 5 (35.71%) were aided by GenAI in Peer Assessment 3. Meanwhile, the Sustained Users offered 17 feedbacks, all of which (100%) were facilitated by GenAI in Peer Assessments 1, 2 and 3.

**Table 1.** Record of GenAI-facilitated feedback in peer assessment (PA)

| Participants | GenAI-facilitated feedback | | | Number of text feedbacks given* | | | Proposed Assessor Type |
|---|---|---|---|---|---|---|---|
| | PA1 | PA2 | PA3 | PA1 | PA2 | PA3 | |
| S1 | Yes | Yes | No | 6 | 1 | 1 | Self-sufficient Master |
| S2 | Yes | Yes | No | 10 | 1 | 5 | |
| S3 | No | No | Yes | 2 | 4 | 2 | Cautious Adopter |
| S4 | No | No | Yes | 1 | 2 | 3 | |
| S5 | Yes | Yes | Yes | 3 | 3 | 2 | Sustained User |
| S6 | Yes | Yes | Yes | 4 | 3 | 2 | |

Note. Total count of peer writings that every participant has provided text feedback to during a peer assessment task, where one piece of text feedback is counted for every piece of peer writing, regardless of the length of the feedback provided. Note that students could retrieve and review as many peer writings as they wanted.

Within these feedbacks, the assessors have represented a minor variation in their feedback focus, which were coded, calculated and presented in Fig. 1.

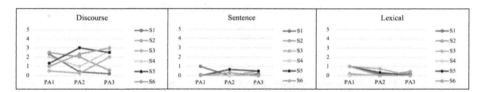

**Fig. 1.** The six assessors' feedback focus in the three peer assessments (PA)

Figure 1 presents the feedback focus identified by three types of assessors across discourse, sentence, and lexical levels in three separate peer assessment tasks. Notably, all of the three types of assessors shared a similar preference in their feedback focus, with a greater emphasis on the discourse level (see Table 2).

Further analysis revealed that the Self-sufficient Masters' quantity of feedback across the three dimensions (discourse, sentence, and lexical) gradually decreased as they transitioned from a GenAI-facilitated to a non-GenAI-facilitated condition. Meanwhile, the Cautious Adopters demonstrated a tendency towards heightened focus on commenting at the discourse and sentence levels as they shifted from a non-GenAI-facilitated to a GenAI-facilitated condition. However, the Sustained Users of GenAI assistance exhibited a consistent increase in their focus on discourse, accompanied by a decrease in their focus on sentences and lexical aspects when providing feedback.

This indicates that the GenAI-facilitated condition might be beneficial in enabling assessors to broaden their focus, encompassing discourse, sentence, and lexical aspects, particularly at the discourse level, which relates to the overall structure, coherence, and logic of the text.

**Table 2.** Example quotes of the three types of assessors on the discourse level

| Assessors | Example Quotes | |
|---|---|---|
| Self-sufficient Master | S1 | "The full text revolves around the theme that college students should adjust their learning strategies to adapt to the times as the times develop, and specifically explained how to adjust learning strategies from different aspects." |
| | S2 | "Clear structure: The article is divided into three main points, explaining three aspects of university learning methods that need to be adjusted." |
| Cautious Adopter | S3 | "The structure of this essay is clear, and the viewpoints are clear, with both positive comments on AI and warnings about its potential risks." |
| | S4 | "Your essay is well-structured and flows logically." |
| Sustained User | S5 | "This article is well-reasoned and proposes solutions to the current situation of students lacking planning. There are sufficient arguments and evidence, with a clear structure and accurate cohesion." |
| | S6 | "It is recommended to add transition sentences between paragraphs to make the whole article more coherent." |

**Feedback and Feedforward Strategies Applied by the Assessors.** The feedback and feedforward strategies applied by three consistent groups of assessors across three distinct peer assessment tasks, as indicated in the two conditions of feedbacks (GenAI-facilitated and non GenAI-facilitated), were presented in Figs. 2 and 3.

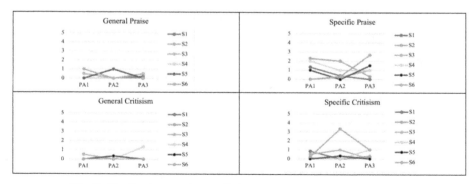

**Fig. 2.** Feedback strategies applied in the three peer assessments (PA)

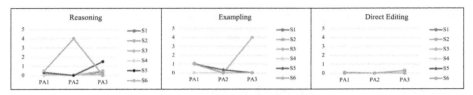

**Fig. 3.** Feedforward strategies applied in the three peer assessments (PA)

As depicted in Fig. 2, following the peer assessment training that distinguished between helpful feedback (specific praise/criticism) and unhelpful feedback (general praise/criticism), the six assessors' feedback shifted towards offering more specific praise and criticism rather than general ones.

Further examination uncovers a nuanced pattern: The Self-sufficient Masters witnessed a gradual decline in their use of specific praise as they transitioned from a GenAI-facilitated to a non-GenAI-facilitated environment. In contrast, among the Cautious Adopters, S3 exhibited a trend towards offering more specific praise and reducing both general and specific criticism, whereas S4 showed an increase in both types of criticism alongside an elevation in general praise upon shifting from a non-GenAI-facilitated to a GenAI-facilitated setup. Lastly, the Sustained Users of GenAI assistance consistently increased their delivery of specific praise and criticism, paralleled by a decrease in general praise and criticism during the feedback process.

This suggests that the GenAI-facilitated condition might be supportive in guiding and enabling the assessors to provide more specific praise and criticism.

A comparison of Figs. 2 and 3 reveals that fewer assessors used feedforward strategies compared to those who use feedback strategies. Moreover, the total amount of feedforward strategies employed by all assessors was considerably less than the amount of feedback strategies applied. This observation may indicate a lack of awareness or ability among the assessors to offer feedforward suggestions.

Upon further analysis of Fig. 3, it becomes evident that the Sustained Users, who consistently utilized GenAI assistance across the three peer assessment tasks, gave the most extensive feedforward, with S6 offering reading and example-based explanations, direct editing, and S5 providing reasoning and examples. Additionally, one of the Cautious Adopters (S3) provided examples during Peer Assessment 3, after transitioning from a non-GenAI-facilitated to a GenAI-facilitated condition.

These findings suggest that the GenAI-facilitated condition might be beneficial in assisting assessors in applying feedforward strategies, potentially enhancing their ability to provide constructive and detailed feedback.

### 4.2 Assessors' Strategies in Formulating GenAI-Facilitated Feedback

Subsequent interviews were undertaken to understand the six assessors' approaches to generating feedback. This section presents insights from their experiences with GenAI-assisted feedback giving.

**Utilizing GenAI for Feedback Formulation.** Participants sought help from GenAI during peer assessment mainly because they encountered some difficulties and challenges when facing the task of peer assessment. Specifically, these commonalities can be summarized as follows:

(1) Insufficient EFL ability: The participants expressed a common sentiment that their English proficiency hindered their ability to conduct a comprehensive and insightful evaluation of their peers' writings. This was evident in responses like, "My language expression and organizational skills are not very good, and my ability to identify problems is also limited" (S3), as well as, "Given my poor English level, it's quite challenging for me to assess each other's English compositions" (S6).
(2) Aspiration for Enhanced Logicality and Depth in Feedback: The participants expressed a desire to offer more insightful and comprehensive critiques. One participant (S2), in particular, voiced her hope that "GenAI could offer preliminary comment frameworks or suggestions on my peers' writings", highlighting their intention to elevate the quality of their feedback.

The interviews also revealed that with the clear target of assessment feedback in mind, the participants strategically interacted with GenAI to formulate feedback. Specifically, their feedback strategies could be summarized as follows:

(1) Clarity in Prompts and Requirements: The participants emphasized the importance of articulating their needs and instructions to the GenAI with utmost clarity to ensure it operates in alignment with their expectations. Examples of such prompts included, "Please provide a comment on the structural arrangement of this writing, taking into account the following content" (S2) and "Kindly assist me in evaluating this composition" (S4).
(2) Iterative Interaction and Fine-tuning: When the initial response from the GenAI did not meet the participants' satisfaction, they engaged in multiple rounds of interaction, refining their instructions to optimize the outcomes and align them with their expectations. This process involved switching between AI tools (S1), posing questions from alternative angles, and modifying the prompt to solicit more specific suggestions, as exemplified by S1, "Your wording seems a bit broad. Could you please offer some more practical recommendations?".

**Acceptance and Adoption of GenAI Suggestions.** The participants mainly used three ways to formulate their feedbacks, namely: direct adoption of GenAI text, integration of GenAI text and personal insights, refinement and enhancement of GenAI texts.

(1) Direct Adoption of GenAI Text: A portion of participants chose to directly utilize the text generated by GenAI as their own feedback, recognizing its comprehensiveness and advanced nature. As S4 remarked, "GenAI provides English feedback that is quite comprehensive and advanced. I have selected some of the feedback as my own, without adding any personal comments."
(2) Integration of GenAI Text and Personal Insights: When incorporating GenAI-generated texts, participants often blended them with their own thoughts and insights, rather than copying them verbatim. This approach was evident in the statements of S1 and S6, who noted that while AI results could be mechanical, they added their own

ideas to enrich the feedback. S6 further mentioned that if unsatisfied with GenAI's output, they would supplement it with their own comments.
(3) Refinement and Enhancement of GenAI Texts: Recognizing the potential of GenAI's initial feedback as a starting point, participants would then make modifications and improvements to personalize and elevate the quality of their feedback. This was reflected in comments like S1's, who stated that she formulated feedback inspired by GenAI's results, and S2's, who first let GenAI generate preliminary comments, which she then carefully reviewed and refined based on her own understanding and judgment.

### 4.3 Challenges and Opportunities Assessors Encountered While Using GenAI

This section delves into the challenges and opportunities that emerged from the assessors' adoption of GenAI assistance, as revealed through their narratives.

**Limitations of GenAI-assisted Feedback Giving.** When it come to the limitations of GenAI-assisted feedback giving, the participants' responses in the interview highlights two limitations.

(1) Request of clear prompt: The participants generally reported that the accuracy and clarity of clear prompt were crucial when using GenAI to assist in writing comments. Unclear prompt often led to GenAI generating answers that were either off-target or vague. According to S1, "The main issue lied in the prompt. It required multiple attempts and adjustments of my prompt to get the desired answer,". Similarly, S2 expressed frustration with uncertainty around the optimal prompt, stating, "Sometimes I don't know what kind of prompt to input to get satisfactory results, so I need to keep trying and adjusting."
(2) Templated and Unspecific GenAI texts: The participants raised concerns about the tendency of GenAI-generated texts to be overly templated and unspecific. S3 observed, "The comments from GenAI are not specific. Many of the comments for different writings are similar. It feels like it's operating in the background and applying a template," revealing a lack of personalization and tailored feedback. S5 echoed this sentiment, noting that the positivity of the comments can be limiting, stating, "Sometimes, AI only gives positive comments, which I don't find very helpful. I need to know my weaknesses and areas for improvement." Additionally, S5 emphasized the importance of specificity, suggesting, "It would be better if it could directly point out which sentence or part needs to be revised," highlighting the desire for GenAI to provide more direct and actionable guidance.

**Advantages of GenAI-assisted Feedback Giving.** Despite the above-mentioned limitations, the participants indicate that GenAI-assistance substantially saved their time and provided valuable inspiration and professional feedback, enhancing the efficiency and quality of their feedback.

(1) Time-Saving Efficiency: Participants consistently highlighted the substantial time savings achieved through GenAI. S2 attested, "It saved my time and enabled me to provide feedback for more writings in a shorter period of time," while S3 concurred, emphasizing how GenAI helped "quickly find the cutting point for evaluation."

(2) Inspiration and Professional Advice: Beyond time management, GenAI emerged as a source of inspiration and professional guidance. S1 acknowledged the creative spark it provided, stating, "The results provided can bring me inspiration," while S3 praised its ability to elevate feedback through "recommending more advanced words and sentence patterns."
(3) Enhanced Understanding of Complex Texts: Finally, GenAI demonstrated its effectiveness in assisting participants to better comprehend and evaluate intricate language structures. S1 credited GenAI's translation and feedback for correcting her understanding of challenging texts, while S4 highlighted its ability to identify logical issues in peers' writings.

## 5 Discussion and Conclusion

The present study investigated the effect of utilizing GenAI tools to facilitate feedback giving in peer assessment of EFL writing. Three types of GenAI assessor behaviour were noted across the three-month study and labelled as: Self-sufficient Master, Cautious Adopter and Sustained User.

The analysis of the assessors' feedback tentatively indicates that the GenAI-facilitated condition has an impact on improving feedback quality, as evidenced by the feedback focus and the feedback and feedforward strategies employed by the assessors. Post-course interviews revealed that participants primarily sought GenAI assistance during peer assessment due to (English language) difficulties encountered. They strategically utilized GenAI's suggestions in three ways: full adoption, partial incorporation, or modification. Despite acknowledging GenAI's limitations, such as a lack of personalization and potential inaccuracies in the generated feedback, the assessors perceived that it could substantially save time and provide valuable feedback, thereby enhancing efficiency and quality.

These findings indicate that the approach used to measure the nature of feedback provided shows promise and offers an approach to further explore how GenAI technology could integrate into peer assessment processes. This may have a number of direct and indirect positive influences on the quality and effectiveness of the feedback and feedforward provided but this should not be assumed. In addition, as part of the investigation, PeerGrader – a specially developed software application – was used to manage the peer assessment and providing research data and seemed to perform well.

The implications of these findings are potentially important for both educators and researchers. For educators, the results highlight the need for improved training and guidance for learners to effectively learn to integrate GenAI into their peer assessment practices. For researchers, the study highlights the need for further investigation into the optimal ways to integrate GenAI tools into current peer assessment systems and modify GenAI-facilitated peer assessment.

Obviously, the main limitation of this study was a small-scale mixed-methods study into the use of GenAI tools by six undergraduate students who volunteered to participate in three peer assessment tasks each spaced a month apart. While our sample size was small, by triangulating the quantitative objective data of three rounds of peer assessment data with subsequent qualitative data of interviews, our findings did indicate subtle differences of the impact of GenAI usage on facilitated feedback. Future research would benefit from upscaling our initial findings with a larger and more diverse sample population, which is warranted to validate and expand upon the findings.

In conclusion, this study highlights the importance for future GenAI-facilitated peer assessment designs, emphasizing the importance of enhancing the participants' abilities to collaborate with GenAI in providing nuanced and constructive feedback. This preliminary exploration contributes to advancing understanding of GenAI's role in peer assessment, emphasizing both its challenges and the potential benefits of implementation in educational settings, including the long-term effects of GenAI-facilitated peer assessment and integration of different GenAI tools.

**Acknowledgement.** We would like to thank all the participants for making this research possible. This work was supported by the Higher Education Teaching Research and Reform Project of the Guangdong Province (Grant No. JG2021002) and Collaborative Education Project of Industry-University Cooperation of the Ministry of Education (Grant No. 231001282100813).

# Appendix

### Appendix I. Feedback Focus Checklist

| Focus | Description |
|---|---|
| Discourse | • Organization (within paragraphs, within an essay)<br>• Paragraphing (changes to whole paragraphs; creating new paragraphs from existing ones) |
| Sentence | • Sentence components (subject, predicate, object, predicative, attribute, adverbial, complement, appositive, etc.)<br>• Sentence types (simple sentence, compound sentence, and complex sentence)<br>• Temporal forms (present perfect, past perfect, future perfect, past perfect future, present continuous, past continuous, present perfect continuous, past perfect continuous, etc.)<br>• Voice (active voice, passive voice) |
| Lexical | • Vocabulary/word choice (e.g., on the other hand → however; effectively → easily)<br>• Word-form corrections (Pluralization: two piece of chalk → two pieces of chalk; Subject-verb agreement: Everyone have → Everyone has; Verb-tense: I go → I went)<br>• Spelling (including typographical errors) (e.g., thise → these)<br>• Capitalization (e.g., while…, → While…)<br>• Punctuation (add or delete a comma, a period, etc.) |

## Appendix II. Feedback and Feedforward Strategies Checklist

| Strategies | Sub-strategies | Descriptions | Examples |
|---|---|---|---|
| Feedback | General praise | General praise for the reviewed work | Good! |
| | Specific praise | Praise the strengths in the reviewed work | Very good! The example you used is very convincing to demonstrate the environmental changes in China |
| | General criticism | General criticism on the reviewed work | Your essay needs revising |
| | Specific criticism | Directly point out or request clarification for sections that are unclear or difficult to understand | You wrote incomplete sentence, for example, "But in recent years, with the impact of …" |
| Feedforward | Reasoning | Briefly explain a certain knowledge point or grammar point | This article requires telling stories about the past, so pay attention to using the past tense |
| | Exampleing | Give examples to illustrate how to improve | You may try to use more specific words to illustrate your point. For example, refine "get our understanding" as "deepen our understanding" |
| | Direct editing | Help the author edit the expression | You may consider changing "whom" in the first sentence as "whose" |

# References

Adachi, C., Hong-Meng Tai, J., Dawson, P.: Academics' perceptions of the benefits and challenges of self and peer assessment in higher education. Assess. Eval. High. Educ. **43**(2), 294–306 (2018)

Alemdag, E., Yildirim, Z.: Design and development of an online formative peer assessment environment with instructional scaffolds. Educ. Tech. Res. Dev. **70**(4), 1359–1389 (2022)

Alier, M., García-Peñalvo, F., Camba, J.D.: Generative artificial intelligence in education: from deceptive to disruptive. Int. J. Interact. Multimed. Artif. Intell. **8**(5), 5–14 (2024)

Baker, K.M.: Peer assessment as a strategy for improving students' writing process. Act. Learn. High. Educ. **17**(3), 179–192 (2016)

Coleman, C., King, J., Ruth, M.H.: Developing higher-order thinking skills through the use of technology. Access Inform. **54**, 20–26 (2001)

Darvishi, A., Khosravi, H., Sadiq, S., Gašević, D.: Incorporating AI and learning analytics to build trustworthy peer assessment systems. Br. J. Edu. Technol. **53**(4), 844–875 (2022)

Darvishi, A., Khosravi, H., Abdi, S., Sadiq, S., Gašević, D.: Incorporating training, self-monitoring and AI-assistance to improve peer feedback quality. In: Proceedings of the ninth ACM conference on learning@ scale, pp. 35–47 (2022b)

Divjak, B., Rienties, B., Iniesto, F., Vondra, P., Žižak, M.: Flipped classrooms in higher education during the COVID-19 pandemic: findings and future research recommendations. Int. J. Educ. Technol. High. Educ. **19**(1), 9 (2022)

Giannakos, M., et al.: The promise and challenges of generative AI in education. Behav. Inform. Technol. 1–27 (2024)

Gielen, M., De Wever, B.: Scripting the role of assessor and assessee in peer assessment in a wiki environment: Impact on peer feedback quality and product improvement. Comput. Educ. **88**, 370–386 (2015)

Govaerts, J.B., van de Wiel, M.W.J., van der Vleuten, C.P.M.: Quality of feedback following performance assessments: Does assessor expertise matter? Eur. J. Train. Dev. **37**(1), 105–125 (2013)

Hattie, J., Timperley, H.: The power of feedback. Rev. Educ. Res. **77**(1), 81–112 (2007). https://doi.org/10.3102/003465430298487

Hovardas, T., Tsivitanidou, O.E., Zacharia, Z.C.: Peer versus expert feedback: an investigation of the quality of peer feedback among secondary school students. Comput. Educ. **71**, 133–152 (2014)

Kim, J., Yu, S., Detrick, R., Li, N.: Exploring students' perspectives on Generative AI-assisted academic writing. Educ. Inform. Technol. 1–36 (2024)

Kollar, I., Fischer, F.: Peer assessment as collaborative learning: a cognitive perspective. Learn. Instr. **20**(4), 344–348 (2010)

Limna, P., Jakwatanatham, S., Siripipattanakul, S., Kaewpuang, P., Sriboonruang, P.: A review of artificial intelligence (AI) in education during the digital era. Adv. Knowl. Executives **1**(1), 1–9 (2022)

Mendoza, L.B., Ortega, M.P., Hormaza, J.M., Soto, S.V.: Trends the use of Artificial Intelligence techniques for peer assessment. In: Proceedings of the 6th International Conference on Engineering & MIS 2020, pp. 1–7 (2020)

Nelson, G.L., Carson, J.G.: ESL students' perceptions of effectiveness in peer response groups. J. Second. Lang. Writ. **7**(2), 113–131 (1998)

Oliveira, E., Rios, S., Jiang, Z.: AI-powered peer review process: An approach to enhance computer science students' engagement with code review in industry-based subjects. ASCILITE Publications, pp. 184–194 (2023).

Ou, C., Thajchayapong, P., Joyner, D.: Open, Collaborative, and AI-Augmented Peer Assessment: Student Participation, Performance, and Perceptions. In *Proceedings of the Eleventh ACM Conference on Learning@ Scale* (pp. 496–500) (2024, July)

Owoc, M.L., Sawicka, A., Weichbroth, P.: Artificial intelligence technologies in education: benefits, challenges and strategies of implementation. In: Owoc, M.L., Pondel, M. (eds.) AI4KM 2019. IAICT, vol. 599, pp. 37–58. Springer, Cham (2021). https://doi.org/10.1007/978-3-030-85001-2_4

Planas Lladó, A., et al.: Student perceptions of peer assessment: an interdisciplinary study. Assess. Eval. High. Educ. **39**(5), 592–610 (2014)

Rienties, B., Domingue, J., Duttaroy, S., Herodotou, C., Tessarolo, F., Whitelock, D.: What distance learning students want from an AI Digital Assistant. Distance Educ. 1–17 (2024)

Strijbos, J.W., Sluijsmans, D.: Unravelling peer assessment: methodological, functional, and conceptual developments. Learn. Instr. **20**(4), 265–269 (2010)

Suzuki, M.: Japanese learners' self revisions and peer revisions of their written compositions in English. TESOL Q. **42**(2), 209–233 (2008)

Topping, K.J.: Peer assessment. Theory Into Pract. **48**(1), 20–27 (2009)

Topping, K.J.: Using Peer Assessment to Inspire Reflection and Learning. Routledge, New York and London (2018)

Topping, K.J.: Digital peer assessment in school teacher education and development: a systematic review. Res. Papers Educ. **38**(3), 472–498 (2021). https://doi.org/10.1080/02671522.2021.1961301

Topping, K.J., Ehly, S.: Peer Assisted Learning. Erlbaum, Mahwah, NJ (1998)

Van den Bos, A.H., Tan, E.: Effects of anonymity on online peer review in second-language writing. Comput. Educ. **142**, 103638 (2019)

Yu, S., Lee, I.: Peer feedback in second language writing (2005–2014). Lang. Teach. **49**(04), 461–493 (2016)

Ware, P., O'Dowd, R.: Peer feedback on language form in telecollaboration. Lang. Learn. Technol. **12**(1), 43–63 (2008)

Weaver, R.L., Cotrell, H.W.: Peer evaluation: a case study. Innov. High. Educ. **11**, 25–39 (1986)

# Institutional Strategies and Practices

# Assessing College Students' Peer Feedback Literacy

Wenyi Chen(✉) and Linlin Jia

Zhongkai University of Agriculture and Engineering, No. 501, Zhongkai Road, Guangzhou, Guangdong Province, China
`winniecwy@126.com`

**Abstract.** Peer feedback activities encompass both the provision and reception of feedback. This research delves into the realm of peer feedback literacy among first-year undergraduate students enrolled in an EFL writing course and try to evaluate peer feedback literacy through four dimensions: feedback-related knowledge and skills (FKA), cooperative learning ability (CLA), appreciation of peer feedback (APF), and willingness to participate (WP). The study enlisted 306 participants from a Chinese university and employed a mixed-method approach involving both descriptive and quantitative analyses. Findings indicate a commendable level of peer feedback literacy overall, with students exhibiting favorable self-assessment regarding the reception and provision of feedback. Moreover, positive associations were identified among each dimension, implying that forthcoming pedagogical interventions should prioritize the enhancement of students' attitudes and conduct to foster heightened engagement and evaluation precision.

**Keywords:** formative assessment · college students · peer feedback literacy · EFL writing

## 1 Introduction

Feedback stands as a foundational pillar in augmenting students' learning processes (Hattie and Timperley, 2007). Student feedback literacy, a pivotal element of the learner-centered feedback model, has garnered increasing attention from various academics (Zhe et al., 2023; Zhan, 2021; Molloy, Boud, and Henderson, 2020; Carless and Boud, 2018; Sutton, 2012). Zhe et al. (2023) introduced peer feedback literacy as the cognitive and attitudinal proficiencies essential for effective involvement in diverse peer feedback exercises. The constituent elements of student feedback literacy have recently sparked intense scholarly discourse (e.g., Carless and Boud, 2018; Malecka, Boud, and Carless, 2020; Wood, 2021; Yu and Liu, 2021).

Providing feedback to peers, as well as receiving and utilizing peer feedback, poses cognitive and socio-emotional challenges for students (McConlogue, 2015; Molloy, Boud, and Henderson, 2020; Nicol, 2010; Nicol, Thomson, and Breslin, 2014). There exists a burgeoning body of literature advocating for the integration of feedback literacy within specific domains like academic writing (Winstone, Balloo, and Carless, 2022; Yu and Liu, 2021; Li and Han, 2022). This research conceptualizes peer feedback literacy as students' competencies and attitudes in delivering and receiving peer feedback and it endeavors to investigate college students' peer feedback literacy in an EFL writing context.

## 2 Literature Review

Expanding on existing research, peer feedback literacy generally consists of four fundamental dimensions or factors: feedback-related knowledge and skills (FKA), cooperative learning ability (CLA), appreciation of peer feedback (APF), and willingness to participate (WP). This section will delve into the current research findings and limitations within these four perspectives.

### 2.1 Feedback-Related Knowledge and Abilities (FKA) in Peer Feedback Literacy

Feedback-related knowledge and abilities (FKA) is integral to fostering effective feedback exchanges among students. Drawing from Social Cognitive Theory, where learning is influenced by observation and modeling, and Self-Determination Theory, emphasizing intrinsic motivation, FKA development in peer feedback literacy thrives on structured training programs and peer modeling.

Studies by Topping (1998) advocate for structured training to enhance specific feedback skills, while research by Van Den Berg et al. (2006) underscores the significance of peer modeling in FKA development. These strategies equip students with the necessary skills to provide detailed, relevant, and actionable feedback, as demonstrated by Nicol and Macfarlane-Dick (2006). Students with higher FKA not only offer quality feedback but also exhibit improved self-regulatory skills, allowing them to reflect on and utilize feedback effectively (Carless, 2011). FKA plays an important role in enhancing feedback quality, promoting self-regulation, and ultimately supporting students in cultivating essential feedback skills for meaningful learning interactions.

### 2.2 Cooperative Learning Ability (CLA) in Peer Feedback Literacy

Cooperative learning ability (CLA) is vital in fostering collaborative skills and enriching feedback interactions within peer feedback literacy. Grounded in Social Interdependence Theory (Johnson and Johnson, 2009) and Community of Practice concepts (Lave and Wenger, 1991), CLA development in peer feedback settings is essential for effective collaboration and learning.

To enhance CLA, engaging students in collaborative tasks and promoting peer collaboration through structured exercises are key strategies. Research by Slavin (1990) and Topping (2005) highlights the benefits of collaborative tasks and peer assessment activities in cultivating cooperative learning skills. Developed CLA contributes to improved feedback quality, as students offer more insightful feedback for enhanced learning outcomes (Van den Bossche et al., 2006). Moreover, CLA promotes critical thinking by stimulating students' ability to analyze feedback effectively and apply it to their own work (Webb, 2009). Therefore, fostering cooperative learning ability (CLA) in peer feedback literacy environments is crucial for enhancing collaborative skills, improving feedback quality, and nurturing critical thinking among students.

## 2.3 Willingness to Participate (WP) in Peer Feedback Literacy

Willingness to participate (WP) is a pivotal factor in peer feedback literacy, shaping student engagement and the quality of feedback interactions. Drawing from Self-Determination Theory and Social Exchange Theory, understanding students' intrinsic motivation and reciprocal relationships is key to fostering WP in peer feedback settings. Creating a supportive peer environment that values constructive feedback and providing structured training on feedback processes are crucial for developing WP.

Scholars like Falchikov and Goldfinch (2000) emphasize nurturing a positive feedback culture to enhance students' willingness to engage, while studies by Carless and Boud (2018) underscore the impact of feedback training programs on boosting participation. Higher levels of WP lead to increased engagement and richer discussions in peer feedback exchanges, ultimately contributing to improved learning outcomes (Topping, 1998). Students demonstrating strong WP benefit from diverse perspectives and reflective practices, enhancing their overall learning experience (Nicol, 2010). WP is essential for meaningful student engagement, quality feedback interactions, and enhanced learning outcomes.

## 2.4 Appreciation of Peer Feedback (APF) in Peer Feedback Literacy

Grounded in Social Learning Theory and Attribution Theory, the appreciation of peer feedback (APF) emphasizes observational learning, social reinforcement, and attributing value to peer feedback based on its credibility. Encouraging feedback reflection and establishing peer feedback norms are key strategies to nurture APF.

Research by Hattie and Timperley (2007) underscores the importance of feedback reflection in enhancing student learning outcomes, while studies by Boud and Molloy (2012) highlight the role of peer feedback norms in cultivating APF. A high level of APF enhances trust, collaboration, and feedback quality among peers (Falchikov and Goldfinch, 2000), empowering students in the feedback process and fostering personal growth (Carless and Boud, 2018). It plays a vital role in shaping a positive feedback culture, trust, and collaborative learning experiences within peer feedback literacy.

In previous literature, emphasis has been placed on the aforementioned four dimensions of Peer Feedback Literacy. Nevertheless, qualitative investigations into peer feedback literacy across these dimensions are still scarce. To our knowledge, Zhe et al. (2023) were the first to introduce and validate a peer feedback literacy scale designed to evaluate this proficiency. This scale serves as a pragmatic instrument for educators and researchers to assess students' aptitude in peer feedback. Leveraging this tool, the present study delves into the peer feedback literacy of first-year undergraduate students enrolled in an EFL writing course.

## 3 Research Design

Drawing from previous studies (Sutton, 2012; Carless and Boud, 2018; Joughin et al., 2021; Ketonen, Nieminen, and Hähkiöniemi, 2020; Han and Xu, 2021; Molloy, Boud, and Henderson, 2020; Song, 2022; Yu, Zhang, and Liu, 2022; Zhan, 2022a; Zhan, 2022b;

Liang, 2019; Man, Kong, and Chau, 2022), with particular emphasis on the work of Zhe et al. (2023), this study constructs the aforementioned research framework (refer to Fig. 1).

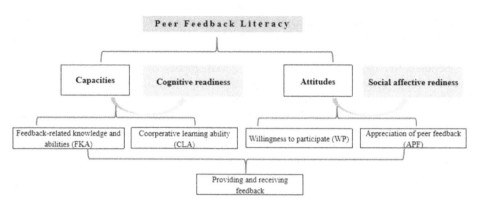

**Fig. 1.** The present research framework

It posits that peer feedback literacy encapsulates both the provision and reception of feedback. Four distinct PFL dimensions underpin these aspects: feedback-related knowledge and abilities (FKA), willingness to participate (WP), cooperative learning ability (CLA), and appreciation of peer feedback (APF). FKA and CLA represent cognitive readiness through capacities such as knowledge and skills, while WP and APF reflect social-affective readiness through attitudes.

In a writing workshop, students demonstrate FKA by providing specific, constructive feedback on their peers' drafts, focusing on areas such as structure, clarity, and supporting evidence. They showcase their ability to discern strengths and weaknesses in writing and offer actionable suggestions for improvement.

During a group project, students with high CLA effectively collaborate with team members, actively listening to diverse perspectives, contributing ideas, delegating tasks, and ensuring everyone's input is valued. They demonstrate effective communication, coordination, and mutual support within the team.

In a classroom discussion, students with high WP actively engage by asking questions, sharing insights, and participating in group activities. They demonstrate enthusiasm for learning, contribute meaningfully to discussions, and take initiative in collaborative tasks, fostering a dynamic and interactive learning environment.

After receiving peer feedback on an essay, a student shows APF by reflecting on the comments with an open mind, acknowledging the valuable insights provided, and using the feedback to revise and enhance their work. They recognize the benefits of peer input in improving their writing skills. All the above four dimensions pertain to the processes of providing and receiving peer feedback.

## 3.1 Research Questions

To gain a comprehensive understanding of college students' peer feedback literacy across the four dimensions within an EFL writing course, the following research questions were formulated:

1. What is the current status of students' comprehensive peer feedback literacy across the four scales based on the questionnaire results?
2. Are there correlations among students' peer feedback literacy levels across the four scales?

## 3.2 Participants

The study comprised 306 randomly selected undergraduate students from a Chinese university enrolled in an EFL course. These first-year non-English majors, had finished College English I in the first semester. Engaging in two computer-mediated peer feedback activities in EFL classes, they previously experienced peer feedback. Pre-survey, the instructor guided a feedback exercise in an EFL writing class, followed by survey completion. The questionnaire was shared via WeChat, with instructors explaining research goals and confidentiality guidelines. The participants were on average, around 19 years old.

## 3.3 Research Instrument

The research instrument utilized in this study is a questionnaire derived from the Peer Feedback Literacy Scale Questionnaire (PFLS-Q, Zhe et al., 2023). Initially comprising 20 items distributed across four scales: feedback-related knowledge and abilities (FKA, 7 items, $\alpha = 0.89$), cooperative learning ability (CLA, 4 items, $\alpha = 0.80$), appreciation of peer feedback (APF, 4 items, $\alpha = 0.81$), and willingness to participate (WP, 5 items, $\alpha = 0.88$). The questionnaire underwent adaptation and translation into Chinese by the authors to facilitate comprehension and enhance validation for EFL learners. Prior to the investigation, the questionnaire underwent the consolidation of items with similar functions, deletion of certain items, resulting in a final questionnaire comprising 18 items (refer to Table 1).

**Table 1.** Questionnaire adapted from SOL-Q-R

| PFL-Q scales | Phases | No. of items | Items |
|---|---|---|---|
| feedback-related knowledge and abilities (FKA) | Capacities (Cognitive readiness) | 7 | 8, 13, 14, 15 17, 26, 30 |
| cooperative learning ability (CLA) | | 5 | 11, 20, 22, 28,31 |
| appreciation of peer feedback (APF) | Attitudes (social affective readiness) | 4 | 3, 5, 25, 29 |
| willingness to participate (WP) | | 4 | 2, 9, 12, 18 |

The students were directed to assess their conduct in the peer feedback activity using a 7-point Likert scale (1 = Strongly Disagree to 7 = Strongly Agree).

## 3.4 Data Collection and Analyses

An online questionnaire tool, Wenjuan Wang (https://www.wenjuan.com), was employed to administer the questionnaire and facilitate data collection. The study utilized a mixed-method approach encompassing descriptive analysis and quantitative analysis. Additionally, a Pearson correlation analysis was conducted to examine the relationships among the four scales of peer feedback literacy. Statistical methods such as M-score and Pearson correlation analysis were applied in the study.

# 4 Results and Discussion

## 4.1 Overall Performance of Students' PFL

The statistics outlined in Table 2 delineate the students' scores in the Peer Feedback Literacy Scales (PFLS). Results indicate that the participants' overall peer feedback literacy is good.

**Table 2.** The minimum, maximum, mean and standard deviation of the students' scores in PFLS.

| PFLQ scales | Min | Max | M | SD |
| --- | --- | --- | --- | --- |
| Global Scale | 1.06 | 7.00 | 4.98 | 0.95 |
| Feedback-related knowledge and abilities (FKA) | 1.17 | 7.00 | 4.62 | 0.96 |
| Cooperative learning ability (CLA) | 1.00 | 7.00 | 4.86 | 1.12 |
| Appreciation of peer feedback (APF) | 1.00 | 7.00 | 5.13 | 1.23 |
| Willingness to participate (WP) | 1.00 | 7.00 | 5.47 | 1.13 |

The Global Scale ranges from 1.06 to 7.00, with a mean score of 4.98 and a standard deviation of 0.95. In terms of feedback-related knowledge and abilities (FKA), scores spanned from 1.17 to 7.00, with a mean of 4.62 and a standard deviation of 0.96, demonstrating that the majority of students exhibit proficient skills in providing and assessing feedback. Within cooperative learning ability (CLA), scores ranged between 1.00 and 7.00, with an average score of 4.86 and a standard deviation of 1.12, indicating that most students hold a favorable self-assessment regarding their capacity to receive peer evaluations and offer review feedback.

Appreciation of peer feedback (APF) scores fell within the 1.00 to 7.00 range, with a mean score of 5.13 and a standard deviation of 1.23. Students generally perceive participation in peer review activities as beneficial for enhancing English proficiency and cultivating interest in learning the language. Willingness to participate (WP) scores ranged from 1.00 to 7.00, with a mean score of 5.47 and a standard deviation of 1.13. This distribution indicates that a significant portion of participants demonstrate heightened enthusiasm for engagement. Factors influencing students' willingness to participate and engage in review processes as outlined in the study by Dörnyei & Ushioda (2013) encompass intrinsic motivation, self-efficacy beliefs, goal orientation, interest in the subject matter, perceived activity value, teacher-student relationship, and classroom atmosphere. These factors likely contribute to the observed high levels of WP in this investigation.

## 4.2 Students' Level in the Four Scales

### 4.2.1 Over All Performance

Utilizing descriptive statistics, Fig. 2 displays box plots illustrating the overall peer feedback literacy and its four factors in the current study. Box plots were preferred over bar graphs due to skewed distributions present in some scales, revealing intriguing patterns within specific segments of the distributions.

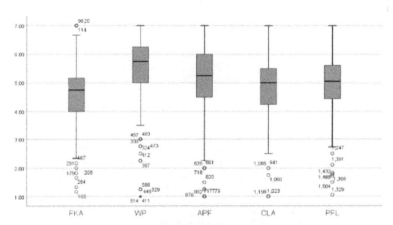

**Fig. 2.** The boxplot of overall peer feedback literacy and its four factors in the present study

Figure 2 illustrates the interquartile range with a median line, where the bars represent the full range excluding outliers, and the circles and asterisks denote statistical outliers and extreme outliers (each outlier is labeled with a corresponding case ID). Boxplots were selected over bar graphs due to skewed distributions in some scales, revealing intriguing patterns across various segments of the distributions as scrutinized by different researchers. Willingness to participate exhibited the highest values, with students' scores typically ranging from 5 to 6.25 in the WP dimension. This discovery is consistent with the results documented in Johnson & Johnson's study (2009), which emphasized the positive influence of cooperative learning on student interactions and academic achievements. It underscores the pivotal role of cooperative learning behaviors in shaping feedback provision skills. While the other scales displayed positive yet more moderate values between 4.75 and 5.2. Overall, students expressed greater willingness and positive attitudes towards peer feedback but demonstrated relatively lower levels of proficiency in knowledge and abilities associated with peer feedback, aligning with the findings observed in Zhe et al.'s (2023) study.

By juxtaposing the findings of Zhe et al. (2023) (refer to Fig. 3) with the outcomes of this study (refer to Fig. 2), a more profound insight into the performance of EFL writing learners is attained. Notably, despite employing different rating scales (a 6-point scale in Zhe et al. and a 7-point scale in this study), both investigations unveiled similar trends. This consistency underscores recurring patterns intrinsic to the EFL writing learning process.

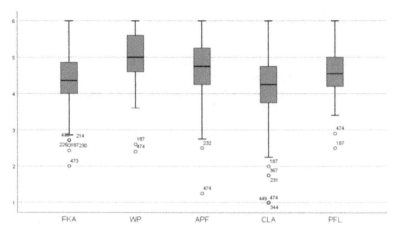

**Fig. 3.** The boxplot of overall peer feedback literacy and its four factors in Zhe et al.'s study

Across both studies, congruent trends were observed in the overall peer feedback literacy and its constituent scales—willingness to participate (WP), appreciation of peer feedback (APF), feedback-related knowledge and abilities (FKA), and cooperative learning ability (CLA). This confluence implies shared developmental pathways among EFL writing learners in these pivotal domains, irrespective of their backgrounds. Particularly, both inquiries highlighted WP as the most proficient domain for students, closely trailed by APF, underscoring the significance of adept writing skills and autonomous learning strategies for EFL learners. This underscores the necessity for educators to accentuate these facets when formulating instructional strategies and materials.

Nonetheless, disparities exist, notably in feedback perception (FKA) and cognitive load awareness (CLA) performances. While Zhe et al. (2023) identified superior FKA over CLA, this study revealed the converse, with CLA exhibiting superior performance over FKA. These variations may arise from diverse factors including students' individual backgrounds, learning milieu, and pedagogical approaches employed by instructors.

Remarkably, the students in this study excelled in CLA. Rooted in cognitive load theory (Sweller, 1988), which posits that learners have finite cognitive capacities during learning, effective management of cognitive load emerges as a pivotal skill for learners. The exemplary performance of students in CLA underscores their adeptness in adjusting learning strategies when confronted with intricate learning tasks, thus optimizing learning outcomes. Through the comparative analysis of Zhe et al. and the current study, we get implications for shaping EFL writing teaching practices, particularly in tailoring teaching strategies to cater to students' specific requirements.

### 4.2.2  A Detailed Look into FKA

Employing the statistical methods of M-score, the survey captured items with mean scores below 4.5 and above 5.5 from statistical analysis. The data indicates that all these identified items are situated within the dimension of feedback-related knowledge and abilities (FKA), as depicted in Table 3.

**Table 3.** The identified items with mean scores lower than 4.5, and above 5.5 (N = 306)

| Items | Min | Max | Mean | SD |
|---|---|---|---|---|
| Feedback-related knowledge and abilities (FKA) | | | | |
| 1. I am able to offer specific revision solutions to peers' writing | 1 | 7 | 4.284 | 1.242 |
| 2. I have the knowledge of how to provide valuable comments | 1 | 7 | 4.408 | 1.233 |
| 3. I have enough linguistic knowledge to participate in peer feedback activities | 1 | 7 | 4.327 | 1.227 |
| 4. I am responsible for the feedback that I provide to peers | 1 | 7 | 5.533 | 1.281 |
| 5. I am meticulous in dealing with the feedback that I have received | 1 | 7 | 5.51 | 1.247 |

Three items within FKA scoring below 4.5 underscore crucial deficiencies in students' feedback capabilities. The first item exposes a lack of confidence in providing tailored revision suggestions to peers, indicating a shortfall in offering specific and beneficial feedback essential for effective peer review processes. Similarly, the second item reveals students' perceived inadequacy in delivering insightful comments to peers, suggesting room for growth in providing substantive critiques that enhance peers' writing quality. Furthermore, the third item highlights a perceived insufficiency in linguistic knowledge necessary for active participation in peer feedback activities, potentially hindering students' ability to provide comprehensive feedback on language-related aspects of written work.

Conversely, the robust performance of two standout items scoring above 5.5 in FKA reflects exemplary strengths among students in certain aspects of feedback provision. The high mean scores signify a strong sense of accountability and meticulousness in delivering and handling feedback within peer interactions. Students' elevated levels of responsibility and conscientiousness in feedback provision, coupled with their meticulous approach to processing received feedback, demonstrate a deep commitment to leveraging feedback for learning and academic enhancement. These positive attitudes and behaviors not only enhance the effectiveness and value of peer feedback exchanges but also foster a culture of support and continuous improvement among learners.

### 4.3 Correlation Between the Four Scales

A Pearson correlation study is conducted to examine the relationship among the four scales of the PFL based on the survey result of the questionnaire.

**Table 4.** Correlation between the four Scales of PFL measured.

| Scale | FKA | WP | CLA | APF |
|---|---|---|---|---|
| FKA | 1 | 0.574 | 0.635 | 0.603 |
| WP |  | 1 | 0.683 | 0.708 |
| CLA |  |  | 1 | 0.803 |
| APF |  |  |  | 1 |

Table 4 presents the correlations among the four dimensions of peer feedback literacy, elucidating the interplay between feedback-related knowledge and abilities (FKA), willingness to participate (WP), cooperative learning ability (CLA), and appreciation of peer feedback (APF).

Positive correlations were observed between each pair of scales, with the strongest correlation identified between CLA and APF, followed by WP and APF, then WP and CLA. FKA exhibited positive correlations with WP ($r = 0.574$), CLA ($r = 0.635$), and APF ($r = 0.603$), indicating moderate correlations. Similarly, WP displayed positive correlations with CLA ($r = 0.683$) and APF ($r = 0.708$), reflecting stronger associations.

Moreover, CLA demonstrated the most robust positive correlation with APF ($r = 0.803$). These correlation coefficients also suggest that students with higher levels of feedback-related knowledge and abilities tend to also showcase increased willingness to participate, cooperative learning proficiency, and appreciation of peer feedback within peer feedback literacy.

## 5 Conclusion and Implications

This study assumes that peer feedback literacy included both the providing and the receiving aspects. While strengths were evident in aspects like accountability and meticulousness in feedback handling, weaknesses were identified in providing tailored revision suggestions and delivering valuable comments.

### 5.1 Potential Challenges Students May Encounter

First, they may receive biased or inaccurate feedback. Students may receive feedback that is subjective, inaccurate, or biased due to varying levels of understanding, preferences, or relationships between peers. This can lead to confusion and hinder the usefulness of feedback for improvement.

Secondly, peers may struggle to provide specific, constructive criticism, opting for vague or overly positive feedback to avoid conflict or discomfort. Without actionable suggestions, students may find it difficult to make meaningful revisions.

Thirdly, students may face challenges in receiving feedback objectively, especially if it contradicts their own perceptions or challenges their ideas. Emotional reactions such as defensiveness or skepticism can impede their ability to benefit from constructive feedback.

## 5.2 Research Implication

The robust correlations between cooperative learning abilities (CLA) and appreciation for peer feedback (APF) suggest that proficient cooperative learners value peer feedback. This aligns with research by Slavin (1990), indicating how cooperative learning can boost academic performance through collaborative learning and peer engagement. Understanding these links offers insights into peer feedback literacy's complex dynamics within education.

Identifying disparities in feedback-related knowledge and abilities (FKA) sheds light on areas for improving students' peer feedback literacy. Targeted interventions can enhance revising skills, comment-giving abilities, and language proficiency, crucial for elevating peer feedback quality. Training programs can effectively develop these competencies, as suggested by Price et al. (2010).

Students' proactive attitudes in managing feedback highlight the need for fostering responsibility and attentiveness in feedback processes. Addressing deficiencies in feedback provision and comment-giving skills is key to enhancing peer feedback literacy and fostering a culture of effective interactions and improved learning outcomes. Tailored training can strengthen feedback-related competencies, refining peer feedback practices and enriching the academic experience.

Exploring the intricate nature of peer feedback literacy can aid educators in optimizing teaching methods to enhance cooperative learning and promote peer feedback appreciation. This can create a supportive educational environment conducive to student development. Future research can focus on assessing the longitudinal impact of interventions and innovative strategies to promote effective feedback exchanges in diverse educational contexts.

## 6 Limitation

The study's limitations include a homogenous sample from a single Chinese university. To ensure broader insight into peer feedback literacy among university students, future research should diversify participants across cultural backgrounds and academic levels. Furthermore, incorporating behavioral assessments can validate self-perceptions of peer feedback competencies, bridging empirical gaps in understanding.

## References

Boud, D., Molloy, E.: Rethinking models of feedback for learning: the challenge of design. Assess. Eval. High. Educ. **37**(3), 279–290 (2012)

Carless, D.: From testing to productive student learning: Implementing formative assessment in Confucian heritage cultures. Routledge (2011)

Carless, D., Boud, D.: The development of student feedback literacy: enabling uptake of feedback. Assess. Eval. High. Educ. **43**(8), 1315–1325 (2018)

Dörnyei, Z., Ushioda, E.: Teaching and Researching Motivation. Routledge (2013)

Falchikov, N., Goldfinch, J.: Student peer assessment in higher education: a meta-analysis comparing peer and teacher marks. Rev. Educ. Res. **70**(3), 287–322 (2000)

Han, J., Xu, L.: Peer feedback literacy in EFL writing: a case study of Chinese university students. Asian J. Appl. Linguist. **8**(2), 165–183 (2021)

Hattie, J., Timperley, H.: The power of feedback. Rev. Educ. Res. **77**(1), 81–112 (2007)

Johnson, D.W., Johnson, R.T.: An educational psychology success story: social interdependence theory and cooperative learning. Educ. Res. **38**(5), 365–379 (2009)

Joughin, G., et al.: Exploring peer feedback literacy in undergraduate students. Stud. High. Educ. **46**(6), 1123–1140 (2021)

Ketonen, J., Nieminen, P., Hähkiöniemi, M.: Peer feedback literacy in practice: insights from a computer science course. IEEE Trans. Educ. **63**(3), 194–201 (2020)

Lave, J., Wenger, E.: Situated learning: Legitimate peripheral participation. Cambridge University Press (1991). https://doi.org/10.1017/CBO9780511815355

Li, L., Han, J.: Peer feedback literacy in EFL writing: a case study of college students. J. Second. Lang. Writ. **51**, 100822 (2022)

Liang, M.: Exploring the impact of peer feedback literacy on academic performance: a longitudinal study. Educ. Psychol. **41**(5), 623–639 (2019)

Malecka, K., Boud, D., Carless, D.: Understanding and developing student feedback literacy: a collaborative approach. Teach. High. Educ. **25**(3), 321–337 (2020)

Man, Y., Kong, Q., Chau, K.: Peer feedback literacy development in a virtual classroom: a case study. Comput. Educ. **170**, 104249 (2022)

McConlogue, T.: Challenges in providing and utilizing peer feedback: a cognitive and socio-emotional perspective. J. Educ. Psychol. **110**(3), 487–502 (2015)

Molloy, E., Boud, D., Henderson, M.: Peer feedback dynamics: understanding the complexities of giving and receiving feedback. Stud. High. Educ. **45**(7), 1358–1374 (2020)

Nicol, D.J., Macfarlane-Dick, D.: Formative assessment and self-regulated learning: a model and seven principles of good feedback practice. Stud. High. Educ. **31**(2), 199–218 (2006)

Nicol, D.: From monologue to dialogue: improving written feedback processes in mass higher education. Assess. Eval. High. Educ. **35**(5), 501–517 (2010)

Nicol, D., Thomson, A., Breslin, C.: Rethinking feedback practices in higher education: a transformative model. High. Educ. Res. Dev. **33**(5), 1098–1112 (2014)

Price, M., Handley, K., Millar, J., O'Donovan, B.: Feedback: all that effort, but what is the effect? Assess. Eval. High. Educ. **35**(3), 277–289 (2010)

Slavin, R. E. (1990). Cooperative Learning: Theory, Research, and Practice

Song, Y.: Integrating peer feedback literacy into language learning: a conceptual framework. Lang. Teach. Res. **26**(1), 78–97 (2022)

Sutton, P.: Enhancing feedback practices in higher education. Assess. Eval. High. Educ. **37**(3), 321–334 (2012)

Sweller, J.: Cognitive load during problem solving: Effects on learning. Cogn. Sci. **12**(2), 257–285 (1988)

Topping, K.: Peer assessment between students in colleges and universities. Rev. Educ. Res. **68**(3), 249–276 (1998)

Topping, K.: Trends in peer learning. Educ. Psychol. **25**(6), 631–645 (2005)

Van den Berg, I., Admiraal, W., Pilot, A.: Design principles and outcomes of peer assessment in higher education. Stud. High. Educ. **31**(3), 341–356 (2006)

Van den Bossche, P., Gijselaers, W.H., Segers, M., Kirschner, P.A.: Social and cognitive factors driving teamwork in collaborative learning environments: team learning beliefs and behaviors. Small Group Res. **37**(5), 490–521 (2006)

Webb, N.M.: The teacher's role in promoting collaborative dialogue in the classroom. Br. J. Educ. Psychol. **79**(1), 1–28 (2009)

Winstone, N., Balloo, K., Carless, D.: Integrating feedback literacy in academic writing: a practical guide for educators. Assess. Matters **14**(2), 27–41 (2022)

Wood, R.: Feedback literacy in practice: strategies for enhancing feedback engagement. Stud. High. Educ. **46**(9), 1703–1718 (2021)

Yu, C., Liu, S.: Enhancing feedback literacy in academic contexts: strategies for educators. Educ. Assess. Eval. Account. **34**(1), 87–104 (2021)

Yu, C., Zhang, H., Liu, S.: Peer feedback literacy: an investigation into students' perspectives. Assess. Eval. High. Educ. **47**(2), 324–341 (2022)

Zhan, Q.: Understanding the role of feedback in enhancing student learning. J. Educ. Psychol. **113**(2), 314–328 (2021)

Zhan, L.: Developing feedback literacy through structured training programs: lessons learned from a business school. Educ. Assess. Eval. Account. **34**(3), 489–506 (2022)

Zhan, L.: Peer feedback literacy in cross-disciplinary collaboration: a case study of engineering students. J. Eng. Educ. **211**(4), 567–582 (2022)

Dong, Z., Gao, Y., Schunn, C.D.: Assessing students' peer feedback literacy in writing: scale development and validation. Assess. Eval. High. Educ. (2023). https://doi.org/10.1080/02602938.2023.2175781

# The Relationship Between Mentor Role and Teachers' Practical Knowledge in the Process of Mentor-Apprentice Dialogue – Based on Epistemic Network Analysis

Yating Jin[1], Yaxuan Wang[1], and Ling Chen[1,2](✉)

[1] Faculty of Education, Beijing Normal University, Beijing, China
yaxuanwang@mail.bnu.edu.cn, chenling@bnu.edu.cn
[2] Advanced Innovation Center Future Education, Beijing Normal University, Beijing, China

**Abstract.** This study examines the impact of mentor roles on teachers' practical knowledge generation during mentor-apprentice dialogues, focusing on differences in cognitive network structures across mentoring styles. Using Epistemic Network Analysis (ENA), the study reveals that strategy knowledge and context knowledge play central roles in the development of practical knowledge, while self-knowledge is underdeveloped. The research highlights the importance of integrating expert knowledge transmission with novice teachers' introspection in professional development and provides empirical support for refining mentoring approaches to ensure balanced and effective learning experiences for novice educators.

**Keywords:** teachers' seminar · mentor roles · teachers' practical knowledge · epistemic network analysis

## 1 Introduction

New teachers often face significant challenges in their first few years, particularly in areas such as classroom management and questioning techniques. This period is crucial for their long-term professional development, necessitating various forms of support to help them transition into their roles Zhong et al. (2023). Effective teacher development requires structured training, with the teacher-apprentice model providing an essential framework. Under the guidance of experienced mentors, novice teachers can enhance their professional skills, teaching strategies, and classroom management.

Mentorship, particularly in the form of seminars, accelerates the transition from theory to practice by facilitating mutual learning, experience sharing, and reflective practice. Mentor teachers play different roles in these seminars, significantly influencing the development of novice teachers' practical knowledge. This knowledge, derived from teaching practice, includes understanding content, addressing student needs, and applying effective teaching strategies.

The role of online one-on-one interactions in generating practical knowledge has become increasingly relevant. Cognitive network analysis offers insights into how knowledge is developed through mentor-apprentice interactions, aiding teachers in handling complex classroom situations. By analyzing seminar dialogues, this study explores how different mentoring styles shape the generation of practical knowledge through feedback, demonstration, and reflection.

## 2 Literature Review

### 2.1 The Apprenticeship

The teacher-apprentice model plays a critical role in novice teacher development by offering structured mentoring and opportunities for professional growth Carmi and Tamir (2023). Mentor teachers transfer practical knowledge and classroom management skills, while novices internalize these through dialogue and feedback Jin et al. (2021). This process enhances critical thinking, adaptability, and teaching efficacy Hennissen et al. (2008), while reducing anxiety. Effective mentoring depends on mentor selection, interaction quality, and the ability to foster reflective practices.

Mentor-apprentice dialogues are key to understanding mentoring dynamics. Research has shown that mentor feedback significantly impacts novice teachers' instructional readiness and career development Kuhn et al. (2024). Mentors' roles vary depending on their mentoring strategies and the needs of the novice teachers, influencing their professional growth Carmi (2024).

### 2.2 Mentor Roles' in Teacher Professional Development

Hennissen's MERID (MEntor Roles In Dialogues) Model categorizes mentors into four roles (seeing Fig. 1): Imperator (high directive, active input), Initiator (high directive, reactive input), Advisor (low directive, active input), and Encourager (low directive, reactive input) Crasborn et al. (2011). These roles reflect varying levels of guidance and input in mentor-apprentice interactions, which are essential for adjusting to novice teachers' evolving needs. Research suggests that adapting mentor roles to individual teacher requirements leads to more effective professional development Beek et al. (2019). However, there is a lack of performance-based assessments to objectively evaluate the effectiveness of these mentoring strategies Michos and Petko (2024).

### 2.3 Teachers' Practical Knowledge

Practical knowledge, deeply explored in educational research, is central to teacher growth. Elbaz (1983). Identified five domains of this knowledge: self, environment, subject matter, curriculum development, and teaching. Clandinin and Connelly (1987) emphasize the importance of personal experiences and reflection in shaping practical knowledge, while Chen (2003) expanded this to include educational beliefs, self-knowledge, strategic knowledge, and critical reflection.

This knowledge is crucial for teachers' professional growth, particularly for novices, and distinguishes expert teachers from others. Mentorship allows novice teachers to acquire and adapt expert knowledge, fostering their professional development Nielsen et al. (2022) but there is still a need for further in-depth discussion and research on how the specific mentoring role of the mentor teacher in the dialogue affects the development of novice teachers' practical knowledge and how these interactions contribute to the improvement of teaching practice.

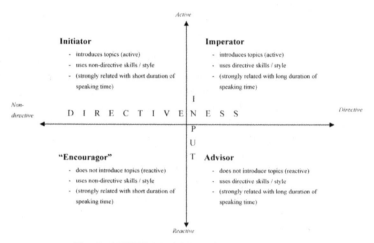

**Fig. 1.** MERID Model Hennissen et al. (2008).

### 2.4 Research Question

Existing research highlights the importance of mentor-apprentice dialogues in teacher development, particularly in how mentor roles influence novice teachers' acquisition of practical knowledge. This study aims to explore the relationship between different mentoring styles and the generation of practical knowledge in novice teachers. Therefore, the following research questions are proposed:

(1) Are there differences in practical knowledge produced between teachers in different mentoring roles?
(2) How do differences in teachers' practical knowledge generation manifest in different mentoring roles?

## 3 Research Design

### 3.1 Research Context and Participants

This study was conducted in City B, which launched an AI and big data-powered online platform to enhance teacher training and offer tailored professional development. The two-month program involved 146 novice teachers from remote districts and experienced mentors from urban areas, many of whom were award-winning educators. These participants engaged in one-on-one online interactions to address common teaching challenges, such as curriculum design and classroom questioning. To investigate variations in novice teachers' practical knowledge under various mentoring roles, we used Purposive Sampling to select workshop dialogues reflecting different mentoring styles.

### 3.2 Coding Framework

Dialogues were coded in accordance with the MERID model. Transcribed seminar dialogues yielded 986 data pieces, from which 745 meaningful segments were analyzed, averaging 30–60 min each, to examine practice-based knowledge. We adopted and adapted Chen Xiangming's framework for practical knowledge, which has been widely used in the study of teachers' practical knowledge in China Chen (2003). Two researchers independently coded the seminar texts, discussed discrepancies, and reached consensus to ensure data analysis reliability before proceeding with epistemic network analysis.

### 3.3 Data Analysis Methods

Epistemic network analysis (ENA), as a quantitative ethnographic methodology, allows for the construction of network diagrams of learners' behaviors, interactions and cognitive processes. Where nodes in the network represent elements in a cognitive framework and edges represent connections between elements, metrics can help to understand interactions between groups of learners Shaffer et al. (2016). Practical knowledge is a dynamic development process, and it is difficult to capture the dynamic generation of teachers' practical knowledge over time in dialogues, ENA has some application potential in revealing teachers' knowledge interactions and promoting teachers' professional development Zhang et al. (2019); Sun et al. (2022).

In this study, a total of 987 pieces of data were generated, 745 pieces of meaningful data were retained after cleaning, and the coding of these data was completed in EXCEL and imported into the ENA web tool (http://app.epistemicnetwork.org) for analysis.

## 4 Results

### 4.1 Are There Any Differences in Practical Knowledge Produced Between Teachers in Different Mentoring Roles?

A t-test was conducted to compare the cognitive networks of novice teachers guided by different mentor roles. The results showed significant differences between the Imperator and Initiator groups on the Y-axis ($p = 0.03$), and between the Imperator and Encourager groups on the X-axis ($p = 0.04$). Additionally, the Initiator and Encourager groups differed significantly on the Y-axis ($p = 0.05$), indicating that the cognitive structures of practical knowledge vary depending on the mentoring role.

In ENA, the centroid plot represents the weighted average position of all nodes in the network model, and is able to characterize changes and trends in the level of professional development or cognitive structure. Further analysis of the centroid plot (Fig. 2) revealed that the Imperator group's cognitive network was distinct from the other three groups, suggesting that more directive mentoring leads to different patterns of practical knowledge generation.

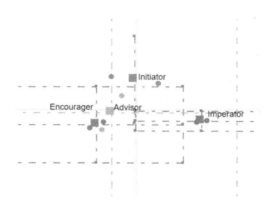

**Fig. 2.** Gravity Centre of the Four Groups

### 4.2 How Do the Differences in Practical Knowledge Generation Manifest Under the Guidance of Different Mentors?

Figure 3 plots the average epistemic network model for the Imperator, Initiator, Advisor and Encourager groups, with node size representing how many connections are established between the surrounding cognitive elements, and line thickness representing the strength of the connections between the nodes. It is clear from the figure that the Imperator is significantly different from the other three categories.

To further compare the differences in the cognitive network models of the different mentoring roles, we plotted a superimposed subtraction graph. Figure 4 shows the cognitive network stacked subtraction diagrams of the Imperator group with the other three groups. Imperator group constructed more interpersonal, belief, situational, knowledge and strategy knowledge but less critical reflection knowledge compared to the other three mentoring roles.

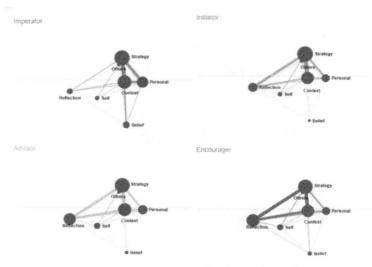

**Fig. 3.** Imperator, Initiator, Advisor and Encourager ENA Model

To compare the practical knowledge elements among different mentor groups, we calculated the cognitive network connectivity coefficients. We set a minimum edge weight of 0.2 to focus on significant connections and better observe relationships between main nodes. The results reveal distinct differences among the groups. The Imperator group had strong connections between strategy and personal knowledge (0.47) and between personal and context knowledge (0.38). The Initiator group showed the highest co-occurrence between strategy and context knowledge (0.66), reflecting their focus on adapting strategies to various situations. The Encourager group had the strongest link between reflection and strategy (0.51), indicating a focus on integrating reflective practices into teaching adjustments. Encourager mentors used a passive, non-directive approach, guiding novice teachers through questions and shared experiences to promote self-exploration. They emphasized integrating reflection with strategy development and adjustment, allowing teachers to adapt methods to their developmental needs.

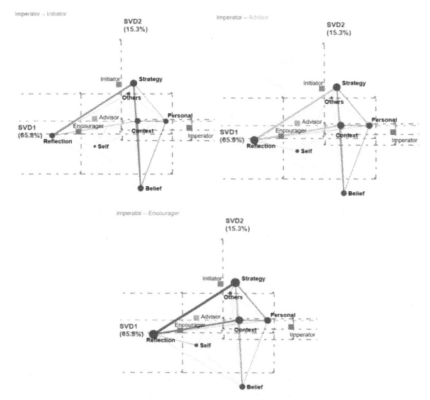

**Fig. 4.** ENA of the "Imperator Group" with the Other Three Groups

## 5 Discussion

### 5.1 The Effect of Different Mentoring Roles on Teachers' Cognitive Network Models of Practical Knowledge

The study shows that different mentor roles significantly affect novice teachers' cognitive networks of practical knowledge. Imperators, with its directive style, fostered strong connections between strategic, interpersonal, belief, and contextual knowledge. Initiators, using a non-directive approach, enhanced alignment between instructional strategies and contexts, resulting in greater co-occurrence of strategy and context knowledge. Advisors, focusing on personal reflection, strengthened links between reflective and interpersonal knowledge. The Imperator group's extensive guidance and diverse knowledge connections highlight the impact of directive mentoring on practical knowledge networks. In contrast, Initiators promoted deeper thinking and context alignment, while Advisors tailored guidance to individual needs and encouraged reflection. These findings underscore the importance of mentoring styles in shaping novice teachers' professional development and suggest that effective mentoring involves balancing directive and reflective practices to support comprehensive knowledge growth Jin et al. (2021); Ellis et al. (2020).

Furthermore, the results showed significant differences in cognitive network structures across mentor groups. T-tests revealed that the Imperator group differed notably from the Initiator and Encourager groups in terms of practical knowledge development. The center of mass analysis confirmed that the cognitive structure of the Imperator group was distinct, likely due to the active input and directive nature of their mentoring style. Imperators' leadership in workshops facilitated a more structured exchange, leading to stronger interpersonal and personal belief knowledge development Crasborn et al. (2011). Consequently, this role promotes a complex and diverse array of knowledge connections within teachers' cognitive networks.

### 5.2 Transitions Between Types of Teachers' Practical Knowledge

Cognitive network diagrams show that knowledge of strategies and contexts is central to teachers' practical knowledge development across all instructional roles. Teaching requires adaptable strategies for varying contexts Hoffman et al. (2015). Both expert and novice teachers focus on student development, adjusting strategies to meet students' needs and teaching environments. Contextual knowledge helps understand current scenarios, while strategic knowledge provides solutions. Teacher-apprentice dialogues often include "reflection-after-action," where contextual knowledge aids understanding and strategic knowledge supports adjustments. However, self-knowledge generation was low in this seminar, likely due to an overemphasis on teaching strategies and less focus on personal teaching philosophies and self-reflection Jin et al. (2021). Novice teachers' dependence on expert guidance may also have hindered their self-knowledge development. Future seminars should integrate reflection mechanisms, such as reflective journals or peer feedback, to enhance teachers' self-knowledge and its impact on their teaching practices.

## 6 Conclusion

This study examined how different mentoring styles impact teachers' cognitive networks using epistemic network analysis (ENA). Findings revealed that Imperator mentors, through their extensive guidance and interventions, fostered more complex and interconnected cognitive networks compared to Initiator and Encourager mentors. Limitations include a small sample size and a focus on cognitive structure without addressing dynamic changes. Future research should explore the long-term effects of training, optimize mentoring styles for better reflection and knowledge integration, and investigate the link between cognitive networks and teaching effectiveness to improve student outcomes.

## References

Beek, G.J., Zuiker, I., Zwart, R.C.: Exploring mentors' roles and feedback strategies to analyse the quality of mentoring dialogues. Teaching and Teacher Education **78**, 15–27 (2019). https://doi.org/10.1016/j.tate.2018.10.006

Carmi, T.: Reframing high-quality mentoring: between teacher mentoring and visions of teaching as a profession. J. Teacher Educ. **75**(2), 186–202 (2024). https://doi.org/10.1177/00224871231200276

Carmi, T., Tamir, E.: An emerging taxonomy explaining mentor-teachers' role in student-teachers' practicum: What they do and to what end? Teach. Teach. Educ. **128**, 104121 (2023). https://doi.org/10.1016/j.tate.2023.104121

Chen, X.: Practical knowledge: The knowledge base for teachers' professional development. Peking University Education Review **01**, 104–112 (2003). https://doi.org/10.19355/j.cnki.1671-9468.2003.01.019

Clandinin, D.J., Connelly, F.M.: Teachers' personal knowledge: what counts as personal in studies of the personal. J. Curric. Stud. **19**, 487–500 (1987)

Crasborn, F., Hennissen, P., Brouwer, N., Korthagen, F., Bergen, T.: Exploring a two-dimensional model of mentor teacher roles in mentoring dialogues. Teaching and Teacher Education **27**(2), 320–331 (2011). https://doi.org/10.1016/j.tate.2010.08.014

Elbaz, F.L.: Teacher thinking: A study of practical knowledge. Croom Helm, London (1983)

Ellis, N.J., Alonzo, D., Nguyen, H.T.M.: Elements of a quality pre-service teacher mentor: a literature review. Teach. Teach. Educ. **92**, 103072 (2020). https://doi.org/10.1016/j.tate.2020.103072

Hennissen, P., Crasborn, F., Brouwer, N., Korthagen, F., Bergen, T.: Mapping mentor teachers' roles in mentoring dialogues. Educational Research Review **3**(2) (2008). https://kns.cnki.net/kcms2/article/abstract?v=S8jPpdFxNHgE18GC34ABzDKsE7Xygo_HGcjSLS-gUvaYx WEEXGJch3yIe1pSjh6IV-Uh4Ey_eoQWr_oyzaMOzj-bLIirHE5nWNDCdc2TVA_fcydW_o 58rWo1RaAJxhGmo2LiDuxgHDEDWi2ljbIv0g==&uniplatform=NZKPT&language=gb

Hoffman, J.V., et al.: What can we learn from studying the coaching interactions between cooperating teachers and preservice teachers? a literature review. Teach. Teacher Educ. **52**, 99–112 (2015)

Jin, X., Li, T., Meirink, J., Van Der Want, A., Admiraal, W.: Learning from novice-expert interaction in teachers' continuing professional development. Professional Develop. Educ. **47**(5), 745–762 (2021). https://doi.org/10.1080/19415257.2019.1651752

Kuhn, C., Hagenauer, G., Gröschner, A., Bach, A.: Mentor teachers' motivations and implications for mentoring style and enthusiasm. Teach. Teacher Educ. **139**, 104441 (2024). https://doi.org/10.1016/j.tate.2023.104441

Michos, K., Petko, D.: Reflection using mobile portfolios during teaching internships: tracing the influence of mentors and peers on teacher self-efficacy. Technol. Pedag. Educ. 1–21 (2024). https://doi.org/10.1080/1475939X.2024.2311798

Nielsen, W., Tindall-Ford, S., Sheridan, L.: Mentoring conversations in preservice teacher supervision: knowledge for mentoring in categories of participation. Mentoring & Tutoring. Partnership in Learning **30**(1), 38–64 (2022). https://doi.org/10.1080/13611267.2022.2030185

Shaffer, D.W., Collier, W., Ruis, A.R.: A Tutorial on Epistemic Network Analysis: Analysing the Structure of Connections in Cognitive, Social, and Interaction Data. J. Learn. Anal. (2016)

Sun, Z., Xu, R., Deng, L., Jin, F., Song, Z., Lin, C.: Beyond coding and counting: Exploring teachers' practical knowledge online through epistemic network analysis. Comput. Educ. **192**, 104647 (2022)

Zhang, S., Liu, Q., Cai, Z.: Exploring primary school teachers' technological pedagogical content knowledge (TPACK) in online collaborative discourse: an epistemic network analysis. br. J. Educ. Technol. **50**, 3437–3455 (2019)

Zhong, Y., Cao, J., Zhang, Z.Y.: The current situation and optimisation path of professional learning of new teachers in primary and secondary schools - A data analysis based on 3,150 teachers in Beijing. Journal of Beijing Institute of Education **37**(1), 40–47 (2023)

# Graduate Study Program Improvement: A Case Study of Industrial Engineering Programs

Pongthorn Ruksorn[1], Naraphorn Paoprasert[2](✉), Kongkiti Phusavat[2], and Pornthep Anussornnitisarn[2]

[1] Department of Applied Science, Faculty of Science and Technology, Phranakhon Si Ayutthaya Rajabhat University, 96 Pratuchai, Phra Nakhon Si Ayutthaya 13000, Thailand
`pongthorn.r@ku.th`

[2] Department of Industrial Engineering, Faculty of Engineering, Kasetsart University, 50 Ngamwongwan Road, Lat Yao, Chatuchak, Bangkok 10900, Thailand
`{naraphorn.p,pornthep.a}@ku.th, fengkkp@ku.ac.th`

**Abstract.** Graduate study programs face many challenges. Not only the motivations in pursuing graduate studies that affect graduate program management, internal management, opportunities, and threats could help improve the program. This study used the Department of Industrial Engineering programs as a case study. With the rapid pace of technological advancements, it is essential to continually update curricula to ensure that graduates have the knowledge and skills to meet market demands. This study explores ways to enhance international programs at the master's and doctoral levels by examining the factors that influence decision-making for students in these programs, along with SWOT analysis and competitor benchmarking. The survey findings indicate that pursuing a master's degree is often motivated by a desire to deepen knowledge in industrial engineering. In contrast, the desire to fulfill their life goals ranked the highest as the reason to pursue a doctoral degree.

**Keywords:** industrial engineering · curriculum improvement · SWOT · engineering education

## 1 Introduction

Pursuing graduate study may offer several benefits, including obtaining research skills, advancing and deepening knowledge, broadening career opportunities, and many others. However, it requires great dedication, both in time and money. Greene et al. (2020) investigated the motivations for pursuing a Master of Arts in Education in North Carolina, USA, considering recruitment strategies, program duration, loyalty to the university, accreditation, lifelong learning, and increased professional opportunities. Their findings revealed that the most influential factors were the desire for more professional opportunities and a commitment to lifelong learning. Similarly, Teowkul et al. (2009) developed a questionnaire to identify the factors influencing participants' decisions to pursue higher education in Thai business administration graduate programs.

Economies worldwide, including Thailand, have been rated poorly (Clancy and Lippert, 2024). Moreover, many students prefer to continue their graduate studies abroad. These reasons led to a decline in the number of graduate program students in most programs in Thailand over the past decade. However, we still have opportunities to recruit students who prefer to stay in Thailand, international students living in Thailand, and international students in neighboring countries due to the great potential of jobs in Industrial Engineering.

The curriculum utilized for instruction and learning must be continuously improved to keep up with the fast pace of modern technology and innovations to offer attractive graduate-level industrial engineering programs. Many countries offer courses in industrial engineering, with each institution needing to tailor its curriculum to meet the specific requirements of its region. According to US News and World Report, the top ten graduate programs in Industrial Engineering in the United States include Cornell University, Georgia Institute of Technology, Northwestern University, Pennsylvania State University, Purdue University, Stanford University, University of California—Berkeley, University of Michigan—Ann Arbor, University of Wisconsin, and Virginia Tech, all of which emphasize Manufacturing Systems (Aamer et al., 2017). Shafeek et al. (2014) note that eight Saudi Arabian companies recommend that Industrial Information Systems and Engineering Mechanics be integral components of industrial engineering programs. These programs should encompass all essential subjects that an industrial engineer should master, such as change management, programming, production planning, and control, report writing in English, and quality management. Additionally, according to Schrippe et al. (2016), there is a varied distribution of industrial engineering courses focusing on industrial and more developed regions, particularly in Brazil's Southeast and South.

Many educational institutions in Thailand offer courses in industrial engineering, a field dedicated to the design, development, planning, control, and management of production processes to enhance efficiency. As management skills become increasingly important, the curriculum has evolved to include manufacturing-related topics and organizational management skills such as data analysis, financial analysis, and supply chain management. At Khon Kaen University, the Marketing Engineer course incorporates Problem-Based Learning (PBL), as demonstrated through a case study. PBL is instrumental in helping students develop critical thinking skills, preparing them for real-world challenges, enhancing collaboration and communication, and maintaining their enthusiasm for learning (Nitisiri et al., 2023).

The Department of Industrial Engineering at Kasetsart University offers two international graduate programs: the Master of Engineering in Industrial Engineering and Engineering Management (IEEM) and the Doctor of Industrial Engineering. These programs are designed to equip students with transdisciplinary expertise in engineering and management. However, the number of students enrolling in these master's and doctoral programs has declined significantly, particularly in international programs. This decrease highlights the need to actively promote the curriculum to attract more international students, especially from neighboring Southeast Asian nations.

Given the rapid changes in today's world, relying solely on the current faculty to update the curriculum to meet market demands may not be feasible. Therefore, this research explored the factors influencing students' decisions to pursue a master's or doctoral degree in industrial engineering via feedback from alumni and current students. A Strengths, Weaknesses, Opportunities, and Threats (SWOT) analysis was conducted to analyze both programs further internally and to look for opportunities together with the threats that may arise externally. A comparison of program characteristics to competitors was also illustrated. Additionally, this study assessed whether the courses offered in the IEEM Master's and Doctor of Engineering programs align with learners' current needs.

## 2 Data Collection and Research Methodology

This work aims to develop an effective Industrial Engineering curriculum at Kasetsart University in Bangkok, Thailand. To achieve this, the opinions, experiences, and expectations of students, professors, and alumni were carefully considered.

The initial section of this research involves collecting data from former and current participants of the Master of Engineering and Doctor of Engineering programs, including Thai and international students. A questionnaire was mainly obtained from Teowkul et al. (2009) and Greene et al. (2020) in collaboration with the course's lecturers to explore the motivations and reasons of students and alumni for choosing to pursue graduate studies, as shown in Tables 1 and 2. In June 2024, an online survey was conducted using Google Forms, targeting alumni and current students who provided their consent to participate. Responses were measured using a five-point Likert scale: (1) strongly disagree, (2) disagree, (3) neither agree nor disagree, (4) agree, and (5) strongly agree. Additionally, open-ended questions were included to allow students and graduates to share their views on the programs.

A SWOT analysis is valuable for identifying and evaluating an organization's strengths, weaknesses, opportunities, and threats (Puyt et al., 2023). This method has been widely applied in education to assess and enhance curricula, especially during the COVID-19 pandemic, which led to the transition of many courses to online formats (Hergüner, 2021). Therefore, this study utilizes a framework that examines internal strengths and weaknesses alongside external opportunities and threats, providing a clear and practical approach to evaluating potential curricular developments. This method allows planners to assess the program's possible outcomes realistically.

Following the SWOT analysis, both curricula were compared with similar programs at other universities. A comparison of the curricula offered in industrial engineering programs at various educational institutions will help to identify the strengths and areas for improvement in each. This can inform potential adaptations to our own curriculum, including updates to the subjects offered, the number of credits required, the program duration, English language proficiency requirements, tuition fees, and the availability of scholarships. For instance, the Mendoza-Mendoza et al. (2024) study examines the effectiveness of industrial engineering curricula across various higher education institutions in Colombia. This evaluation compares proficiencies in crucial areas such as quantitative reasoning, critical reading, English language proficiency, mathematics and statistics, engineering projects, and production design across three primary domains: institutional type (public versus private), the location of the academic facility, and program accreditation status.

## 3 Result and Discussion

### 3.1 Results of the Survey

Following the distribution of the surveys to alumni and current students, eighteen respondents were received for the Master of Engineering program—eleven from graduates and seven from current students. For the Doctor of Engineering program, there were seven respondents, including three alumni and four current students.

#### 3.1.1 Master of Engineering Program

In Table 1, it was observed that the primary motivation for both current and former students to enroll in the Master of Engineering program was a desire to deepen their knowledge in this field of study (Mean = 4.67). Additionally, many alumni pursued this program as earning a master's degree was their significant life goal (Mean = 4.44). The university's strong reputation also played a notable role in attracting students (Mean = 4.44). Conversely, the least influential factor in pursuing a master's degree was the opportunity to attend classes with friends (Mean = 2.06), followed by the majority of individuals around them attending graduate school. (Mean = 2.11). Furthermore, most students disagreed that Thai should be the language of instruction in the classroom (Mean = 2.22). This may be because the respondents have already decided to study in our program; they may prefer to study in English. However, preliminary interviews reflected that many other Thai students prefer to study in the Thai language. This evidence is shown in the number of students studying in the same program that is taught in Thai.

Students were also asked to select five subjects they were most interested in studying. The top five interesting classes were Data Engineering and Analytics, Financial Analysis and Control Systems, Leadership and Entrepreneurship, and Operations Modeling in Supply Chain. Consequently.

Additionally, open-ended questions were included to gather insights on market demand. The researcher summarized the responses as follows:

Q1: *Please list the engineering research tools (software, theoretical concepts, and principles) you want to learn from this course.*

A1: Many students expressed an interest in learning financial analysis tools, including financial statements, key performance measures, and financial models, as well as computer programs such as Python, MATLAB, R, and ARENA Simulation. Additionally, some students showed interest in studying logistics and supply chain topics.

Q2: *Please specify what you hope to gain from this program upon graduation.*

A2: Some students are drawn to this program because they believe it will equip them with the knowledge necessary for their professional careers. Many students also wanted to visit factories and network with others. Ultimately, teaching and learning should be adaptable, incorporating both in-class instruction and video recordings for later review.

The open-ended questions revealed that students were interested in learning more about financial analysis. Consequently, the curriculum should be expanded to include courses on financial analysis relevant to industry and financial institutions. Additionally, the current curriculum offers instruction in computer programming languages such as Python, MATLAB, R, and ARENA Simulation. However, the lessons will be revised to apply these tools to real-world scenarios.

Factory visits are essential for enhancing the effectiveness of industrial engineering education. Therefore, the curriculum will be revised to include visits to various industrial facilities.

**Table 1.** Results of the survey for the Master of Industrial Engineering program.

| Question | Mean | S.D. |
| --- | --- | --- |
| 1. To accomplish the life's objectives | 4.44 | 0.62 |
| 2. To bring pride to the family | 3.56 | 1.38 |
| 3. Accompany a friend | 2.06 | 1.21 |
| 4. Since everyone around me is enrolled in graduate school | 2.11 | 1.23 |
| 5. It is essential to have a good reputation because employment necessitates education | 2.44 | 1.29 |
| 6. To give me more chances to progress in their existing position | 3.94 | 1 |
| 7. To increase your chances of finding a new and better job | 4 | 1.19 |
| 8. To expand this field's network | 3.89 | 1.28 |
| 9. I want my coworkers to respect me | 2.78 | 1.17 |
| 10. To make the present position more secure | 3.28 | 1.07 |
| 11. To enhance communication abilities in English | 3.61 | 1.04 |
| 12. Kasetsart University's reputation is one reason I applied for a degree in Industrial Engineering and Engineering Management | 4.44 | 0.62 |
| 13. I want to learn more about this field of study, so I chose the Industrial Engineering and Engineering Management degree and am interested in applying | 4.67 | 0.49 |
| 14. If possible, I would like to enroll in a program that only requires coursework—no thesis | 3.11 | 1.41 |
| 15. If possible, I would like the program to be taught in Thai | 2.22 | 1.4 |
| 16. I am satisfied with teaching online since no travel will be involved | 3.06 | 1.26 |
| 17. I would prefer weekday classes to relax on Saturdays and Sundays | 2.83 | 1.72 |
| 18. Even without scholarships, I still pursue this program | 4 | 0.87 |

### 3.1.2 Doctor of Engineering Program

In the past, the number of doctoral students has been relatively low. This prompted the researcher to investigate the factors that motivate individuals to pursue doctoral studies. As shown in Table 2, it was found that students primarily chose to obtain a doctorate to fulfill their life goals (Mean = 4.71). An intriguing finding is that current and former students expressed interest in enrolling in the Doctor of Engineering program to improve their English communication skills (Mean = 4.57). These results may arise from the fact that in the past, we used to have only Thai doctoral students, and by studying in an

English-speaking program, they may view the study as an "English-learning" program along with their doctoral study. It is also possible that fewer students worldwide are currently expressing interest in pursuing doctoral degrees. Consequently, prestigious universities must actively attract exceptional students to research positions. Given this, applicants to the program may not always have the highest level of English proficiency. Therefore, the program can support current students such as offering them to take more English classes to improve their English skills.

Interestingly, the desire to establish a professional reputation or make their families proud did not significantly motivate doctoral students (Mean = 2.86). Another interesting finding is that the reason to make the present position more secure did not receive a high score. This could be because we have accepted quite a small number of existing faculty members who only had their master's degrees. It would be interesting to explore this market further since many faculty members in Southeast Asian universities have only acquired master's degrees.

**Table 2.** Results of the survey for the Doctor of Engineering program

| Question | Mean | S.D. |
|---|---|---|
| 1. To achieve the goals in life | 4.71 | 0.49 |
| 2. To make the family proud | 2.86 | 1.77 |
| 3. Follow a companion | 3.29 | 1.38 |
| 4. Because everyone in my immediate vicinity is a graduate student | 3.14 | 1.35 |
| 5. To establish trustworthiness because of my job responsibilities | 2.86 | 1.35 |
| 6. To expand the current work's prospects for progression | 3.86 | 1.35 |
| 7. To increase your prospects of getting another job | 4.29 | 0.76 |
| 8. To expand this field's network | 3.29 | 1.25 |
| 9. Desire esteem from colleagues | 3.43 | 1.40 |
| 10. To make the present position more secure | 3.57 | 1.40 |
| 11. To improve English communication skills | 4.57 | 0.53 |

In addition to the rating scale questionnaire, the researcher administered an open-ended survey covering the following topics:

- Among the seven students who responded to the survey, six expressed a desire for scholarship opportunities. Therefore, clearly outlining the availability and likelihood of scholarships in the curriculum may enhance the program's attractiveness.
- The potential of the department's faculty and the university's reputation influenced students' decisions to pursue this program.
- Students, particularly international students, emphasized the importance of forming networks and engaging in meaningful research.
- The students suggested collaboration between lecturers, current students, and alumni could strengthen the program. They also emphasized the need for discussions and exchanges on relevant research to foster innovative and engaging projects.
- Finally, students felt that the graduation requirements were too high with four publications: Two international conference proceedings and two international journal publications.

## 3.2 SWOT Analysis

The program's committee brainstormed to conduct a SWOT analysis, which is presented in Tables 3 and 4. Both programs share similarities, including affordability and strong international collaboration. The department's faculty members have also established industry connections, allowing students to research real-world problems. These connections also facilitate the publication of research papers supported by a network of editors in international journals.

### 3.2.1 SWOT Analysis for the Master Program in IEEM

- Strengths: The program is considered to be affordable at 200 thousand baht, making it accessible to many students. Moreover, the curriculum is enriched by collaborations with several international educational institutions, fostering a productive exchange of ideas in academics and research. These exchanges offer international students flexibility in their pursuit of academic excellence. The department's faculty members also have strong industry connections, enabling students to research real-world challenges. Since the program can accept full-time and exchange international students, classes offer ethnic diversity, allowing students to learn from many perspectives and cultures. Finally, the program continuously researches new pedagogy and adopts in-trend techniques such as project-based learning in many classes.
- Weaknesses: A significant weakness of this program is the lack of resources to help students enhance their English language skills. Consequently, many students struggle with writing research papers in English, leading them to prefer presenting at international academic conferences over submitting manuscripts to international journals. Additionally, most graduate students are employed full-time, which limits their capacity to engage in research. Finally, since the existing program offers classes on the weekend and is taught in English, the teaching cost is much higher than the standard Thai classes during weekday working hours.
- Opportunities: Online teaching removes the need for students to attend classes in person, offering greater flexibility. This may also attract international students from other countries, especially Asian countries. Additionally, the program's network of partnerships with overseas universities provides students with more opportunities for further studies and internships. The expansion of international corporations operating in Thailand has also increased employment opportunities for graduates. Finally, the lifelong learning attitude nowadays allows us to offer a flexible program that could potentially increase the number of qualified students.
- Threats: Since most industries in Thailand do not require graduate-level skills, they prefer to hire candidates with only a bachelor's degree mainly due to the lower salary. This phenomenon discourages many undergraduate students from pursuing their master's degrees. Additionally, there is a general lack of understanding about the practical applications of industrial engineering, which further discourages students from continuing their studies. The presence of several Thai educational institutions offering master's degrees in industrial engineering has also increased competition, resulting in lower enrollment in the program.

**Table 3.** SWOT Analysis for the Master Program in IEEM

| Strengths | Opportunities |
|---|---|
| - Affordability<br>- International partnership worldwide<br>- Flexibility in pursuing academic excellence<br>- Industrial connections for real-world applications<br>- Student diversity - international students<br>- Continuously adopt new pedagogies | - Online<br>- Internship/exchange abroad<br>- Number of international companies<br>- Life-long learning |
| Weaknesses | Threats |
| - Lack of mechanism to assist English proficiency<br>- Reliance on part-time students<br>- Teaching cost for English program is relatively high | - Many companies in Thailand require only at least a Bachelor's degree<br>- Lack of understanding of the industrial engineering profession<br>- Lack of interest in graduate study<br>- Similar programs from well-known institutions also offer certificates |

### 3.2.2 SWOT Analysis for Doctoral Program in Industrial Engineering

- Strengths: The program shares several strengths with the master's degree program, including affordable tuition, partnerships with foreign universities, and strong industrial collaboration. Additionally, doctoral students in this program have the opportunity to publish in international journals because many faculty members are heavily committed to conducting research studies, which creates a strong network.
- Weaknesses: Some students lack a prior degree in industrial engineering, making it challenging to engage with doctoral-level courses effectively. Consequently, students with limited or no background in industrial engineering may need to take master-level classes first. Additionally, their English proficiency may not be fluent enough to start conducting a research thesis effectively. As a result, students often face difficulties writing their research papers in English. Therefore, the department should consider implementing support mechanisms to help improve students' English proficiency.
- Opportunities: Doctoral degrees are increasingly necessary for higher academic positions among university instructors in Asian nations. A few companies with rigorous research units, which could be domestic or international, also require doctoral degrees. This could also result in the preference of international companies who may prefer an English language degree.
- Threats: Competing educational institutions offer full scholarships and monthly stipends to attract students to their PhD programs. As a result, many top students also choose to apply to other universities. Also, since a few students work full-time, they may not entirely commit to the program.

**Table 4.** SWOT Analysis for the Doctoral Program in Industrial Engineering

| Strengths | Opportunities |
|---|---|
| - High chance of acceptance rate to publish academic papers<br>- Affordability<br>- International partnership worldwide<br>- Industrial connections for real-world applications<br>- High-profile faculty members | - Universities require a Ph.D<br>- The need for research units in many domestic and international organizations<br>- International companies may prefer an English language degree |
| Weaknesses | Threats |
| - Lack of mechanism to assist English proficiency<br>- Relatively low entry requirement | - Other countries/universities offer scholarships to attract good Ph.D. students<br>- Lack of total commitment by students |

### 3.3 Compare the Curriculum with Those Offered by Other Institutions

This section compares the Master of Engineering program and the Doctor of Engineering program with other institutions that employ similar teaching models and offer courses in English. Table 5 compares the Master of Engineering program with those at other universities. While the total number of credits is consistent with other institutions, attendance at seminar courses is currently mandatory. It may be worth considering removing this requirement to enhance the curriculum, though these seminars could be offered as discussion sessions that do not count toward credit. Table 6 shows that the number of credits varies across courses when comparing the Doctor of Engineering program to those at other universities. Since doctoral studies mainly depend heavily on research conduct, the number of required credits seems to have little influence on the selection of programs.

**Table 5.** Comparison of the Master of Engineering program to other institutions

| Item | Kasetsart University | Institution A | Institution B |
|---|---|---|---|
| Required courses (credits) | 0 | 9 | 0 |
| Required elective courses (credits) | 0 | 15 | 0 |
| Elective courses (credits) | 21 | 0 | 36 |
| Thesis (credits) | 12 | 12 | 0 |
| Seminar courses (credits) | 2 | 0 | 0 |
| Research methodology (credits) | 1 | 0 | 0 |
| Total (credits) | 36 | 36 | 36 |

(*continued*)

**Table 5.** (*continued*)

| Item | Kasetsart University | Institution A | Institution B |
|---|---|---|---|
| Tuition fee (THB) | 2,36,000 | 3,60,000 | 6,60,000 |
| Duration (Years) | 2–3 | 2–3 | 1.5–3 |
| Part-time | Yes | No | Yes |
| Class time | Sunday (all day) | Weekdays | 5 full days consecutively per model |
| Selling point | Have partners all over the world | Logistics and Supply Chain, focus on research | Dual degree program with the University of Warwick, UK |
| Class type | Modular | Spreading throughout a semester | Modular |
| Degree name(s) | Industrial Engineering and Engineering Management | Logistics and Supply Chain | Engineering Business Management- Supply Chain and Logistics Management |

**Table 6.** Comparison of the Doctor of Engineering program to other institutions

| Item | Industrial Engineering, Kasetsart University | Engineering and Technology, Institution A | Logistics and Engineering Management, Institution C | Industrial and Manufacturing Engineering, Institution D |
|---|---|---|---|---|
| Required courses (credits) | 3 | 3 | 9 | 12 |
| Elective courses (credits) | 9 | 9 | 3 | |
| Thesis (credits) | 36 | 48 | 36 | 72 |
| Seminar courses (credits) | 4 | | | |
| Total (credits) | 52 | 60 | 48 | 84 |
| Tuition fee (THB) | 328,000++ | 550,000++ | 570,000++ | 1,495,800 |
| Admission requirement | TOEFL score of 450 or higher or 190 in the Computer-Based Test | - TOEFL (PBT 400+, or IBT 32+) or IBT (Home Edition 32+)<br>- IELTS 4.5+<br>- TU-GET (PBT 400+, or CBT 32+) or<br>- TOEIC 500+ | TOEFL score report of 500 or TOEIC of 173 or IELTS of 5.5 or higher Proposed research | AIT-EET: 6; IELTS Academic: overall 6 (writing 6); TOEFL iBT: overall 80 (writing 21–23); & PTE Academic: overall 52 (writing 62–73) |
| Minimum Duration | Not specific | Not specific | 4 Years | Not specific |
| Maximum Duration | Not specific | 6 Years | 6 Years | Not specific |
| Fully Funded Scholarship (prior to arrival) | No | Yes | No | Yes |

## 4 Discussion and Conclusions

This study surveyed current students and alumni to explore their reasons for pursuing their English-language master's or doctoral degrees at the Department of Industrial Engineering. Although the sample size was small due to the historically small number of students, we could still explore the underlying reasons from the questionnaire answers. SWOT analysis and competitor benchmarking were also conducted to explore the paths for the two curricula of interest: Industrial Engineering and Engineering Management (IEEM) and the Doctor of Industrial Engineering.

The results overall found that perhaps the reason why we continuously had a small number of students in both programs may be because we targeted the wrong market. From the opportunity of online classes for the master's degree and the demand for doctoral degrees of many faculty members around ASEAN, it would be beneficial to move teaching and learning activities to weekdays. This adjustment would give international students more time to study and research, especially doctoral students. This improvement could further be extended to the rigorous offer of hybrid learning. The curriculum could include a hybrid approach, utilizing video recordings. This would enhance accessibility for Thai students who work full-time and offer overseas students more flexibility to review materials or return to their home countries.

This study could shed light on the broader topic of engineering education design. Findings related to curriculum and content in our study could help strengthen the content that will be delivered to current and future graduate students. Hence, teaching techniques that were claimed to be effective for engineering education, such as project-based learning (Mills, 2003) and challenge-based learning (Doulougeri et al., 2022), should continuously be reviewed, and promising techniques should then be adopted.

Regarding the additional improvement in the master's degree, the program committee could focus on conducting a market analysis study. The aim was to identify potential candidates who are willing to study in the field of IEEM and who are also willing to study and write their thesis in English. With suitable target identification, the committee can decide whether the program should be regular or special (weekend). Scholarship opportunities should also be clearly announced and updated on the program website.

Although the teaching expense in this type of program is generally higher than the one for the Thai program, the program could offer another side of benefits apart from only financial benefits, such as good-quality publications and the opportunities to attract more students to support faculty members to assist in their research projects. As suggested by the ASEE (2003), one leg of responsibility should also come from government support to maintain high-quality graduate programs in Thailand and develop an efficient science and engineering workforce. With good scholarship opportunities, in a broader picture, any program in Thailand could potentially attract top Thai and international students to continue their studies in their program.

## References

Aamer, A., Greene, B., Toney, C.: An empirical study of industrial engineering curriculum. Int. J. Indus. Eng. Manage. **8**(1), 39 (2017)

American Society for Engineering Education (ASEE): Engineering Education and the Science and Engineering Workforce. In: Government-University-Industry Research Roundtable (US); National Academy of Sciences (US); National Academy of Engineering (US); Institute of Medicine (US); Fox MA, editor. Pan-Organizational Summit on the US Science and Engineering Workforce: Meeting Summary. Washington (DC): National Academies Press (US) (2003). https://www.ncbi.nlm.nih.gov/books/NBK36351/

Clancy, L., Lippert, J.: Economic ratings across 34 countries are more negative than positive. Pew Research Center (2024). https://www.pewresearch.org/short-reads/2024/06/07/economic-ratings-across-34-countries-are-more-negative-than-positive/

Doulougeri, K., Vermunt, J.D., Bombaerts, G., Bots, M.: Challenge-based learning implementation in engineering education: a systematic literature review. J. Eng. Educ. 1–31 (2024)

Greene, C., Zugelder, B.S., Warren, L.L., L'Esperance, M.: What factors influence motivation for graduate education? Critical Questions in Education **11**(1), 21–37 (2020)

Hergüner, B.: Rethinking public administration education during the pandemic: Reflections of public administration students on online education through a SWOT analysis. Thinking Skills and Creativity, 41, 100863 (2021)

Mendoza-Mendoza, A., Mendoza-Casseres, D., De La Hoz-Domíngez, E.: Comparison of industrial engineering programs in Colombia based on standardized test results. Eval. Program Plann. **103**, 102415 (2024)

Mills, J., Treagust, D.: Engineering education: is problem-based or project-based learning the answer? Australasian Journal of Engineering Education, 3 (2003)

Nitisiri, K., Jamrus, T., Sethanan, K., Chetchotsak, D., Nakrachata-Amon, T.: Problem-based learning in marketing engineer course: a case study from industrial engineering curriculum. In: Leveraging Transdisciplinary Engineering in a Changing and Connected World, pp. 691–700. IOS Press (2023)

Puyt, R.W., Lie, F.B., Wilderom, C.P.: The origins of SWOT analysis. Long Range Plan. **56**(3), 102304 (2023)

Schrippe, P., Medeiros, F.S.B., Weise, A.D., Sturm, C.H., Koschek, J.F.: Mapping of the undergraduate and graduate curriculum in industrial engineering in Brazil. Int. J. Eng. Educ. **32**(3), 1250–1259 (2016)

Shafeek, H., Gutub, S.A., Miski, A.G.: Industrial engineering curriculum restructuring. Int. J. Sci. Eng. Res. **5**(9), 434–446 (2014)

Teowkul, K., Seributra, N.J., Sangkaworn, C., Jivasantikarn, C., Denvilai, S., Mujtaba, B.G.: Motivational factors of graduate Thai students pursuing master's and doctoral degrees in business. RU Int. J. **3**(1), 25–56 (2009)

# Specific Aspects of MOOC's Use in Czech Universities

Miloslava Cerna and Petra Poulova[✉]

Faculty of Informatics and Management, University of Hradec Kralove, Hradec Kralove, Czech Republic
{Miloslava.Cerna,Petra.Poulova}@uhk.cz

**Abstract.** The paper discusses selected aspects of the MOOC innovative phenomenon that enable universities to enhance educational offerings through strategic planning and resource allocation. The article approaches the issue as a specific form of student mobility study at the Faculty of Informatics and Management. Authors have gained a lot of experience and they intend to share it through the presentation of the scenario. In this case study, authors present in detail a proven functional scenario for the implementation of Coursera courses into the university study system. A total of 1,214 courses were enrolled by individual users between October 2022 and May 2023. 658 of these courses were successfully completed by May 10, 2023. As of this date, 50 students earned credits under the terms of the Dean's directive. As traditional educational paradigms shift towards more inclusive and technology-driven models, the role of platforms like Coursera becomes increasingly critical in shaping the future of education.

**Keywords:** Coursera · COVID-19 · MOOC · online learning · student satisfaction

## 1 Introduction

The COVID-19 pandemic catalysed the widespread adoption and integration of online MOOC in higher education, both globally and in the Czech Republic. This shift not only ensured educational continuity during the pandemic, but also paved the way for a more flexible and accessible future in education.

Many universities around the world, including selected universities in the Czech Republic, have started to recognize MOOC as part of their academic programs. Universities have incorporated a MOOC platform such as Coursera to enrich students with their educational offerings, allowing students to take these courses as part of their degree programs. For example, some universities offer Coursera courses as electives or supplementary learning materials (Coursera, 2023). In the rapidly evolving landscape of modern education, MOOC learning platforms such as Coursera have emerged as vital tools in democratizing access to quality education. These platforms offer a diverse array of courses across various disciplines, enabling learners from different geographical locations and socio-economic backgrounds to acquire new skills and knowledge.

This contribution is about embedding MOOC into the university system so that students earn not only benefits associated with acquiring additional knowledge and the completion of prestigious courses on the given platform, including a certificate of completion of the Coursera course, but students also earn credits at their mother university.

This case study shows the solution to the issue of the institutional implementation of Coursera courses into the study system at the Faculty of Informatics and Management, University of Hradec Králové. The University of Hradec Králové offers high-quality tertiary education in a wide range of study fields at the following faculties: the Faculty of Informatics and Management, the Faculty of Education, at the Faculty of Science, and at the Philosophical Faculty. University of Hradec Králové is located in the old European city of the same name with the history going back to the 11th century. However, the university itself is young and dynamic. University of Hradec Kralove is one of the top public universities in Hradec Králové, It is ranked #1001–1200 in QS World University Rankings 2025 (TOPUNIVERSITIES, 2024). The University of Hradec Králové offers students a number of study programs such as computer science, business studies, teacher education, mathematics, chemistry, history, and social studies. At the same time, the University actively encourages students to engage in Coursera courses. The Faculty of Informatics and Management, University of Hradec Králové had a substantial edge because it has been actively involved in e-learning since the turn of the millennium. It has a sophisticated technology and personnel side of the e-learning issue, with hundreds of deployed e-courses. (Cerna and Poulova, 2012).

The paper discusses selected aspects of the MOOC innovative phenomenon that enables universities to enhance educational offerings through strategic planning and resource allocation. Authors approach the issue as a specific form of student mobility, so-called virtual mobility at the Faculty of Informatics and Management. Virtual mobility is when a student studies a course/curriculum at another institution without physically leaving their home university (Valtins and Muracova, 2019). In this case, the study takes place online. The Faculty of Informatics and Management had experience with virtual mobilities already before the COVID pandemic. In 2005, together with several other Czech universities, it was one of the founders of the RIUS project (The Start-up of Inter-University Studies in a Network of Selected Universities in the Czech Republic), a network of Czech universities enabling students of participating departments to study selected subjects online at partner universities. Based on the experience gained, the original national network was extended to the European level thanks to the EVENE project (Erasmus Virtual Economics & Management Studies Exchange). (Poulova et al., 2009) The project's consortium was composed, apart from three Czech universities, the same ones as in the RIUS project, of another five European partners from Ireland, Great Britain, Finland, Latvia, and Italy. The core aim of this project was, the creation of a seminal impulse for a network of traditional higher education institutions for the purpose of a mutual exchange and sharing of courses and educators and the possibility of providing these to students in a distance education supported by eLearning format. These networks were operating until 2011, when they were phased off due to the economic conditions following the 2008 financial crisis.

Given this experience, the faculty was open to the possibility of using virtual mobility also during COVID. After initial experiments with the use of the COURSERA platform, it was decided to continue using this platform. In this case study, authors present in detail a proven functional scenario for the implementation of Coursera courses into the university study system at the Faculty of Informatics and Management, University of Hradec Králové from the Dean's directive to students' feedback.

## 2 Literature Review

The Coursera platform (https://www.coursera.org) and the delivery of its courses can be understood as a model of study mobility. The following characteristics represent a set of key points to consider when implementing this mobility into the university system: access to global education and global market, cultural exchange, flexibility and convenience, skill development, collaboration and networking. Coursera courses often focus on practical skills and professional development, which are highly valued in the global job market. This aligns with the goals of study mobility programs that aim to enhance students' employability and global competencies. (Coursera, n.d.).

Potential issues are quality assurance and recognition of credits because transferring credits from online courses to traditional degree programs are sometimes found rather complicated (Umar, 2021).

### 2.1 Potential - Internationalization

There is an enormous desired potential in this Coursera virtual student study mobility program that can foster intercultural competencies among students even if students do not physically leave for a stay in a foreign university. Like short-term study programs, this virtual mobility can facilitate personal growth in various areas of the globalized world, supporting the development of cultural awareness and intercultural knowledge (Nguyen, 2017), (Bartunek, 2023).

Francisco's (2022) paper describes virtual mobility as a chance for internationalisation. She shares her experiences with the introduction of virtual mobility from the perspective of students at the Ilocos Sur Polytechnic State College in the Philippines, which began their International Credit Transfer Program with its Indonesian university partner electronically. These students did not regard the usage of online platforms as a barrier; rather, they felt that the platforms helped them develop the abilities of 21st-century educators. It is advantageous that this publication includes policy recommendations for strengthening and sustaining the program.

Not everyone is entirely convinced that virtual student mobility is a smart solution to a sustainable international education program. What worked during the pandemic may not work completely in the post-pandemic era. The authors concluded their research with the need to reconsider virtual student mobility (Schueller and Şahin, 2022).

## 2.2 Challenges

Based on the literature review, we have defined three areas of challenges that can hinder effectiveness of implementing MOOC in a university setting. These challenges encompass technological (Bailes 2012), managerial (Ramiz, 2024). And curricular aspects (Bustos et al., 2023), (Cooper, 2017).

Bustos et al.'s (2023) research is closely related to our research and overlaps in many ways. They discuss the challenges of implementing Coursera in a university setting. They find curriculum adaptation a critical issue. Adapting existing curricula to include online courses can be challenging, especially in terms of ensuring alignment with educational standards and learning outcomes while respecting and taking into account diverse student characteristics. (Bustos et al., 2023). They claim that continuous improvement processes are essential but often difficult to establish, especially in rapidly changing educational environments and navigating unforeseen circumstances like the pandemic, as shown in their research. (Bustos et al., 2023).

The integration of online platforms like Coursera requires robust ICT support, which may not be uniformly available across institutions, leading to disparities in access and engagement (Bailes, 2012).

In the turning point of the Covid pandemic, a tsunami of various attempts by educational institutions, universities and libraries was launched to best convey educational content to students in a situation where they could not physically attend classes. There were a lot of better or worse prepared study texts, a number of YouTube educational channels, the opening of databases of professional resources to free course offers on already established commercial platforms such as Coursera.

## 2.3 Possible Approaches

During the pandemic, colleges in the Czech Republic attempted to make self-study as simple as possible for students and the public. Many schools have worked to increase the amount of free content available in Czech and foreign e-book and magazine databases. Teachers streamed lectures online, and not only for students. And, despite being closed, university libraries scanned books and put them outside the door or sent them. The Czech Republic's universities closed on March 11, 2020, to avoid the spread of the coronavirus. However, in the virtual world, they were more open than ever before. A number of colleges have compensated for the cancellation of classes by distributing their online resources to their students and the public, free and with access.

Here is a list of selected universities in the Czech Republic that actively started supporting MOOCs (Massive Open Online Courses) in 2020 and have significantly expanded services of university libraries or transferred their services to other media platforms: Charles University (UK), Czech Technical University in Prague (CTU), Palacký University in Olomouc (UPOL), Mendel University in Brno (MENDELU), Masaryk University in Brno (MUNI), Jan Evangelista Purkyně University, The Silesian University in Opava, Technical University of Ostrava, and University of Hradec Králové (UHK).

Czech Technical University in Prague also transferred teaching and resources to the online environment; they streamed lectures and organized video conferences, organized e-learning courses on Moodle. Teachers prepared self-study materials for students with a number of links and often created instructional videos. For example, the Faculty of Electrical Engineering has created an entire YouTube channel with a series of lectures on various topics, from cybernetics and mathematics to philosophy for technicians (CVUT-FEL, n.d.). This Faculty of Electrical Engineering, Czech Technical University in Prague channel is still active and has 22.4 thousand subscribers.

Palacký University in Olomouc (UPOL) also has set up a YouTube channel where its teachers gave lectures. For example, students of the Faculty of Education learned how to create an online test for their students (Univerzita Palackého, n.d.). Moodle became a popular and frequently used platform, as well.

Mendel University in Brno made thousands of Czech specialist books available through the Flexibooks Department of Scientific and Pedagogical Information and Services (MENDELU, n.d.)

The cost of borrowing was covered by the university library. There were more than 195,000 titles available, the library was negotiating with suppliers to expand the number of concurrently working users to an unlimited one. The e-mail assistance service was widely used, where librarians provided students with advice and instructions, they answered questions or searched for available books on the topic. With so-called contactless borrowing, the student requested the preparation of books in advance by e-mail, told the date of the visit, and the librarian then prepared the publications at the tables at the entrance.

Masaryk University was flexible and responded quickly to the restrictive situation. Masaryk University in Brno made thousands of books available online, so students could access them from home and continue their work. The most helpful for students was the so-called e-repository, which allowed them to borrow fifteen thousand of the most requested books that the university had physically purchased and scanned in the past (MUNILib, n.d.).

The e-learning support center at Charles University launched a pilot operation of the MOOC platform to make interesting knowledge available to the general public. The MOOC course platform of Charles University uses the open source software MOODLE and is located at mooc.cuni.cz. (Univerzita Karlova, 2019). Charles University's electronic provided consolidated information about all the eResources available at Charles University. These eResources were available to students (EIZ, n.d.). The Faculty of Mathematics and Physics of Charles University simply sent the necessary books to the students by a classic postal package. Many UK librarians have also been involved in promoting distance learning, coordinating the offer and helping with video learning tools such as Adobe Connect software or MS Teams for online teamwork.

Jan Evangelista Purkyně University, The Faculty of Art and Design streamed lectures on art, moderated discussions with external guests - artists, designers, art and design theorists, curators, philosophers or journalists on YouTube. The Research Library of University has extended its online databases for science and research to students. Students were introduced to use the EBSCO Discovery Service (EDS) search tool, which can efficiently search most of the electronic information resources available at the University from one place, both within licensed and a number of free databases on the Internet (UJEP, n.d.).

The Silesian University in Opava also switched to distance learning during the pandemic. In addition to making all the materials available to students in the form of e-learning and making available the digital collection of the university library, the e-shop of publications or the repository of final theses, it has also launched the university's Internet educational television (Lucerna TV, n.d.). It contains educational videos and documentaries, for some of which original study materials or methodological materials for teaching are also available.

At the Technical University of Ostrava in addition to access to the Krameria of the National Library or the online library Bookport.cz, they also managed the institutional repository DSpace VŠB-TUO, where scientific articles of university journals were archived and accessible together with full texts of university qualification theses. They have also launched an e-learning portal with links to the e-learning system and the library catalogue (VŠB-TUO, n.d.).

The above examples show that the pandemic has accelerated knowledge distribution at various spheres: in teaching, in the presentation of study material or in access to resources. The university provided resources and support to help students and staff adjust to the new learning environment. The dominant changes were in transition to online learning toward massive knowledge distribution and support for students and staff. The pandemic era was a time of rapid change and adaptation for the universities in the Czech Republic leading to lasting transformations in their educational practices.

The pandemic accelerated the use of massive knowledge distribution (De Moura et al., 2021).

## 3 Methodology

The aim of the article is to present a proven functional scenario for the implementation of MOOC courses into the university study system.

The individual stages will be described, graphically illustrated and supplemented with authentic documents and comments.

To cope with the pandemic, the Faculty of Informatics and Management, University of Hradec Kralove was faced with the question of how to proceed with online study within full-time study programmes. Although the faculty was generally well prepared for online learning, having more than 20 years of experience in creating e-learning courses and utilizing blended learning concept, the total onset of online learning in March 2020 proved challenging. (Cerna and Poulova, 2019). However, the situation was successfully managed, the blended learning materials were supplemented so that they were usable for full distance learning, synchronous tools such as videoconferencing were incorporated into the educational process. The technological aspect is not a problem at our faculty, as we are an established Faculty of Informatics and Management with a long history of success in implementing e-courses into teaching. (Poulová et al., 2010), (Poulova et al., 2013), (Poulova et al., 2022). Access to necessary technology and reliable internet connectivity are not a barrier for students of our faculty.

Despite the fact that the educational process went smoothly, the fatigue from online study was gradually growing on the part of both learners and teachers. The fatigue may be attributed to the constraints of social contacts, the difficulties of self-study and the laborious preparation of digital study materials. In the last semester of face-to-face teaching restrictions in the summer semester 2021/22, the faculty took advantage of COURSERA's offer of free licenses for students and gained valuable experience.

FIM has always placed great emphasis on students gaining international experience. Before COVID-19, 200 students went to study at foreign universities every year with the support of the faculty. The same number of foreign students studied at FIM.

Unfortunately, the COVID-19 outbreak has severely limited the possibilities of travel and face-to-face teaching. Since FIM has had experience creating and using e-learning courses to enhance teaching since 1999, we were very happy to use the COURSERA offer. In the spring of 2022, we registered and enabled our students to study.

Before the start of the academic year 2022/23, the faculty was faced with the question of whether, despite the fatigue of the online environment, to build on the positive experience with Coursera and invest in the purchase of licenses for students.

**Research Question**
*Are the courses offered by the COURSERA platform appealing enough to students in the post-COVID era?*

The attractiveness of MOOCs on the COURSERA platform as virtual mobility will be compared with students' interest in traditional mobility.

## 4 Results and Findings

In order to verify the research question, it was decided to purchase 150 licenses for the students of the faculty.

In addition to ensuring the license, it was necessary to prepare processes for integrating virtual mobility into the curriculum.

As for the scenario, we will start with the Dean's directive because it gives the legal weight to the initiative to incorporate completion of the course into the study system and it is binding.

### 4.1 Dean's Directive

The directive clarifies the possibility of completing virtual mobilities for both students and employees. The process begins with an explanation of what is involved, followed by a general description of the platform and material structure. Following that, there is a structured section dedicated to participation in virtual study mobility. The final section informs how subjects are recognized and how students earn credits.

### 4.2 Participation in the Virtual Mobility Program on the Coursera Platform

First, the Coursera platform itself is introduced as one of the world's largest online education platforms, where prestigious universities and major multinational companies offer more than 5,000 courses in 19 languages (https://www.coursera.org). Based on the partnership between Coursera and the Faculty of Informatics and Management of the University of Hradec Králové, students and employees have access to these study materials and certificates proving completion.

Every FIM UHK student can join the program. Coursera provides students with certificates of course completion. This section of the Dean's direction consists of two core parts: Organization of student selection in the Coursera licensing program and Study under the Coursera license program.

### 4.3 Organization of Student Selection in the Coursera Licensing Program

The announcement of the tender for time-limited licenses is published on the UHK website and Facebook. Students apply for individual selection procedures via the study mobility website by the deadline for the selection procedure published in the announcement.

The stage of registering for the competition includes the following determining points: addressing the students on the university website, allocation scheme of licenses, mandatory completion of at least one course, recognition of Coursera virtual mobility and conversion to ECTS credits in the university study system, status as a regular student and instructions on how to register for the competition, or who to turn to if necessary.

Students were directly approached on the university's website to apply for the competition. The information fully corresponds to the dean's directive. First, students are on the web provided with general background information about the Coursera educational platform. They are instructed that not only content of the courses varies but also their completion from simple tests to complex tasks or projects. Successful graduates in most cases receive a digital certificate with confirmation of completion, which is free or for a fee.

The key on the basis of which licenses are allocated is important for students. Allocation of licences is based on student's study results. Applicants who have not yet participated in the program will be given priority.

This year, the competition was announced for the sixth time under the name Virtual Mobility COURSERA – UHK.

### 4.4 Study Under the Coursera License Program

In case of a successful selection procedure and a free license, the student is informed about the license allocation by e-mail together with an invitation to register/log in to Coursera.

The license is assigned to the student for a limited period of time given in the tender announcement (usually 3 months). Within this period, the student can study any number of courses, but he is obliged to complete at least one. If he does not complete any course, he will be placed at the bottom of the order in the next selection procedure.

If the student does not respond to the invitation and does not register for any course in Coursera within 7 calendar days, his license will be revoked and he will be placed at the bottom of the order in the next selection process.

Another "vital" piece of information is the access time to the course, and perhaps the most important is the value of virtual mobility expressed in ECTS. A student can study any number of courses, but must complete at least one. Successfully completed courses will be recognized for students of bachelor's and master's study programs as so-called Coursera virtual mobility up to a total of 10 ECTS per academic year.

During virtual mobility, the applicant must be registered as a regular FIM UHK student and must not have closed or interrupted studies. Further conditions of participation and information about the program are given in Dean's Directive No. 2/2022 (Fig. 1).

**Fig. 1.** Scenario for the implementation of Coursera courses into the university study system.

## 4.5 Completion

A total of 1,214 courses were enrolled by individual users between October 2022 and May 2023. 658 of these courses were successfully completed by May 10, 2023. As of this date, 50 students earned credits under the terms of the Dean's directive.

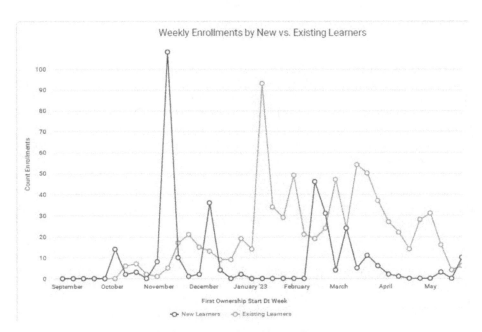

**Fig. 2.** Number of weekly enrollments

Figure 2 shows how users logged into the system. There are noticeable fluctuations related to individual selection procedures.

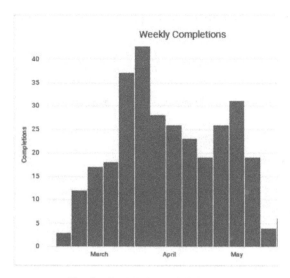

**Fig. 3.** Completions of Courses.

Figure 3 demonstrates the number of courses successfully completed from February to May 2023.

**4.6 Student Satisfaction**

The decision to use the COURSERA platform turned out to be excellent from the student's point of view as well. Their positive reaction testifies to this fact:

"*COURSERA exceeded my expectations. I completed several courses with a different focus - from HR, marketing, digital footprints to project management. Both beginners and advanced students will find it useful. In addition, the courses are from well-known universities and companies. I like the range, what the platform offers, as well as the form that is unique for each course (combination of video, texts, control tests, creation in programs,...) I like to supplement my knowledge here and expand my overview in the areas that interest me, but they are not taught (or not so much in-depth) at our university.*

*The obtained certificates are then taken out not only in the CV but also on the LinkedIn professional network, where they complete the overall impression. The platform is very clear and intuitive, and it is also possible to use a mobile application. Another advantage that I have to highlight about this platform is the use of the English language. I have noticeably improved in it. I am very grateful to have the opportunity to use Coursera and learn in many areas. I would definitely recommend all students to take advantage of this opportunity, because it brings a lot of possibilities and new knowledge.*"

Lucie

"*COURSERA as a platform was definitely beneficial. It contains a large number of courses from many different areas, which was very beneficial because I could try courses from programming to marketing to healthy nutrition. I think the selection of courses from the university was also quite well chosen for my study program. I am also glad that the* subjects were evaluated. I got the most from the Digital marketing course from Meta; the area was explained with practical examples and was well structured and supported by videos.

In general, I can only recommend the course and I am very happy that the university provides this option."

Jaroslav

## 5  Discussion and Conclusion

Mobility is important for students within a brick and mortar university, as it enables students to acquire knowledge, develop their intercultural skills and develop personally from the point of view of independence. Unfortunately, a number of objective reasons do not allow all students to gain international experience. The reasons can be economic, social or personal. Virtual mobilities are an opportunity to convey this experience to a much larger group of students.

A good option within virtual mobility is the use of MOOC courses. One of the platforms that offers a large number of quality courses is Coursera, which we chose. As far as physical mobilities are concerned, a limited number of students can travel, but within the framework of virtual mobilities there is a chance to satisfy the majority of genuine applicants.

The reality of the pandemic led us to an elaborate system of virtual mobility. At least something good came out of something very bad.

The significance of online learning platforms lies not only in their ability to provide flexible and self-paced learning opportunities but also in their potential to bridge educational gaps and foster lifelong learning. As traditional educational paradigms shift towards more inclusive and technology-driven models, the role of platforms like Coursera becomes increasingly critical in shaping the future of education.

**A Look into the Future**
Virtual mobility has the potential to further develop and become a common part of higher education. With the increasing emphasis on digitization and internationalization of education, more universities are expected to integrate MOOCs and virtual mobilities into their strategies.

## References

Bailes. A.P.: ERA challenges for Australian University ICT. Proceedings of the Thirty-fifth Australasian Computer Science Conference, pp. 63–72. Australian Computer Society (2012)

Bartunek, P.: Enhancing college students' intercultural competence through international electronic-service-learning. Rupkatha Journal on Interdisciplinary Studies in Humanities **15**(1) (2023)

Bustos, P.M., Avendaño, J.F., Valdivieso, A.: Implementation of curricular innovations in undergraduate engineering programs: scope and challenges. In: 2023 World Engineering Education Forum - Global Engineering Deans Council (WEEF-GEDC). IEEE, Monterrey (2023)

Cerna, M., Poulova, P.: Social software application and their role in the process of education from the perspective of university students. In: Proceedings of 11$^{th}$ European conference on e-learning, pp. 87–96. ACAD Conferences, Reading (2012)

Cerna, M., Poulova, P.: Reflection of students' language needs analysis in the e-course—comparative study. In: Uskov, V., Howlett, R., Jain, L. (eds.) Smart Education and e-Learning 2019. Smart Innovation, Systems and Technologies, vol 144. Springer, Singapore (2019)

Cooper, T.: Curriculum renewal: barriers to successful curriculum change and suggestions for improvement. J. Educ. Train. Stud. **5**(11), 115–128 (2017)

Coursera: Coursera for Campus (n.d.). https://www.coursera.org/campus

Coursera: What Are College Credits? (2023). https://www.coursera.org/articles/what-are-college-credits

CVUTFEL: Fakulta elektrotechnická ČVUT v Praze. Záznamy přednášek, promovidea kateder a výzkumných skupin, akce, výzkumné výsledky aj (n.d.). https://www.youtube.com/user/CVUTFEL/playlists

De Moura, F.V., De Souza, A.C., Noronha, A.B.: The use of Massive Open Online Courses (MOOCs) in blended learning courses and the functional value perceived by students. Computers & Education 161 (2021)

EIZ: Charles University's eResources Portal (n.d.). https://cuni.primo.exlibrisgroup.com/discovery/search?vid=420CKIS_INST:DB&lang=en

Francisco, A.B.: Virtual mobility: the lived experience of exchange students in a higher education institution in Asia. In: Proceeding of the 2nd International Conference on Education and Technology. Atlantis Press, Madiun (2022)

Lucerna, T.V.: Internet educational television (n.d.). https://www.lucernatv.cz/

MENDELU: Department of Scientific and Pedagogical Information and Services (n.d.). https://uvis.mendelu.cz/en/dspis-about-department

MUNILib: Electronic Information Resources Portal at MU (n.d.). https://ezdroje.muni.cz/index.php?lang=en

Nguyen, A.: Intercultural competence in short-term study abroad. Frontiers: The Interdisciplinary Journal of Study Abroad **29**(2), 109–127 (2017)

Poulova, P., Cerna, M., Svobodova, L.: University Network – Efficiency of Virtual Mobility. In: EDUTE 2009: Proceedings of the 5$^{th}$ WSEAS/IASME International Conference on Educational Technologies, pp. 87–92. WSEAS, Athens (2009)

Schueller, J., Şahin, B.B.: Considering the complexities of virtual student mobility as an approach to inclusive internationalisation in the post-pandemic period. Perspectives: Policy and Practice in Higher Education **27**(3), 96–104 (2022)

TOPUNIVESRITIES: University of Hradec Kralove (2024). https://www.topuniversities.com/universities/university-hradec-kralove#p2-rankings

UJEP: ELECTRONIC RESOURCES UJEP (n.d.). https://knihovna.ujep.cz/cs/4399/elektronicke-zdroje-ujepUJEP

Umar, A.W.: Challenges of implementing European credit transfer system at university of Raparin. J. Lang. Stud. **5**(1), 181–186 (2021)

Univerzita Karlova: E-learningové vzdělávání na UK (2019). https://cuni.cz/UK-10080.html

Univerzita Palackého: Nejsledovanější videokanál mezi vysokými školami v ČR! (n.d.). https://www.youtube.com/@PalackyUniversity

Valtins, K., Muracova, N.: Virtual mobility for students, going from distance learning to live participation. Periodical of Engineerings and Natural Sciences. **7**(1), 222–227 (2019)

VŠB-TUO: EDUDOCS (n.d.). https://www.vsb.cz/e-vyuka/en

# Learning Analytics in Education

# Identification of Potential At-Risk Students Through an Intelligent Multi-model Academic Analytics Platform

Kam Cheong Li, Billy T. M. Wong[✉], and Mengjin Liu

Institute for Research in Open and Innovative Education, Hong Kong Metropolitan University. Ho Man Tin, Kowloon, Hong Kong SAR, China
{kcli,tamiwong,mjliu}@hkmu.edu.hk

**Abstract.** The identification of students potentially at risk of having learning difficulties is of utmost importance for the provision of timely support. This paper presents an intelligent academic analytics platform which features a multi-model prediction approach to identify students potentially at risk of failing a course. The platform aims to help instructors identify potential at-risk students at the beginning of a course so that appropriate learning support can be provided early. It employs three supervised machine learning algorithms – linear regression, XGBoost, and decision tree – to build predictive models. A student's risk level is based on the predicted grade s/he will receive for a course, determined by integrating the prediction results of the three models using a majority vote method. The platform also provides supplementary information about students, such as past course grades and factors contributing to the predicted risk levels, for instructors' reference to inform learning support strategies. Preliminary evaluation results show that the platform correctly identified about 39% of students who failed their courses. The results suggest that some students who were predicted as having a high risk of failing at the beginning of a course would eventually pass with the learning support provided after early identification. This demonstrates the effectiveness of the platform in enhancing student success through proactive support enabled by early prediction of academic risk.

**Keywords:** At-risk students · prediction · learning analytics · academic analytics · student support

## 1 Introduction

The identification of students potentially at risk of having learning difficulties is crucial for providing timely and effective support. By identifying at-risk students at an early stage of a course, instructors can implement proactive measures to address potential challenges encountered by the students before the challenges escalate, so that the students' learning experience and outcomes could be enhanced. Relevant research has consistently shown that early intervention can significantly improve students' academic performance and retention rates (Franco et al., 2017; Gordanier et al., 2019; Lizzio and Wilson, 2013; Villano et al., 2018).

Learning analytics has emerged as a powerful tool for predicting academic risk and informing educational interventions (Sghir et al., 2023). Leveraging vast amounts of student data from various sources, educators can gain comprehensive insights into learning behaviours and identify students who may struggle in their courses. This facilitates data-informed decisions about resource allocation, instructional strategies, and personalised support in a timely manner. For example, prediction models were proposed using in-class clicker data and students' prior learning data to identify at-risk students, enabling early interventions to increase success rates (Choi et al., 2018). Other examples include alert systems that provide real-time insights and early warnings based on predictive analysis of student risk factors (Akçapınar et al., 2019; Cechinel et al., 2024; Jayaprakash et al., 2014).

This study aims to contribute to the growing body of research in this field by presenting an intelligent platform that employs a multi-model prediction approach to identify students potentially at risk of course failure. The platform combines three supervised machine learning algorithms using a majority vote method to provide a comprehensive assessment of student risk levels. Moreover, efficient and user-friendly dashboards were developed to visualise the predictive results for course instructors.

## 2 Related Work

Learning analytics draws upon a diverse array of data sources to identify at-risk students and predict academic performance, ranging from traditional academic records to digital footprints in learning management systems. From an analysis of 233 related studies, Li et al. (2024) observed that the common types of data include students' academic performance, socio-demographics, and learning behaviours. The types and sources of data used for learning analytics typically depend on factors such as the learning environment, institutional data infrastructure, course design, and technology integration (Elouazizi, 2014).

For example, Zhao et al. (2020) developed an academic performance prediction model based on students' behavioural data collected from multiple sources, including SPOC platform data (e.g., online learning frequency and duration, and learning emotions), Smart Card data (e.g., library interactions), and Wi-Fi data (e.g., frequency and duration in study areas, and attendance in class). With the rich profiles of students, the proposed model offered an insightful overview of students' behavioural patterns and demonstrated high accuracy in predicting academic performance. Tempelaar et al. (2020) examined the strengths and weaknesses of various data types in designing predictive models for academic performance. They found that data collected from surveys were significantly affected by response style bias, while trace data, particularly those of the product type, remain independent of these biases, which can enhance the accuracy of predictive models.

As reported in the literature, a variety of machine learning techniques and algorithms have been applied to create models to predict at-risk students. As identified by Li et al. (2024), the most popular algorithms include decision tree (e.g., Matzavela and Alepis, 2021; Sithole et al., 2023), neural networks (e.g., Yang et al., 2020; Latif et al., 2021), and Bayesian networks (e.g., Hao et al., 2022; Lakho et al., 2022). They all belong to the classification methods, which organise objects with similar characteristics into classes. Classification is regarded as "one of the most frequently used methods in machine learning to find at-risk students in educational environments" (Huang et al., 2019, p. 208).

Some studies employed multiple machine learning methods to determine the one which yields the most accurate prediction results for identifying at-risk students. For example, Bayazit et al. (2022) created a model to predict at-risk students in an online flipped course. They utilised five algorithms (i.e., k-nearest neighbours, decision tree, naïve Bayes, random forest, and support vector machines) and found that the naïve Bayes algorithm showed the best performance. By comparing the performance of six algorithms, Queiroga et al. (2022) selected random forest to develop models to predict students at risk of failure or dropping out in the K-12 context.

Ensemble learning techniques were also used to combine high-performing models to achieve precise estimations. Pek et al. (2022) constructed a model to identify at-risk students in high schools using data on academic and demographic characteristics, as well as course grades. They integrated seven machine learning algorithms with the ensemble stacking method to produce the best prediction results. Kustitskaya et al. (2024) trained and validated four algorithms to predict learning performance, and then developed a weighted average ensemble approach to combine these algorithms, leveraging the strengths of each model for better prediction quality.

Despite a range of related work on learning analytics has been carried out for identifying at-risk students, there have been limitations that the current study seeks to address. One limitation is the underutilisation of ensemble learning techniques which have shown promise in other fields but their use remain limited in predicting student performance. Additionally, many articles on this topic focused on illustrating theoretical frameworks without offering details about data processing or visualisations of learning analytics tools. These limitations hinder the effective transformation of relevant research into meaningful interventions that support struggling students.

To address these limitations, this study proposes an exploratory method that integrates the prediction results of three distinct models using a majority vote technique. Dashboards were developed and utilised to present related information to instructors with the aim of facilitating timely interventions and personalised support for students identified as potentially at risk.

## 3 Development of an Intelligent Academic Analytics Platform

### 3.1 Data Collection

For developing an intelligent academic analytics platform, the data collected include students' socio-demographic data, general academic records, and previous academic achievements. These data were collected from the university's data warehouse and transformed into the format required by the platform. Table 1 shows the major types of the collected data.

### 3.2 Multi-model Prediction Approach

Supervised machine learning techniques were adopted for building predictive models to identify students who are at risk of failing a course. Students who are predicted to receive a final grade of C or below for a course are considered at a high risk of failing the course, those with a predicted grade between C+ and B− are at a medium risk, and those with a predicted grade of B or above are considered at a low risk.

**Table 1.** Major types of students' data collected for development of the platform

| Data category | Data item | Description |
|---|---|---|
| Socio-demographic data | Residential area | Indicating the living locations of students |
| | Local/non local | Indicating if a student is local or non-local |
| | Marital status | Indicating if a student is single, married, or divorced |
| | Gender | Indicating a student's gender |
| | Age | Age of the student |
| General academic records | Year of study | Year of study in a programme |
| | Programme | Programme title |
| | Total credits taken | Total credits taken in the term |
| | Term | Term (Spring/Summer/Autumn) |
| | Subject | Course subject area |
| | Scholarship amount | Cumulated amount of scholarship obtained |
| | No. of course taken in the term | Number of courses taken in the term |
| | No. of awards obtained | Number of scholarship/awards obtained |
| | No. of attempts of the course | Number of attempts in the course |
| | Credits | Credits of the course |
| | Course level | Course level (Foundation/Middle/Higher) |
| | Course duration | Duration of the course |
| Previous academic achievements | GPA change | GPA change over last two terms |
| | Course passing rate_last term | Course passing rate in last term |
| | CGPA_last term | CGPA of last term |
| Dependent variables | Course grade point | Grade point obtained by the student for the course |
| | Course letter grade | Letter grade obtained by the student for the course |

During the development phase of the intelligent academic analytics platform, a number of machine learning algorithms that support classification and regression were tested. Three algorithms were finally chosen for deployment as they were shown to provide relatively high interpretability for prediction, efficient model training performance, and stable performance in terms of accuracy. The following describes the three selected machine learning algorithms.

- **Linear Regression**: It is a linear approach for modelling, which aims to identify a linear function that explains the dependent variable (i.e., final grade) by the independent variable(s) (e.g., CGPA of the student). Linear Regression is popular because it produces accurate predictions and is very easy to apply (Al-Fairouz and Al-Hagery, 2020).
- **Decision Tree**: It is "a method for classifying by looking for differences between classes and dividing them using attributes by making a diagram in the form of a tree" (Priyasadie and Isa, 2021, p. 215). In the tree structure, each internal node represents a test on an attribute, each branch indicates an outcome of the test, and each leaf node denotes a class label. Decision Tree (DT) generates an "IF-THEN" decision rule to find the prediction results, which is simple and easy to comprehend.
- **XGBoost**: Extreme Gradient Boosting is an extension of Gradient Boosting (GB), which is an ensemble constructed from DT models that performs classification with speed and scale. XGBoost is able to handle extensive datasets by making use of multiple decision trees to perform prediction. Unlike DT that trees are built sequentially, trees are built in parallel with XGBoost so that learning can occur in parallel during training.

The three machine learning algorithms are run separately, and a total of three predictive models are created. A multi-model prediction approach is employed, with each model having equal weight in the final decision. The risk level is determined by majority vote: if at least two models predict a high risk, the student is classified as having a high risk.

### 3.3 Dashboards

Power BI was used as the visualisation tool for this intelligent multi-model academic analytics platform. Mock data have been used in the figures below to present the dashboard design. Figure 1 shows the main page of the dashboards, which displays an overview of the selected course for an instructor, including the course summary, prediction summary, and student data. Specifically, the prediction summary allows users to view the distribution of students by risk level, programme, or year of study. Additionally, users can view the relevant details of a selected student on this page. The risk level of a student is displayed in three colours, in which red represents a high risk of failing the course, amber indicates a moderate risk, and green indicates a low risk.

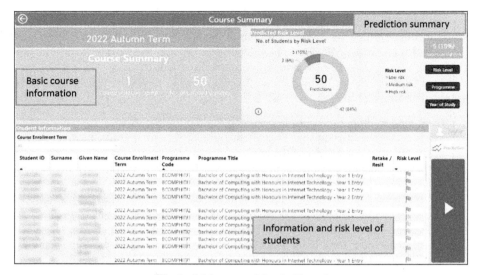

**Fig. 1.** Main page of the dashboard

Figure 2 presents the dashboard of prediction results for a course. Prediction quality is indicated by the number of stars at the top. A larger number of stars represents higher accuracy in the predictions. The maximum number of stars is four, implying that the Mean Absolute Error (MAE) of the prediction is less than one sub-grade. The number of stars decreases by one when the MAE increases by one sub-grade. The risk level of each student is presented in the last column based on the aforementioned majority vote method.

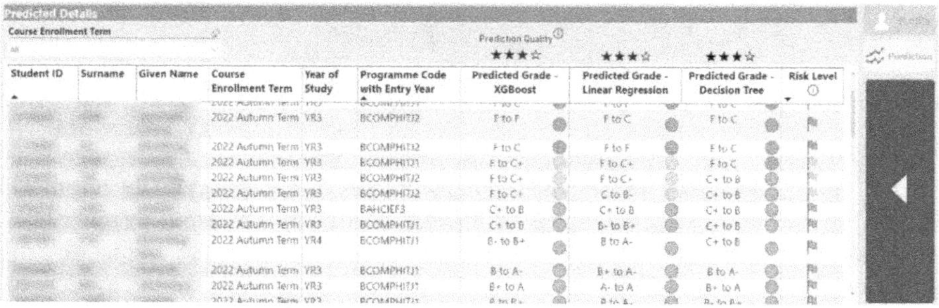

**Fig. 2.** Dashboard of prediction results for a course

Figure 3 shows the view of a student profile. The basic information section at the top shows the student's name, address, email, current year of study, gender, and number of courses at high risk. The course enrolment records section at the bottom left corner provides an overview of the courses the student has taken, along with their respective grades. Additionally, the CGPA (Cumulative Grade Point Average) and GPA

Identification of Potential At-Risk Students    205

(Grade Point Average) section at the bottom right corner offers insights into the student's academic performance over time, allowing for easy tracking of progress.

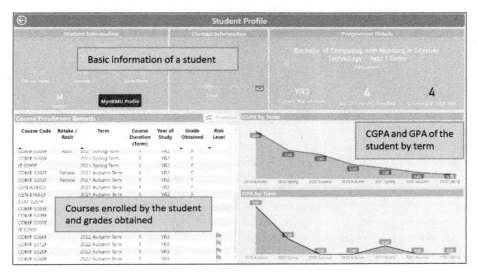

Fig. 3. Dashboard of a student profile

Figure 4 shows the dashboard of prediction results for each student. It displays the CGPA of a student by term in the top left corner. The top right section presents the selected courses for the current term, along with the predicted grades by each of the three predictive models. When a course is selected in this section, the prediction information

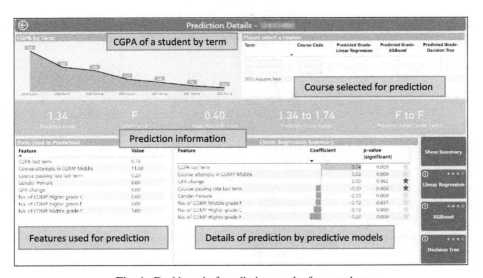

Fig. 4. Dashboard of prediction results for a student

is shown in the middle, including the predicted grade, MAE, and predicted grade range. The dashboard also allows instructors to view the factors used in predicting the student's grade and details of predictions by each predictive model.

## 4 Preliminary Evaluation Results

A preliminary evaluation for the platform was conducted at the beginning of a Spring term. The dataset used for the evaluation included student data from three previous terms (Spring, Summer, and Autumn), covering 105 courses with a total sample size of 65,841 course enrolments. Eighty percent of the dataset was randomly selected for model training, and the remaining 20% was used for testing.

The performance of the multi-model prediction approach was measured by several evaluation metrics, including accuracy, precision, recall, and F1 score. These metrics were calculated based on statistical measures of true positive (TP), true negative (TN), false positive (FP), and false negative (FN). In this study, since the aim of the prediction was to identify students who are at risk of failing a course, those who were predicted to be at high risk of failing were regarded as "positive" cases, while those who were predicted to be at medium or low risk are considered "negative" cases. The medium- and low-risk students were grouped together, and the high-risk students were put as a separate group, because the platform was designed primarily for identifying the high-risk students to support effective resource allocation and targeted interventions tailored for these students who are mostly in need. Table 2 presents a confusion matrix of the prediction results for the Spring term for evaluation.

**Table 2.** Confusion matrix of the prediction results for evaluation

|  |  | Predicted results | |
|---|---|---|---|
|  |  | High risk | Medium/Low risk |
| **Actual results** | Fail | TP (n = 571) | FN (n = 886) |
|  | Pass | FP (n = 1012) | TN (n = 676) |

The four evaluation metrics were measured based on the following formulas. Table 3 presents the preliminary evaluation results. The performance metrics of the predictive model reveal a modest level of accuracy and balanced performance. The accuracy result shows that the model correctly predicted the outcomes for 40% of cases. The recall result indicates that the model successfully identified 39% of the actual at-risk students, highlighting its performance to detect students who need support. However, the precision result suggests that only 36% of the students predicted to be at risk were indeed at risk, revealing a relatively high number of false positives. The F-measure, which balances precision and recall, stands at 0.37, reflecting a consistent but modest performance across these metrics.

$$\text{Accuracy} = \frac{TP + TN}{TP + TN + FP + FN}$$

$$\text{Recall} = \frac{TP}{TP + FN}$$

$$\text{Precision} = \frac{TP}{TP + FP}$$

$$\text{F1 Score} = 2 \times \frac{\text{Precision} \times \text{Recall}}{\text{Precision} + \text{Recall}}$$

**Table 3.** Performance of the multi-model prediction approach in the preliminary evaluation

| Performance metrics | Values |
|---|---|
| Accuracy | 40% |
| Recall | 0.39 |
| Precision | 0.36 |
| F-measure | 0.37 |

## 5  Discussion and Conclusion

This paper presents an intelligent academic analytics platform that utilises a multi-model prediction approach to identify students at risk of failing courses. By employing three supervised machine learning algorithms and integrating their predictions through a majority vote method, the platform facilitates early identification and timely support for at-risk students.

The preliminary evaluation results, showing 39% of students who were correctly identified to have failed their courses, should be interpreted in light of the platform's practical implementation. This modest rate does not necessarily indicate poor predictive performance, but may reflect the positive impact of early interventions. These students were predicted as high-risk at the beginning of courses, and their course instructors were informed of these students for offering timely support and targeted interventions. Part of these students may have eventually passed their courses, making the initial risk assessment appear less accurate than it actually was. This outcome aligns with research by Bin Mat et al. (2013) and Arnold and Pistilli (2012), which emphasises the critical role of early and targeted support in improving academic success. The platform thus demonstrates its value not just as a predictive tool, but as an effective driver for timely learning support.

The platform has been constrained by its scope of data. The prediction was conducted at the beginning of a term on the basis of learning performance of the preceding courses, omitting potentially important real-time data generated during the learning process of the current course, such as ongoing assignment performance, class participation, and engagement metrics. The inclusion of these dynamic indicators would enhance prediction accuracy, allowing for a more comprehensive and timely assessment of student risk factors (Qiu et al., 2022; Lin et al., 2024). By continuously feeding real-time data, the predictive models can better adapt to changes in student behaviours and performance. This allows the predictions to reflect more accurately the latest trends and patterns, leading to more reliable assessments of student risk factors and potential outcomes.

Future work should focus on addressing these limitations by incorporating real-time data to enable continuous prediction throughout a course. Additionally, more sophisticated ensemble methods, such as weighted voting or stacking, should be explored to improve prediction accuracy. Furthermore, investigating user experiences will be crucial for further refinement and validation, ensuring that the platform realises its full potential in supporting at-risk students.

**Acknowledgment.** The work described in this paper was partially supported by a grant from Hong Kong Metropolitan University (CP/2022/04).

## References

Akçapınar, G., Altun, A., Aşkar, P.: Using learning analytics to develop early-warning system for at-risk students. Int. J. Educ. Technol. Higher Educ. **16**(1) (2019). https://doi.org/10.1186/s41239-019-0172-z

Al-Fairouz, E.I., Al-Hagery, M.A.: Students performance: From detection of failures and anomaly cases to the solutions-based mining algorithms. Int. J. Eng. Res. Technol. **13**(10), 2895–2908 (2020)

Arnold, K.E., Pistilli, M.D.: Course signals at Purdue: Using learning analytics to increase student success. In: Proceedings of the 2nd international conference on learning analytics and knowledge, pp. 267–270 (2012)

Bayazit, A., Apaydin, N., Gonullu, I.: Predicting at-risk students in an online flipped anatomy course using learning analytics. Education Sciences **12**(9), 581 (2022)

Bin Mat, U., Buniyamin, N., Arsad, P.M., Kassim, R.: An overview of using academic analytics to predict and improve students' achievement: A proposed proactive intelligent intervention. In: 2013 IEEE 5th conference on engineering education (ICEED), pp. 126–130. IEEE (2013)

Cechinel, C., et al.: LANSE: a cloud-powered learning analytics platform for the automated identification of students at risk in learning management systems. In: International Conference on Artificial Intelligence in Education, pp. 127–138. Springer Nature Switzerland, Cham (2024)

Choi, S.P., Lam, S.S., Li, K.C., Wong, B.T.: Learning analytics at low cost: At-risk student prediction with clicker data and systematic proactive interventions. J. Educ. Technol. Soc. **21**(2), 273–290 (2018)

Elouazizi, N.: Critical factors in data governance for learning analytics. J. Learn. Anal. **1**(3), 211–222 (2014)

Franco, V., Melo, M., Santos, G., Apolónio, A., Amaral, L.: A national early intervention system as a strategy to promote inclusion and academic achievement in Portugal. Front. Psychol. **8**, 1137 (2017)

Gordanier, J., Hauk, W., Sankaran, C.: Early intervention in college classes and improved student outcomes. Econ. Educ. Rev. **72**, 23–29 (2019)

Hao, J., Gan, J., Zhu, L.: MOOC performance prediction and personal performance improvement via Bayesian network. Educ. Inf. Technol. **27**(5), 7303–7326 (2022)

Huang, A.Y.Q., Lu, O.H.T., Huang, J.C.H., Yin, C.J., Yang, S.J.H.: Predicting students' academic performance by using educational big data and learning analytics: evaluation of classification methods and learning logs. Interact. Learn. Environ. **28**(2), 206–230 (2019)

Jayaprakash, S.M., Moody, E.W., Lauría, E.J., Regan, J.R., Baron, J.D.: Early alert of academically at-risk students: an open source analytics initiative. J. Learn. Anal. **1**(1), 6–47 (2014)

Kustitskaya, T.A., Esin, R.V., Vainshtein, Y.V., Noskov, M.V.: Hybrid approach to predicting learning success based on digital educational history for timely identification of at-risk students. Education Sciences **14**(6), 657 (2024)

Lakho, S., Jalbani, A.H., Memon, I.A., Soomro, S.S., Chandio, A.A.: Development of an integrated blended learning model and its performance prediction on students' learning using Bayesian network. J. Intel. Fuzzy Sys. **43**(2), 2015–2023 (2022)

Latif, G., Alghazo, R., Pilotti, M.A., Brahim, G.B.: Identifying" At-Risk" Students: An AI-based Prediction Approach. Int. J. Comp. Digi. Sys. **11**(1), 1051–1059 (2021)

Li, K.C., Wong, B.T.M., Liu, M.: A survey on predicting at-risk students through learning analytics. Int. J. Inno. Learn. **36**(5), 1–15 (2024)

Lin, C.C., Cheng, E.S., Huang, A.Y., Yang, S.J.: DNA of learning behaviors: A novel approach of learning performance prediction by NLP. Comp. Educ. Artif. Intel. **6**, 100227 (2024)

Lizzio, A., Wilson, K.: Early intervention to support the academic recovery of first-year students at risk of non-continuation. Innov. Educ. Teach. Int. **50**(2), 109–120 (2013)

Matzavela, V., Alepis, E.: Decision tree learning through a predictive model for student academic performance in intelligent m-learning environments. Comp. Educ. Artif. Intel. **2**, 100035 (2021)

Pek, R.Z., Özyer, S.T., Elhage, T., Özyer, T., Alhajj, R.: The role of machine learning in identifying students at-risk and minimizing failure. IEEE Access **11**, 1224–1243 (2022)

Priyasadie, N., Isa, S.M.: Educational data mining in predicting student final grades on standardized Indonesia Data Pokok Pendidikan data set. Int. J. Adv. Comput. Sci. Appl. **12**(12), 212–216 (2021)

Qiu, F., et al.: Predicting students' performance in e-learning using learning process and behaviour data. Sci. Rep. **12**(1), 453 (2022)

Queiroga, E.M., Batista Machado, M.F., Paragarino, V.R., Primo, T.T., Cechinel, C.: Early prediction of at-risk students in secondary education: a countrywide k-12 learning analytics initiative in Uruguay. Information **13**(9), 401 (2022)

Sghir, N., Adadi, A., Lahmer, M.: Recent advances in Predictive Learning Analytics: A decade systematic review (2012–2022). Educ. Inf. Technol. **28**(7), 8299–8333 (2023)

Sithole, S.T., Ran, G., De Lange, P., Tharapos, M., O'Connell, B., Beatson, N.: Data mining: will first-year results predict the likelihood of completing subsequent units in accounting programs? Acc. Educ. **32**(4), 409–444 (2023)

Tempelaar, D., Rienties, B., Nguyen, Q.: Subjective data, objective data and the role of bias in predictive modelling: Lessons from a dispositional learning analytics application. PLoS ONE **15**(6), e0233977 (2020)

Villano, R., Harrison, S., Lynch, G., Chen, G.: Linking early alert systems and student retention: a survival analysis approach. High. Educ. **76**, 903–920 (2018)

Yang, Z., Yang, J., Rice, K., Hung, J.L., Du, X.: Using convolutional neural network to recognize learning images for early warning of at-risk students. IEEE Trans. Learn. Technol. **13**(3), 617–630 (2020)

Zhao, L., et al.: Academic performance prediction based on multisource, multifeature behavioral data. IEEE Access **9**, 5453–5465 (2020)

# An Investigation into the Application of Learning Analytics in Collaborative Learning

Billy T. M. Wong[✉], Kam Cheong Li, and Mengjin Liu

Institute for Research in Open and Innovative Education, Hong Kong Metropolitan University.
Ho Man Tin, Kowloon, Hong Kong SAR, China
{tamiwong,kcli,mjliu}@hkmu.edu.hk

**Abstract.** Collaborative learning has been recognised for its potential to enhance learning outcomes. With the advent of relevant data collection and analysis techniques, learning analytics has emerged as a powerful tool to support and enhance collaborative learning experiences. This paper offers a comprehensive review of the application of learning analytics in enhancing collaborative learning. A total of 89 research articles, published between 2014 and 2023 and related to the use of learning analytics in collaborative learning, were sourced from Scopus for analysis. The review focused on various aspects including the settings, objectives, data types, and techniques associated with the use of learning analytics in collaborative learning. The findings indicate that online learning environments are the most common setting for collaborative learning activities supported by learning analytics, followed by blended and face-to-face settings. The primary objectives of learning analytics include monitoring and understanding collaborative processes, assessing engagement and participation, and predicting and improving performance. The most frequently used data types include behavioural and interaction data, as well as communication data, primarily collected from learning management systems, collaborative learning platforms, cameras, and sensors. The most prevalent learning analytics techniques include machine learning, network analysis, and statistical analysis. The results of this study contribute to informing the design and implementation of effective collaborative learning activities. By leveraging data-driven insights, instructors can optimise engagement, participation, and learning outcomes in collaborative learning settings.

**Keywords:** Learning analytics · collaborative learning · systematic review · online learning environment

## 1 Introduction

Collaborative learning refers to a set of teaching and learning strategies involving learners working together to achieve shared learning goals (Dillenbourg, 1999; Le et al., 2018). It contrasts with traditional teacher-led instruction by emphasising student interaction, cooperation, and mutual support. Collaborative learning has been recognised for its potential to improve learning outcomes, in terms of expanding students' perspectives, encouraging debate and idea elaboration, and thereby enhancing critical thinking skills (Tedla and Chen, 2024). By providing opportunities for exchanging and organising knowledge with others, collaborative learning can also promote students' learning attitudes, motivation, achievement, and self-efficacy (Sung and Hwang, 2013).

Analysing data generated through the collaborative learning process provides important insights into student interactions, engagement levels, and learning outcomes. With the development of advanced data collection and analysis techniques, learning analytics has emerged as a powerful tool to enhance and support collaborative learning experiences. Through collecting and interpreting data on student participation, communication patterns, and group dynamics, learning analytics plays a crucial role in measuring learning engagement and social interaction (Xing et al., 2023; Sharma et al., 2023), providing personalised feedback to students (Cornide-Reyes et al., 2020; Zheng et al., 2022), predicting learning gains and performance (Cen et al., 2016; Olsen et al., 2020), and assisting instructors in providing timely interventions (Tlili et al., 2021; Kasepalu et al., 2023).

Despite much research on the application of learning analytics in collaborative learning contexts, only a limited number of studies have been conducted to systematically analyse relevant work (Dado and Bodemer, 2017; Kaliisa et al., 2022; Yan et al., 2023; Ouyang and Zhang, 2024). Relevant studies are constrained by their focus on specific types of learning analytics techniques, such as social network analysis and artificial intelligence, as well as their emphasis on particular learning environments, including face-to-face and computer-supported collaborative learning contexts. These limitations highlight the need for a broader investigation that encompasses a wider range of learning analytics approaches and diverse educational settings to understand comprehensively their application and effectiveness for collaborative learning. The present study addresses the limitations by covering the following research questions:

- What learning modes have been adopted in collaborative learning activities supported by learning analytics?
- What objectives have been achieved by learning analytics in collaborative learning?
- What types of data and analytical techniques have been utilised to facilitate collaborative learning?

## 2 Related Work

Collaborative learning is rooted in the sociocultural theory (Vygotsky, 1978) which emphasises the crucial role of social interactions in the learning process. It broadly covers a variety of instructional approaches that engage learners in collective intellectual endeavours. Key elements of collaborative learning include positive interdependence, significant interaction, individual accountability, social skills, and group processing (Laal and Laal, 2012). Several review studies have specifically explored these elements, examining topics such as group formation strategies and techniques (Maqtary et al., 2019; Putro et al., 2020), learners' self-regulation (Sharma et al., 2024), and interaction promotion (Strauß and Rummel, 2020; Huang and Lajoie, 2023).

Collaborative learning has gained growing popularity due to technological advancements. Related reviews have explored various tools and techniques that facilitate collaborative learning. For example, Al-Samarraie and Saeed (2018) analysed publications on cloud computing tools for collaborative learning. They categorised relevant tools into synchronised tools, learning management systems, and social networking tools, which support collaborative learning activities such as sharing, editing, communication, and discussion. Tan et al. (2022) reviewed related literature to examine the aspects of collaborative learning supported by artificial intelligence (AI), including collective performance, learning contents, sentiments and emotions, discourse patterns and talk moves, learner characteristics and behaviours. They also identified the AI techniques that serve the purposes of discovering, learning, and reasoning. Paulsen et al. (2024) investigated the use of immersive virtual reality in collaborative learning, highlighting its potential as a shared experience in an immersive, virtually mediated environment where learners engage with a common goal or problem.

Over the past decade, learning analytics has gained widespread adoption in the education domain, leading to a surge in review studies on this topic. These reviews have examined various aspects, including the applications, trends, and challenges of learning analytics across different educational levels, with a particular emphasis on higher education (Wong, 2017; Wong et al., 2018; Cerratto Pargman and McGrath, 2021; Stojanov and Daniel, 2024) and K-12 settings (Paolucci et al., 2024). Some studies have explored specific learning analytics tools and techniques, such as visual analytics (Vieira et al., 2018), video analytics (Yürüm et al., 2023), machine learning (Tahiru et al., 2023; Pandian et al., 2023), and dashboards (Ramaswami et al., 2023; Paulsen and Lindsay, 2024). Others have concentrated on students' performance and success (Costa et al., 2020; Ifenthaler and Yau, 2020), as well as the prediction of dropout and at-risk students (de Oliveira et al., 2021; Li et al., 2023).

There has been growing interest in the integration of learning analytics with learning theories and pedagogical approaches, such as self-regulated learning (Wong et al., 2019; Heikkinen et al., 2023), game-based learning (Alonso-Fernández et al., 2019; Banihashem et al., 2023), and personalised learning (Wong et al., 2023; Khor and K, 2023). Reviews have also examined the adoption of learning analytics in collaborative learning. For example, Dado and Bodemer (2017) surveyed 89 publications related to the application of social network analysis (SNA) in computer-supported collaborative learning (CSCL) and found that the applications primarily focused on one-mode networks of learners connected by communication-based ties, providing mostly descriptive results. The authors recommend including technical, instructional, and knowledge artefacts as SNA actors and relating SNA findings to cognitive, social, and motivational outcomes using statistical analysis. Based on a systematic review of 36 studies on social learning analytics (SLA), Kaliisa et al. (2022) found that SLA has been predominantly utilised in formal online settings, in which SNA was primarily employed to understand students' learning processes through a social constructivist lens. Yan et al. (2023) identified key opportunities provided by socio-spatial learning analytics (SSLA), including unobtrusive research methodologies, support for classroom orchestration and learner reflection, development of new theories on collaborative learning, and empowerment of stakeholders with quantitative data for evaluating learning spaces. Ouyang and Zhang (2024) reviewed AI-driven learning analytics applications and tools in CSCL, revealing that while existing tools primarily focus on students' cognitive engagement and utilise various data types, there is a need for more comprehensive design principles, advanced

AI techniques for multi-source and multimodal data analysis, and improved support for instructional interventions in CSCL contexts.

These review studies on the use of learning analytics in collaborative learning however have limitations, such as being restricted to specific types of learning analytics techniques (e.g., SLA, SNA, SSLA, and AI) and focusing on specific learning environments only (e.g., face-to-face and CSCL contexts). To address the literature gap, this study is aimed to provide a comprehensive investigation into various learning analytics applications and tools in collaborative learning settings, including face-to-face, online, and blended learning, in order to reveal how learning analytics can be effectively integrated into collaborative learning practices.

## 3 Methodology

### 3.1 Data Collection

For this study, relevant publications were collected from the Scopus database. A set of keywords [("learning analytics" OR "data mining" OR "machine learning") AND "collaborative learning"] was used to search for journal articles published in the period from 2014 to 2023. An initial search returned 441 results, which were then screened according to the following selection criteria: (i) the article reports an empirical study of collaborative learning supported by learning analytics; (ii) it describes the collaborative learning activities and learning analytics methods in detail; (iii) it was set in a school context; (iv) it was written in English; (v) it was available in full text. Publications that fail to meet any of these criteria were excluded from the present study. A total of 89 articles were finally selected for analysis.

### 3.2 Data Analysis

A content analysis approach was employed to analyse the selected articles. Each article was checked to identify and categorise the information about the contexts and features of learning analytics approaches applied in collaborative learning, including learning modes, objectives of learning analytics, data types, data sources, and learning analytics techniques. The coding process involved two researchers: one focused on identifying and categorising information, and the other was responsible for verification. Further reviews were conducted for conflicting cases until a consensus was achieved.

## 4 Results

### 4.1 Number of Publications

Figure 1 shows the number of the publications between 2014 and 2023. The number remained low in the early years, with no more than three publications in each year between 2014 and 2016. There was an increase in the number, particularly since 2021. The upward trend continued into 2023, reaching a peak of 24 articles. The results indicate a growing interest in learning analytics in collaborative learning over the past decade, with particularly rapid expansion in the most recent years.

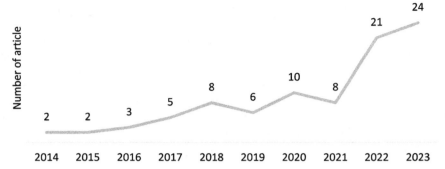

**Fig. 1.** Number of publications between 2014 and 2023

## 4.2 Learning Modes

Figure 2 presents the distribution of learning modes for collaborative learning activities supported by learning analytics. Online learning accounts for the largest proportion (52%), while blended learning and face-to-face learning represent 26% and 22%, respectively. The results reveal the diverse needs and preferences in collaborative learning environments.

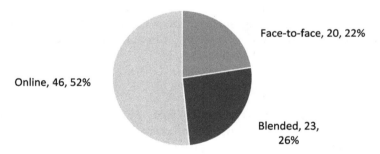

**Fig. 2.** Learning modes of collaborative learning activities

## 4.3 Objectives of Learning Analytics

Figure 3 shows the various objectives of learning analytics in collaborative learning activities. The most frequent one was monitoring and understanding of collaborative processes in learning, which underscores the importance of comprehensively observing and analysing the dynamics of collaboration. This was followed by assessing engagement and participation, indicating a strong interest in measuring active involvement and ensuring all participants contribute meaningfully. Other commonly identified objectives include predicting and improving performance, and providing feedback and support, highlighting the necessity of guidance and timely interventions to enhance collaboration. The remaining objectives consist of assessing collaboration quality, group formation and management, analysing discourse and content, and visualising collaboration, each representing specialised areas that contribute to a holistic understanding of collaborative learning.

**Fig. 3.** Objectives of learning analytics in the activities

## 4.4 Types of Data Used for Analytics

Figure 4 presents the diverse types of data analysed to comprehend and enhance collaborative learning experiences. Behavioural and interaction data (e.g., clickstream data, system logs, and participation in discussion and collaborative problem-solving) were most frequently used. This is followed by three types of communication data, namely textual data, audio and speech data, and visual and video data, which provided insights into text-based communication, verbal interactions, and non-verbal cues, respectively. Other data types, including assessment and performance data, physiological and biometric data (e.g., eye-tracking data and electrodermal activity data), artefact and product data, survey and self-report data, and metadata (e.g., student characteristics), were relatively less common but revealed the multifaceted nature of learning analytics for collaborative learning environments.

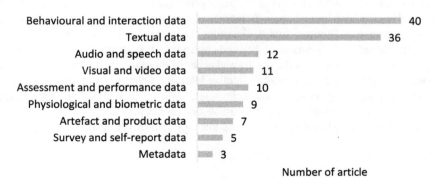

**Fig. 4.** Types of data used for learning analytics in the studies

## 4.5 Data Sources for Analytics

Figure 5 shows the frequency of data sources used for learning analytics in collaborative learning environments. Learning management systems, together with specialised collaborative platforms, were the most common data sources used to capture learner interactions and engagement in online settings. Video and audio capture, as well as sensors, were major sources of data on learner interaction and communication in face-to-face learning environments. Other data sources include messaging and communication tools, surveys, and simulation and gaming tools. The variety of data sources demonstrates the complex and multidimensional aspects of learning analytics in collaborative learning.

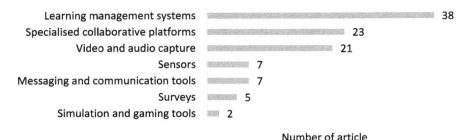

**Fig. 5.** Data sources for learning analytics in the studies

## 4.6 Learning Analytics Techniques

Figure 6 illustrates the analytical methods employed in the studies of collaborative learning. Machine learning was the most widely used technique, reflecting its effectiveness in uncovering patterns and insights from complex data sets. This is closely followed by network analysis, which was used to analyse the relationships and interactions among learners within collaborative environments. Another commonly used technique was statistical analysis (e.g., descriptive statistics, correlation analysis, and meta-analysis), which helped quantify learner interactions, engagement levels, and outcomes. Discourse and content analysis examine the content and patterns of learner interactions to evaluate collaboration quality and communication strategies, while sequential and process analysis focus on the timing and order of these interactions to reveal critical moments and processes that enhance effective learning. Other techniques, such as natural language processing, visualisation techniques, multimodal analysis, and data mining, further emphasise the diverse toolkit available for researchers and educators aiming to enhance collaborative learning experiences through data-driven insights.

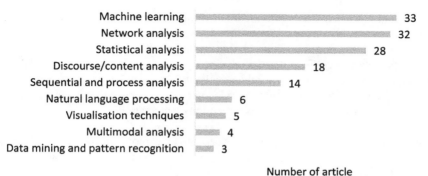

**Fig. 6.** Learning analytics techniques used in the studies

## 5 Discussion and Conclusion

The findings of this study reveal the diverse applications of learning analytics in collaborative learning. The results highlight a preference for online learning environments in relevant work, where learner interaction and engagement were effectively supported (Chen et al., 2021), and learning data was readily accessed (Kew and Tasir, 2022). The presence of blended and face-to-face learning indicates that traditional methods still play an important role, suggesting a need for balance between these approaches to accommodate various learner needs, as well as the development of novel learning analytics tools and techniques to facilitate collaborative learning in different environments.

The major objectives of learning analytics in collaborative learning activities primarily focused on monitoring collaborative processes and assessing engagement, revealing the importance of understanding the dynamics of collaboration and ensuring active participation among learners. Overall, the objectives addressed in related studies cover the key elements of collaborative learning, such as meaningful interaction, individual accountability, and effective group processing (Laal and Laal, 2012), which contribute to improving learning outcomes.

The results also highlight the diverse data types and sources used in learning analytics for collaborative learning. Behavioural and interaction data from learning management systems and collaborative platforms are the most prevalent, providing insights into online engagement. Communication data (text, audio, and video) captures both verbal and nonverbal interactions. Less common ones are physiological data and artefact analysis. This multimodal approach allows an understanding of the dynamic and complex collaborative processes, going beyond surface-level observations to reveal deeper insights into learner interactions, engagement, and knowledge construction in both online and face-to-face settings (Yan et al., 2024).

The findings regarding the analytical approaches used in collaborative learning show that machine learning and network analysis are the most popular techniques, reflecting their ability to uncover intricate patterns and relationships in collaborative data (Järvelä et al., 2020; Dado and Bodemer, 2017). The use of advanced techniques like natural language processing and multimodal analysis highlights the field's evolution towards more sophisticated data-driven insights.

The findings of this study provide implications for designing effective collaborative learning activities. By taking into consideration various factors related to learning modes, data types, and learning analytics techniques, educators can devise and apply more targeted approaches to collecting and analysing diverse data throughout the collaborative learning process. This could foster the creation of data-rich learning environments that facilitate the generation of insights into learner interactions and engagement for supporting the development of tailored interventions that meet the unique needs of learners in different contexts.

Building on these insights, future work might explore the potential of artificial intelligence and deep learning to enhance real-time analysis and personalised interventions in collaborative settings. Additionally, there is a need for longitudinal studies that employ these analytical techniques to track the long-term impacts of collaborative learning strategies.

**Acknowledgment.** The work described in this paper was partially supported by a grant from Hong Kong Metropolitan University (CP/2022/04).

## References

Al-Samarraie, H., Saeed, N.: A systematic review of cloud computing tools for collaborative learning: opportunities and challenges to the blended-learning environment. Comput. Educ. **124**, 77–91 (2018)

Alonso-Fernández, C., Calvo-Morata, A., Freire, M., Martínez-Ortiz, I., Fernández-Manjón, B.: Applications of data science to game learning analytics data: a systematic literature review. Comput. Educ. **141**, 103612 (2019)

Banihashem, S.K., Dehghanzadeh, H., Clark, D., Noroozi, O., Biemans, H.J.: Learning analytics for online game-based learning: A systematic literature review. Behaviour & Information Technology (2023). https://doi.org/10.1080/0144929X.2023.2255301

Cen, L., Ruta, D., Powell, L., Hirsch, B., Ng, J.: Quantitative approach to collaborative learning: Performance prediction, individual assessment, and group composition. Int. J. Comput.-Support. Collab. Learn. **11**, 187–225 (2016)

Cerratto Pargman, T., McGrath, C.: Mapping the ethics of learning analytics in higher education: a systematic literature review of empirical research. J. Learn. Analy. **8**(2), 123–139 (2021)

Chen, S., Ouyang, F., Jiao, P.: Promoting student engagement in online collaborative writing through a student-facing social learning analytics tool. J. Comput. Assist. Learn. **38**(1), 192–208 (2021)

Cornide-Reyes, H., et al.: A multimodal real-time feedback platform based on spoken interactions for remote active learning support. Sensors **20**(21), 6337 (2020)

Costa, L.A., Pereira Sanches, L.M., Rocha Amorim, R.J., Nascimento Salvador, L.D., Santos Souze, M.V.D.: Monitoring academic performance based on learning analytics and ontology: A systematic review. Informatics in Education **19**(3), 361–397 (2020)

Dado, M., Bodemer, D.: A review of methodological applications of social network analysis in computer-supported collaborative learning. Educ. Res. Rev. **22**, 159–180 (2017)

de Oliveira, C.F., Sobral, S.R., Ferreira, M.J., Moreira, F.: How does learning analytics contribute to prevent students' dropout in higher education: a systematic literature review. Big Data and Cognitive Computing **5**(4), 64 (2021)

Dillenbourg, P.: What do you mean by collaborative learning? In: Dillenbourg, P. (ed.) Collaborative-learning: Cognitive and Computational Approaches, pp. 1–19. Elsevier, Oxford (1999)

Heikkinen, S., Saqr, M., Malmberg, J., Tedre, M.: Supporting self-regulated learning with learning analytics interventions–a systematic literature review. Educ. Inf. Technol. **28**(3), 3059–3088 (2023)

Huang, X., Lajoie, S.P.: Social emotional interaction in collaborative learning: Why it matters and how can we measure it? Social Sciences & Humanities Open **7**(1), 100447 (2023)

Ifenthaler, D., Yau, J.Y.K.: Utilising learning analytics to support study success in higher education: a systematic review. Edu. Tech. Res. Dev. **68**(4), 1961–1990 (2020)

Järvelä, S., Gašević, D., Seppänen, T., Pechenizkiy, M., Kirschner, P.A.: Bridging learning sciences, machine learning and affective computing for understanding cognition and affect in collaborative learning. Br. J. Edu. Technol. **51**(6), 2391–2406 (2020)

Kaliisa, R., Rienties, B., Mørch, A.I., Kluge, A.: Social learning analytics in computer-supported collaborative learning environments: A systematic review of empirical studies. Comp. Edu. Open **3**, 100073 (2022)

Kasepalu, R., Chejara, P., Prieto, L.P., Ley, T.: Studying teacher withitness in the wild: comparing a mirroring and an alerting & guiding dashboard for collaborative learning. Int. J. Comput.-Support. Collab. Learn. **18**(4), 575–606 (2023)

Kew, S.N., Tasir, Z.: Learning analytics in online learning environment: A systematic review on the focuses and the types of student-related analytics data. Technol. Knowl. Learn. **27**(2), 405–427 (2022)

Khor, E.T., K, M.: A systematic review of the role of learning analytics in supporting personalized learning. Education Sciences **14**(1), 51 (2023)

Laal, M., Laal, M.: Collaborative learning: what is it? Procedia Soc. Behav. Sci. **31**, 491–495 (2012)

Le, H., Janssen, J., Wubbels, T.: Collaborative learning practices: teacher and student perceived obstacles to effective student collaboration. Camb. J. Educ. **48**(1), 103–122 (2018)

Li, K.C., Wong, B.T., Chan, H.T.: Prediction of At-Risk Students Using Learning Analytics: A Literature Review. In: International Conference on Technology in Education, pp. 119–128. Springer Nature Singapore, Singapore (2023)

Maqtary, N., Mohsen, A., Bechkoum, K.: Group formation techniques in computer-supported collaborative learning: a systematic literature review. Technol. Knowl. Learn. **24**, 169–190 (2019)

Olsen, J.K., Sharma, K., Rummel, N., Aleven, V.: Temporal analysis of multimodal data to predict collaborative learning outcomes. Br. J. Edu. Technol. **51**(5), 1527–1547 (2020)

Ouyang, F., Zhang, L.: AI-driven learning analytics applications and tools in computer-supported collaborative learning: A systematic review. Educ. Res. Rev. **44**, 100616 (2024)

Pandian, B.R., Aziz, A.A., Subramaniam, H., Nawi, H.S.A.: Exploring the role of machine learning in forecasting student performance in education: An in-depth review of literature. Multidisciplinary Reviews **6**, e2023ss043 (2023)

Paolucci, C., Vancini, S., Bex, R.T., II., Cavanaugh, C., Salama, C., de Araujo, Z.: A review of learning analytics opportunities and challenges for K-12 education. Heliyon **10**(4), e25767 (2024)

Paulsen, L., Dau, S., Davidsen, J.: Designing for collaborative learning in immersive virtual reality: a systematic literature review. Virtual Reality **28**(1), 63 (2024)

Paulsen, L., Lindsay, E.: Learning analytics dashboards are increasingly becoming about learning and not just analytics-A systematic review. Educ. Inf. Technol. (2024). https://doi.org/10.1007/s10639-023-12401-4

Putro, B.L., Rosmansyah, Y., Suhardi, S.: An intelligent agent model for learning group development in the digital learning environment: A systematic literature review. Bulletin of Electr. Eng. Informat. **9**(3), 1159–1166 (2020)

Ramaswami, G., Susnjak, T., Mathrani, A., Umer, R.: Use of predictive analytics within learning analytics dashboards: A review of case studies. Technol. Knowl. Learn. **28**(3), 959–980 (2023)

Sharma, K., Nguyen, A., Hong, Y.: Self-regulation and shared regulation in collaborative learning in adaptive digital learning environments: A systematic review of empirical studies. Br. J. Edu. Technol. **55**, 1398–1436 (2024)

Sharma, P., Akgun, M., Li, Q.: Understanding student interaction and cognitive engagement in online discussions using social network and discourse analyses. Educ. Tech. Res. Dev. (2023). https://doi.org/10.1007/s11423-023-10261-w

Stojanov, A., Daniel, B.K.: A decade of research into the application of big data and analytics in higher education: a systematic review of the literature. Educ. Inf. Technol. **29**(5), 5807–5831 (2024)

Strauß, S., Rummel, N.: Promoting interaction in online distance education: designing, implementing and supporting collaborative learning. Info. Learn. Sci. **121**(5/6), 251–260 (2020)

Sung, H.Y., Hwang, G.J.: A collaborative game-based learning approach to improving students' learning performance in science courses. Comput. Educ. **63**, 43–51 (2013)

Tahiru, F., Parbanath, S., Agbesi, S.: Machine learning-based predictive systems in higher education: a bibliometric analysis. J. Scientomet. Res. **12**(2), 436–447 (2023)

Tan, S.C., Lee, A.V.Y., Lee, M.: A systematic review of artificial intelligence techniques for collaborative learning over the past two decades. Comp. Educ. Artif. Intel. **3**, 100097 (2022)

Tedla, Y.G., Chen, H.L.: The impacts of computer-supported collaborative learning on students' critical thinking: a meta-analysis. Educ. Inf. Technol. (2024). https://doi.org/10.1007/s10639-024-12857-y

Tlili, A., et al.: A smart collaborative educational game with learning analytics to support English vocabulary teaching. Int. J. Interact. Multim. Artif. Intel. **6**(6), 215–224 (2021)

Wong, B.T.M.: Learning analytics in higher education: an analysis of case studies. Asian Ass. Open Univ. J. **12**(1), 21–40 (2017)

Wong, B.T.M., Li, K.C., Choi, S.P.M.: Trends in learning analytics practices: a review of higher education institutions. Interact. Technol. Smart Educ. **15**(2), 132–154 (2018)

Wong, B.T.M., Li, K.C., Cheung, S.K.: An analysis of learning analytics in personalised learning. J. Comput. High. Educ. **35**(3), 371–390 (2023)

Wong, J., Baars, M., Davis, D., Van Der Zee, T., Houben, G.J., Paas, F.: Supporting self-regulated learning in online learning environments and MOOCs: A systematic review. Int. J. Human-Comp. Interact. **35**(4–5), 356–373 (2019)

Vieira, C., Parsons, P., Byrd, V.: Visual learning analytics of educational data: A systematic literature review and research agenda. Comput. Educ. **122**, 119–135 (2018)

Vygotsky, L.S.: Mind in society. Harvard University Press, Cambridge, MA (1978)

Xing, W., Zhu, G., Arslan, O., Shim, J., Popov, V.: Using learning analytics to explore the multifaceted engagement in collaborative learning. J. Comput. High. Educ. **35**(3), 633–662 (2023)

Yan, L., Zhao, L., Gašević, D., Li, X., Martinez-Maldonado, R.: Socio-spatial learning analytics in co-located collaborative learning spaces: a systematic literature review. J. Learn. Analy. **10**(3), 45–63 (2023)

Yan, L., et al.: Evidence-based multimodal learning analytics for feedback and reflection in collaborative learning. Br. J. Edu. Technol. (2024). https://doi.org/10.1111/bjet.13498

Yürüm, O.R., Taşkaya-Temizel, T., Yıldırım, S.: Predictive video analytics in online courses: A systematic literature review. Technol. Knowl. Learn. (2023). https://doi.org/10.1007/s10758-023-09697-z

Zheng, L., Zhong, L., Niu, J.: Effects of personalised feedback approach on knowledge building, emotions, co-regulated behavioural patterns and cognitive load in online collaborative learning. Assess. Eval. High. Educ. **47**(1), 109–125 (2022)

# Enhancing a Probabilistic Auto-regressive Model with Gaussian Noise and Savitzky–Golay Filter for the Data Generation of Small-Scale Education Datasets

Kwok Tai Chui[1]($\boxtimes$), Jackson Tsz Wah Chan[1], Ramidayu Yousuk[2], Lap-Kei Lee[1], and Fu Lee Wang[1]

[1] School of Science and Technology, Hong Kong Metropolitan University, Ho Man Tin, Kowloon, Hong Kong, China
`{jktchui,lklee,pwang}@hkmu.edu.hk, chantwah1231@gmail.com`
[2] Faculty of Engineering, Department of Industrial Engineering, Kasetsart University, 50 Ngamwongwan Road, Lat Yao, Chatuchak, Bangkok 10900, Thailand
`ramidayu.y@ku.th`

**Abstract.** Sufficient samples are important to train accurate and robust machine learning models. In education datasets, common applications, including learning analytics, innovative learning, educational administration, and knowledge management, require models that can support small-scale training datasets. These applications limit the choices of algorithms, are prone to model overfitting and bias, and lack generalizability; thus, they possess room for research and enhancement. In this paper, a research work was presented on the data generation algorithm for the enhancement of small-scale education datasets. A probabilistic auto-regressive model was implemented and enhanced by merging it with Gaussian noise and Savitzky–Golay filter. The overall data distribution was improved, and more helpful training data is available. This approach also enabled the data generation of multiple variables simultaneously because incorporating the mutual dependence of variables enhances the characterization ability. Future research directions were also suggested.

**Keywords:** artificial intelligence · auto-regressive model · data generation · education dataset · Gaussian noise · learning analytics · Savitzky–Golay filter · small-scale dataset

## 1 Introduction

In today's digital era, the adoption of digitization, sensor networks, information and communication technology (ICT), and the Internet of Things (IoT) provide data collection and continual monitoring, thus yielding the realization of smart city applications by turning data into valuable applications. As always, it is desired to have sufficient samples to train accurate and robust artificial intelligence models. Nevertheless, small-scale dataset environments can be found in many daily life applications; for example, we devoted effort to educational datasets in this research paper. Small-scale dataset environments can easily be found in education datasets attributable to various reasons: (i) small class size (Shen and Konstantopoulos, 2021), (ii) limited samples, e.g., assessment components, throughout the semester or academic year (Albreiki et al., 2021), (iii) privacy issues (Korir et al., 2023), (iv) no consent (Yan et al., 2024), and (v) lack of budget (Ang et al., 2020).

Typical approaches to solving for small-scale datasets include transfer learning (Wang et al., 2023a), few-shot learning (Qin et al., 2024), downsampling of the majority classes (Veiga and Rodrigues, 2024), and data generation (Chui et al., 2020). The first approach relies on the concept of borrowing knowledge from a source model (usually trained with a large-scale dataset) to a target model (using a small-scale education dataset). It requires a good linkage between source and target domains and domain knowledge of both datasets. The second and third approaches retain the challenging nature of the small-scale environment. In our research, we focus on the last approach because it enhances the foundation of machine learning research, having more training data in the data postprocessing stage.

The organization of the paper is as follows. Section 2 presents the literature review. The following section shows the methodology of three data generation algorithms. In Sect. 4, performance evaluation and comparison will be conducted. Finally, a conclusion is drawn, and future research directions are discussed.

## 2 Literature Review

The auto-regressive and its variants are well-known algorithms in forecasting models (Czapaj et al., 2022; Despotovic et al., 2024). Attention is drawn to an emergent research direction, i.e., their usage in data generation. Text-to-image generation was achieved using autoregressive video generation with diffusion models (Weng et al., 2024). It facilitated the reduction in Frechet video distance and increment of the average CLIP similarity between video frames and text. Another work (Zhou et al., 2020) generated vibration signals of machines and diagnosed fault machines using an integrated nonlinear auto-regression neural network and 2D convolutional neural network. It achieved accuracies of 99.3% and 98% in two benchmark datasets, significantly outperforming the generative adversarial network-based approach by 5.64% and 9.25%, respectively. A research study (Wang et al., 2023b) suggested that incorporating both generative adversarial networks and auto-regressive algorithms enhanced the generation performance of long time-series sequences. It was applied in three applications: disease, population, and energy. Performance evaluation revealed that the algorithm made enhancements in the Frechet distance, mean square error, and mean average error. In addition, auto-regressive image generation was investigated with the aid of a large language model (Pourreza et al., 2023). Single-object and multi-object scenarios were considered. Four metrics were used to evaluate the performance of the model, including reproduce/remove-partial/remove-all peak signal-to-noise ratio and classification accuracy.

After reviewing the latest developments in auto-regressive-based data generation, it is necessary to investigate the effectiveness of auto-regressive algorithms in education datasets. Noise insertion and filtering techniques will also be investigated to support the data generation via an auto-regressive algorithm. It is worth noting that, theoretically, the algorithm can be applied to similar data types with customization (Iglesias et al., 2023).

## 3 Methodology

This research extends the probabilistic auto-regressive model by a three-fold data generation approach to enhance the diversity and reliability of generated data. It comprises three parts: (i) A probabilistic auto-regressive model, (ii) Gaussian noise insertion, and (iii) Savitzky-Golay filtering.

### 3.1 A Probabilistic Auto-regressive Model

The model was recently established (Jun. 2022) with enhancements to the traditional probabilistic auto-regressive models using customized loss functions and conditional inputs (Zhang et al., 2022). It worked well in multi-sequence datasets (e.g., multiple signals in a dataset).

There are two scenarios in the data generation using the probabilistic auto-regressive model: (i) In a non-sequential dataset, additional steps are needed to proxy sequential data generation. In the first stage (modeling), knowledge is learnt from the identical multi-sequence table. As the model lacks an understanding of inter-row dependencies (or sequences in general), it treats the sequence index and sequence key as a continuous value and a categorical variable, respectively. The number of epochs requires further evaluation. In the second stage (sampling), an identical number of rows of real data will be generated. The sequence key is used for sequencing separation, whereas the sequence index serves as row reordering, and (ii) In the modelling phase, multi-sequence datasets are learned using context columns, sequence index, and sequence key. The next phase is to generate identical sequence lengths (as of the source dataset), along with the specification of the numbers of sequences.

The probabilistic autoregressive model provides various adjustable parameters that allow for precise customization of the data generation process. Various parameters contribute to the model construction: (i) One such parameter is "enforce_min_max_values," which ensures that the generated values adhere to some minimum and maximum thresholds, (ii) Another parameter, "enforce_rounding," applies specific rounding rules to the generated data., (iii) the "locales" parameter sets the locale for the synthetic data, (iv) In contrast, the "context_columns" parameter designates columns that offer contextual information during the data generation process, (v) the "verbose" parameter controls the level of detail in the model's output, and (vi) the "cuda" parameter enables the utilization of CUDA-based hardware acceleration.

After generating the initial synthetic data with the probabilistic auto-regressive model, two additional components were employed to further enhance the synthetic dataset.

## 3.2 Multivariate Gaussian Noise Insertion

Gaussian noise (one of the famous statistical noises) is then inserted into the generated data (using the probabilistic auto-regressive model). The noise increases the randomness and variations from a Gaussian distribution manner. The use of Gaussian noise ensures that the statistical properties of the noise, such as mean and variance, align with those of actual noise, contributing to more accurate data generation. Thus, It provides a realistic representation of noise that is often encountered in real-world data, making it suitable for simulating practical scenarios, i.e., student exam performance datasets in this research. There are two major advantages of Gaussian noise insertion (Nandan et al., 2024; Wang et al., 2023c), including (i) Versatility: Gaussian noise insertion can be easily adjusted by modifying its parameters, allowing for flexibility in generating data with different noise levels and characteristics, and (ii) Computational efficiency: The generation of Gaussian noise is computationally efficient, making it suitable for generating large datasets and simulations. As education datasets are generally multivariate, the Gaussian noise insertion is extended to a multivariate version.

The standard formulation of the probability density function (*pdf*) of a Gaussian random variable $g$ (of random vector $G$) is defined as:

$$pdf(g) = \frac{1}{\sigma\sqrt{2\pi}} e^{-\frac{(g-\mu)^2}{(2\sigma^2)}} \tag{1}$$

where $\sigma$ and $\mu$ are the standard deviation and mean of the distribution, respectively.

$$pdf_m(g) = \frac{1}{|\beta|^{\frac{1}{2}}(2\pi)^{\frac{n}{2}}} e^{-\frac{1}{2}(g-\mu)^T \beta^{-1}(g-\mu)} \tag{2}$$

where $\beta$ is the covariance matrix and $n$ is the dimensionality of the symmetric positive definite. The covariance matrix is defined as:

$$\beta = E\left[(G-\mu)(G-\mu)^T\right] = E\left[GG^T\right] - \mu\mu^T \tag{3}$$

## 3.3 Savitzky-Golay Filtering

The Savitzky-Golay filter is used to enhance data generation further. It smooths the dataset by fitting successive segments of data points with a low-degree polynomial. In addition, it helps to maintain the underlying patterns and trends in the data while reducing noise, making the synthetic data more representative of real exam performance trends.

The major advantages of Savitzky-Golay filter are fivefold (Liu et al., 2024; Ochieng et al., 2023): (i) Preserves peak shapes: The filtering method is effective in preserving the shapes of peaks in the data so that it is useful in signal processing and spectral analysis, (ii) Noise reduction: It effectively reduces noise in the data while preserving important features, which reflects its robustness for denoising applications, (iii) Smoothing: The approach provides effective smoothing of data while maintaining important data characteristics, (iv) Computational efficiency: Savitzky-Golay filtering is computationally efficient, which is capable of supporting real-time applications and large-scale datasets, and (v) Localized nature: It operates on localized data segments, which supports localized analysis.

The key parameter in the filter design is the smoothing parameter. To optimally design the parameter, a common technique is adopted, which first studies the power spectrum of the featureless area and second suppresses noise below certain thresholds. It is worth noting that effort is devoted to selecting appropriate areas and parameters. The ideal process is to dynamically design the filter in different areas of the multivariate datasets.

## 4 Performance Evaluation and Comparison

The benchmark education dataset is first illustrated. The analysis of the twofold data generation comprises three parts, including validity analysis, consistency check, and statistical similarity analysis. A comparison is also carried out to study the effectiveness of different data generation algorithms.

### 4.1 A Wearable Exam Stress Dataset

Datasets with skin conductance recordings from experiments using artificial stimuli can be found online. However, there is a lack of longer recordings during real-world cognitive stressors. The "A Wearable Exam Stress Dataset" (Amin et al., 2022a; Amin et al., 2022b; Goldberger et al., 2020) aimed to connect the existing knowledge about the human stress response, primarily based on laboratory-acquired data, with the actual fluctuations in people's skin conductance during real-life stressful exam experiences. The dataset includes accelerometer readings, interbeat interval, skin surface temperature, blood volume pulse, heart rate, and electrodermal activity recorded during three assessments (1.5-h midterm 1, 1.5-h midterm 2, and 3-h finals) of ten participants using wearable devices (Empatica E4 wristband), along with the corresponding grades. Its purpose was to evaluate the influence of stress on exam performance.

### 4.2 Analysis of Twofold Data Generation Algorithms

The multivariate signals comprise temperature, blood volume pulse, heart rate, and electrodermal activity. As mentioned, the analysis of data generation algorithms involves validity analysis, consistency check, and statistical similarity analysis. The metrics in these analyses were widely adopted in the literature (Chan et al., 2024; Jaeger and Banks, 2023; Shrestha, 2021).

#### 4.2.1 Validity Analysis

There are three key metrics in the validity analysis:

- Primary Key Uniqueness and Non-Null Constraint: It is important to verify that primary keys in both the real and synthetic datasets are unique and not empty. This check is essential to maintain data integrity and prevent the occurrence of duplicate or missing values in key identifiers.

- Continuous Value Range Adherence: Check that continuous values in the synthetic data fall within the specified minimum and maximum ranges observed in the real, which is crucial to validate. Deviations from these ranges may indicate errors in the data generation process or insufficient fidelity in capturing the digital distribution.
- Discrete Value Categories Alignment: Make sure that the discrete values in the generated data correspond to the categories found in the actual data. This pertains to categorical variables such as types of exams, subject areas, and student demographics. Consistency in categories maintains the meaningfulness and interpretability of the data.

### 4.2.2 Consistency Check

The consistency check aims to ensure that the column names between the ground truth and generated multivariate signals align. Verifying that the column names in the synthetic dataset correspond to those in the real dataset is important. Consistency in column names is crucial for seamless data integration, analysis, and interpretation across various datasets and environments. This practice ensures that the data can be effectively compared and analyzed, regardless of the source.

### 4.2.3 Statistical Similarity Analysis

The statistical similarity metric is commonly used to assess the likeness between a genuine data column and its synthetic counterpart. The evaluation is carried out by comparing key summary statistics such as the mean, median, and standard deviation. It is specifically designed for continuous numerical data, including the conversion of date-time values into numerical representations.

It is worth noting that it disregards missing values, focusing solely on the available data. Once the comparison is completed, the metric yields a score ranging from 0.0 to 1.0. A score of 1.0 signifies that there is an exact match between the statistical characteristics of the real and synthetic data. On the other hand, a score of 0.0 indicates a significant disparity between the two sets of data. This metric provides valuable insights into the quality and accuracy of synthetic data generation processes, enabling data scientists and analysts to make informed decisions about the usability of synthetic data for various applications.

### 4.2.4 Numerical Results and Comparisons

Validity analysis and consistency checks are grouped for evaluation. Table 1 summarizes the results using three approaches (i) a probabilistic auto-regressive model, (ii) a probabilistic auto-regressive model with Gaussian noise insertion, and (iii) a probabilistic auto-regressive model with Savitzky-Golay filtering. It can be seen from the results that perfect data validity and consistency checks in all three approaches. It reveals the feasibility of these approaches, particularly adding Gaussian noise and applying the Savitzky-Golay filter as second-tier data generation.

The statistical similarity analysis is then performed. The results of the three data generation approaches are summarized in Tables 2, 3 and 4. The following observations can be drawn:

**Table 1.** Numerical results of the validity analysis and consistency check for three data generation approaches. DV stands for data validity and DS stands for data structure.

| Subjects | Data generation approaches, validity analysis, and consistency checks | | | | | | | | |
|---|---|---|---|---|---|---|---|---|---|
| | A probabilistic auto-regressive model | | | A probabilistic auto-regressive model with Gaussian noise insertion | | | A probabilistic auto-regressive model with Savitzky-Golay filtering | | |
| | DV | DS | Overall | DV | DS | Overall | DV | DS | Overall |
| S1 | 100% | 100% | 100% | 100% | 100% | 100% | 100% | 100% | 100% |
| S2 | 100% | 100% | 100% | 100% | 100% | 100% | 100% | 100% | 100% |
| S3 | 100% | 100% | 100% | 100% | 100% | 100% | 100% | 100% | 100% |
| S4 | 100% | 100% | 100% | 100% | 100% | 100% | 100% | 100% | 100% |
| S5 | 100% | 100% | 100% | 100% | 100% | 100% | 100% | 100% | 100% |
| S6 | 100% | 100% | 100% | 100% | 100% | 100% | 100% | 100% | 100% |
| S7 | 100% | 100% | 100% | 100% | 100% | 100% | 100% | 100% | 100% |
| S8 | 100% | 100% | 100% | 100% | 100% | 100% | 100% | 100% | 100% |
| S9 | 100% | 100% | 100% | 100% | 100% | 100% | 100% | 100% | 100% |
| S10 | 100% | 100% | 100% | 100% | 100% | 100% | 100% | 100% | 100% |

- Table 2: The average of metrics for ten subjects is: blood volume pulse (99.61%, 99.93%, 98.25%), electrodermal activity (88.40%, 90.99%, 86.36%), heart rate (85.86%, 83.15%, 88.62%), and temperature (56.02%, 49.99%, 73.36%). Given in the results of Table 1 that data validity and data structure are ensured, the generated data distribution is better spreading in temperature, followed by heart rate, electrodermal activity, and blood volume pulse.
- Table 3: The average of metrics for ten subjects is: blood volume pulse (99.59%, 99.87%, 98.59%), electrodermal activity (88.40%, 91.03%, 86.13%), heart rate (85.77%, 83.14%, 83.13%), and temperature (56.03%, 49.91%, 76.53%). A similar observation is found in Table 2.
- Table 4: The average of metrics for ten subjects is: blood volume pulse (99.60%, 99.30%, 97.55%), electrodermal activity (88.40%, 90.63%, 86.91%), heart rate (86.86%, 83.14%, 84.37%), and temperature (56.03%, 49.98%, 71.00%). A similar observation is found in Table 2.

**Table 2.** Numerical results of the statistical similarity analysis using a probabilistic auto-regressive model.

| Subjects | Blood volume pulse | | | Electrodermal activity | | | Heart rate | | | Temperature | | |
|---|---|---|---|---|---|---|---|---|---|---|---|---|
| | Mean | Median | Std. | Mean | Median | Std. | Mean | Median | Std. | Mean | Median | Std. |
| S1 | 99.92% | 99.97% | 98.93% | 84.04% | 93.25% | 81.08% | 87.89% | 87.58% | 89.85% | 54.61% | 50.28% | 72.53% |
| S2 | 99.93% | 99.87% | 98.44% | 92.40% | 98.44% | 87.83% | 86.06% | 84.62% | 90.37% | 59.16% | 68.49% | 68.92% |
| S3 | 99.91% | 99.93% | 97.24% | 86.70% | 88.89% | 84.53% | 85.03% | 83.75% | 91.91% | 58.17% | 56.53% | 74.97% |
| S4 | 99.82% | 99.91% | 98.16% | 93.15% | 97.59% | 87.55% | 85.55% | 78.83% | 85.78% | 55.06% | 43.62% | 77.96% |
| S5 | 99.83% | 99.84% | 98.90% | 85.40% | 80.65% | 87.36% | 85.23% | 84.14% | 91.44% | 53.26% | 32.59% | 75.06% |
| S6 | 99.89% | 99.95% | 99.06% | 89.75% | 93.77% | 88.17% | 83.69% | 81.92% | 87.06% | 58.86% | 68.9% | 71.94% |
| S7 | 99.91% | 99.96% | 98.32% | 89.54% | 95.26% | 85.51% | 89.63% | 86.8% | 85.79% | 59.24% | 43.54% | 75.96% |
| S8 | 99.94% | 99.96% | 98.08% | 87.22% | 90.42% | 84.41% | 81.19% | 76.07% | 87.16% | 57.05% | 43.25% | 73.76% |
| S9 | 99.97% | 99.94% | 97.80% | 81.12% | 77.71% | 82.80% | 84.12% | 80.29% | 88.99% | 48.59% | 31.91% | 71.98% |
| S10 | 96.97% | 99.94% | 97.52% | 94.65% | 93.90% | 94.38% | 90.18% | 87.53% | 87.85% | 56.24% | 60.75% | 70.49% |

**Table 3.** Numerical results of the statistical similarity analysis using a probabilistic auto-regressive model with Gaussian noise insertion.

| Subjects | Blood volume pulse | | | Electrodermal activity | | | Heart rate | | | Temperature | | |
|---|---|---|---|---|---|---|---|---|---|---|---|---|
| | Mean | Median | Std. | Mean | Median | Std. | Mean | Median | Std. | Mean | Median | Std. |
| S1 | 99.90% | 99.88% | 99.44% | 84.04% | 93.26% | 81.01% | 87.80% | 87.53% | 87.70% | 54.60% | 50.46% | 75.06% |
| S2 | 99.87% | 99.82% | 97.91% | 92.40% | 98.44% | 87.78% | 85.94% | 84.28% | 83.81% | 59.10% | 68.36% | 70.94% |
| S3 | 99.91% | 99.84% | 97.88% | 86.70% | 88.80% | 84.84% | 85.25% | 83.84% | 84.00% | 58.24% | 56.34% | 78.31% |
| S4 | 99.82% | 99.87% | 98.91% | 93.15% | 97.56% | 86.90% | 85.33% | 78.92% | 78.72% | 55.06% | 43.31% | 82.98% |
| S5 | 99.75% | 99.65% | 98.77% | 85.40% | 80.98% | 86.03% | 84.81% | 83.96% | 83.51% | 53.45% | 32.79% | 79.42% |
| S6 | 99.94% | 99.92% | 98.88% | 89.75% | 93.77% | 88.16% | 83.81% | 81.89% | 81.82% | 58.83% | 68.73% | 74.49% |
| S7 | 99.91% | 99.90% | 99.02% | 89.54% | 95.30% | 85.45% | 89.51% | 86.73% | 86.65% | 59.35% | 43.77% | 78.85% |
| S8 | 99.92% | 99.90% | 98.72% | 87.22% | 90.61% | 83.99% | 81.04% | 76.46% | 76.72% | 56.89% | 42.56% | 77.59% |
| S9 | 99.94% | 99.92% | 98.02% | 81.12% | 77.71% | 82.73% | 84.19% | 80.09% | 80.15% | 48.55% | 31.96% | 74.77% |
| S10 | 96.96% | 99.97% | 98.32% | 94.65% | 93.90% | 94.37% | 89.97% | 87.73% | 88.25% | 56.25% | 60.83% | 72.85% |

**Table 4.** Numerical results of the statistical similarity analysis using a probabilistic auto-regressive model with Savitzky-Golay filtering.

| Subjects | Blood volume pulse | | | Electrodermal activity | | | Heart rate | | | Temperature | | |
|---|---|---|---|---|---|---|---|---|---|---|---|---|
| | Mean | Median | Std. | Mean | Median | Std. | Mean | Median | Std. | Mean | Median | Std. |
| S1 | 99.92% | 93.94% | 98.29% | 84.04% | 93.26% | 81.17% | 87.89% | 87.53% | 85.68% | 54.61% | 50.39% | 70.63% |
| S2 | 99.93% | 99.94% | 97.70% | 92.40% | 94.44% | 87.89% | 86.06% | 84.28% | 85.70% | 59.16% | 68.54% | 67.46% |
| S3 | 99.91% | 99.87% | 96.73% | 86.70% | 88.80% | 86.47% | 85.03% | 83.84% | 86.32% | 58.17% | 56.45% | 72.56% |
| S4 | 99.82% | 99.80% | 97.24% | 93.15% | 97.56% | 88.39% | 85.55% | 78.92% | 82.30% | 55.07% | 43.58% | 74.05% |
| S5 | 99.83% | 99.84% | 98.10% | 85.40% | 80.98% | 89.11% | 85.22% | 83.96% | 87.09% | 53.26% | 32.87% | 71.75% |

(*continued*)

**Table 4.** (*continued*)

| Subjects | Blood volume pulse | | | Electrodermal activity | | | Heart rate | | | Temperature | | |
|---|---|---|---|---|---|---|---|---|---|---|---|---|
| | Mean | Median | Std. | Mean | Median | Std. | Mean | Median | Std. | Mean | Median | Std. |
| S6 | 99.89% | 99.89% | 98.17% | 89.75% | 93.77% | 88.18% | 83.69% | 81.89% | 83.00% | 58.86% | 68.80% | 69.95% |
| S7 | 99.91% | 99.91% | 97.71% | 89.54% | 95.30% | 85.60% | 89.63% | 86.73% | 82.23% | 59.24% | 43.70% | 73.87% |
| S8 | 99.94% | 99.96% | 97.40% | 87.22% | 90.61% | 85.01% | 81.19% | 76.46% | 82.62% | 57.05% | 42.80% | 71.01% |
| S9 | 99.93% | 99.92% | 97.21% | 81.12% | 77.71% | 82.88% | 94.12% | 80.09% | 85.34% | 48.59% | 31.81% | 69.86% |
| S10 | 96.94% | 99.97% | 96.94% | 94.65% | 93.90% | 94.40% | 90.18% | 87.73% | 83.44% | 56.24% | 60.81% | 68.86% |

## 5 Conclusion

In conclusion, the research work presented a data generation algorithm to enhance small-scale education datasets. By implementing a probabilistic auto-regressive model and enhancing it with Gaussian noise and Savitzky–Golay filter, the overall data distribution was improved, providing more helpful training data on the education dataset. This approach also enabled the data generation of multiple variables simultaneously (blood volume pulse, electrodermal activity, heart rate, and temperature), enhancing the characterization ability. Future research directions include (i) investigating the commons and differences of generated data in three data generation algorithms and (ii) analyzing the quality of data generation when more portions of data are generated.

**Funding.** The work described in this paper was fully supported by a grant from Hong Kong Metropolitan University (RIF/2021/05).

## References

Albreiki, B., Zaki, N., Alashwal, H.: A systematic literature review of student'performance prediction using machine learning techniques. Education Sciences **11**, 552 (2021)

Amin, M.R., Wickramasuriya, D., Faghih, R.T.: A Wearable Exam Stress Dataset for Predicting Cognitive Performance in Real-World Settings (version 1.0. 0). PhysioNet (2022)

Amin, M.R., Wickramasuriya, D.S., Faghih, R.T.: A wearable exam stress dataset for predicting grades using physiological signals. In: 2022 IEEE Healthcare Innovations and Point of Care Technologies (HI-POCT), pp. 30–36. IEEE (2022)

Ang, K.L.M., Ge, F.L., Seng, K.P.: Big educational data & analytics: Survey, architecture and challenges. IEEE Access **8**, 116392–116414 (2020)

Chan, J.T.W., Chui, K.T., Lee, L.K., Paoprasert, N., Ng, K.K.: Data generation using a probabilistic auto-regressive model with application to student exam performance analysis. In: 2024 International Symposium on Educational Technology (ISET), pp. 87–90. IEEE (2024)

Chui, K.T., Liu, R.W., Zhao, M., De Pablos, P.O.: Predicting students' performance with school and family tutoring using generative adversarial network-based deep support vector machine. IEEE Access **8**, 86745–86752 (2020)

Czapaj, R., Kamiński, J., Sołtysik, M.: A review of auto-regressive methods applications to short-term demand forecasting in power systems. Energies **15**, 6729 (2022)

Despotovic, M., Voyant, C., Garcia-Gutierrez, L., Almorox, J., Notton, G.: Solar irradiance time series forecasting using auto-regressive and extreme learning methods: Influence of transfer learning and clustering. Appl. Energy **365**, 123215 (2024)

Goldberger, A.L., et al.: PhysioBank, PhysioToolkit, and PhysioNet: components of a new research resource for complex physiologic signals. Circulation **101**, e215–e220 (2000)

Iglesias, G., Talavera, E., González-Prieto, Á., Mozo, A., Gómez-Canaval, S.: Data augmentation techniques in time series domain: a survey and taxonomy. Neural Comput. Appl. **35**, 10123–10145 (2023)

Jaeger, A., Banks, D.: Cluster analysis: a modern statistical review. Wiley Interdisciplinary Reviews: Computational Statistics **15**, e1597 (2023)

Korir, M., Slade, S., Holmes, W., Héliot, Y., Rienties, B.: Investigating the dimensions of students' privacy concern in the collection, use and sharing of data for learning analytics. Computers in Human Behavior Reports **9**, 100262 (2023)

Liu, S., Xu, T., Du, X., Zhang, Y., Wu, J.: A hybrid deep learning model based on parallel architecture TCN-LSTM with Savitzky-Golay filter for wind power prediction. Energy Convers. Manage. **302**, 118122 (2024)

Nandan, D., Kanungo, J., Mahajan, A.: An error-efficient Gaussian filter for image processing by using the expanded operand decomposition logarithm multiplication. J. Ambient. Intell. Humaniz. Comput. **15**, 1045–1052 (2024)

Ochieng, P.J., Maróti, Z., Dombi, J., Krész, M., Békési, J., Kalmár, T.: Adaptive Savitzky-golay filters for analysis of copy number variation peaks from whole-exome sequencing data. Information **14**, 128 (2023)

Pourreza, R., et al.: Painter: teaching auto-regressive language models to draw sketches. In: Proceedings of the IEEE/CVF International Conference on Computer Vision, pp. 305–314 (2023)

Qin, A., Chen, F., Li, Q., Song, T., Zhao, Y., Gao, C.: Few-shot remote sensing scene classification via subspace based on multiscale feature learning. IEEE Journal of Selected Topics in Applied Earth Observations and Remote Sensing **17**, 13292–13307 (2024)

Shen, T., Konstantopoulos, S.: Estimating causal effects of class size in secondary education: evidence from TIMSS. Res. Pap. Educ. **36**, 507–541 (2021)

Shrestha, N.: Factor analysis as a tool for survey analysis. Am. J. Appl. Math. Stat. **9**, 4–11 (2021)

Veiga, R.J., Rodrigues, J.M.: Fine-grained fish classification from small to large datasets with vision transformers. IEEE Access **12**, 113642–113660 (2024)

Wang, H., Li, Z., Hou, X.: Versatile denoising-based approximate message passing for compressive sensing. IEEE Trans. Image Process. **32**, 2761–2775 (2023)

Wang, L., Zeng, L., Li, J.: AEC-GAN: adversarial error correction GANs for auto-regressive long time-series generation. In: Proceedings of the AAAI Conference on Artificial Intelligence, pp. 10140–10148 (2023)

Wang, Z., Liu, X., Yu, J., Wu, H., Lyu, H.: A general deep transfer learning framework for predicting the flow field of airfoils with small data. Comput. Fluids **251**, 105738 (2023)

Weng, W., et al.: ART-V: Auto-Regressive Text-to-Video Generation with Diffusion Models. In: Proceedings of the IEEE/CVF Conference on Computer Vision and Pattern Recognition, pp. 7395–7405 (2024)

Yan, L., et al.: Practical and ethical challenges of large language models in education: A systematic scoping review. Br. J. Edu. Technol. **55**, 90–112 (2024)

Zhang, K., Patki, N., Veeramachaneni, K.: Sequential models in the synthetic data vault (2022). arXiv preprint arXiv:2207.14406

Zhou, Q., Li, Y., Tian, Y., Jiang, L.: A novel method based on nonlinear auto-regression neural network and convolutional neural network for imbalanced fault diagnosis of rotating machinery. Measurement **161**, 107880 (2020)

# Smart Learning Environments

# Review Study "Virtual Reality in Biology Education"

Michaela Toman and Marie Hubálovská(✉)

Department of Applied Cybernetics, Department of Technics, University of Hradec Králové, Rokitanskeho 62, Hradec Kralove, Czech Republic
{michaela.toman,marie.hubalovska}@uhk.cz

**Abstract.** The review article evaluates the efficacy of virtual reality (VR) as a teaching tool compared to traditional methods, such as lectures, in biology education. This study analyzes research findings from English and Czech sources, aiming to present a comprehensive summary of VR's impact on learning outcomes, student motivation, and perceptions in biology and medical education. The research addresses several critical questions: the difference between traditional and VR-based teaching, the potential of VR to enhance motivation and knowledge acquisition, student opinions on VR use, variations in student feedback, and factors influencing VR implementation in biology education. Key search terms included "Virtual Reality in Biology Education" and "VR in Medical Education," focusing on publications from 2019 to 2023 sourced from databases like EBSCO, Web of Science, ResearchGate, and Google Scholar. Out of 255 sources identified, 26 studies met the inclusion criteria, while 229 were excluded due to irrelevance or focus on non-VR educational technologies. The studies reviewed demonstrate a consistent pattern: VR generally enhances student motivation and learning outcomes. For instance, Chuang et al. (2023) found that VR improved high school students' understanding of human organs, though some experienced dizziness. Christopoulos et al. (2023) noted increased motivation with VR but no significant difference in knowledge retention compared to video instruction. Thompson et al. (2020) and Bennett et al. (2019) reported positive student feedback and improved comprehension of biological concepts, such as cell organelles and cellular processes. In conclusion, the integration of VR into biology education appears to significantly boost student engagement and understanding, despite some logistical and financial constraints. The overall positive student reception suggests a promising future for VR in educational contexts, provided these challenges are addressed effectively.

**Keywords:** virtual reality in teaching biology · virtual reality in teaching biology · virtual reality in teaching medicine · technology for teaching biology

## 1 Introduction

Education is a dynamic field that is constantly adapting to evolving societal needs and pedagogical methods. As societies change and new challenges emerge, the educational landscape must continuously evolve to meet these demands. Paradoxically, the Covid-19 pandemic, despite its widespread disruptions, has had a positive impact on the development of new educational techniques and methods. The sudden shift to remote learning compelled educators and institutions to innovate rapidly, resulting in the adoption of diverse digital tools and approaches that have since become integral to modern education.

Currently, several major trends are influencing education, with the widespread use of contemporary technologies and digital platforms at the forefront. These technologies have revolutionized how education is delivered and received. Online learning platforms, e-learning courses, and interactive digital learning resources have facilitated flexible and independent learning, allowing students to acquire knowledge according to their individual needs and schedules. This shift toward personalized learning represents a significant departure from the traditional one-size-fits-all approach, empowering learners to take control of their educational journeys.

Among the technological advancements reshaping education, virtual reality (VR) has emerged as a transformative technology with enormous potential in various fields, including education. VR's ability to create highly immersive and realistic environments makes it a powerful tool for teaching complex concepts and skills. As Hamad and Jia (2022) note, VR's verisimilitude allows learners to experience challenging activities and situations in a manner that is both realistic and believable, making the learning process more effective and the acquired knowledge more transferable to real-world scenarios.

Through immersive experiences, interactive simulations, and 3D visualizations, VR offers unique opportunities to enhance learning processes. The use of technologies such as VR increases students' interest in learning content and promotes their active engagement in the educational material, as they become fully immersed in a virtual environment (Lau and Lee, 2012). This heightened engagement is crucial in fostering a deeper understanding of the subject matter and in making learning more enjoyable and meaningful.

VR provides students with a highly engaging and interactive learning environment that goes beyond traditional methods. It allows them to virtually explore historical events, scientific phenomena, and complex concepts in a manner that is not possible through conventional teaching methods. By visualizing abstract ideas, manipulating objects, and engaging in simulations, students can achieve a deeper and more intuitive understanding of the material being discussed. This hands-on approach to learning is particularly beneficial in subjects that involve intricate processes or require the development of practical skills.

Moreover, VR simulations allow students to practice skills and techniques in a safe and controlled environment. This aspect of VR is particularly valuable in fields where mistakes in the real world could have serious consequences, such as in medical or technical training. Virtual reality can also address accessibility issues by creating an inclusive learning environment. For students with disabilities or physical limitations, VR can offer opportunities to fully participate and perform activities that may have previously been difficult or impossible for them. By tailoring content, pace, and level of difficulty to meet individual learning needs, VR ensures that education is accessible to all, promoting equity in the learning experience (O'Connor and Domingo, 2017).

In addition, VR facilitates collaborative learning and allows students to interact with peers, teachers, and experts from around the world. This global connectivity fosters a sense of community and encourages the exchange of ideas, which is essential for developing critical thinking, problem-solving, creativity, decision-making, and spatial awareness skills. Through interactive challenges and real-life simulations, students can apply theoretical knowledge and develop the practical skills needed in their chosen fields, bridging the gap between classroom learning and real-world application (Hamilton et al., 2020).

The review study "Virtual Reality in Biology Teaching" focuses on the comparison of traditional teaching methods (mainly lecture-based frontal teaching) with VR teaching in biology. This study will summarize relevant sources, evaluate their results, and consolidate the content of the selected sources. The aim of the paper is to provide a comprehensive summary of current knowledge in the field of research solutions applied in biology and medical education. The search for relevant literature will be conducted in both English and Czech sources, ensuring a broad and inclusive review of the available evidence.

This study aims to highlight the potential benefits of VR in enhancing the teaching and learning of biology, a subject that often involves complex processes and intricate details. By comparing VR with traditional methods, the study seeks to demonstrate how immersive technologies can make abstract biological concepts more tangible and accessible, ultimately improving student outcomes and fostering a deeper understanding of the subject.

## 2 Criteria and Methodology for the Selection of Sources

To successfully search for sources, it is essential to establish criteria that allow us to obtain the most accurate results while filtering out inappropriate sources. Given the narrowly specified research topic, it is crucial to specify the research questions as much as possible. These questions include the following areas:

1. Is there a difference between traditional teaching and virtual reality teaching?
2. Can the use of virtual reality in biology education increase student motivation and the amount of knowledge gained?
3. How do students feel about the use of virtual reality in teaching biology?
4. Are there differences in students' opinions about the use of virtual reality in biology education?
5. What influences the introduction of virtual reality in biology education?

It is also important to determine relevant keywords for effective search. The following keywords will be used in this research: "Virtual reality in biology education", "VR in biology education", "Virtual reality in medical education" and "VR in medical education".

Another important parameter for the search is the time period in which the sources were published. For this research, sources published between 2019 and 2023, a period of five years, will be used.

The search for relevant resources will be conducted in EBSCO, Web of Science, ResearchGate and Google Scholar databases.

## 3 Publications

A total of 255 sources were found during the search, from which 26 studies were selected. The number of excluded studies that did not meet the criteria was 229. Some sources focused on VR software development for education and were therefore not used. Another reason for exclusion was the use of other educational software or games for which it was not possible to determine the effect of VR on student achievement. EBSCO, Web of Science, ResearchGate, and Google Scholar databases were used to search for resources.

### 3.1 The Main Differences Between Traditional Biology Teaching and Virtual Reality (VR) Teaching

For decades, traditional biology teaching has relied on classical methods such as lectures, textbooks, and laboratory exercises. These methods have formed the backbone of biology education, providing a structured approach to learning that has been used across generations. However, Smith et al. (2022) point out that while these methods are well-established and have a long track record of success, they often limit students' ability to fully understand complex biological concepts. The reliance on two-dimensional diagrams and static images in textbooks, while useful, can be less interactive and insufficiently stimulating for students who may struggle to grasp the intricacies of biological structures and processes. This traditional approach often results in students learning in a predominantly passive manner, where they receive information rather than actively engaging with it. Such passivity can lead to lower levels of engagement and reduced knowledge retention, as students may find it challenging to connect theoretical knowledge with real-world applications.

The potential of virtual reality (VR) in transforming biology education is further developed by Jones et al. (2021), who highlight how VR offers an interactive and immersive environment that allows students to participate directly in the learning experience. Unlike traditional methods, VR provides three-dimensional visualizations and simulations that enable students to "travel" inside a cell, examine biological processes up close, or perform virtual dissections. These experiences, which are not achievable through conventional methods, offer students a more comprehensive understanding of complex systems and the dynamic nature of biological processes. By enabling learners to explore biological environments in an immersive manner, VR helps bridge the gap between abstract concepts and tangible experiences, fostering a more intuitive grasp of the subject matter.

Brown et al. (2020) underscore the importance of simulations within VR, emphasizing that they allow students to conduct experiments in an environment that closely resembles reality but without the risks and costs associated with physical experiments. This feature of VR is particularly advantageous in educational settings where resources may be limited or where certain experiments might pose safety risks. In a virtual environment, students can repeat experiments, observe their results, and immediately see the consequences of their actions, providing a learning experience that is both safe and cost-effective. This iterative process of experimentation and observation enhances students' understanding of scientific principles, as they can engage with the material in a hands-on manner that is not possible in a traditional classroom setting.

Johnson et al. (2023) further highlight that VR has the potential to revolutionize the understanding and retention of knowledge in biology education. The immersive nature of VR, combined with the ability to repeatedly engage with the material through direct interaction and visual experiences, allows students to retain information more easily and effectively. This method of learning goes beyond simply memorizing facts; it promotes a deeper understanding by encouraging students to interact with biological concepts in a meaningful way. By engaging multiple senses and providing a rich, interactive learning environment, VR helps students internalize complex information and apply it in various contexts, leading to more enduring and impactful learning outcomes.

## 3.2 The Impact of Using VR on Student Motivation and Knowledge Acquisition

Student motivation is a key factor in educational success, as it drives the willingness to learn and the perseverance needed to overcome challenges. Smith et al. (2022) highlight that the interactive and immersive environment of virtual reality (VR) significantly increases student motivation by engaging them in the learning process in a fun and stimulating way. Unlike traditional methods, where students may passively absorb information, VR transforms learning into an active experience, making it more enjoyable and inherently motivating. This motivation is not just superficial; it plays a crucial role in deepening students' commitment to their studies. When students are more engaged, they are more likely to invest the necessary time and energy into their learning, which in turn leads to better educational outcomes. This engagement can be particularly impactful in subjects like biology, where complex concepts often require a high level of attention and dedication to fully comprehend.

Supporting this idea, Jones et al. (2021) argue that VR not only increases motivation but also directly contributes to improved learning outcomes. The immersive nature of VR creates a learning environment that is both captivating and educationally effective. Students using VR tend to perform better on tests and retain knowledge more effectively than those who rely solely on traditional learning methods. This improvement is largely attributed to VR's ability to create an experiential learning environment, where students learn through direct experience rather than passive observation. By participating in virtual experiments, simulations, and explorations, students can actively engage with the material, which enhances their understanding and improves their ability to apply the knowledge they have gained in practical settings. This experiential learning approach is particularly beneficial in scientific disciplines, where hands-on practice is essential for mastering complex concepts and procedures.

Brown et al. (2020) add that one of the key factors contributing to improved knowledge acquisition through VR is its ability to provide immediate feedback. In a traditional classroom, feedback often comes with a delay, which can hinder the learning process. Students may not fully understand their mistakes or the reasons behind them until much later, reducing the effectiveness of the feedback. In contrast, VR environments allow students to receive instant feedback on their actions and decisions during simulations or experiments. This immediate feedback loop is crucial for reinforcing learning, as students can quickly correct their mistakes and understand the impact of their choices in real-time. This process of immediate reflection and adjustment helps to solidify their understanding and leads to a more effective and lasting learning experience.

Extending this analysis, Johnson et al. (2023) report that VR also promotes long-term learning by allowing students to revisit learning materials as often as needed. The ability to repeatedly engage with content in a VR environment helps students to better consolidate their knowledge and skills. This repeated practice is particularly valuable when studying complex and challenging topics that require ongoing review and reinforcement. For example, in biology, where concepts like cellular processes or anatomical structures can be difficult to grasp, the ability to revisit and interact with these concepts in a VR environment can lead to a deeper and more lasting understanding. This iterative learning process supports long-term retention and ensures that students are better prepared to apply their knowledge in real-world scenarios, whether in advanced studies or professional practice.

### 3.3 Student Perceptions of the Use of VR in Biology Education

Students generally have positive attitudes towards the use of virtual reality (VR) in biology education, recognizing its potential to enhance their learning experience. Smith et al. (2022) report that students particularly value the interactivity and visual appeal of VR. These features transform the learning environment, making it not only more engaging but also more meaningful. Through VR, students can interact with complex biological processes and structures in ways that traditional methods, such as textbooks and lectures, simply cannot offer. This direct experience allows students to better grasp abstract concepts, as they can visualize and manipulate three-dimensional models of cells, organs, and ecosystems. The ability to "experience" biology in this immersive way helps bridge the gap between theoretical knowledge and practical understanding, leading to a more comprehensive and lasting learning experience.

Jones et al. (2021) confirm that most students find VR a fun and exciting alternative to traditional methods. The novelty and dynamic nature of VR make it a refreshing change from the conventional classroom setting, where learning is often passive. Students appreciate the opportunity to explore biological processes and structures in a three-dimensional environment, which not only deepens their understanding but also sustains their interest in the subject matter. This immersive exploration often serves as a powerful motivator, encouraging students to delve deeper into biology and fostering a genuine interest in the field. The sense of adventure and discovery that VR offers can transform how students perceive biology, making it more accessible and appealing as a field of study.

However, it is important to acknowledge that not all students have exclusively positive experiences with VR. Brown et al. (2020) point out that some students experience physical discomfort when using VR, such as dizziness, nausea, or eyestrain. These symptoms, often referred to as "cybersickness," can occur due to the disconnect between what the eyes perceive and what the body feels, especially during prolonged use of VR. Such discomfort can significantly limit a student's ability to fully engage with the VR content, detracting from the overall learning experience. For these students, the negative physical effects may overshadow the educational benefits, leading to a less favorable impression of VR as a learning tool. It is crucial for educators to be aware of these potential issues and to provide alternative learning options or shorter VR sessions to accommodate students who may be sensitive to VR environments.

Johnson et al. (2023) also highlight that technical issues, such as poor image quality, slow device response, or software glitches, can negatively affect the student experience with VR. These problems can disrupt the learning process, leading to frustration and reduced engagement. While the majority of students perceive VR positively, these technical challenges can detract from the immersive experience that VR is intended to provide. To ensure that students can fully benefit from VR in education, it is essential for schools and institutions to invest in high-quality, reliable technology. Regular maintenance and updates, along with adequate technical support, are necessary to minimize these issues and to ensure that the VR experience is as smooth and effective as possible.

In conclusion, while students generally respond positively to the use of VR in biology education, appreciating its interactivity and the deepened understanding it provides, it is important to address the challenges that some students may face. By being mindful of physical discomfort and technical issues, educators can maximize the benefits of VR, ensuring that it serves as an effective and inclusive tool in the biology classroom.

### 3.4 Differences in Students' Views on the Use of VR in Biology Education

Smith et al. (2022) suggest that differences in students' views on the use of virtual reality (VR) in education may be attributed to a variety of factors, including individual preferences, technical proficiency, and personal experience with technology. These differences highlight the diverse ways in which students engage with learning tools and the varying degrees of comfort they have with new technologies. For some students, the simplicity and predictability of traditional learning methods—such as textbooks and lectures—may be more appealing because these methods align with their established study habits and offer a sense of familiarity. In contrast, other students may be drawn to the innovative and dynamic approach that VR offers, appreciating its ability to make learning more interactive and immersive. This variation in preferences underscores the need for a flexible approach in education that accommodates different learning styles and preferences.

Jones et al. (2021) further elaborate on the challenges some students face when adapting to VR technology, particularly those who are not accustomed to working with advanced technologies. For these students, the transition from traditional learning tools to VR can be daunting. They may feel insecure or uncomfortable when using VR, which can negatively affect their perception of the technology. This discomfort may stem from a lack of familiarity with VR interfaces, difficulty in navigating virtual environments, or anxiety about using new and unfamiliar tools. As a result, these students might find it challenging to fully engage with the VR content, leading to a less positive experience compared to their more tech-savvy peers. This highlights the importance of providing adequate support and training to help all students become comfortable with VR technology, ensuring that it can be used effectively as a learning tool.

Brown et al. (2020) add that students' views on VR may also be influenced by health issues associated with its use, such as dizziness, nausea, or eye strain—commonly known as "cybersickness." Some students may be more sensitive to these issues, which can significantly impact their willingness to use VR as a learning tool. The physical discomfort experienced by these students can create a barrier to their engagement with the technology, leading them to prefer more traditional learning methods that do not pose such risks. This sensitivity to VR-induced discomfort is an important consideration for educators when integrating VR into the curriculum, as it can affect not only the effectiveness of the technology but also the overall well-being of students.

Johnson et al. (2023) highlight that despite these differences in opinion, the majority of students still perceive VR positively. They recognize the potential of VR to enhance their learning experiences through its interactive and immersive capabilities. However, Johnson et al. emphasize the importance of educators being mindful of individual student needs and preferences when incorporating VR into the classroom. To ensure that VR is accessible and beneficial to all students, it is essential to adopt a differentiated approach that takes into account the diverse range of experiences and comfort levels students have with the technology. This might include offering alternative learning methods for those who are less comfortable with VR, providing additional support for students who struggle with the technology, and addressing health-related concerns by limiting VR usage time or adjusting the content to minimize discomfort.

In conclusion, while VR holds significant promise as a transformative educational tool, its implementation in the classroom must be handled with care. Educators should strive to create an inclusive learning environment where all students, regardless of their technical proficiency, preferences, or sensitivities, can benefit from the advantages that VR offers. By considering individual differences and providing appropriate support, educators can help ensure that VR enhances the learning experience for all students, rather than becoming a source of frustration or discomfort.

### 3.5 Factors Influencing the Implementation of VR in Biology Education

Implementing virtual reality (VR) in biology education presents several challenges and opportunities that need to be carefully considered by educators and administrators. Smith et al. (2022) emphasize that one of the most significant barriers to the widespread adoption of VR in schools is the cost associated with purchasing and maintaining the necessary equipment. High-quality VR systems, including headsets, controllers, and compatible computers or consoles, are expensive, and the ongoing maintenance and potential need for regular updates add to the financial burden. For schools with limited budgets, these costs can be prohibitive, making it difficult to justify the investment, especially when weighed against other educational needs. This financial barrier can also exacerbate existing inequalities between well-funded schools and those with fewer resources, potentially leading to disparities in access to cutting-edge educational tools like VR.

In addition to the financial costs, Jones et al. (2021) highlight the importance of investing in training for both teachers and students to use VR technologies effectively. The introduction of VR into the classroom is not as simple as just providing the equipment; it requires a significant commitment to ensuring that educators are comfortable and proficient in using the technology. Teachers need to understand not only how to operate the VR systems but also how to integrate them into their teaching strategies in a way that enhances learning outcomes. This training process demands time and resources, as educators may need to attend workshops, participate in professional development programs, and spend time experimenting with the technology before they can confidently use it in the classroom. For students, especially those who are less familiar with advanced technologies, there may also be a learning curve, requiring additional support to help them navigate and fully benefit from VR-based learning experiences.

Brown et al. (2020) stress the importance of thoughtfully integrating VR content into existing biology curricula. To be effective, VR must be more than just an add-on; it needs to be carefully aligned with specific learning objectives and seamlessly integrated into the curriculum. This means that educators may need to modify existing lesson plans and develop new didactic materials that take advantage of the unique capabilities of VR. For instance, while traditional methods might involve students reading about cell division, a VR module could allow them to virtually observe and interact with the process in three dimensions. However, creating such content requires collaboration between curriculum developers, subject matter experts, and technology specialists to ensure that the VR experiences are educationally valuable and aligned with curriculum standards. This can be a complex and time-consuming process, further adding to the challenges of VR implementation.

## 4 Conclusion

Traditional biology teaching has long relied on classical methods such as lectures, textbooks and laboratory exercises. These methods have their advantages, are well established and familiar to both teachers and students. However, their limitations lie in their lack of interactivity and passive approach to learning. The two-dimensional diagrams and static images in textbooks can be less engaging for students and do not allow a full understanding of complex biological concepts. For example, complex cellular structures or the dynamics of biological processes are difficult to explain in a traditional learning environment, which can lead to lower student engagement and knowledge retention.

On the other hand, Virtual Reality (VR) is revolutionizing biology education by offering an immersive and interactive environment. VR allows students to engage with learning in new ways - for example, they can 'travel' inside a cell, examine biological processes up close or conduct simulated experiments. These possibilities are unattainable in traditional education. VR provides 3D visualizations and simulations that allow students to better understand complex biological systems and processes. Such experiences promote active learning, leading to a deeper understanding of the material.

Student motivation is a key factor in educational success and VR significantly increases student motivation to learn. The interactive and visually appealing environment that VR offers draws students into the learning process in a fun and stimulating way. This increased motivation isn't just superficial - students who are more engaged in learning through VR are more willing to invest time and energy in their studies, leading to better learning outcomes. VR improves student learning outcomes and knowledge retention by enabling learning through direct experience.

Another advantage of VR is its ability to provide instant feedback. In a simulated environment, students can immediately see the consequences of their decisions, which promotes more effective learning than traditional methods that often provide delayed feedback. The ability to revisit learning materials repeatedly in a VR environment also promotes long-term learning, which is particularly useful when studying complex and challenging topics.

Students generally have a positive view of the use of VR in biology education. They particularly appreciate the interactivity and visual appeal that VR brings. This way of teaching makes the material more engaging and meaningful because students can better understand complex concepts through direct experience. Many students see VR as a fun and exciting alternative to traditional methods, which promotes their interest in biology and science in general.

However, not all students have only positive experiences with VR. Some may experience physical discomfort, such as dizziness, nausea or eyestrain, which can affect their ability to fully engage in the learning experience. Technical issues such as poor image quality or slow device response can also negatively affect students' VR experience. These factors highlight the need for quality technical equipment and support when using VR in education.

Students' views on using VR may vary depending on their individual preferences, technical skills and previous experience with technology. While some students may prefer traditional forms of learning for their simplicity and predictability, others may appreciate the innovative and dynamic approach that VR offers. Students who are not used to working with advanced technologies may find it difficult to adapt to VR, which may affect their perception of the technology.

Health issues such as dizziness or eyestrain can also affect some students' views of virtual reality. These students may be less willing to use VR as a learning tool, highlighting the need for an individual approach when integrating this technology into the classroom. Despite these differences, most students perceive VR positively, but educators should take into account individual student needs and preferences to ensure that the technology is accessible and beneficial to all.

Implementing VR in biology education presents several challenges. One of the main obstacles is the cost of purchasing and maintaining VR equipment, which can be costly for many schools. In addition to purchasing hardware and software, it is also necessary to invest in training teachers and students to use the technology effectively. This process requires time and resources, which can be an additional challenge for schools.

Another key issue is the integration of VR content into existing biology curricula. In order to use VR effectively, the content must be tailored to specific learning objectives and aligned with the requirements of the school curriculum. This may require modifications to existing lesson plans and the creation of new didactic materials, which can be time consuming and requires collaboration between educators and VR experts.

In addition to these challenges, the health aspects associated with the long-term use of VR should also be taken into account. Schools should ensure that students are not subjected to undue stress or discomfort when using VR and should provide clear guidelines for the safe and effective use of this technology. Overall, the introduction of VR into the classroom is promising but requires careful planning and support to be successful and beneficial for all students.

**Acknowledgements.** The article is supported by Specific research project of Faculty of Education, University Hradec Kralove, 2024, No. 2126.

# References

Bennett, J.A., Saunders, C.P.: Virtual cell tour: The impact of virtual reality on student learning and engagement in stem cell classes. J. Microbiol. Biol. Educ. **20**(2) (2019). https://doi.org/10.1128/jmbe.v20i2.1658

Hamad, A., Jia, B.: How virtual reality technology has changed our lives: A review of current and potential applications and limitations. Int. J. Environ. Res. Public Health 19 (2022). https://doi.org/10.3390/ijerph191811278

Hamilton, D.E., McKechnie, J., Edgerton, E., Wilson, C.: Immersive virtual reality as a pedagogical tool in education: a systematic literature review of quantitative learning outcomes and experimental design. J. Comp. Educ. **11** and **8**(1), 1–32 (2022). https://doi.org/10.1007/s40692-020-00169-2

Christopoulos, A., Pellas, N., Qushem, U.B., Laakso, M.: Comparing the effectiveness of video-assisted instruction and stereoscopic 360° virtual reality in high school biology courses. Br. J. Edu. Technol. **54**(4), 987–1005 (2023). https://doi.org/10.1111/bjet.13306

Chuang, T., et al.: The use of virtual reality technology in teaching biology. The œAmerican Biology Teacher **85**(1), 23–32 (2023). https://doi.org/10.1525/abt.2023.85.1.23

Kumar, A., et al.: Gamified learning and assessment using ARCS with integrated 3D animation and next generation AIoMT virtual reality simulation. Electronics **12**(4), 835 (2023). https://doi.org/10.3390/electronics12040835

Lau, K.W., Lee, P.Y.: Using virtual reality to create unusual environmental stimulation to motivate students to explore creative ideas. An Interact. Learn. Environ. **23**(1), 3–18 (2012). https://doi.org/10.1080/10494820.2012.745426

Li, F., et al.: Application of sustainability teaching in engineering education: A case study of Undergraduate course design of Raman Spectroscopy based on Virtual Reality (VR) technology. Sustainability **15**(3), 1782 (2023). https://doi.org/10.3390/su15031782

Liu, F., Yeh, C.: The influence of Competency-Based VR learning materials on Problem-Solving behavioral Intentions-Taking environmental issues in junior high schools as an example. Sustainability **14**(23), 16036 (2022). https://doi.org/10.3390/su142316036

O'Connor, E., Domingo, J.A.: A practical guide with theoretical foundations for creating effective virtual reality learning environments. J. Educ. Technol. Sys. **45**(3), 343–64 (2017). https://doi.org/10.1177/0047239516673361

Thompson, M.M., et al.: The impact of virtual reality on high school students' conceptions of cells. J. Univ. Comput. Sci. **26**(8), 929–946 (2020). https://doi.org/10.3897/jucs.2020.050

Thompson, M., et al.: Immersion positively affects learning in virtual reality games compared to equally interactive 2d games. Info. Learn. Sci. **122**(7/8), 442–463 (2021). https://doi.org/10.1108/ils-12-2020-0252

Webb, M., et al.: Haptically supported collaborative learning in virtual reality for schools. Educ. Inf. Technol. **27**(1), 937–960 (2021). https://doi.org/10.1007/s10639-021-10639-4

# Use of Virtual Reality for Improving Students' Learning Attention in Higher Vocational Education

Xiaojun Liu[1], Liang Liu[2], Yong Cai[1], and Simon K. S. Cheung[3,4](✉)

[1] Shenzhen Institute of Technology, Shenzhen, Guangdong Province, China
[2] City University of Macau, Taipa, Macau SAR, China
[3] Hong Kong Metropolitan University, Hong Kong SAR, China
kscheung@hkmu.edu.hk
[4] Shenzhen City Polytechnic, Shenzhen, Guangdong Province, China

**Abstract.** One of the challenges being faced in higher vocational education is to improve students' learning attention which impacts their learning performance. This paper investigates a solution through the use of virtual reality. Specifically, we study whether immersive experiential teaching can help improve students' learning attention, based on two experiments separately conducted to two higher vocational universities in China. By random sampling, 82 students from one university and 66 students from the other university were selected to participate the first and second experiments respectively. Structural equation modeling was employed to assess the causal relationship among four variables, namely, students' behavioral intention to use virtual reality, learning satisfaction, learning motivation, and learning attention. The results affirmed that students' behavioral intention to use immersive virtual reality technology would positively correlate to improvement of their learning attention.

**Keywords:** virtual reality; learning attention · higher vocational education · learning motivation

## 1 Introduction

The use of virtual reality (VR) in vocational education is generally believed to be a promising approach to enhancing student engagement, motivation, and practical skills. It is also evidenced that VR can address some known challenges faced by vocational education, including the need of practical, hands-on learning experiences, and the limitations imposed by conventional instructional media.

One of the primary benefits of VR in vocational education is its ability to provide immersive and interactive learning environments that closely simulate real-world work scenarios (Ravichandran and Mahapatra, 2023). This immersive aspect is crucial for vocational education, where practical skills and knowledge are essential. For instance, the development of a VR application for the two-stroke engine replication demonstrates how VR can facilitate the learning of complex mechanical systems that might be difficult or impossible to access in traditional settings (Sholichin et al., 2020). Hanson and Shelton (2008) showed that allowing a student to manipulate a 3D object in a virtual space offers them control over what they saw and when they saw it.

The use of VR could raise the students' learning engagement and motivation by providing realistic simulations that allow students to visualize and interact with concepts in a way that is impossible with conventional 2D interfaces (Babu et al., 2018; Rafiq et al., 2022). The integration of daily life experiences with course materials has been demonstrated to be an effective method for capturing learners' attention in the initial stages of instruction (Hung et al., 2023). This increased engagement can lead to better retention of knowledge and improved learning outcomes. The use of VR in vocational education also offers the potential to overcome geographical and resource constraints, enabling students to engage in practical learning experiences regardless of their physical location or the availability of equipment and tools (Regivaldo et al., 2021).

However, it is important to note that, while participation is highly valued, there are critiques regarding its implementation and its potential to become an ideological construct that may not always align with students' actual experiences or needs (Gourlay, 2015). This critique points to the need for a nuanced understanding of participation and engagement, considering the complexities of day-to-day practices and the diverse ways in which students engage in their learning.

Accordingly, our study aims to address the above-mentioned gap in existing research and contribute to the literature on virtual reality technology and vocational education. The primary research question in our study is whether utilizing VR technology in an educational setting would impact the motivation and attention of students enrolled in vocational programs? A quantitative methodology was used for collection and analysis of data to address this research question.

## 2 Literature Review

The immersive nature of VR is critical to capturing and maintaining student attention. The immersive environment created by VR can make learning more engaging and interactive, leading to better focus on the content being taught. Eye-tracking studies have shown that VR environments can effectively capture students' attention by manipulating visual elements such as objects of interest, influencing where students look within the virtual classroom (Bozkir et al., 2021). Students are very interested in VR-based learning methods (Liu et al., 2024).

In recent years, there has been a rising need of smart learning for learning flexibility, effectiveness, efficiency and engagement (Cheung et al., 2021). Satisfaction in digital learning environments is closely linked to both motivation and attention. Research has found that motivation and satisfaction are significantly correlated, with stronger motivations leading to higher satisfaction levels. VR's ability to provide immersive and interactive learning experiences significantly improves learning satisfaction. Studies have shown that immersive VR learning environments can lead to higher levels of learner satisfaction due to the increased engagement and emotional connection they foster. For example, using VR to teach computer hardware components resulted in high levels of student satisfaction due to the immersive and interactive nature of the learning experience (Cheng-Hsiu, 2023). Furthermore, the design principles of immersive VR micro-lessons highlight the importance of sensory simulation, scene construction, and human-computer interaction increasing learner satisfaction with the learning process. Furthermore, the quality of the learning experience, including aspects like course design, support services, and the use of engaging content, can enhance both motivation and satisfaction (Lin et al., 2017).

Behavioral intentions are closely related to the overall effectiveness of VR in education. The development of a Learning Management System (LMS) for VR education demonstrates an effort to align VR content with appropriate instructional design, indicating a focus on integrating VR with pedagogical strategies to influence learners' behavioral intentions toward learning (Kim et al., 2019). In addition, the exploration of VR MOOCs highlights the potential of VR to provide personalized learning experiences that may influence learners' decisions to enroll in further education or specific courses (Li et al., 2022). VR holds promise for increasing attention, motivation, and satisfaction with learning in educational settings.

## 2.1 Research Hypothesis

We establish the following hypothesis statements, based on the relationship among four variables learned from the literature review, namely, behavioral intention to use virtual reality, learning satisfaction, learning motivation, and learning attention.

H1: Behavioral intention to use virtual reality has a positive impact on learning motivation.
H2: Behavioral intention to use virtual reality has a positive impact on learning satisfaction.
H3: Behavioral intention to use virtual reality has a positive impact on learning attention.
H4: Learning motivation plays an intermediary role between behavioral intention to use virtual reality and learning attention.
H5: Learning satisfaction plays an intermediary role between behavioral intention to use virtual reality and learning attention.

## 2.2 The Proposed Theoretical Model

With a theoretical basis for investigating the relationship among behavioral intention to use virtual reality, learning motivation, learning satisfaction, and learning attention, Fig. 1 illustrates the hypothetical relationship between the research model and the various structures of all indicators tested in our research.

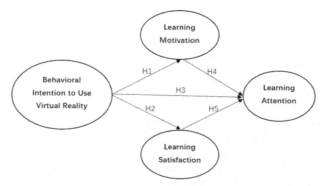

**Fig. 1.** The proposed hypothetical model.

## 3 Research Method

### 3.1 Data Collection and Sample Characteristics

This research was based on data from two samples of 82, and 66 s-year college students studying information technology at the Shenzhen Institute of Technology and Shenzhen City Polytechnic. The participants were selected from a diverse range of genders and age groups and were selected through a convenient sampling method, and data were collected through a questionnaire survey. The survey items were presented on a 7-point Likert-type scale, ranging from "strongly disagree" to "strongly agree". The data were analyzed using the statistical software package SPSS 24.0 together with the structural equation modeling software PLS 4. The data collection period was conducted on the Friday following the midterm examination, enabling students to contrast the diverse experiences of VR technology-based instruction with those of conventional teaching methodologies. This was undertaken on 17 May, and 24 May 2024.

### 3.2 Measurements

The evaluation of various aspects of the proposed model, including behavioral intention to use virtual reality, learning satisfaction, learning motivation, and learning attention, was conducted using a measurement scale derived from existing literature. To measure learning motivation, five items from a study by Law et al. (2019) were utilized, demonstrating good reliability with an internal consistency coefficient of Cronbach $\alpha = 0.87$. Similarly, four items from a study by Bhattacherjee (2001) were adopted to assess learning satisfaction, exhibiting good reliability with an internal consistency coefficient of Cronbach $\alpha = 0.91$. Behavioral intention to use virtual reality was evaluated using four items from a study by Cabero and Pérez (2018), which displayed good reliability with an internal consistency coefficient of Cronbach $\alpha = 0.88$. Furthermore, a four-item Perceived Coolness Scale adapted from Keller (2010) was employed, showing good reliability with an internal consistency coefficient of Cronbach $\alpha = 0.89$. All items were measured using a 7-point Likert scale.

## 3.3 Pilot Test

To assess the accuracy and consistency of the scales implemented, a questionnaire was created, and a preliminary investigation was conducted in May 2024. During this pilot study, a group of 30 students were surveyed and asked to provide feedback on the clarity of the scales. The results revealed that all variables met the predetermined standards for validity and reliability, thereby confirming the dependable nature of the developed scale in gauging students' acceptance levels towards VR technology in higher education. This conclusion was further supported by the composite reliability, Cronbach's alpha, and reliability coefficients, all of which exceeded 0.7, as well as the average variance extracted (AVE), which surpassed 0.5. Thus, it was demonstrated that the experimental scale exhibits strong reliability and validity.

## 3.4 Research Result

### 3.4.1 Demographic Information

To commence the survey at Shenzhen Institute of Technology, participants were asked to provide their demographic information. A grand total of 82 questionnaires were distributed, all were returned, resulting in a flawless recovery rate of 100%. Out of the respondents, the majority consisted of females, accounting for 67.1% or 55 students, while males made up the remaining 32.9%, totaling 27 students. Among the entire sample, 76.8% were students aged 18 years old. The remaining 23.2% were composed of 19 students who were above the age of 19.

### 3.4.2 Convergent Validity Testing

A reliable model fit analysis considers the convergent validity of items, measuring how closely they align with each other. According to Table 1, composite reliability values range from 0.876 to 0.982, indicating that they all exceed the recommended threshold of 0.70. Furthermore, the Cronbach's alpha values surpass the suggested value of 0.70, ranging from 0.818 to 0.977. An alpha value of 0.70–0.80 or higher indicates an exceptional level of reliability (Ursachi et al., 2015). The AVE values range from 0.638 to 0.915, all exceeding the recommended value of 0.50 as suggested by Fornell and Larcker (1981).

**Table 1.** Convergent validity.

|    | Cronbach's alpha (CA) | Composite reliability (CR) | Average variance extracted (AVE) |
|----|----------------------|---------------------------|----------------------------------|
| BI | 0.812                | 0.876                     | 0.638                            |
| LM | 0.977                | 0.982                     | 0.914                            |
| LS | 0.962                | 0.972                     | 0.898                            |
| LA | 0.954                | 0.970                     | 0.915                            |

Note: BI: Behavioral Intention to Use Virtual Reality; Learning Motivation; LS: Learning Satisfaction; LA: Learning Attention.

### 3.4.3 Discriminant Validity Testing

After we get the reliability and validity of the model, we then analyze the internal relations of the model. Table 2 showed that there was a significant positive correlation between Behavioral Intention to Use Virtual Reality on Learning Motivation ($\gamma = 0.333$, $P < 0.01$), Learning Satisfaction ($\gamma = 0.358$, $P < 0.001$), and Learning Attention ($\gamma = 0.469$, $P < 0.01$); Learning motivation was positively correlated with Learning Satisfaction ($\gamma = 0.928$, $P < 0.01$), and Learning Attention ($\gamma = 0.872$, $P < 0.01$). Lastly, Learning Satisfaction was positively correlated with Learning Motivation ($\gamma = 0.910$, $P < 0.01$) These revealed results might provide initial support for our proposed hypotheses.

**Table 2.** Differentiation validity test.

| Dimension | BI | LM | LS | LA |
|---|---|---|---|---|
| BI | 1 | 0.333** | 0.358** | 0.469** |
| LM | | 1 | 0.928** | 0.872** |
| LS | | | 1 | 0.910** |
| LA | | | | 1 |

Note: BI: Behavioral Intention to Use Virtual Reality; Learning Motivation; LS: Learning Satisfaction; LA: Learning Attention.

### 3.4.4 Testing Hypotheses and the Intermediary Effect

Table 3 showed that Behavioral intention to use virtual reality had a significantly positive effect on Learning motivation ($\gamma = 0.328$, $t = 4.538$, $P < 0.001$), supporting H1; Behavioral intention to use virtual reality had a significantly positive effect on either Learning satisfaction ($\gamma = 0.360$, $t = 4.687$, $P < 0.001$) or Learning attention ($\gamma = 0.414$, $t = 5.999$, $P < 0.001$), supporting H2 and H3.

Next, we analyze the variable relationship of indirect influence. We utilized the bootstrapping method in process to examine the potential mediation of Learning strategies and Learning motivation. Based on the confidence level of 95% calculated with the number of bootstrap samples set to 5000 (Hayes, 2009) and the indirect effect measurement method (Hayes and Preacher, 2014; Montoya and Hayes, 2016). Learning motivation significantly positive influence between Behavioral intention to use virtual reality and Learning attention ($\gamma = 0.107$, $t = 2.043$, $P < 0.05$) supporting H4. Learning satisfaction significantly positive influence between Behavioral intention to use virtual reality and Learning attention ($\gamma = 0.210$, $t = 3.340$, $P < 0.001$) supporting H5. This means that Learning motivation and Learning satisfaction plays an intermediary role between Behavioral intention to use virtual reality and Learning attention.

**Table 3.** Hypothesis testing (primary experiment).

|  | Original sample (O) | T statistics | P values |  |
|---|---|---|---|---|
| BI → LM | 0.328 | 4.538 | 0.000 | H1 Support |
| BI → LS | 0.360 | 4.687 | 0.000 | H2 Support |
| BI → LA | 0.414 | 5.999 | 0.000 | H3 Support |
| BI → LM → LA | 0.107 | 2.043 | 0.041 | H4 Support |
| BI → LS → LA | 0.210 | 3.340 | 0.001 | H5 Support |

Note: BI: Behavioral Intention to Use Virtual Reality; Learning Motivation; LS: Learning Satisfaction; LA: Learning Attention.

### 3.4.5 Structural Model Result

After verifying the research hypothesis, we analyze and sort out the obtained data according to PLS 4 software and improve it to our structural model, as shown in Fig. 2, which is the structural result of our model.

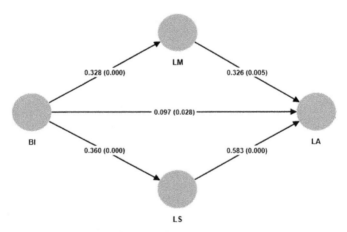

Note: BI: Behavioral Intention to Use Virtual Reality; Learning Motivation; LS: Learning Satisfaction; LA: Learning Attention.

**Fig. 2.** Structural model (primary experiment).

Following the verification above, the utilization of VR technology in vocational education classrooms can potentially enhance students' learning motivation, satisfaction, and attention. This has significant implications for the future development of our teaching design. To corroborate the findings of the preceding research, a second study was conducted at an alternative vocational institution with the objective of re-certifying results.

### 3.4.6 Secondary Experiment to Verify the Results

A grand total of 66 questionnaires were distributed at Shenzhen City Polytechnic, all were returned, resulting in a recovery rate of 100%. Out of the respondents, the majority consisted of females, accounting for 56.1% or 37 students, while males made up the remaining 43.9%, totaling 29 students. Among the entire sample, 75.8% were students aged 18 years old. The remaining 24.2% were composed of 16 students who were above the age of 19.

Table 4 showed that Behavioral intention to use virtual reality had a significantly positive effect on Learning motivation ($\gamma = 0.366$, $t = 4.413$, $P < 0.001$), supporting H1; Behavioral intention to use virtual reality had a significantly positive effect on either Learning satisfaction ($\gamma = 0.397$, $t = 4.677$, $P < 0.001$) or Learning attention ($\gamma = 0.158$, $t = 2.976$, $P < 0.05$), supporting H2 and H3.

Next, we analyze the variable relationship of indirect influence. Learning motivation significantly positive influence between Behavioral intention to use virtual reality and Learning attention ($\gamma = 0.146$, $t = 2.050$, $P < 0.05$) supporting H4. Learning satisfaction significantly positive influence between Behavioral intention to use virtual reality and Learning attention ($\gamma = 0.184$, $t = 2.672$, $P < 0.05$) supporting H5. This means that Learning motivation and Learning satisfaction plays an intermediary role between Behavioral intention to use virtual reality and Learning attention.

Table 4. Hypothesis testing (secondary experiment).

|  | Original sample (O) | T statistics | P values |  |
|---|---|---|---|---|
| BI → LM | 0.366 | 4.413 | 0.000 | H1 Support |
| BI → LS | 0.397 | 4.677 | 0.000 | H2 Support |
| BI → LA | 0.158 | 2.976 | 0.003 | H3 Support |
| BI → LM → LA | 0.146 | 2.050 | 0.040 | H4 Support |
| BI → LS → LA | 0.184 | 2.672 | 0.008 | H5 Support |

Note: BI: Behavioral Intention to Use Virtual Reality; Learning Motivation; LS: Learning Satisfaction; LA: Learning Attention.

After hypothesis verification, we obtained the structural model in Fig. 3, which is consistent with the structural model results in Fig. 2 above, indicating that our research has been successfully verified again.

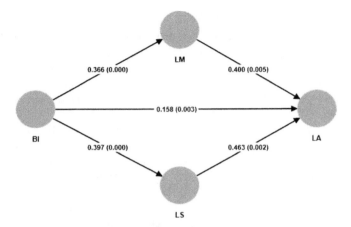

Note:  BI: Behavioral Intention to Use Virtual Reality; Learning Motivation; LS: Learning Satisfaction; LA: Learning Attention.

**Fig. 3.** Structural model (secondary experiment).

## 4 Discussion and Conclusion

Our findings indicate that utilizing virtual reality (VR) technology in vocational education can potentially enhance students' motivation and attention. Further research could be conducted in the future on the use of immersive VR in vocational education to develop more effective learning strategies and methods. However, the adoption of VR in vocational education is not without challenges. These include the high cost of VR equipment and software, the need for specialized technical support, and the limited understanding and enthusiasm among educators regarding the benefits of VR technology (Ravichandran and Mahapatra, 2023; Hendra, 2022). Additionally, the effectiveness of VR-based learning depends on the quality of the VR content and the pedagogical strategies employed to support student learning (Chen, 2019).

Despite the challenges, evidence strongly supports the potential of VR technology to enhance vocational education. VR can provide students with valuable practical experiences, increase their motivation and engagement, and prepare them for the demands of modern workplaces (Belani, 2020; Maulana et al., 2021; Prasolova-Førland et al., 2019). To maximize the benefits of VR in vocational education, it is essential to invest in appropriate infrastructure, develop high-quality VR content, and provide training for educators on how to effectively integrate VR into their teaching practices (Ravichandran and Mahapatra, 2023; Hendra, 2022).

In conclusion, VR technology represents a significant opportunity to transform vocational education by offering immersive, interactive, and practical learning experiences. While there are challenges to overcome, the evidence suggests that with careful planning and implementation, VR can significantly enhance the quality of vocational education and better prepare students for their future careers.

# References

Babu, S.K., Krishna, S., Unnikrishnan, R. and Bhavani, R.R.: Virtual reality learning environments for vocational education: A comparison study with conventional instructional media on knowledge retention. In: 2018 IEEE 18th International Conference on Advanced Learning Technologies (ICALT), pp. 385–389. IEEE (2018)

Belani, M.: Evaluating virtual reality as a medium for vocational skill training. In: Extended Abstracts of the 2020 CHI Conference on Human Factors in Computing Systems, pp. 1–8 (2020)

Bhattacherjee, A.: Understanding information systems continuance: an expectation-confirmation model. MIS Q. **25**, 351–370 (2001)

Bozkir, E., et al.: Exploiting object-of-interest information to understand attention in VR classrooms. In: 2021 IEEE Virtual Reality and 3D User Interfaces (VR), pp. 597–605. IEEE (2021)

Chen, L.W., Tsai, J.P., Kao, Y.C., Wu, Y.X.: Investigating the learning performances between sequence-and context-based teaching designs for virtual reality (VR)-based machine tool operation training. Comput. Appl. Eng. Educ. **27**(5), 1043–1063 (2019)

Cheung, S.K.S., Wang, F.L.: The continuous pursuit of smart learning. Australas. J. Educ. Technol. **37**(2), 1–6 (2021)

Cabero-Almenara, J., Pérez-Díez-de-los-Ríos, J.L.: Validación del modelo TAM de adopción de la Realidad Aumentada mediante ecuaciones estructurales. Estudios sobre Educación. **34**, 129–153 (2018)

Fornell, C., Larcker, D.F.: Structural equation models with unobservable variables and measurement error: algebra and statistics. J. Mark. Res. **18**, 382–388 (1981)

Gourlay, L.: 'Student engagement' and the tyranny of participation. Teach. High. Educ. **20**(4), 402–411 (2015)

Hanson, K., Shelton, B.E.: Design and development of virtual reality: analysis of challenges faced by educators. J. Educ. Technol. Soc. **11**(1), 118–131 (2008)

Hayes, A.F.: Beyond Baron and Kenny: Statistical mediation analysis in the new millennium. Commun. Monogr. **76**(4), 408–420 (2009)

Hendra, J.: Potential utilization of virtual reality learning for vocational school teachers. World J. Adv. Eng. Technol. Sci. **7**(02), 054–061 (2022)

Hung, C.Y., Lin, Y.T., Yu, S.J., Sun, J.C.Y.: Effects of AR-and VR-based wearables in teaching English: The application of an ARCS model-based learning design to improve elementary school students' learning motivation and performance. J. Comput. Assist. Learn. **39**(5), 1510–1527 (2023)

Keller, J.M.: Motivational design for learning and performance. Springer, US (2010)

Kim, H., Nah, S., Oh, J., Ryu, H.: VR-MOOCs: A learning management system for VR education. In: 2019 IEEE Conference on Virtual Reality and 3D User Interfaces (VR), pp. 1325–1326. IEEE (2019)

Law, K.M.Y., Geng, S., Li, T.M.: Student enrollment, motivation and learning performance in a blended learning environment: the mediating effects of social, teaching, and cognitive presence. Comput. Educ. **136**, 1–12 (2019)

Li, P., Fang, Z., Jiang, T.: Research Into improved Distance Learning Using VR Technology. Frontiers in Education **7**, 757874 (2022)

Liu, X., Zhang, H., Liu, L.: The perceived coolness of using virtual reality technology in blended learning performance can improve learning motivation and learning satisfaction. Frontiers in Education **9**, 1346467 (2024)

Lin, M.H., Chen, H.C., Liu, K.S.: A study of the effects of digital learning on learning motivation and learning outcome. Eurasia J. Math. Sci. Technol. Educ. **13**(7), 3553–3564 (2017)

Maulana, F.I., et al.: Contribution of virtual reality technology to increase student interest in vocational high schools. In: 2021 International Seminar on Intelligent Technology and its Applications (ISITIA), pp. 283–286. IEEE (2021)

Prasolova-Førland, E., Fominykh, M., Ekelund, O.I.: Empowering young job seekers with virtual reality. In: 2019 IEEE Conference on Virtual Reality and 3D User Interfaces (VR), pp. 295–302. IEEE (2019)

Ravichandran, R.R., Mahapatra, J.: Virtual reality in vocational education and training: challenges and possibilities. J. Digi. Learn. Educ. **3**(1), 25–31 (2023)

Rafiq, A.A., Triyono, M.B., Djatmiko, I.W.: Enhancing student engagement in vocational education by using virtual reality. Waikato Journal of Education **27**(3), 175–188 (2022)

Regivaldo, S.F., Aparecido, C.X.R., Sandro, R.A.A.: Virtual reality as a tool for fundamental and vocational education. Metaverse **2**(1), 12 (2021)

Sholichin, F., et al.: November. Virtual reality learning environments for vocational education: a comparative study with conventional instructional media on two-stroke engine. In: IOP Conference Series: Materials Science and Engineering, Vol. 979, No. 1, p. 012015. IOP Publishing (2020)

Ursachi, G., Horodnic, I.A., Zait, A.: How reliable are measurement scales? External factors with indirect influence on reliability estimators. Procedia Economics and Finance **20**, 679–686 (2015)

# A Study on the Effectiveness of a VR Training Programme in the Property Management Industry

Yan-Wai Chan[1], Simon K. S. Cheung[2], Kwan-Keung Ng[3](✉), Aaron S. Y. Chiang[4], Pius Lam[4], and Kwok Tai Chui[2]

[1] The Education University of Hong Kong, Hong Kong SAR, China
kevinywchan@hkic.edu.hk
[2] Hong Kong Metropolitan University, Hong Kong SAR, China
{kscheung,jktchui}@hkmu.edu.hk
[3] Shenzhen City Polytechnic, Shenzhen, China
ngkwankeung@outlook.com
[4] Hong Yip People Development Academy, Hong Kong SAR, China
{sychiang,kllam1}@hongyip.com

**Abstract.** The aim of this study is to evaluate the effectiveness of virtual reality (VR) training in managing accidental incidents within shopping malls, commercial properties, and residential properties. It also aimed to share the experiences and feedback obtained from the VR training program within the property management industry in Hong Kong. The research focused on employees of a reputable yet representative property management company in Hong Kong. We employed the Unified Theory of Acceptance and Use of Technology (UTAUT) model as the research methodology to construct the survey. An online survey was anonymously distributed to staff members who underwent VR training via the property management company's multi-media platform, aiming to assess the effectiveness of the training and their inclination to apply the acquired knowledge when dealing with accidental incidents in the workplace. With 279 completed survey responses from the trainees, the findings revealed that the VR training program effectively facilitated the application of learned skills in real-life situations. Overall, this research provides insights into the increasing significance and effectiveness of VR training in the property management industry, offering valuable perspectives on the application and impact of innovative training methods in real-life scenarios.

**Keywords:** Artificial Intelligence · Property Management Industry · Unified Theory of Acceptance and Use of Technology (UTAUT) · Virtual Reality (VR)

## 1 Introduction

In Hong Kong, property management companies are integrating technology into their service delivery, driven by the Hong Kong Smart City Blueprint 2.0 (Hong Kong Smart City Blueprint 2.0, 2020) and the need for smart education and training advancements. The densely populated living environment presents challenges in effectively training practitioners in the property management industry without leveraging technological tools. The industry's 24/7 nature presents difficulties in providing focused training and response to real-life scenarios. Property management encompasses a spectrum of building-related services, and the obligations outlined in property management contracts vary, leading to diverse contract types and scheduling challenges (Wong and Lai, 2021).

Our research work evaluates the effectiveness of virtual reality (VR) training in managing accidental incidents within the property management industry in Hong Kong. The research focuses on employees of a property management company and employs the Unified Theory of Acceptance and Use of Technology (UTAUT) model to construct the survey, which UTAUT is a famous theory applied in educational research (Faqih and 2021). An online survey was distributed to staff members who underwent VR training via the company's internet platform to assess the training's effectiveness and their inclination to apply the acquired knowledge in dealing with accidental incidents in the workplace. The findings suggest that the VR training program effectively facilitated the application of learned skills in real-life situations. The study aims to share the experiences and feedback obtained from the VR training program within the property management industry in Hong Kong, Hong Yip Service Company Limited (Hong Yip), providing insights into the increasing significance and effectiveness of VR training. Hong Yip established in 1967 as a wholly owned subsidiary of Sun Hung Kai Properties Limited, is a leading property and facilities management company with over 50 years of experience in Hong Kong (Hong Yip, 2024). Through pioneering service and technological innovations, the company has consistently brought its management practices and business operations in line with international standards, earning them an enviable status in the property management industry in Hong Kong.

This research study emphasises the increasing significance and effectiveness of VR training in the property management industry. The use of VR training has been beneficial in managing accidental incidents, and the study offers valuable insights into the application and impact of innovative training methods in real-life scenarios (Chan et al., 2024).

## 2 Virtual Building Platform for Integrated Emergency Handling

This research work is a part of the "Virtual Building Platform for Integrated Emergency Handling" project that received funding from the Hong Kong Institute of Vocational Education (IVE), with the contribution of professional knowledge and on-site scenarios from Hong Yip. The Hong Kong Institute of Vocational Education (IVE) is a leading institution in vocational education, renowned for its dedication to providing high-quality training tailored to various industries, including property management. Through collaboration with industry stakeholders, IVE ensures that its curriculum is in line with current market demands, equipping students with practical skills directly applicable in the workplace. Concurrently, Hong Yip Service Company Limited, one of the largest property management firms in Hong Kong, is committed to the continuous professional development of its staff. The company actively invests in cutting-edge training solutions, such as AR, VR and MR technology, to enhance employee skills and preparedness. As a prominent industry player, Hong Yip is the pioneer in the application of the latest technology in its business operations, and its practices set the industry standards, making its involvement in the research crucial for understanding the effectiveness of VR training and its implications for workforce development in property management.

The property management industry faces numerous challenges in providing comprehensive training and responding to real-life scenarios, such as the dynamic nature of emergencies, time constraints from operating 24/7, limited resources, engagement issues with traditional training methods, and difficulty in simulating realistic conditions. VR training effectively addresses these challenges by offering immersive simulations that allow employees to practice various emergency responses in a safe environment, enhancing their understanding and retention of critical skills. The flexibility of VR training accommodates irregular schedules, while its interactive nature increases engagement and motivation among trainees. Additionally, VR reduces logistical burdens related to physical training resources, making it a cost-effective solution for preparing employees to handle real-life incidents confidently and proficiently.

Traditionally, VR training has centred on single-event scenarios (Pottle, 2019). By bolstering user motivation to participate, VR technology can deliver more effective education at a reduced cost and in less time compared to oral or text-based methods. This approach enhances the precision of messaging and diminishes the need for reeducation (Chiang et al., 2022). Hong Yip has constructed and refined an innovative technology training platform, actively engaging in partnerships with external universities and technology firms to leverage their expertise in facilitating this collaboration.

In recent years, VR technology advancements have created new training opportunities (Conrad et al., 2024; OSHC, 2024). VR provides an immersive and safe environment for training in special or hazardous operations that would be unsafe in real-life scenarios. It also enables learners to practice tasks repeatedly, thereby enhancing their proficiency. While VR-based training is primarily utilized to improve technical skills and ensure more effective performance assessments, it is equally crucial to assess and train non-technical skills such as decision-making, situational awareness, and alertness (Liu et al., 2021). In order to enhance realism, the current VR virtual building—F.A.S.T. comprehensive emergency event training platform—incorporates multiple virtual building scenes, props, and roles, each simulating different emergency situations. The acronym F.A.S.T. stands for "Fire-handling" (Fig. 1), "AED application," "Suspicious object handling," and "Traffic accident handling" (Figs. 2 and 3). Furthermore, the captioned VR training content has been integrated into the advanced properties management emergency handling module (99.5 learning hours) within the course module grouping of "Property service management in advanced diploma in integrated property services management (QF level 4)" as well as the "Properties management emergency handling module (91 learning hours) in diploma in integrated property services management (QF level 3)".

The implementation of VR training in the property management industry has had a positive impact on the practical application of skills in real-life situations. This is achieved by immersing employees in realistic emergency scenarios, which enhances their situational awareness and improves their decision-making abilities during actual incidents. Trainees have reported increased confidence and preparedness, enabling them to act decisively when faced with emergencies. The immersive environment also promotes better retention of critical skills through repeated practice, while immediate feedback during simulations reinforces correct procedures. Additionally, VR training facilitates realistic scenario practice for rare events, fosters team coordination and communication, and reduces response times. Collectively, these benefits contribute to a more capable workforce that is better equipped to handle emergencies effectively (Zarantonello & Schmitt, 2023; Ng et al., 2019).

**Fig. 1.** Screenshots of VR – Fire emergency situations. The VR pictures show the interface of a virtual building in which various emergency cases will occur. (Source: Hong Yip).

In addition, these scenarios encompass a diverse array of stakeholders, including members of the general public, firefighters, law enforcement officers, and emergency medical personnel. This requires trainees to demonstrate their capacity to address and resolve intricate, multifaceted emergencies efficiently. The VR virtual building integrates various educational components, such as instructional videos, system prompts, verbal guidance, and practical experiences, to provide a comprehensive training setting. Certain modules incorporate voice recognition functionality for interacting with virtual characters and employ the Nitrol smart tool, a mobile application for staff patrol purposes. Upon completion of the training, the system autonomously assesses the response process and safety, reinforcing the learning process's efficacy. This approach is devised to mitigate casualties and losses by bolstering trainees' ability to respond to emergency situations, thus enhancing safety awareness. Hong Yip has also created an introductory video on the aforementioned training platform, and it has been uploaded to the Property Management Services Authority (PMSA) YouTube channel (PMSA, 2024) for sharing with practitioners in the property management industry.

This programme offers numerous advantages to both employees and the general public. By providing structured and continuous learning opportunities, it is expected that safety awareness will increase, the occurrence of injuries will decrease, and the skills and

**Fig. 2.** Screenshots of VR – VR versus Real-Life Scenario. The VR pictures and photos are the comparison between real-life and virtual view spots. (Source: Hong Yip).

**Fig. 3.** Screenshots of VR – Integrated Emergency Handling Platform. The emergency cases have to be handled with the support of virtual equipment and staffing. (Source: Hong Yip).

effectiveness of employees and customers in managing incidents will improve, thereby ensuring their safety and well-being. Ultimately, VR training enhances safety awareness, reduces the likelihood of workplace injuries, and establishes a risk-free virtual training environment. This approach not only meets industry standards but also contributes to the cultivation of property management talent, ultimately boosting the company's reputation and cutting costs and manpower when compared to traditional training methods.

VR training significantly enhances the effectiveness of managing accidental incidents in the property management industry compared to traditional training methods. VR training provides immersive, realistic simulations that enable trainees to practice emergency response skills in a safe environment, leading to better retention and application of knowledge. It addresses both technical and non-technical skills, such as decision-making and situational awareness, while offering immediate feedback and adaptability to diverse scenarios. In contrast, traditional training methods, which often rely on theoretical learning and standardized curricula, fail to effectively engage trainees and may leave them unprepared for the complexities of real-life emergencies. Overall, this study highlights VR training as a transformative approach that improves safety awareness and reduces workplace injuries in the property management sector.

## 3 UTAUT Model

The UTAUT model, developed in 2003 (Venkatesh et al., 2003), is a widely used framework that helps understand the factors that affect users' acceptance and adoption of technology. It integrates several existing theories, including the Theory of Reasoned Action (TRA), the Technology Acceptance Model (TAM), the Theory of Planned Behavior (TPB), and the Social Cognitive Theory (SCT). The model considered key factors such as Perceived Usefulness (PE), Effort Expectancy (EE), Social Influence (SI), and Facilitating Conditions (FC) to provide a comprehensive understanding of users' behavioural intentions and actual usage (Venkatesh, 2022). The UTAUT model identified these key factors that influence users' acceptance and adoption of technology. Perceived Usefulness relates to users' belief that a technology will enhance their job performance or make tasks easier, while Effort Expectancy refers to the ease of use associated with the technology. Social Influence considers the impact of social factors on adoption, and Facilitating Conditions involve the resources and support available to users. User's Behavioral Intentions are central to the model and are influenced by attitudes, perceived usefulness, ease of use, and subjective norms. Studies have shown that these factors significantly affect users' intention to adopt various technologies (Venkatesh et al., 2003).

The UTAUT model provides a comprehensive framework for understanding users' technology adoption behaviour. It offers valuable insights into technology adoption behaviour by considering factors such as perceived usefulness, perceived ease of use, user intentions, effort expectancy, social influence, and facilitating conditions. Numerous studies have supported the relationships proposed by the UTAUT model, highlighting its relevance and applicability in various technological contexts (Bayaga and du Plessis, 2024; Ng et al., 2022).

The UTAUT model significantly enhances the understanding of VR training effectiveness in the property management industry by providing a structured framework to evaluate critical factors influencing employees' acceptance and use of this technology. The model's constructs—Perceived Usefulness (PU), Effort Expectancy (EE), Social Influence (SI), and Facilitating Conditions (FC)—help assess how trainees perceive the value of VR training, its ease of use, the influence of peers and management, and the availability of necessary resources and support. High scores in these areas correlate with positive Behavioural Intentions (BI), indicating a willingness to apply learned skills in real-life situations. Additionally, the UTAUT model facilitates feedback for the continuous improvement of the training program and ensures its relevance to employees' specific needs within the property management sector.

## 4 Methodology

This research study aims to assess the impact and efficacy of VR training on employees' ability to manage accidental incidents in shopping malls, commercial areas, and residential properties. The study focuses on staff members of a property management company in Hong Kong.

The UTUAT model will be utilised to evaluate user intentions subsequent to the participation of Hong Yip staff in the VR training mentioned above. This evaluation will involve the measurement of demographic attributes, such as role/position, education level, workplace characteristics (type of building), and age group, as well as the attitudes of the staff members (users) towards Perceived Usefulness (PU), Effort Expectancy (EE), Social Influence (SI), Facilitating Conditions (FC), and Behavioral Intention (BI) through an online questionnaire. Participation in the questionnaire is voluntary.

The following research questions were asked to the staff who attended the VR training course and measured how effective the VR Training Programme to be applied in the staff's workplace:

a. What are the strengths of the VR training courses in preparing the staff to handle accidental cases in their workplaces?
b. What are the areas where the staff think the VR training courses could be improved to better assist them in handling accidental cases in their workplaces?
c. Have they faced any challenges or barriers to applying the techniques learned from the VR Training course in real-life accidental cases?

## 5 Research Findings

During the research period from 1 July 2022 to 30 June 2024, a total of 38 classes were conducted for the VR training courses. These classes accommodated 409 trainees, of whom 279 completed and returned their questionnaires, resulting in a 68% response rate. Among the 279 trainees, 153 (55%) were male and 126 (45%) were female. Table 1 shows the demographic details whereas Table 2 presents the UTAUT details:

**Table 1.** Demographic Details

| Position of the Trainees | | | Education Level | | |
|---|---|---|---|---|---|
| Management | 123 | 44.1% | Secondary | 142 | 50.9% |
| Supervisor | 23 | 8.3% | Matriculation | 27 | 9.7% |
| Technical | 15 | 5.4% | Bachelor | 88 | 31.5% |

(*continued*)

**Table 1.** (*continued*)

| Position of the Trainees | | | Education Level | | |
|---|---|---|---|---|---|
| Administration | 25 | 8.9% | Graduate | 2 | 0.7% |
| Others | 93 | 33.3% | Others | 20 | 7.2% |
| Total | 279 | 100.0% | Total | 279 | 100.0% |
| **Workplace (Type of Building)** | | | **Age Group** | | |
| Shopping mall | 51 | 18.3% | 20–29 | 24 | 8.6% |
| Commercial | 36 | 12.9% | 30–39 | 51 | 18.3% |
| Residential | 96 | 34.4% | 40–49 | 69 | 24.7% |
| Composite | 15 | 5.4% | 50–59 | 82 | 29.4% |
| Other | 81 | 29.0% | 60 or above | 53 | 19.0% |
| Total | 279 | 100.0% | Total | 279 | 100.0% |

**Table 2.** UTAUT Details

| Constructs | Means (5-Point Likert Scales) |
|---|---|
| Perceived Usefulness (PU) | 4.37 |
| Effort Expectancy (EE) | 4.33 |
| Social Influence (SI) | 4.26 |
| Facilitating Conditions (FC) | 4.23 |
| Behavioural Intention (BI) | 4.31 |

## 6 Discussion and Analysis

Based on the UTAUT survey model, trainees have rated PE, EE, SI, FC, and BI highly, with scores ranging from 4.23 to 4.37 on a 5-Point Likert Scale. Additionally, the user's intentions to adopt technology, also known as behavioural intention (BI), received a score of 4.31. This indicates that a majority of the trainees agree that the knowledge and skills acquired from VR training are valuable for handling accidental cases in their workplaces. Moreover, over 77% of the trainees (216) expressed willingness to recommend colleagues to the VR training courses.

The property management industry in Hong Kong faces challenges in attracting young professionals to pursue careers within this sector. As evidenced by the survey, over 48% of the trainees (135) are over 50 years of age, and among them, 19% are over 60 (53). Additionally, more than 61% of the trainees (169) do not hold a degree. Notably, over 85% of the trainees (236) have not previously received VR training. Therefore, providing VR training to prepare trainees to handle accidental cases in their workplaces may significantly benefit them, particularly for mature trainees without tertiary education backgrounds.

The following are the findings from the trainees' responses regarding the following three research questions:

a. *What are the strengths of the VR training courses in preparing the staff to handle accidental cases in their workplaces?*

Through VR training, people can gain a preliminary understanding of events, increase their sense of realism, and clearly process procedures and methods. This is easier for people to understand than just textbook learning. VR training can simulate emergency situations, let people know that accidents can be avoided, and allow them to feel the scene under unexpected circumstances. This increases knowledge and allows actual practice in a safe environment without feeling unfamiliar.

In VR simulations, people can preview potential situations so that when actual situations occur, they can immediately apply what they have learned. Even for very rare occurrences, people can practice VR and gain experience from it. Compared to just theoretical learning, VR training provides more opportunities for practical application, allowing people to become more proficient in relevant skills. In summary, VR training can help people handle various unexpected situations in a timely and specific manner, improving their emergency response capabilities.

b. *What are the areas where the staff think the VR training courses could be improved to better assist them in handling accidental cases in their workplaces?*

The company can provide a larger space to facilitate VR training better. They can consider adding more diverse simulated scenarios to help trainees expand their thinking. Additionally, they can incorporate sound effects and collect feedback from trainees after they complete the training. Since some of the videos may be outdated, adding more virtual environments will help provide a more immersive experience for the trainees.

Providing more accessories and supporting equipment will allow more colleagues to experience the VR training. They can design training for different types of emergencies and promptly collect feedback to make improvements. Overall, the VR training is already quite impressive, and they can continue to add more scenarios to heighten the sense of alertness. At the same time, they should encourage trainees to continuously review and refresh their knowledge to maintain their emergency response capabilities.

c. *Have they faced any challenges or barriers to applying the techniques learned from the VR Training course in real-life accidental cases?*

On-site situations are constantly changing, requiring flexible thinking in teaching and practical operations. In addition to increasing knowledge to solve problems, trainees also need to truly understand their work environment so that they will not feel lost in emergencies. For example, in the case of a fire alarm, while VR training simulates the visual effects, it cannot let trainees feel the actual heat, so training on some rare emergency situations is still necessary to improve their response capabilities.

While issues like equipment problems and colleagues easily forgetting key points also need attention, this VR training enables trainees to solve problems and accumulate experience in communication. Overall, continuous observation and practice are needed to continuously improve the training program and enhance trainees' safety awareness and adaptability.

The research findings from the 279 participants indicate that VR training significantly enhances emergency preparedness in the property management industry. It provides a realistic and immersive learning experience, leading to a better understanding of procedures, practical application of skills in a safe environment, and the ability to practice various emergency scenarios repeatedly. However, areas for improvement were identified, including the need for more diverse scenarios, incorporation of sensory elements, regular content updates, and increased accessibility to VR resources. Participants also noted challenges in applying learned techniques due to the dynamic nature of real-life situations, the necessity of familiarising themselves with physical environments, and potential technical issues with the VR equipment. Overall, the insights underscore the effectiveness of VR training while also highlighting opportunities for improvement and the importance of ongoing practice to maintain skills.

Employees who participated in VR training provided positive feedback regarding their experiences. They emphasised that the immersive simulations significantly improved their comprehension of emergency procedures and allowed for the practical application of skills in a secure environment, thereby enhancing their confidence in managing real-life incidents. The opportunity for repeated practice facilitated the internalisation of responses to rare emergencies, and the immediate feedback provided valuable insights into their performance. Trainees found the interactive nature of VR to be more engaging than traditional methods. However, they suggested potential enhancements, such as broadening the variety of simulated scenarios and incorporating sensory elements. Despite recognising the benefits, employees acknowledged challenges in applying learned techniques to dynamic real-world situations, underscoring the necessity for ongoing practice to sustain readiness.

It is recommended that further research be conducted to explore the effectiveness of VR training in the property management industry. These could include conducting longitudinal studies to assess long-term skill retention, comparing VR training with other modalities, and customising training scenarios to reflect specific organisational contexts. Furthermore, exploring the impact of group dynamics during VR training, integrating emerging technologies such as augmented reality and artificial intelligence, evaluating the broader organisational outcomes of VR training, and examining feedback mechanisms for continuous improvement could yield valuable insights. Addressing these research directions can emphasise the necessity for ongoing exploration to enhance training effectiveness and emergency preparedness in the industry.

## 7 Conclusion

In conclusion, property management entities seeking to implement VR training for emergency response include expanding training scenarios to cover diverse emergencies, enhancing realism by incorporating sensory elements, customising training for different facilities, and collecting continuous feedback for improvement. These steps aim to better prepare trainees to handle various on-site challenges and improve the effectiveness of the VR-based emergency response training program.

The research has demonstrated the effectiveness of virtual reality (VR) training in enabling staff to apply their learning in real-life scenarios in the property management industry in Hong Kong. The study utilised the UTAUT model to develop a survey, and the findings from 279 completed responses indicated a positive inclination of staff members to apply the acquired knowledge from VR training when dealing with accidental incidents in the workplace. The implementation of VR training has not only proven beneficial for staff but has also received recognition and endorsement from various entities and authories in the industry. This research aims to disseminate the experiences and feedback derived from the VR training program and contribute to the advancement of training practices within the property management industry in Hong Kong.

Overall, this research contributes to the body of knowledge surrounding VR training in the property management industry and emphasises the importance of ongoing innovation and adaptation in training practices. The insights gathered from this study hope to guide future developments and investments in VR training, ultimately leading to the adoption of safer and more effective property management practices in Hong Kong and beyond.

**Funding.** The work described in this paper was fully supported by a grant from the Hong Kong Institute of Vocational Education (IVE) (Project Number: TY000797).

## References

Bayaga, A., du Plessis, A.: Ramifications of the Unified Theory of Acceptance and Use of Technology (UTAUT) among developing countries' higher education staffs. Educ. Inf. Technol. **29**(8), 9689–9714 (2024)

Chan, Y.W., Tsang, Y.F., Cheung, S.K., Ng, K.K., Yuen, C.W.: A study on the design and implementation of the smart site safety system from the stakeholders' perspectives. In: International Conference on Blended Learning, pp. 287–299. Springer Nature, Singapore (2024)

Chiang, D.H., et al.: Immersive virtual reality (VR) training increases the self-efficacy of in-hospital healthcare providers and patient families regarding tracheostomy-related knowledge and care skills A prospective pre-post study. Medicine (Baltimore) **101**(2), E28570-e28570 (2022)

Conrad, M., Kablitz, D., Schumann, S.: Learning effectiveness of immersive virtual reality in education and training: A systematic review of findings. Computers & Education: X Reality **4**, 100053 (2024)

Faqih, K.M., Jaradat, M.I.R.M.: Integrating TTF and UTAUT2 theories to investigate the adoption of augmented reality technology in education: Perspective from a developing country. Technol. Soc. **67**, 101787 (2021)

Hong Kong Smart City Blueprint 2.0: Innovation and Technology Bureau, HKSAR Government (2020). https://www.smartcity.gov.hk/modules/custom/custom_global_js_css/assets/files/HKSmartCityBlueprint(ENG)v2.pdf

Hong Yip Service Company Limited: Hong Yip Service Company Limited official website (2024). https://www.hongyip.com/Pages/home

Liu, Y., et al.: VR-based Training on Handling LNG Related Emergency in the Maritime Industry. In: *2021 International Conference on Cyberworlds* (CW), pp. 159–165. IEEE, France (2021)

Ng, K.S.P., Lai, I.K.W., Ng, S.K.K.: The acceptance of the online gamification learning platform by higher education students in hospitality and tourism. Int. J. Innov. Learn. **31**(3), 330–347 (2022)

Ng, R.Y.K., Ng, S.K.K., Liu, B.: An Empirical Study on the Usefulness, Effectiveness and Practicability of Vocational and Professional Education and Training's (VPET) Open Educational Resources (OER) in the Hotel Industry. In: Cheung, S., Lee, L.K., Simonova, I., Kozel, T., Kwok, L.F. (eds.) Blended Learning: Educational Innovation for Personalized Learning. ICBL 2019. Lecture Notes in Computer Science, vol 11546, pp. 265–276. Springer, Cham (2019)

OSHC: Occupational Safety and Health Council. The OSH Innovation & Technology Expo, March 7–8, (2024). https://sms.oshc.hk/expo2024/eng/highlight.html

Pottle, J.: Virtual reality and the transformation of medical education. Future Healthcare Journal **6**(3), 181–185 (2019)

Property Management Services Authority (PMSA): 智能物管系列 - 物管從業員創新培訓體驗 (Intelligent Property Management Series - Innovative training experience for property management practitioners) (2024). https://www.youtube.com/watch?v=WNKtesCT6pQ&list=PLSBpn70-tDQPy2tFxCyEMsCEQnnnfP2Xl&index=3

Wong, P., Lai, J.: On the property management services ordinance of hong kong: concerns and implications. Prop. Manag. **39**(5), 600–617 (2021)

Venkatesh, V.: Adoption and use of AI tools: a research agenda grounded in UTAUT. Ann. Oper. Res. **308**, 641–652 (2022)

Venkatesh, V., Morris, M.G., Davis, G.B., Davis, F.D.: User acceptance of information technology: toward a unified view. MIS Q. **27**(3), 424–478 (2003)

Zarantonello, L., Schmitt, B.H.: Experiential AR/VR: a consumer and service framework and research agenda. J. Serv. Manag. **34**(1), 34–55 (2023)

# A Virtual Reality Serious Game for Improving Pet Dog Care Skills

Lap-Kei Lee[1]($\boxtimes$), Yukai Cai[1], Ho-Yin Chui[1], Chun-Hei Lam[1], Edmond King Sing Fong[1], Praewpran Prayadsab[2], and Nga-In Wu[3]

[1] School of Science and Technology,
Hong Kong Metropolitan University, Ho Man Tin, Hong Kong SAR, China
{lklee,eksfong}@hkmu.edu.hk
[2] Faculty of Engineering, Department of Industrial Engineering, Kasetsart University,
50 Ngamwongwan Road, Lat Yao, Chatuchak, Bangkok 10900, Thailand
praewpran.p@ku.th
[3] College of Professional and Continuing Education, The Hong Kong Polytechnic University,
Hong Kong SAR, China
ngain.wu@cpce-polyu.edu.hk

**Abstract.** This paper addresses the important issue of canine welfare, particularly in Hong Kong, where dog ownership is prevalent. With the rise in dog-related accidents due to inadequate pet care knowledge and skills, there is a critical need for improved education among dog owners. This study presents a novel solution in the form of a Virtual Reality (VR) serious game designed to enhance pet care skills. The game provides tutorials on key aspects of dog ownership: cleaning, feeding, housing, and dog-walking. Three VR games specifically address the latter three aspects, which educates users on appropriate food for dogs, creating a safe living environment, and dog walking etiquette. The design of these serious games is expected to provide valuable insights for education practitioners on utilizing VR technology to enhance pet welfare, extending beyond dogs.

**Keywords:** virtual reality · serious game · pet dog care skills · canine welfare · pet welfare

## 1 Introduction

The well-being of domestic canines is a globally pertinent issue, with particular relevance in regions such as Hong Kong where dogs are one of the most popular pets. As per the Thematic Household Survey (THS) of 2019, conducted by the Census and Statistics Department (C&SD) of the Hong Kong SAR Government (C&SD, 2019), it was deduced that approximately 147,500 households were dog owners in 2018. This figure represents 5.7% of the total households in Hong Kong during that period. Furthermore, the total number of dogs owned by these households was estimated to be around 221,100.

As the demographic of dog owners expands, the subsequent increase in incidents related to canine mishaps can present a substantial societal issue. These incidents encompass a variety of accidents, predominantly stemming from a lack of adequate pet dog care knowledge and skills. For instance, food poisoning is a common mishap. Certain foods, such as chocolate and grapes, are toxic to dogs (Kovalkovičová et al., 2009). However, due to a lack of awareness, owners often inadvertently feed these harmful substances to their pets, leading to fatal consequences. Another common issue is heatstroke, particularly in regions like Hong Kong, where the summer climate is hot and humid. As reported by Paige (2015), dogs can succumb to heatstroke after less than an hour of outdoor activity. Unfortunately, novice dog owners often overlook these potential hazards.

A significant contributing factor to the rise in canine-related accidents is the lack of adequate dog care skills among many owners, both new and experienced. This deficiency in knowledge can lead to irresponsible pet ownership, potentially resulting in harm or even death of the dogs. A number of studies have highlighted the necessity for improved education among prospective and current dog owners (Blackwell et al., 2008; The All-Party Parliamentary Group for Animal Welfare, 2009; Rooney et al., 2009). The Agriculture, Fisheries and Conservation Department (AFCD) of the Hong Kong SAR Government has been actively promoting responsible dog ownership through various educational and publicity programs aimed at enhancing public awareness (AFCD, 2024). Similarly, the Society for the Prevention of Cruelty to Animals (spca.org.hk) has been advocating for dog welfare, preventing cruelty, and alleviating suffering through educational initiatives, such as courses on dog care and common medical issues. Other existing solutions, including mobile applications and books, offer some level of instruction on dog care skills, yet these solutions have proven to be insufficient (see Sect. 2 for more details). Consequently, there is an urgent need for innovative solutions.

Virtual Reality (VR) technology emerges as a potential solution to this critical issue. VR is a sophisticated computer technology that generates a three-dimensional virtual environment, thereby convincingly simulating the user's physical presence within a virtual world (Elmqaddem, 2019). The past decade has witnessed considerable advancements in VR hardware and software, leading to enhanced affordability and user accessibility. This progress has catalyzed a significant surge in its application within the educational sector, e.g., the work by Ng et al. (2020); the readers may also refer to the surveys by Radianti et al. (2020) and Lee et al. (2024) for additional examples. Another effective educational technology is *serious games*, which are characterized as digital games designed not only to entertain but also to accomplish at least one supplementary objective, such as facilitating learning or promoting health (Dörner et al., 2016). These games have demonstrated efficacy in fostering learning and engagement across various educational contexts; examples include the works of Tsikinas et al. (2018) and Lee et al. (2019a, 2019b).

**Our Contribution.** This paper presents the design and implementation of a Virtual Reality (VR) serious game aimed at enhancing the pet care skills of prospective dog owners. The serious game incorporates tutorials in the form of multiple-choice questions and video demonstrations, covering four critical aspects of dog ownership: cleaning, feeding, housing, and dog-walking. Three VR serious games have been specifically designed to address the latter three aspects. The VR feeding game educates learners about the appropriate and potentially harmful foods for dogs; the VR housing game instructs learners on creating a safe and comfortable environment for their pets; and the VR dog-walking game imparts knowledge on dog walking etiquette and managing unexpected situations during a walk. It is anticipated that the design and implementation of these serious games will offer valuable insights to education practitioners on leveraging VR technology to improve welfare of pets in general, not limited to only dogs.

**Organization of the Paper.** Section 2 reviews existing and related solutions for enhancing dog care knowledge and skills. Section 3 details the design and implementation of our VR serious game for enhancing dog care skills for prospective dog owners. Section 4 presents some preliminary evaluation results, and Sect. 5 concludes the paper with future work directions.

## 2 Existing Solutions for Enhancing Dog Care Knowledge

This section reviews existing and related solutions for enhancing dog care knowledge of prospective and existing dog owners.

The Internet has emerged as a prevalent platform for pet care advice, yet the potential for misinformation poses significant risks. If the quality of the information procured is substandard, dog owners may unintentionally make decisions that jeopardize their pets' welfare (Kuhl et al., 2022). This highlights the critical need for reliable, evidence-based resources in the area of pet care, particularly for dog owners.

Many books on dog care have been published, such as those by Pinkwater and Pinkwater (2002) and Dodman and Lindner (2007), which provide extensive and credible knowledge on dog care skills and offer in-depth and comprehensive content for prospective and current dog owners. In today's digital age, maintaining consistent reading habits has become increasingly challenging due to the overflow of easily digestible, "bite-sized" content from the Internet and smartphones; this shift towards "shallow" reading can hinder the absorption of more complex and nuanced information found in longer texts (Spjeldnæs and Karlsen, 2022). Additionally, while these books provide valuable knowledge, their practical application is limited for individuals who do not yet own a dog.

An alternative method for acquiring dog care knowledge is through participation in specialized courses. For instance, in Hong Kong, the Society for the Prevention of Cruelty to Animals (SPCA) offers a course titled "Canine First Aid" (SPCA, 2023). This course equips participants with the necessary skills to respond appropriately to their dogs' medical and surgical emergencies. Upon completion, participants receive a certificate and a First Aid Kit. However, the frequency of this course is limited, often resulting in extended waiting periods for interested individuals. Additionally, with a cost of around US$ 200, the course may be financially inaccessible for some individuals.

To the best of our knowledge, there is a noticeable absence of Virtual Reality (VR) applications designed to enhance dog care skills. However, numerous mobile applications cater to this need. For instance, "11pets: Pet Care" (11pets.com) is a mobile application that assists pet owners in managing their pets' health. It enables tracking of weight and nutrition, scheduling of vaccinations and veterinary visits, and storage of medical history. Users can pay to upgrade to the premium version, which provides access to round-the-clock veterinary support and engagement with the user community.

## 3 Design and Implementation of Our VR Serious Game

This section details the design and implementation of our serious game for enhancing dog care skills for prospective dog owners, which leverages virtual reality to create an immersive environment for acquiring different skills on pet dog care. The system was developed and tested using PICO 4 Pro (picoxr.com/cn/products/pico4-pro), which is a standalone VR headset that operates independently without the need for a computer connection and equipped with two controllers.

Translated text:

Cleaning game
Feeding game
House-tidying game
Dog-walking game
Back

**Fig. 1.** Primary selection menu showing the four critical aspects of dog ownership: cleaning, feeding, housing, and dog-walking.

Our serious game covers four critical aspects of dog ownership: cleaning, feeding, housing, and dog-walking, as shown in the primary selection menu within the VR environment of our serious game (Fig. 1). Recall that the feeding module educates learners about suitable and potentially harmful dietary choices for dogs; the housing module provides guidance on creating a secure and comfortable habitat for the pet dog; and the dog-walking module imparts knowledge on proper dog-walking etiquette and strategies for handling unforeseen circumstances during a walk. The cleaning module focuses on the correct methods of cleaning dogs. However, we encountered challenges in enabling learners to perform detailed tasks such as cleaning within the VR environment. Thus, a VR game for this module was not included. Upon choosing a specific topic, learners have the option to engage in the Tutorial mode or the VR game mode (excluding the cleaning module).

### 3.1 Tutorial Mode

The tutorial mode equips the learners with the fundamental knowledge for each module, enabling them to apply this understanding within the corresponding VR serious game. Two types of tutorials are offered: the multiple-choice questions and video tutorials.

**Multiple-choice Questions.** This tutorial presents ten multiple-choice questions related to the selected module, one at a time (refer to Fig. 2). Users can utilize the VR controller to move the pointer and select their answers. In line with the principles of gamification theory, which emphasize the importance of feedback and rewards, explanations and scores are provided for correct answers (refer to Figs. 3 and 4 below for examples of selecting a correct and incorrect answer, respectively).

A Virtual Reality Serious Game for Improving Pet Dog Care Skills 273

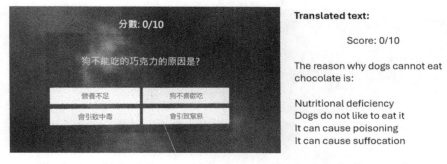

**Translated text:**

Score: 0/10

The reason why dogs cannot eat chocolate is:

Nutritional deficiency
Dogs do not like to eat it
It can cause poisoning
It can cause suffocation

**Fig. 2.** A multiple-choice question in the tutorial mode of the feeding module.

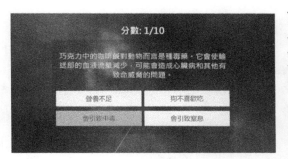

**Translated text:**
Score: 1/10
The caffeine in chocolate is a poison to animals. It can reduce the blood flow in the transport system, which may cause heart disease and other life-threatening problems.

Nutritional deficiency
Dogs do not like to eat it
**It can cause poisoning (*in green*)**
It can cause suffocation

**Fig. 3.** Explanation is shown after selecting a correct answer in a multiple-choice question.

**Translated text:**
Score: 1/10
Onions contain sulfoxides and disulfides, which can damage red blood cells and cause anaemia.

Dog food
***Boiled chicken (in red)***
***Onion (in green)***
White rice

**Fig. 4.** Explanation and the correct answer (in green) are shown after selecting an incorrect answer (in red) in a multiple-choice question.

Upon completion of all the ten questions, the end screen is displayed, as shown in Fig. 5. This screen provides hints, the total score, and buttons that navigate to other parts. The hints, which are the answers to incorrectly answered questions, aid users in reinforcing their knowledge. The total score, reflecting the number of correctly answered questions, allows learners to assess their performance and determine whether they need to revisit the tutorial, return to the main menu, or commence the serious game or a video tutorial.

Translated text:

Score: 6/10

Remember:
Different sizes of dogs need different types of dog food.
Dogs cannot eat onions.
Dogs cannot eat cherries because it can cause rapid breathing and shock.
Dogs cannot eat chocolate because it can cause poisoning.

Play again
Back to selection menu
Play game

**Fig. 5.** End screen for the multiple-choice question tutorial mode.

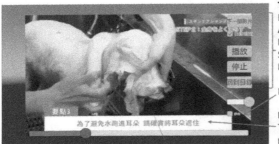

Translated text:
Next video
Auto-play
Play
Stop
Back to selection menu

Mute

Point 3
To avoid water from entering the ears, please make sure to cover them properly.

**Fig. 6.** Control menu interface for videos in the video tutorial mode.

**Video Tutorial.** We offer video tutorials tailored to the selected module. To maintain learner engagement and prevent loss of interest due to excessive length, these tutorials are approximately 10 min in duration. Learners can interact with the video using the VR controller, which when clicked, brings up the control menu interface as shown in Fig. 6.

### 3.2 VR Game Mode

There are three VR serious games for the feeding, housing, and dog-walking module, respectively.

**VR Serious Games for the Feeding Module.** Figure 7 illustrates the user interface of this VR game. Various food items are classified as either inedible or edible for dogs, displayed on the left and right sides, respectively. These food items will randomly appear and move towards the learner. The learner is equipped with two VR controllers, functioning as virtual swords. The left sword, colored red, is used to strike the inedible and potentially harmful food, while the right sword, colored green, is used to strike the edible and safe food. If the learner uses an incorrect sword to strike a food item or fails to strike it (i.e., it bypasses the learner), the life points will decrease. When life points reach zero, the game is over. We anticipate that this game design will effectively train learners to rapidly distinguish between suitable and unsuitable food for their pet dogs.

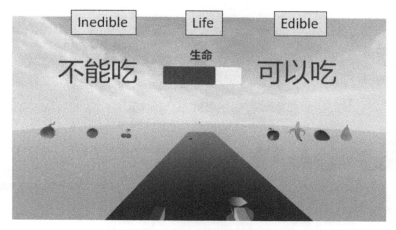

**Fig. 7.** User interface of the VR serious game for the feeding module.

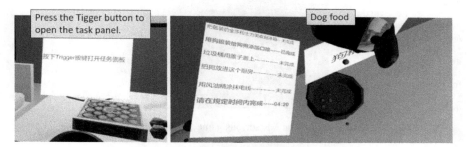

**Fig. 8.** User interface of the VR serious game for the housing module.

**VR Serious Games for the Housing Module.** The VR environment for this serious game replicates a typical dog owner's home, with a 3D room scene designed to reflect the standard room size and conditions in Hong Kong. The scene incorporates various small items such as chocolates, electrical wires, a trash can, as well as an AI dog that roams around the room. Figure 8 depicts the user interface of this game. As indicated on the left of Fig. 8, learners can press the "trigger" button on the controller to open a task panel. This panel contains a list of tasks related to maintaining a safe and comfortable environment for the pet dog and a timer (refer to Fig. 9 below). As shown on the right of Fig. 8, learners can use the controller to interact with the items in the scene, e.g., picking up a bag of dog food to refill the tray. Upon completion of a task, its status in the task panel will switch from "incomplete" to "completed". Learners must complete all tasks within a five-minute timeframe; failure to do so results in a game over.

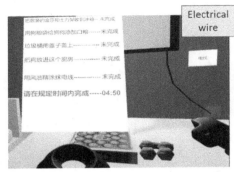

**Fig. 9.** Task list in the task panel and a timer in the VR serious game for the housing module.

**Fig. 10.** Start screen in the VR serious game for the dog-walking module.

**Fig. 11.** The dog died in an accident in the VR serious game for dog-walking.

**VR Serious Games for the Dog-Walking Module.** The VR environment for this serious game replicates a real-life park, providing learners with a simulated experience of walking their dogs. An AI dog, programmed to always walk ahead of the player, may also randomly defecate, consume food found along the path, and interact with other dogs within the scene. Figure 10 displays the game's start screen, with the left side providing instructions on controller operation, and the right side presenting a real-time task list.

The initial task involves safely holding the dog leash and crossing the road. During this crossing, learners must remain vigilant and adhere to traffic signals; failure to do so will result in the dog being involved in a vehicular accident, leading to game termination, as depicted in Fig. 11.

**Translated text:**

Tasks
• Hold the dog leash firmly.
• Take the puppy for a walk in the park.
• **Avoid entering the lawn and bushes. (Failed)**
• Do not collide with pedestrians.

**Fig. 12.** A failure in a normal task for dog-walking.

Upon entering the park, learners are tasked with guiding the dog along a designated walkway. Various standard tasks will appear in the real-time task list, designed to reinforce fundamental dog-walking knowledge, such as avoiding bushy areas to prevent parasite exposure. Failure to complete these standard tasks will not result in game termination, but their status will be marked as "failed" on the task panel, providing learners with areas for improvement in the next attempts of the game (e.g., see Fig. 12).

Additionally, unexpected "emergency tasks" may also arise, simulating real-life dog-walking emergencies. These emergency tasks, of which there are three types, each have a specific time limit. A timer, displayed at the top of the screen, will only appear when an emergency task is initiated and will disappear upon task completion.

**Fig. 13.** Emergency task on cleaning up after the dog.

The first type of emergency task involves cleaning up after the dog, which may defecate at any given moment. To prevent environmental pollution, learners must select the appropriate tool to clean up the waste (a newspaper for feces or a water bottle for urine). Figure 13 shows two screen captures of the gameplay of this emergency task.

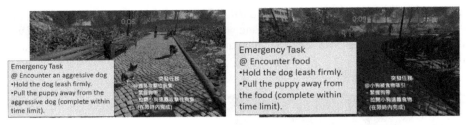

**Fig. 14.** Emergency tasks on encountering an aggressive dog (left) and roadside food (right).

**Fig. 15.** Explanation is shown after completing (left) or failing (right) an emergency task.

Another emergency task educates learners on handling aggressive dogs, and the final emergency task instructs learners on what to do when their dogs are attracted to roadside food (Fig. 14). The aggressive dogs and roadside food appear randomly. When the dog approaches an aggressive dog or roadside food, the corresponding task is triggered. Learners must quickly grasp the leash and pull the dog away to prevent game failure due to the dog being attacked or poisoned by roadside food; upon task completion, whether successful or failed, an explanation is provided to ensure learners fully understand how to handle these unexpected situations. (Fig. 15). The serious game concludes with a summary screen, providing learners with feedback on areas for improvement based on failed tasks (see Fig. 16 below).

**Fig. 16.** End-game summary screen with feedback on failed tasks.

## 4 Preliminary Evaluation

To validate the effectiveness of our VR serious game in enhancing pet dog care skills, we invited 15 participants to play the serious game and complete an individual survey. Some participants were also invited to a focus group interview. The survey employed a 5-point Likert scale (1: strongly disagree, 2: disagree, 3: neutral, 4: agree, 5: strongly agree). Table 1 presents the survey items along with the corresponding results.

**Table 1.** Distribution of participant responses on the Likert scale in the survey results.

| Item | 1 | 2 | 3 | 4 | 5 |
|---|---|---|---|---|---|
| **1. The game mechanics is easy to follow** | | | | | |
| 1a. Feeding game | 0% | 0% | 20.0% | 40.0% | 40.0% |
| 1b. Housing game | 0% | 0% | 33.3% | 46.7% | 20.0% |
| 1c. Dog-walking game | 0% | 0% | 33.3% | 53.3% | 13.3% |
| **2. The game content is interesting** | | | | | |
| 2a. Feeding game | 0% | 0% | 20.0% | 40.0% | 40.0% |
| 2b. Housing game | 0% | 6.7% | 46.7% | 40.0% | 6.7% |
| 2c. Dog-walking game | 0% | 6.7% | 40.0% | 40.0% | 13.3% |
| **3. The game graphics is attractive** | | | | | |
| 3a. Feeding game | 6.7% | 26.7% | 40.0% | 26.7% | 0% |
| 3b. Housing game | 0% | 20% | 40.0% | 40.0% | 0% |
| 3c. Dog-walking game | 0% | 20% | 26.7% | 46.7% | 6.7% |
| **4. It effectively enhances my skills in dog care** | | | | | |
| 4a. Tutorials | 0% | 0% | 13.3% | 46.7% | 40.0% |
| 4b. Feeding game | 0% | 20.0% | 33.3% | 40.0% | 6.7% |
| 4c. Housing game | 0% | 0% | 33.3% | 40.0% | 26.7% |
| 4d. Dog-walking game | 0% | 6.7% | 33.3% | 46.7% | 13.3% |
| **5. I would recommend this VR game to others** | 0% | 13.3% | 33.3% | 46.7% | 6.7% |

The majority of participants agreed that the game mechanics of the three serious games were intuitive and easy to understand (survey items 1a to 1c).

While the feeding game was deemed engaging by most participants (survey item 2a), approximately half expressed neutrality or disagreement regarding the interest level of the housing and dog-walking games (survey items 2b and 2c). Notably, during the focus group interview, some participants suggested that these two games lacked sufficient content.

The dog-walking game was praised for its appealing graphics by most participants (survey item 3c). However, a significant proportion felt that the graphics of the feeding and housing games could be improved (survey items 3a and 3b). Specific feedback included difficulty in identifying the small fruits in the feeding game and experiencing dizziness in the housing game.

The majority of participants agreed that the tutorials, housing, and dog-walking games effectively enhanced their dog care skills (survey items 4a, 4c, and 4d). However, just over half of the participants were neutral or disagreed that the feeding game contributed to their dog care skills (survey item 4b). This may be attributed to the perceived quality of the graphics in the feeding game.

Nevertheless, more than half of the participants indicated that they would recommend this VR serious game to others (survey item 5).

## 5 Conclusion

This paper introduces an innovative approach through a Virtual Reality (VR) serious game, specifically designed to enhance pet care skills for potential dog owners. The game offers comprehensive tutorials on crucial elements of dog ownership, including cleaning, feeding, housing, and dog-walking. Three different VR games focusing on the latter three elements were designed to educate learners on suitable food for dogs, the creation of a secure living habitat, and proper dog-walking practices. The design of these serious games is anticipated to offer useful insights for educational practitioners on the application of VR technology to improve pet welfare, with potential implications extending beyond canine care.

**Future Works.** As suggested in Sect. 4, future works include enriching the agme content and enhancing the graphics of the current implementation of the VR serious games. A more comprehensive evaluation of the VR game's effectiveness is also desirable, potentially employing a pre-post test design with a larger participant pool. Another future work direction is to explore the application of immersive reality in improving dog owners' cleaning skills.

## References

Agriculture, Fisheries and Conservation Department: Proper care of pets - Dogs (2024). Retrieved 1 Sep 2024 from https://www.pets.gov.hk/english/proper_care_of_pets/dogs/before_getting_a_dog.html

Blackwell, E.J., Twells, C., Seawright, A., Casey, R.A.: The relationship between training methods and the occurrence of behavior problems, as reported by owners, in a population of domestic dogs. Journal of Veterinary Behavior **3**(5), 207–217 (2008)

Census and Statistics Department: Keeping of dogs and cats. Thematic Household Survey (Report No. 66) (2019). Retrieved 1 Sep 2024 from https://www.censtatd.gov.hk/en/data/stat_report/product/B1130201/att/B11302662019XXXXB0100.pdf

Dodman, N.H., Lindner, L.: Puppy's first steps: The whole-dog approach to raising a happy, healthy, well-behaved puppy. Houghton Mifflin Harcourt (2007)

Dörner, R., Göbel, S., Effelsberg, W., Wiemeyer, J.: Serious games. Springer, Cham (2016)

Elmqaddem, N.: Augmented reality and virtual reality in education. Myth or reality?. Int. J. Emerg. Technol. Learn. **14**(3) (2019)

Kovalkovičová, N., Šutiaková, I., Pistl, J., Šutiak, V.: Some food toxic for pets. Interdiscip. Toxicol. **2**(3), 169–176 (2009)

Kuhl, C.A., Lea, R.G., Quarmby, C., Dean, R.: Scoping review to assess online information available to new dog owners. Veterinary Record **190**(10), e1487 (2022)

Lee, L.K., et al.: Improving the experience of teaching and learning kindergarten-level English vocabulary using augmented reality. Int. J. Innov. Learn. **25**(2), 110–125 (2019)

Lee, L.K., et al.: A mobile game for learning English vocabulary with augmented reality block builder. In: Technology in Education: Pedagogical Innovations: 4th International Conference, ICTE 2019, pp. 116–128. Springer Singapore (2019b)

Lee, L.K., et al.: A systematic review of the design of serious games for innovative learning: augmented reality, virtual reality, or mixed reality? Electronics **13**(5), 890 (2024)

Ng, S.C., Lee, L.K., Lui, A.K.F., Wong, K.F., Chan, W.Y., Tam, H.H.: Using immersive reality in training nursing students. Int. J. Innov. Learn. **27**(3), 324–343 (2020)

Paige, F.: Heatstroke in dogs: a potential killer that's easy to avoid. South China Morning Post (2015). Retrieved on 1 Sep 2024 from https://www.scmp.com/magazines/post-magazine/article/1773307/heatstroke-dogs-potential-killer-thats-easy-avoid

Pinkwater, J., Pinkwater, D.M.: Superpuppy: How to choose, raise, and train the best possible dog for you. Houghton Mifflin Harcourt (2002)

Radianti, J., Majchrzak, T.A., Fromm, J., Wohlgenannt, I.: A systematic review of immersive virtual reality applications for higher education: Design elements, lessons learned, and research agenda. Comput. Educ. **147**, 103778 (2020)

Rooney, N., Pead, M., Sargan, D., Westgarth, C., Creighton, E., Branson, N.: Pedigree dog breeding in the UK: a major welfare concern?, pp. 1–78. Royal Society for the Prevention of Cruelty to Animals, Hosham, UK (2009)

Society for the Prevention of Cruelty to Animals. (2023). Canine first aid. Retrieved on 1 Sep 2024 from https://www.spca.org.hk/get-involved/pet-care-courses/canine-first-aid/

Spjeldnæs, K., Karlsen, F.: How digital devices transform literary reading: the impact of e-books, audiobooks and online life on reading habits. New Media Soc. **26**(8), 4808–4824 (2024)

The All-Party Parliamentary Group for Animal Welfare: A healthier future for pedigree dogs (2009). Retrieved on 1 Sep 2024 from http://www.ourdogs.co.uk/special/apgaw.pdf

Tsikinas, S., Xinogalos, S., Satratzemi, M., Kartasidou, L.: Using serious games for promoting blended learning for people with intellectual disabilities and autism: Literature vs reality. In: Interactive Mobile Communication Technologies and Learning: Proceedings of the 11th IMCL Conference, pp. 563–574. Springer International Publishing (2018)

# Author Index

**A**

Anussornnitisarn, Pornthep 173

**B**

Barot, Tomas 41

**C**

Cai, Yong 246
Cai, Yukai 269
Cerna, Miloslava 185
Chan, Jackson Tsz Wah 222
Chan, Yan-Wai 257
Chen, Ling 164
Chen, Wenyi 151
Chen, Zexuan 134
Cheung, Simon K. S. 246, 257
Chiang, Aaron S. Y. 257
Chui, Ho-Yin 269
Chui, Kwok Tai 85, 222, 257
Cross, Simon 134

**D**

Duan, Chenggui 55

**F**

Fong, Edmond King Sing 269

**H**

Huang, Xingyun 112, 124
Hubálovská, Marie 235

**J**

Javorcik, Tomas 41
Jen, Fen-Lan 112, 124
Jia, Linlin 151
Jiao, Jianli 112, 124
Jin, Yating 164

**K**

Kostolanyova, Katerina 41

**L**

Lam, Chun-Hei 269
Lam, Pius 257
Lee, Lap-Kei 71, 85, 222, 269
Li, Kam Cheong 199, 210
Li, Shao-Fu 71
Lian, Yuting 124
Lin, Jzung-Lu 71
Liu, Jiaqi 85
Liu, Liang 246
Liu, Mengjin 199, 210
Liu, Xiaojun 246
Liu, Xiaoting 112
Luk, Louise 71

**N**

Ng, Kwan-Keung 71, 85, 257

**P**

Paoprasert, Naraphorn 85, 173
Phusavat, Kongkiti 173
Poulova, Petra 185
Prayadsab, Praewpran 269

**R**

Rienties, Bart 134
Rohlíková, Lucie 3
Ruksorn, Pongthorn 173

**S**

Saleh, Salmiza 99
Simonova, Ivana 41
Sun, Ningwei 99

**T**
Toman, Michaela  235

**W**
Wang, Fu Lee  222
Wang, Yaxuan  164
Wong, Billy T. M.  199, 210
Wong, Leung Pun  85
Wu, Nga-In  269

**Y**
Yang, Shun-Neng  71
Yousuk, Ramidayu  222

**Z**
Zhan, Zehui  15
Zheng, Jiayi  15
Zhong, Chaocheng  15
Zhong, Weisen  15

Printed in the USA
CPSIA information can be obtained
at www.ICGtesting.com
CBHW081450011224
18277CB00005B/112